Accounting and its business environment

Fundamentals of accounting for business students

Accounting and its business environment

Fundamentals of accounting for business students

by
Fred McLeary

JUTA & CO, LTD
1995

First Published 1985
Second Impression 1987
Second Edition 1990
Third Edition 1992
Fourth Edition 1995

© Juta & Co, Ltd
PO Box 14373, Kenwyn 7790

ISBN 0 7021 3289 6

SET, PRINTED AND BOUND IN THE REPUBLIC OF SOUTH AFRICA BY
THE RUSTICA PRESS (PTY) LTD, NDABENI, CAPE
D3197

Foreword to the first edition

South Africa is unique. It has a unique social system, one that is a mass of contradictions. Different laws apply in different parts of the country and even in respect of different people in the same part of the country so that our country has at least two different economies: a fairly sophisticated first-world economy which is the one known to most whites and to rapidly increasing numbers of others, and a fairly primitive subsistence third-world economy which is almost entirely black. The current period is marked by changes in this social system, with attempts to pull the third-world part of our economy into the first-world part. It follows that the business environment is also unique, and it has a large part to play if this process of change is to lead to greater prosperity for all.

Our business environment's informal sector—the backyard and spare-time businesses—is probably as large, in percentage terms, as in any other country in the world. At the same time we seem in danger of drifting into that form of corporate communism foreseen by Edward Bellamy, with a few large corporations gobbling up any and all of the smaller formal businesses until the stage is reached where half a dozen such corporations control the whole country.

We have a government which loudly proclaims the virtues of free enterprise, but which employs a larger proportion of people in the public sector than many countries which are avowedly socialist. What is more, this excessive employment in the public sector is increasing even while the government preaches the virtues of a more effective civil service and calls upon the private sector to play a greater role in the development of the country.

We have a legal system which is almost unique: Roman-Dutch law applies only in this country and in Sri Lanka. However, our version of Roman-Dutch law has been strongly influenced by the British common law and a great deal of our commercial law is based upon laws which are in effect in the United Kingdom and the United States. This applies particularly to our company law. Our tax law is pretty well unique and so is the subject of a major portion of current South African business literature.

With a melange of characteristics like this it is scarcely surprising that many books, highly regarded in other countries but dealing with the business environments which exist in America, in Britain or in Australia are found to be inadequate and inappropriate when used in this country. This is not meant as a criticism of the quality of these books, it is simply an acknowledgement of the fact that we are different and that anyone studying our business environment therefore needs books with a different, specialised viewpoint.

Very few such books have been published since the smallness of the potential market for books on South African business has in the past discouraged many from trying to meet this need, but the terrifying increase in the cost of books imported from overseas has made the cost of developing a local business literature seem less prohibitive. The tempo of the times has dictated that there should be an emphasis on the field of labour relations, but it is gratifying to note that books on other aspects of the South African business environment are gradually appearing.

This book tries to cover the field of accounting in this country primarily from the point of view of the businessman rather than the accountant, of the potential user of accounting information rather than of the preparer (who is already well served by locally written books). If it helps to improve understanding and communication between the South African businessman and his accountant, it will have achieved its major objective.

Pretoria,
9 September 1985.

Fred McLeary

Foreword to the fourth edition

The world keeps changing at an ever faster rate, and the required body of knowledge for managers and particularly, from my point of view, financial managers, is changing dramatically and growing rapidly. This book has been largely rewritten in response to comments and criticisms based on this perspective. There are changes in virtually every chapter, but the following are the most important:

1. A new section on the basics of financial management has been added and the chapters have been rearranged to some extent to accommodate this.
2. The chapters dealing with basic accounting and with ratio analysis and cash flow analysis have been rewritten, as has the chapter on the requirements of financial reporting for companies.
3. Brief summaries have been given of some important developments in the accounting field, particularly in the field of international accounting which should become more important if South Africa does take a more important role in the international community.
4. A great many new problems and cases have been added, and the test-yourself sections have been modified, hopefully for the better.

For the rest, this book still has its original aims: it is designed for the management student who has no intention of majoring in accounting but does need a good working knowledge of it, and for the non-formal student who wants to have some knowledge of accounting.

Pretoria
June 1994
Fred McLeary

To René, James and Bruce

Table of contents

Part one

The financial environment

This first section sets out the environment in which accounting operates. It looks at the basics of information processing and at the structure of the accounting profession before looking at some of the factors which have determined the directions in which accounting has developed and is developing—tax law, company law and electronic data processing.

Chapter 1

Information and accounting information

The major purpose of an accounting system is to provide information which can be used by the various stakeholders in an undertaking. However, there are other systems which play a part in providing information. This chapter reviews the types of information systems and the stakeholders who would use these.

1. **Prophets of profit**

2. **Information processing and information management**

3. **Information and the reasons it is required**

4. **The information system within the undertaking**

5. **Accounting information and the purpose of accounting**

1. Prophets of Profit

Accounting interacts with society by producing information to meet the needs perceived as necessary by society. While this provision of information has long been argued as a neutral function which does not influence societal actions, this view has been discredited in the last few decades. Information is neutral only in theory. In practice, the selection of information to furnish and the manner of presenting that information leads to perceptions on the part of the recipients of that information. The current double entry system of accounting which is the basis of much of the rest of this book was developed in the north of Italy probably during the twelfth or thirteenth century, but only revealed to the world in 1494 in a book written by an Italian, Fra Luca Pacioli. He described it as "providing information about its (a business entity's) activities which would be useful in administering and managing the business of the entity."[1] It was, in his opinion, to be used solely for the benefit of the owner/manager of the entity. Because of the nature of business at that time he did not even consider the possibility of accounting having any societal impact.

"Change in societal structure over the five centuries which have passed since the publication of Pacioli's work have led to changes in the way in which businesses are viewed in relation to society. A social ecology has developed which sees business as part of society as a whole and which demands that business give account of itself and its actions to the rest of society."[2]

The accounting system was never designed to provide all the information to which society might have a claim, since "financial accounting reports on the economic activities and the economic status of an economic entity . . . it does not provide information about the social activities of the organisation".[3] Accounting reports are combined with written reports on aspects other than these economic activities to provide the totality of information about an undertaking.

Accounting does have a massive effect on societal activities, however. In any market society exchange takes place freely in the marketplace. The market mechanism assumes the role of arbiter of the allocation of societal resources by setting prices. This mechanism is activated by the actions of the participants to the exchange process taking place in the market, and the actions of these participants are determined by the information about the products in the marketplace. For almost all the exchange actions the information is provided by *current accounting practices* which underlie most of the cost and value assumptions made by the participants. This is so obvious that some social analysts have contended that accounting data have superseded competition as the chief arbiter of society's resources. As a result of this accounting has moved from having a purely passive scorekeeping role as envisaged by Pacioli towards being a participant in the exchange process in that accounting information has in itself become a saleable commodity.

[1] McLeary, Frederick *Unpublished inaugural lecture*, University of South Africa 1990
[2] ibid
[3] Anthony, Robert N *Tell it like it was* 1983 Homewood, Illinois: Richard D Irwin

Looking at accounting from the perspective of adjudicating on economic exchanges offers a new way of looking at accounting problems and accounting questions. Accounting no longer appears as the lifeless recording of transactions. Instead, it can be seen as a dynamic player in the economic and social fields by providing information necessary to the other players.

In the light of this perspective it is useful to survey the nature of information and the nature of the users of accounting information.

2. Information processing and information management

One of the catch phrases of today is that we are living in the information age. The United States claims that it has moved from an industrial age into a post-industrial age where more people are employed in processing information than in producing goods or, to use their terminology, there are more white-collar workers than blue-collar workers. It is widely accepted that knowledge is power, that the man who controls the flow of information is the most powerful man around, and an aura of mysticism has surrounded the whole process of turning data into information. Each of us is flooded daily by streams of information, from newspapers, radio and television, streams which are generally very non-specific. It is information which may be of use to the competitors in a radio or television quiz, but which supplies the answers to very few of the problems faced in the daily routine of a business or to any other specific problems. To gain *this* type of information it is necessary to have access to specific information resources. One of these specific resources concerned with a commercial undertaking is the financial reports of that undertaking, reports which are the product of the accounting system employed.

3. Information and the reasons that it is required

Every person spends his life in a way which is determined mainly by the decisions he has made. Those entrusted with the task of caring for the welfare of others, whether as doctors, as politicians, as businessmen or managers or in any other field of endeavour, constantly make decisions which affect not only their own lives but the lives and happiness of their constituents. These decisions have to be made against a background of uncertainty. There is no way in which this uncertainty can be eliminated, since the effects of decisions made depend largely on events which have yet to occur and are beyond the control of the decision-maker. Decisions are seldom made in total uncertainty, however. A doctor, for example, has a store of knowledge, which is assimilated information arranged in an orderly manner, concerning disease. This, combined with the information which he builds up about his patient's physical condition as he performs his examination, enables him to come to a decision concerning the illness and then a second decision on how to treat it. It is obvious that the *information about illness and about the patient* at his disposal enables him to minimise the uncertainty and so come to a well-founded decision.

Information needs to be defined if any discussion of it is to take place. While it can be defined simply as a group of data logically arranged so as to present an intelligible whole, for the purposes of this book it will have a more exacting definition.

Information can be defined as the logical grouping of bits of data into a recognisable pattern, which could be called an item of news. This serves to improve the ability of a decision-maker to reach a well-founded decision by lessening the uncertainty surrounding any decision which he takes. For the item of news to deserve the title of information it must meet certain criteria:

Accuracy: The news must be factual and presented in its proper context. It should ideally be immediately verifiable from another source, but this is all too often impossible without impinging on the third requirement mentioned below;

Relevance: There is no point in gleaning information which has no relevance to the problem or decision under review. This is the greatest problem with the streams of information to which reference was made above. Newspapers and television provide a great deal of information which is of no use under particular circumstances. The age of the computer brought with it the ability to produce massive piles of printouts containing all information concerning an undertaking, and such printouts were supplied to management without thought for relevance or even for ability to assimilate it all! Such irrelevant information often serves as disinformation and clouds the judgement of the decision-maker; and

Timeousness: The information must reach the decision-maker when he needs it. This is the criterion on which many accounting systems stumble, particularly as far as reporting to non-management users or financial users is concerned.

Information must be distinguished from *misinformation*, which is false news, and from *disinformation*, which is the deliberate spreading of false news for purposes of creating or compounding confusion and uncertainty.

4. The information system within the undertaking

Any undertaking, whether a large company formed for the purpose of making a profit or a small charitable society, requires a variety of information in order to carry out its self-appointed task in an adequate manner. The quantity of information required may vary from undertaking to undertaking, as may the types and qualities which are of most use, but a simple comprehensive model can be drawn up for the classification of the information requirements of any undertaking. The diagram (Fig 1.1 on page 5) shows such a model in matrix format, with a few examples of the type of information being referred to in each block of the matrix:

Information flows into the undertaking from its environment and flows within the undertaking as it interacts with its environment and as its members interact with each other. Some of these flows are generated internally while others are internalised after being generated elsewhere in the environment. Some of them are formally created flows, such as those emanating from the accounting system, while others are informal but still of value. The information flows need to be read and understood by the managers of the undertaking and by those who invest in it and interact with it in other ways. Misinformation and disinformation flow in the same ways and have to be sifted out of the information system or they will compound the

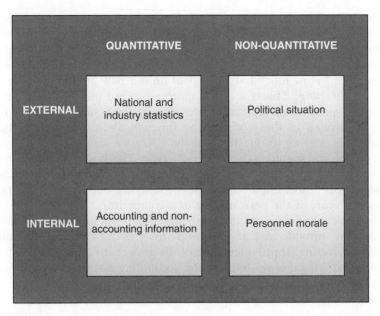

Figure 1.1

difficulties facing those attempting to read the flows and assist in creating the environmental uncertainty with which a manager must deal.

5. Accounting information and the purpose of accounting

The accounting system is part of the total information system of the undertaking. It is concerned solely with the processing of internally generated data which have a direct monetary effect on the undertaking. The accounting system is concerned with recording all monetary transactions within the undertaking, with the sorting and classification of these transactions, and eventually with the presentation of reports which summarise the results of these monetary transactions. These reports are presented in a variety of forms for the edification of a variety of users and primarily form part of the internal information system for the managers and owners of the undertaking; secondly, they are part of the external information network for those parts of its environment with which the undertaking interacts.

5.1 Types of information supplied by the accounting system

The accounting system obviously supplies information of varying types in order to provide the answers to any number of specific questions. Broadly speaking, however, there are only three classifications of accounting information which have been named as follows by Horngren:[4]

---

[4] Horngren, Charles T and Gary Sundem *Introduction to Management Accounting* 7th edition 1987, Prentice Hall, Chapter 1.

1. *Scorekeeping:* This is the most straightforward task of the simple bookkeeping system. It is a simple matter of recording all transactions, listing them and adding them together so as to be able to answer questions concerning the progress of the undertaking such as "What have our total sales been for the year to date?" or "How much have we spent on our new building to date?"
2. *Attention-directing:* This is a rather more advanced task in that it requires an intelligent appraisal of the figures provided by the system, the same figures as those mentioned in the scorekeeping function above. This time the system provides the answer to questions of the "Are we selling enough?" or "How much can we still spend on the building?" type. This is accomplished by drawing comparisons between the actual figures as provided by the scorekeeping system and some sort of ideal figure. This ideal could be a budget, the performance of a previous year, or the performance of a competitor.
3. *Problem-solving:* This is the true managerial information which the accounting system can provide as a follow-up to the information mentioned as attention-directing. It provides some of the answers to questions like "What do we do now?". If sales are too low the accounting system can provide answers about the effect on profits of alternative strategies to increase them. Possible answers would be to cut prices in order to gain increased volume, to employ more salesmen, to increase advertising expenditures or to concentrate on the more profitable lines in order to increase profits even if sales do not reach targets. The accounting system can provide the information necessary to decide which of these, or which combination of these, is most likely to be most beneficial, financially speaking, to the undertaking.

5.2 Users of accounting information

Many user groups exist for whom accounting information is a primary input into their own information systems. Obviously they have different needs and require different information. The extent of their reliance on accounting information and the comparative importance of this information will thus also vary. These user groups can be split into to broad categories:

Internal, ie those concerned with the details of running the undertaking on a day-to-day basis; and

External, ie those concerned with evaluating the overall performance of the undertaking over a period.

Internal users are primarily *Management*, which includes sole owners or partners of small firms and the professional managers of larger undertakings.

External users do not have the same needs; they require mainly scorekeeping information concerning the undertaking, information which is provided by the *financial accounting system*, one of the two major divisions of the accounting system and the one which is the main focus of this book.

External users include the following:

Equity investors:

These are the suppliers of permanent capital who do not have any direct say in the running of the undertaking. They include the shareholders in a large company and the silent partners who invest funds at risk in the hope of a return, but who leave the actual running of the firm to the directors or partners whom they elect to those posts. Their interest in the accounting system is mainly focused on a report telling them how profitable the undertaking is and how strong it is financially in order that they may be able to evaluate their investments. Potential new equity investors, in particular, would be interested in the history of the company, its present operations and some idea of its future plans and the dividend policy followed by the firm.

Long-term lenders:

These people lend money to an undertaking on the understanding that they will receive a pre-determined rate of return on the funds which they lend. They normally play no part whatever in the management of the undertaking, but require that the undertaking should be able to:
1. *Service the loan,* ie meet all interest payments as they fall due and be able to repay the loan on due date; and
2. *Provide adequate security* in case of default so that the lender does not lose his capital. This is the major difference between the lender and the equity investor, whose money is at risk.

The lender is therefore interested in the profitability of the undertaking and especially in the cash flows engendered by this profitability, as well as the financial strength of the undertaking.

The terms of a loan sometimes include provision for the lender to obtain certain managerial powers where the lender has reasonable grounds for believing that the borrower may not be able to meet his obligations in respect of the above requirements, though this type of provision is seldom found except in high-risk loan transactions.

Creditors:

They are the suppliers of the short-term credit which is the lifeblood of commerce. They seldom request accounting information in the normal course of business, but when they do they are interested in the same sort of information as the long-term lenders discussed above. Requests for accounting information are normally forthcoming only when the original application for credit is made. Their information requirements differ from those of long-term lenders purely in timing: they want to know whether cash flows will be sufficient to meet their calls in the immediate future and not necessarily whether there will be large enough cash flows over the longer term.

Government and statutory bodies:

As most people know only too well, they require financial information concerning financial activity. The best known requirement is that of the Receiver of Revenue for income tax purposes. He requires information concerning the profits made by the undertaking so that the taxable income can be determined for the purposes of the fiscus. However, there are other Government bodies which require information from the accounting system, such as the Department of Statistics. Various statutory bodies also require selected information which is provided by the accounting system.

Researchers and academics:

Information for a variety of research projects is required. These often overlap to some extent with the Government bodies mentioned above, but are generally more applicable to private enterprise, to a specific sector of industry or even to a specific enterprise. It is impossible to generalise about the information which they require, since each project has its own goals and requirements.

The needs of these external users are largely met by the annual financial statements prepared by every undertaking, either in terms of the Income Tax Act or in terms of other Acts applicable to the undertaking or, in the case of unincorporated non-profit undertakings, in terms of their own constitutions. The specific requirements of Government bodies and Departments may require that special reports be prepared in addition to these annual financial statements.

Internal users have their needs met largely by the other major division of the accounting system, the *management accounting system*, which provides far more detail than the financial system and will barely be touched on in this book.

Management has requirements different from those of investors primarily in that management must have more detail. For the investor it is sufficient to see that profits are being increased or that they are declining; management must know where, why and how they are changing. Ordinary financial statements do not usually provide all the answers to the questions which managers must raise and supplementary management statements are needed. Ordinary annual statements do provide some of the information required, however, and they certainly act as attention directors. A drop in profits or in the short-term liquidity position can be signalled by the statements; more detailed information can then be requested. The accounting system can be called upon to provide relevant information for management at any time. Regular scorekeeping reports are normally presented to management at fairly short intervals and provide information needed for the day-to-day running of the company. They also act as attention-directors, pointing out the strengths and weaknesses of the firm as they develop.

Key words

Information	Misinformation
Disinformation	Scorekeeping
Attention-directing	Problem-solving
Internal users	External users

Chapter 2

The structure of the accounting profession

1. The variety of accounting qualifications

Accounting has spawned a number of branches on its way to becoming recognised as a profession. This is hardly surprising when one considers the variety of work which accountants are called upon to perform; work which varies from the drudgery of writing up a set of books to the highly technical tasks performed by the auditor when certifying a set of financial statements or preparing a financial forecast for the edification of shareholders. Since many of the tasks are specialised, specialist qualifications have become necessary and it is essential to have some idea of what the various qualifications involve and what particular specialist would be best able to perform a specific task.

2. The Chartered Accountant (SA)

When people speak of a professional accountant they usually have in mind a man with this qualification. This is an accolade which the Chartered Accountant has worked hard to earn, even if it is a little unfair on some of the holders of other qualifications. Chartered Accountants may register to act as public accountants, but many of them work in accounting fields other than that of public practice.

The Chartered Accountant (SA) is a member of the South African Institute of Chartered Accountants. He obtains membership by meeting the requirements regarding professional examinations and experience. These requirements are, briefly, as follows:

2.1 Experience

A period of service in the office of, and under the supervision of, a Chartered Accountant in public practice is necessary. This is a formal period of training attested to by the signing of Training Contract registered with the Public Accountants and Auditors Board, in terms of which the rights and responsibilities of both parties are set out. This period is nominally five years, but a graduate gains a remission of two years from this period and a matriculant who obtains a degree during the training period can gain remission of up to one year.

2.2 Professional examinations

The training function and the examining function, except for a final qualifying examination, have been delegated to participating universities in South Africa. These universities grant successful candidates a Certificate in the Theory of Accounting (CTA), which usually involves the granting of a degree or even an honours degree somewhere along the line. The courses involved in gaining such a Certificate include four courses in accounting, two or three in auditing, at least one in tax, two in commercial law and single courses in such subjects as administration of estates, statistics, economics and business economics. The actual combination of courses varies from university to university, but all the Certificates are theoretically equal at the end of the day.

The possessor of CTA may then apply to write the qualifying examination set by the Public Accountants and Auditors Board. Successful candidates who have complied with the experience requirements may then apply for membership of the Institute.

2.3 The Public Accountants and Auditors Board

This Board is a statutory body set up in terms of the Public Accountants and Auditors Act and charged with regulating the public accounting profession in South Africa. Besides having the duty of setting requirements for training of Chartered Accountants (SA), it is responsible for all disciplinary matters and matters pertaining to ethics. It maintains a register of Public Accountants and is entitled to take disciplinary action against anyone on the register who acts in a way calculated to bring the profession into disrepute. It has unrestricted powers to investigate any act or omission which it feels is not in accordance with the rules. A member of the South African Institute is entitled to apply for registration as a public accountant, but until such registration is confirmed he is not entitled to act as a public accountant since the disciplinary rules cannot be applicable to him until such registration is formalised.

2.4 Duties and responsibilities of the Public Accountant

2.4.1 The primary task of the public accountant is to perform audits. This is the only task which is reserved to him. He may do many other kinds of work, but he will do them in competition with people who are not public accountants. His duty when performing an audit is to present a report on the financial or other statements which are the subject of his audit.

The content of the report may be laid down, as in cases where audits are statutorily required, or may be dictated by the terms of his agreement with his clients. The Companies Act, for instance, lays down the duties of an auditor performing an audit and the form of the report is largely dictated by these duties.

2.4.2 The auditor must report on material irregularities. The responsibility for determining just what constitutes a material irregularity must be that of the auditor, who must draw on his training and experience to decide when an irregularity becomes material. He must first report on the matter to the person in charge of the undertaking. If the matter is not rectified within thirty days he must report it to the Public Accountants and Auditors Board which will decide whether it is necessary to take further action.

2.4.3 To summarise a number of rules and regulations: an auditor must be independent and must not allow himself to be placed in a position where his independence is compromised. This means that he should not audit a firm in which he himself has an interest; he should not accept an appointment which conflicts with the interests of an existing client; he should not develop any close relationship with the personnel of a client and, very important, he should not receive a disproportionate share of his fee income from one client so that he develops a dependence on that client's goodwill.

3. Certified Financial Accountant

The CA (SA) undergoes a long and arduous training which is aimed at making him into a good auditor. Many people who qualify as Chartered Accountants do not remain in the auditing field but do go into practice as public accountants specialising in accounting, secretarial, taxation and consulting services to smaller businesses which would not really benefit from a statutory audit. This means that many CA(SA)'s are actually overqualified for the work which they are doing. There are also many practitioners who would like to spend time developing an auditing practice but who are unable to do so because of the pressure of work: work which could be done by less highly qualified people if they were available. The accounting profession in this country eventually faced up to this problem and decided to create what is effectively a lower tier of professional qualification for people not involved in auditing. This second body was at first known as the Institute of Financial Accounting Technicians. This name failed to meet with any great enthusiasm, possibly because the initials FAT did not really give the impression of a professional body. After due thought, the name was changed to the Institute of Certified Financial Accountants. Members are entitled to call themselves Certified Financial Accountants and add the initial CFA to their names.

The Public Accountants and Auditors Board is responsible for maintaining a record of the members and is also responsible for entrance examinations and enforcement of an ethical disciplinary code. No formal training period is required, but those wishing to obtain the qualification must provide evidence of satisfactory practical experience. The educational requirements are broadly defined. Relevant university degrees are accepted, as is a specially developed course presented by various Technikons.

4. The Chartered Institute of Secretaries and Administrators

This is a specialist qualification totally divorced from the Public Accountants and Auditors Board. Members of this institute are trained in accounting, commercial law, taxation and company secretarial practice. There are no laid-down experience requirements, but the Board of the Institute must be satisfied that the prospective member has had sufficient appropriate practical experience. For registration as a student a matriculation certificate or equivalent is required.

Members of this institute are pre-eminently qualified to act as company secretaries, whether as secretary to a specific company (or group of companies) or in public practice as a secretary of companies. They have suffered in the past when competing with CA (SA)s for public practice secretarial work since the competition has been able to offer a complete range of services including the audit of a company, but this disadvantage has largely fallen away with the introduction of the close corporation which does not require an audit. Members of the CIS are included among those who are entitled to act as accounting officers for this new type of organisation.

The Institute has its own disciplinary procedures which do not differ in spirit from those of the Chartered Accountants (SA) and members who transgress these rules are also subject to suspension and even, in extreme cases, to expulsion from the Institute.

There are two classes of membership, namely Associate and Fellowship. At present the only difference between the two lies in length of membership, but there are proposals that fellowship should only be granted by examination.

5. The Chartered Institute of Management Accountants

This is an Institute which has come up the hard way. It started as a rather looked down upon qualification, suitable for factory clerks, but its image has been improved to the state where it is regarded as very nearly equivalent to the Chartered Accountants qualification. It has also been recognised by the granting of a Royal Charter. In the United Kingdom there is already very close co-operation between the CA and CIMA, with each granting the other large-scale exemptions for examination purposes. In this country the CA is granted exemptions when applying to register as a CIMA student but not vice versa. This matter is largely out of the hands of the accounting bodies, however, because of the nature of the Chartered Accountant's training here which is conducted largely by universities. To date the universities have not been favourably disposed towards granting exemptions based on non-university qualifications.

As implied by the name, the members of this Institute are specialists in the field of management accounting. The examinations are set in the United Kingdom, but where necessary are adapted to suit South African circumstances. A student is entitled to write either the British papers or the South African ones. The South African papers are marked in South Africa only when they differ from the British ones or where they are written in Afrikaans. Subjects covered include financial accounting, several courses in management accounting, commercial law and industrial law, taxation, statistics and data processing.

Appropriate practical experience, attested to by members of the Institute, is also required. Once again there are two classes of membership, based upon length of membership and election by fellow members.

The members of this Institute are obviously ideally trained to be management accountants working within a company, which is where most of them are found. However, there are also quite a few in public practice specialising in such fields as accounting systems design and maintaining records of companies.

The Institute has appropriate ethical standards enforced by disciplinary procedures and its members have also been granted the right to act as accounting officers of close corporations.

6. The Chartered Association of Certified Accountants

As in the case of the CIMA, this is a British body which accepts foreign members and allows a variation in the examination in order to allow South African and some other students to write examinations based on local law and tax. It is a very highly regarded qualification in Britain, being accepted as virtually on par with the various British Chartered Accountant qualifications. Practical experience is necessary but does not have to be obtained in the offices of a practising accountant. Candidates may obtain the required experience in commerce, in the public sector or in industry and are not tied down to obtaining all their experience in only one of these fields. Those who obtain the qualification are entitled to use the designation ACCA (Associate) which automatically changes to FCCA (Fellow) after five years of continuous membership.

7. Conclusion

These bodies are by no means all the accounting bodies active in this country. There are a few very specialised ones, such as the Institute of Municipal Treasurers and Accountants, which are also recognised as maintaining high standards, but most of the rest aim, when looking for members, mainly at those who do not have the background to attempt to gain membership of the bodies mentioned above. They generally have fairly low educational requirements and little control over the activities of their members. This is not to be taken as a flat condemnation of all these bodies: some, like the Institute of Certified Bookkeepers, have contributed to the development of a body of accounting knowledge in the underdeveloped areas where the more highly qualified do not see any profitable business and so have not developed any influence there.

The members of the bodies described above are, however, the most important in terms of our economy as a whole. Each has an area of expertise; his wider knowledge often overlaps with the area of expertise of one of the others, but with a little thought as to one's requirements it should not be too difficult to decide which qualification is the most appropriate for the person one is seeking to perform a particular task.

Key words

Chartered Accountant (SA)	CA (SA)
South African Institute of Chartered Accountants	SAICA
Public Accountants and Auditors Board	PAAB
Association of Commercial and Financial Technicians	ACFT
Chartered Institute of Secretaries and Administrators	CIS
Chartered Institute of Management Accountants	CIMA

Chapter 3

The regulatory environment

Accounting practice is regulated in two ways: there are legal prescriptions and there are regulations laid down by the accounting bodies. These latter are referred to as Generally Accepted Accounting Practices and are the subject of this chapter.

All of these are based upon certain postulates which fulfil the same function as the axiom does in mathematics, even though they may not be self evident. All the regulatory requirements have been developed from them, however, and so this chapter starts off with a short review of them.

1. **Accounting conventions**

2. **Problems and confusion**

3. **Historical development of GAAP**

4. **The development of GAAP in South Africa**

5. **The South African statements of GAAP**

6. **Accounting guidelines**

7. **The future of GAAP in South Africa**

1. Accounting conventions

Accounting is classified as one of the economic sciences. The economic sciences as a whole are not distinguished by their immutability or their exactness, and accounting has these problems in full measure. However, there are certain basic principles upon which the whole study of accounting is based. Since these principles are not natural principles like the axioms of mathematics but are rather derived from practice and observation of the requirements of an accounting system they are referred to as *conventions* rather than as principles. Upon these basic conventions a whole structure of legal requirements and generally accepted practices has been erected, but even they are not immutable and changes in economic reality over the course of, particularly, this last century have led to certain of these basic conventions being questioned.

The following conventions are those which are accepted as basic to the practice of accounting:

1.1 Conventions concerning the environment

The accounting entity convention decrees that the undertaking can and should be separated from its owner or owners for purposes of financial accounting. Separate financial records should be maintained for the undertaking and its owners even in the case of very small businesses where the financial affairs of the owner and the business are often very closely intertwined.

The going concern convention accepts that the entity will continue to operate for the foreseeable future in something like its current form. This is important for such matters as valuation of assets since assets in use in, say, a production line, would almost certainly have a different value from those same assets if they were to be sold off because of the undertaking ceasing to operate.

The accounting period convention decrees that the financial activities of an entity can be partitioned off into arbitrary, convenient time periods, the usual one in terms of tax and other laws being a period of one year. This partitioning into time periods can lead to problems in the case of transactions which are in process at the end of the period.

The stable monetary unit convention is the one which is pre-eminently under siege. The convention worked reasonably well for centuries, but the inflation which is endemic in the politician-run economies of the twentieth century has made a mockery of it at this time. While there are still reasons for retaining aspects of this convention it is generally accepted nowadays that financial records which do not take note of the unstable nature of the purchasing power of money cannot but fail in their attempts to present totally relevant financial information.

1.2 Conventions concerning the operation of the system

The historic cost convention follows on from the stable monetary unit convention mentioned above. All transactions are recorded at actual monetary values at the date of the transaction and are not adjusted in the light of subsequent fluctuations in the value of the monetary unit. This has the benefit for what is called stewardship accounting of showing all the money entrusted to the managers of the concern and the way in which all such money has been invested over the years. However, this is only one aspect of accounting and alternatives to the historic cost convention are currently being developed.

The quantifiability convention follows the historic cost convention to some extent, but actually entails a lot more. This convention states that only items which are quantifiable in terms of money can be recorded in an accounting system. Historical costs actually incurred are obviously easily quantifiable, but the changes in the value of the monetary unit are not always so easily quantifiable. There are also problems caused by attempting to quantify those aspects of an undertaking which are not necessarily the direct result of monetary transactions. This could include such items as the value of an undertaking's brand names or of patents which have been developed as part of ongoing projects and for which the development costs are difficult to identify with any degree of certainty.

The realisation convention follows on from the accounting period convention. When a transaction is in process at the end of a period there must be a convention governing the allocation of profit. A winemaker, for instance, would harvest the grapes in one period, ferment them and mature the resulting wine over one or more periods and sell the wine in yet another period. If the wine is finally sold at a profit, the profit is only taken into account at the time that this profit is realised, which is when it is sold, even if the work involved in making that profit was spread over several periods.

The matching convention may at first glance seem to contradict the realisation convention. This convention decrees that costs must be matched with the revenues they generate. This does not mean that costs incurred in one period must be matched with the income for that period, but that the costs incurred by the winemaker in the production of the wine mentioned above must be carried forward from one period to the next until the wine is actually sold so that the costs of that particular vintage can be matched with the income derived from it. This leads to the concept of *accrual accounting*: costs are accrued in the financial records until such time as the revenues generated by those costs are realised and are only then written off as expenses.

The duality convention is the basis of the double entry accounting system. This convention acknowledges that all financial transactions have at least two aspects, and that this dual nature of the transactions requires that the accounting system record both aspects. For instance, if one were to purchase an asset and pay for it directly in cash, the duality convention would require the recording of the increase in the value of the assets and also the recording of the decrease in amount of cash available.

Conventions relating to the quality of financial records

The convention of objectivity is the one which a great many laymen seem to feel that accountants constantly flout. The records should be maintained strictly on the basis of objectively determinable monetary transactions and should not be creatively modified to present the type of picture which may be desired.

The convention of prudence, which was once referred to as the convention of conservatism, simply decrees that, where it is possible to objectively raise arguments in favour of two different methods of disclosure, that method should be chosen which reflects the less optimistic view. The classic example is that of the valuation of trading stock which is shown at the lower of cost price or realisable value. In other words, an increase in the value of the stock is not recorded until realisation but a decrease is taken into account immediately.

The convention of consistency simply states that financial reports must be prepared on a basis which is consistent with that of previous years in order to allow the users of the financial statements to be able to draw valid comparisons between different accounting periods. This obviously implies that similar transactions taking place in two different accounting periods must be subjected to the same accounting treatment.

The convention of materiality decrees that the accounting treatment of a transaction must take account of its materiality. Small amounts of capital expenditure for such items as wastepaper baskets would be written off immediately as expenses even though they may last for several years and should, in terms of the matching convention, be written off over the period of use. However, the amount involved is regarded as immaterial to the reasonableness of the financial reports and the extra work involved in keeping track of the waste paper basket over its lifetime makes a strict application of the matching principle ludicrous.

There are a few other minor conventions mentioned in some accounts, but these all seem to be restatements of one or other of the above, all of which are basic to the accounting process as we know it. The statements of generally accepted accounting practice which are briefly discussed below are mostly either expansions of the conventions or statements of how the conventions should be applied in particular circumstances where some confusion may exist.

2. Problems and confusion

Accounting has been called the language of business. As with any language, there are regional variations; there are different ways of saying something, some of which you may feel express exactly what you want to say and others which may seem to you not to have quite the same meaning. People living in different places assign slightly different meanings to various words, and these differences can sometimes cause confusion. Various accounting systems have been around for some time. Our double entry systems have been in use for some eight centuries in different countries. Inevitably, some local variations have crept in as the same basic system has been applied to a variety of economic systems and different stages of economic development. Practices which were adequate for recording the progress of the small trader of the pre-industrial age or of the small partnerships which developed might prove wholly incapable of providing meaningful information to the shareholders of large corporations in present times.

To complicate matters further, politicians have interfered in many countries. People with little or no knowledge of financial statements or accounting generally have decided to introduce laws to protect shareholders from unscrupulous businessmen who misstate matters in their financial reports. They have introduced laws to enforce accounting practices which suit their own particular brand of ignorance and so have driven wedges between the accountants of their own countries and those of other countries where accountants have been subjected to the whims of their own politicians. Tax policies have also contributed to the confusion of the accountants of the world, with tax jargon being part of the normal vocabulary of the accountant in most countries today. Unfortunately, tax jargon differs from country to country.

Even within a country differences of opinion arise so that interpretation of financial reports has become a very hazardous occupation. The interpreter constantly runs the risk of reading an item in a way which differs from the way in which the preparer of the statements intended it. However, as with any other medium of communication, there are good ways of presenting information and bad ways. There may be several different good ways of saying what you want to say, and the real task is that of weeding out those ways which are definitely inferior.

Political pressure arose in the United States of America for standardisation of financial statements after the financial collapses of the late nineteen twenties and the early thirties. However, it soon became obvious that this was positively harmful in a developing economy with different types of undertaking being developed, new methods of finance being dreamed up by the more creative bankers and constantly changing economic circumstances. The language of communication in the business world had to be allowed to develop in order to meet the demands of changing circumstances. The problem of various accounting treatments of similar transactions remained, however. Gradually the idea of non-compulsory standards took hold, and reporting on deviations from standard became the norm.

3. Historical development of GAAP

The Accounting Principles Board in the United States was the body which set out to ward off the ogre of government-enforced conformity in accounting. This board issued opinions based on surveys undertaken among practitioners to determine the most appropriate method of reporting various transactions. It was an independent body sponsored by the American Institute of Certified Public Accountants and was not merely a passive collector of information from practitioners; it obtained the agreement of practitioners by proposing a method and only issuing an opinion after due consideration of the reaction to its proposal.

In 1973 this body was replaced by a new body, the Financial Accounting Standards Board (FASB) which is currently responsible for fending off the politicians. The American Congress did decide that some form of standardisation was necessary for investors in publicly held companies and appointed the Securities and Exchange Commission (SEC) to oversee this standardisation. In practice the SEC has delegated this task to the FASB, which is sponsored by various accounting and business bodies.

4. The development of GAAP in South Africa

The principle of Generally Accepted Accounting Practice was introduced into South African law by the Companies Act of 1973, which came into effect on 1 January 1974. This Act required all financial statements for companies to be prepared in accordance with generally accepted accounting practice, something which had not at that stage been defined. There was something to fall back on, as the International Accounting Standards Committee (IASC) had been formed in 1973, charged with the task of promoting international accounting standardisation. Because it represents the viewpoints of members of the accounting profession in no less than twelve major western countries most of the statements of standard practice issued by this body have been fairly generalised, but even so they have given guidelines within which the professional accounting bodies of member countries have been able to formulate their own standards. South Africa was a founder member of the IASC, and has subsequently served on its board, so it could be reasonably argued that these standards form the basis of GAAP in this country. The current position regarding statements issued by the IASC is that International Accounting Standards (IAS) should be adopted by the profession in member countries if they have no equivalent local standard or if the local standard agrees with the IAS; that local standards should only be adopted where they are more restrictive than the IAS; and that where there is conflict between the local and the international standards the professional bodies should 'use their best endeavours' to support compliance with the international standard or at least to ensure disclosure of the extent of non-compliance. South Africa has recently been taken to task for complying with the letter rather than the spirit of this last requirement.

To give substance to a South African set of GAAPs, however, the Accounting Practice Board (APB) was constituted in addition in 1973. This board consists of representatives of organised commerce (SACOB, Die Afrikaanse Handels-instituut), industry (Steel and Engineering Industries Federation of South Africa, the Chamber of Mines) and the major accounting bodies (Public Accountants and Auditors Board, Chartered Institute of Secretaries and Administrators, Chartered Institute of Management Accountants). There are no representatives of other bodies which may be presumed to have some interest in the matter, such as shareholders, organised labour and consumer bodies; the APB consists of the preparers of the statements rather than the users.

Proposed statements of GAAP are prepared by the South African Institute of Chartered Accountants through its Accounting Practices Committee (APC), sometimes after the issue has been aired by way of a discussion paper (DP). These are considered by the APB and after consideration and amendment, if felt necessary, these are circulated in the form of Exposure Drafts (ED) for comment. In the light of comment received the ED will be adopted, possibly with modifications, or possibly rejected or referred back to a committee for further consideration or modification.

There is no law requiring adherence to statements of GAAP. Counsel's opinion on the legal force of these statements was that compliance with these statements was sufficient to satisfy the requirements of the Companies Act, but that non-compliance with the statements was not necessarily non-compliance with the Act. Circumstances could arise which would result in fuller disclosure if some practice were employed other than one specified as GAAP. The auditor would in such cases presumably have to decide whether the financial statements did give full disclosure or whether he should qualify his report on the financial statements.

The APB started issuing statements in late 1973 with the non-controversial 1.001 'Disclosure of Accounting Policies' which came into effect on 1 January 1974. The numbering method used was subsequently changed so that this statement is now known as AC101. Many more Exposure Drafts have been issued which have not yet become statements, and some of these have been issued as guidelines numbered AC200 and up. The guidelines contain those parts on which finalisation has been reached but which are not yet definitive statements because there may be matters still under discussion which will be included in the eventual statement.

5. The South African Statements of GAAP

Summaries of the contents of the first eighteen statements issued in this country are given below. These cover only the salient points and anyone wishing to apply them or to settle any arguments is advised to use the actual statements in all their detail.

5.1 AC101 "Disclosure of Accounting Policies"

This statement was issued in conjunction with AC100 'Preface to statements of Generally Accepted Practice' which sets out the method of preparation and approval of statements, the application of such statements, legal application and the opinion of counsel to which reference was made above. The statement defines *Fundamental Accounting Concepts* (the going-concern convention, the matching convention, the consistency convention and the prudence convention discussed in chapter 4), *Accounting Bases* (which are the various methods developed for applying the accounting concepts in particular circumstances) and *Accounting Policies* (the specific accounting bases adopted by a particular undertaking). It discusses the problems in applying the concepts and especially the significance of the disclosure of accounting policies since different accounting bases (for example in the valuation of stock) can lead to significantly different financial results being shown.

5.2 AC102 "Taxation in the financial statements of companies"

This statement examines disclosure requirements in those odd seeming cases where tax provided does not seem to bear any relationship to the profits disclosed in the financial statements. These differences usually arise because the company is able to take advantage of some specific tax provisions which often have the effect of postponing or deferring the payment of income tax.

There are two broad types of differences:
- Timing differences arise such as those caused by accelerated depreciation allowances, which defer payment of tax to a later period.

● Permanent differences arise when specific incomes are not taxable or specific expenses are not allowable.

In the case of timing differences the statement requires that provision be made for the tax which will be payable at some later date. It accepts the revolving nature of the deferred tax provision which arises when the company continually becomes able to take advantage of new allowances as it keeps buying new plant, for instance. It refers to this phenomenon as "recurring timing differences".

It also places some emphasis on the difference between the partial allocation basis, which only takes tax differences into account to the extent that it is probable that an asset or liability will crystallise in the near future, and the comprehensive allocation basis which takes into account the tax effects of all timing differences.

The comprehensive allocation basis is to be used except where the firm can reasonably estimate the pattern of its future timing differences. To substantiate its ability to estimate this it must present in the notes to the financial statements a statement showing the expected pattern over the next three years.

The statement also takes account of the effect of assessed losses, pointing out that these will affect future tax liability if a profit is made and that where there is a reasonable prospect of this happening the assessed loss should be treated as a deferred tax benefit.

Where minimum companies tax representing prepayment of taxes is payable, the amount paid may be treated as a current asset or as a reduction of deferred tax liability, whichever is more appropriate.

The statement drops the ambivalence of the previous statement concerning the method of providing for deferred tax and specifies that the liability method must be used. It also specifies the information to be given in the notes to the financial statements. This includes a note to the effect that deferred tax is provided, a tax reconciliation statement showing why the effective tax rate differs from the nominal rate and a table of the expected pattern of movements on the deferred tax account for the next three years.

5.3 AC103 "Extraordinary items and prior year adjustments"

This statement defines the following three items:
● Extraordinary items are those material items of income and expense arising from activities outside the ordinary activities of the enterprise, for example the discontinuation of a major part of the business of the enterprise;
● Abnormal items are those which arise from the normal activities of the enterprise but are unusual because of their size, such as unusually high maintenance costs in one particular year;
● Prior year adjustments are corrections of fundamental errors made in prior years or adjustments arising from a change in the accounting base used, such as a change from FIFO to LIFO method of stock valuation.

The reasoning followed by the statement is that the income statement should show not only the results of the operations for the year under review, but also extraordinary items and prior year adjustments. No requirements exists for the separate disclosure of abnormal items, but the income statement should show at least:

- Net income before extraordinary items;
- The net effect of extraordinary items after allowing for any effect on tax and any outside shareholders' interest;
- Net income for the period;
- The net effect of prior year adjustments; and
- Obviously, while not mentioned in the statement, the net amount available for shareholders after all these adjustments have taken place.

5.4 AC104 "Earnings per share"

While the importance of earnings per share (EPS) as a measure of the success of an investment has often been overstated, there is no doubt that a great many people do rely on this figure and that it is therefore important that the method of determining it, if it is disclosed in the financial statements, should be standardised. The statement applies specifically to those companies which are listed on a recognised stock exchange only.

EPS is to be stated in the financial statements and in terms of cents per share, not as a percentage. It is to be calculated by taking into account the full income attributable to equity share capital and dividing this by the weighted average number of shares in issue and ranking for dividend during that period. The method of taking into account changes in share capital is laid down, whether the change is due to new share issues, reduction of share capital or share exchanges, and there is a strict requirement that full tax charges including deferred tax be brought into account. Potential dilution of future EPS by new share issues during the period should be mentioned, but no attempt to quantify the extent of such dilution is necessary.

5.5 AC105 "Disclosure of leases in the financial statements of lessees"

The increasing extent of so called 'off balance sheet' financing after about 1960 led to doubts regarding adequate disclosure. The balance sheet traditionally has included a list of assets *owned* by the enterprise. Many firms were, however, using assets not owned by themselves but leased from others, often under a lease contract which effectively passed ownership to themselves at the conclusion of the lease. These assets were not always reflected on the balance sheet until the effective passing of ownership, with the result that it was not possible to gain an impression of the assets used in the enterprise by looking at the balance sheet. This made interfirm comparison extremely difficult as the firm using the 'off balance sheet' assets would invariably reflect a far greater assets turnover since at least some of its assets would be omitted from the denominator.

This statement proposes to eliminate this problem by looking at the substance of the transaction and starts with two definitions:

- A finance lease is one that transfers substantially all the risks and rewards of ownership to the lessee;
- An operating lease is any lease other than a finance lease.

The statement proposes that finance leases be capitalised, but does not make this compulsory, and that operating leases should not be capitalised. The effect of this is that assets leased under a finance lease will be reflected on the balance sheet in the same way as owned assets, with cost and accumulated depreciation being shown. This obviously changes the legal status of a balance sheet in that amounts are reflected as assets in respect of movables which are actually the property of someone else, the lessor, but it does make the balance sheet more realistic for evaluation purposes. To cater for doubts about the validity of this approach, the statement requires separate disclosure of the amounts owing under leases, details of repayments to be made and the amount of depreciation charged on these assets. Profits or losses arising from disposal of these assets must also be reflected.

If the leases are not capitalised, all expenditure in terms of lease contracts must be stated, including expenditure deferred or provided for as a result of the application of the matching concept.

This statement came into effect on 1 July 1982.

5.6 AC106 "Depreciation Accounting"

This statement seems fairly obvious. It did not state anything new, but clarified a few matters. A depreciable asset is defined as one which has a limited useful life, but which extends over more than one accounting period, and which is held by the enterprise to be used in the production of income from productive activities, services or rentals. Depreciation is the allocation of the cost of that asset over its useful life. Most fixed assets are included in the definition of depreciable assets, but land is specifically excluded except where the value of that land is dependent on the value of minerals which are being extracted from it. Buildings are included, but not very enthusiastically; it is not really necessary to provide depreciation on buildings unless you feel you should. Once an asset is classified as a depreciable asset it must be depreciated and the basis of depreciation should be consistent. The effect of any change in the basis should be quantified, if possible, and disclosed.

The method of depreciation, the estimate of useful life and the estimate of residual value if any, are left to individual judgement. However, full disclosure is required of the method used, the amount of depreciation charged during the year, the gross amount of depreciable assets and the relative accumulated depreciation.

The valuation base on which depreciation is based should also be disclosed, whether at cost or a valuation of some sort.

This statement applies to any financial statements prepared in respect of a period ended on or after 1 January 1983.

5.7 AC107 "Contingencies and events after balance sheet date"

Contigencies are defined as conditions or situations where the ultimate outcome, gain or loss, will only be confirmed if the event does or does not take place, with contingent gains or losses being defined accordingly. An example is a court case where an unfavourable verdict would result in a loss while a favourable one would result in a gain.

The Statement requires disclosure of contingent losses, either by way of a charge in the income statement if a loss, the amount of which can be reasonably estimated, seems the likely outcome, or else by way of a note to the financial statements.

Contingent gains, by an application of the prudence concept, should not be disclosed.

There is usually a lapse of time between the date at which the financial statements are prepared and the date on which they are sent to shareholders. Events between these two dates can have a bearing on the financial statements. There are two kinds of events after the balance sheet date which require disclosure:

● Those which result in greater clarity concerning the valuation of assets or liabilities at the date of the balance sheet, such as a decision in the court case mentioned above. In this case the financial statements should be adjusted to reflect the actual amounts.

● Those which do not affect the financial statements, but which have a bearing on the evaluation of the company on the date at which the financial statements are sent to shareholders. These could include such matters as expropriation of a foreign subsidiary by a new government in the country concerned after the date of the balance sheet. In such a case the financial statements should not be adjusted since they do reasonably present the position at the year end, but a note concerning the event and its effect, if quantifiable, should be added. This type of note customarily forms part of the director's report.

This statement also had an effective date of 1 January 1983.

5.8 AC108 "Valuation and presentation of stock in the context of the historical cost system"

This statement defines stock, including work in progress, to be tangible property held for resale in the ordinary course of business or in the course of production for resale or to be consumed in the production of goods for resale. Generally, the statement requires these goods to be valued for balance sheet purposes at historical cost based on the First in, First out (FIFO) system or the weighted average cost system.

Under the FIFO system, and most others, the actual physical movements of stock items are ignored and it is presumed that the items being sold represent the oldest stock on hand whether or not there is any reason to believe that this is true. The items which remain are therefore the newest items and are valued at the cost of the most recent purchases. The weighted average method calculates an average cost of items purchased during the period under review and uses this as the basis for valuing the remaining items.

The Last in, First out (LIFO) method is favoured in times of rising prices by many firms and was allowed until recently by the tax authorities. Under this system the items sold are presumed to have come from the last batch purchased, so that the remaining items are from earlier batches and should be valued at the prices paid for those. When prices are rising this means that stock valuations are lower under this method because the effect of price increases is largely eliminated. Stated profits are therefore smaller than under FIFO, and more realistic in that an increase in the price of your inputs can scarcely be regarded as a profit. However, the statement requires that undertakings using this system include a note indicating the effect of using this method of valuation rather than the approved methods.

Provision is also made for using the actual cost of an item where this can be ascertained due to the nature of the product. A motor dealer, for instance, should be able to identify the actual cost of each motor vehicle standing on his floor waiting to be sold.

In all cases, where the market value of the stock is lower than the historical cost, stock should be written down to the market value.

Finally, full disclosure should be made of valuation methods used, stocks should be subdivided into different categories (where this is applicable) and the effects of any changes in the basis of valuation. The effective date of his statement was 1 April 1983.

5.9 AC109 "Accounting for construction contracts"

This statement applies to contractors in cases where a contract has activities spread over more than one accounting period. It accepts that a contractor has the right to decide on whether he apportions the profit on the contract over the period of the contract or whether he takes all the profit upon completion of the contract, but states a preference for the apportionment or 'percentage of completion' method as presenting a fuller picture of the operations. Where there is a high level of uncertainty, however, it may be more appropriate to use the completed contract method, and the percentage of completion method cannot be used unless the percentage of completion can be reasonably estimated and costs attributable to the contract can be clearly identified. In the case of cost plus contracts, costs not to be recovered under the contract must also be reasonably determinable.

There are provisions calling for disclosure of the amount of construction work in progress, how much is under fixed cost contracts and how much under cost plus contracts; progress payments received and the method of arriving at turnover, plus of course the accounting method used.

The statement came into effect on 1 January 1984.

5.10 AC110 "Accounting for the results of associated companies and nonconsolidated subsidiaries under the equity method"

This statement defines the two methods of accounting for investments in associated companies and nonconsolidated subdiaries:

● The cost method by which only the cost of acquiring the shares in the investee company is shown on the face of the balance sheet and only dividend income received from it is shown as income;

● The equity method by which changes in the value of the investee company are reflected by showing the relative portion of the investee company's income as income to the investor and adding this amount to the cost of the investment.

Dividends received are then shown as deductions from this cost or, alternatively stated, only the after dividend portion of the total income accruing to the shares is added to the cost.

The statement lays down that where a company either owns more than twenty per cent of the equity share capital of another company or can exercise significant influence over the financial and operating policies of that company, the equity method should be employed. The investor company is entitled to choose either of the criteria for the definition of associated company and must then apply this criterion consistently. This differs from the international statement which only uses the 20 per cent measure as a guideline and not as a basis for definition.

A second factor to be taken into account is the nature of the investment. Where the shares are held for short term or speculative purposes it would be pointless to account for them in any other way than under the cost method.

If a company does not apply the equity method after 1 October 1983 it must state its reasons and give particulars regarding the name and value of the investment as well as the percentage of voting power held.

5.11 AC111 "Revenue recognition"

This statement defines when a transaction should be recognised as being completed so that the revenue flowing from that transaction can prudently be recognised as having been earned. Broadly, revenue from sales of goods is earned when the risks of ownership have passed to the buyer and the collectibility of the revenue is reasonably assured. Where sales of services are concerned, the services should have been performed and use can be made of either the completed contract or percentage of completion method in cases where services are performed under contracts which have not expired at the end of a financial period. Investment income should be recognised on an accrual basis in the case of interest and on the date when shareholders become entitled to dividends in the case of share investments. The appendix gives specific guidelines for various types of transactions where there may be some doubts.

This statement is one which largely codified generally existing practice and came into effect on 1 January 1985.

5.12 AC112 "Accounting for the effects of changes in foreign currency exchange rates"

This statement faces the problems arising from the floating exchange rates which currently reign and lays down guidelines for conversion of the currency amounts in respect of operating income and expenditure and of assets and liabilities.

It starts off by examining the difference in treatment which may be applicable to completed transactions, where there are realised gains or losses, and those which have not been completed during the period. Some of these may have some years to run, and it is impossible to state in advance what the final gain or loss may be. In this case it may be appropriate to take into account unrealised gains or losses relating to the period under review, or it may be more appropriate to take the eventual gain or loss into account when the transaction is finally completed. In the latter case it will be necessary to disclose by way of note the fact that there is a deferred foreign currency transaction. There should also be a disclosure by way of note of the amount of unhedged or uncovered transactions outstanding at balance sheet date.

As far as the mechanics are concerned, assets and liabilities should be brought into account at the exchange rate ruling on the date of the financial statements, while transactions during the year should be recorded at the dates ruling when the transaction took place or at a weighted average rate for the period.

5.13 AC113 "Lessor accounting"

This extends the requirements of AC105 concerning the disclosure in the statements of lessees to the statements of lessors. Its first pertinent point is that the disclosure in the statements of lessors must be based on the substance of the lease and not on its legal form, and uses the same definitions of "operating lease" and "financial lease".

The latter are to be treated as sales, with receipts being treated as repayment of capital and payment of finance charges. The finance portion of the lease payments will be treated as income, whereas total receipts from operating leases must be treated as income.

5.14 AC114 "Capitalisation of borrowing costs"

Interest costs on money borrowed to purchase a productive asset may be treated as part of the cost of that asset. In addition, foreign exchange losses and amortisation of such costs as discounts or premiums arising on the borrowing or repayment of money may be treated the same way. The statement does not require this to be done, but requires a consistent policy of either capitalisation or non-capitalisation to be adopted. It gives a discussion of the pros and cons of capitalisation, and lays down that, if capitalisation is the policy to be adopted, this capitalisation should cease when the asset is ready for its intended use or when operations commence.

The requirements to be met if a policy of capitalisation is adopted are stated, as is the requirement that the policy of capitalisation or non-capitalisation and the amount of borrowing costs identifying the portions capitalised, should be disclosed.

The effective date of this statement is 1 January 1986.

5.15 AC115 "Reporting financial information by segment"

This statement requires the separate disclosure of segment income. The segment can either be geographical, relating to a specific country or group of countries, or industry, relating to different products or services or groups of products or services. It is applicable to listed companies and to other large enterprises, the financial statements of which may be widely distributed.

Total disclosure is not required, but as a minimum the statements must disclose the segment sales or revenue, the segment result and the segment assets employed. Disclosure must also be made of changes in the period to segment identification, segment accounting policy and accounting practices used in reporting segment information.

5.16 AC116 "Disclosure of retirement benefit information in financial statements"

In view of the significant amounts tied up in various company retirement plans it was deemed necessary to report on this aspect so that shareholders could evaluate the significance of the relevant costs in the accounting period and the actual and contingent liabilities at balance sheet date. The statement starts off by discussing various aspects of retirement benefit plans and reviews the differences between the funding objectives and the accounting objectives. Problems such as changes in plans and how they affect both current and retired employees are discussed before the statement itself is set out.

The statement deals only with disclosure requirements. The nature of the plan must be disclosed along with the accounting policies applied and details of the most recent actuarial valuation. Where the fund is not actuarially valued this must be disclosed.

The effective date of this statement is 1 January 1987.

5.17 AC117 "Accounting for discontinued operations"

This statement does not apply to mining operations which are run down over time by their very nature, but to operations or segments of operations which are deliberately discontinued by management either by disposal or abandonment. It requires the disclosure of the profit or loss on discontinuance to be shown as an extraordinary item, this to include the results of discontinued operations from date of discontinuance to effective disposal date, direct costs of discontinuance and proceeds of disposal less net carrying value of assets and liabilities of the discontinued operation.

Separate disclosure should also be made of the identity of the discontinued operation, the expected disposal date where applicable and the remaining assets and liabilities of the discontinued operation.

The effective date of this statement is 1 January 1987.

5.18 AC118 "Cash Flow Information"

The statement is dealt with fully in Chapter 16. "Funds flow and cash flow analysis". Briefly, it deals with the presentation of cash flow information in such a way as to comply with the requirements of the Companies Act for a statement of sources and applications of funds.

The statement applies to all financial statements covering periods commencing on or after 1 October 1988.

6. Accounting guidelines

Non-binding guidelines currently in existence include AC201 "Disclosure of effects of changing prices on financial results" which is discussed in detail in chapter 12 along with the related AC202 "Accounting for fixed asset revaluations" and AC203 "Valuation of real estate assets".

AC204 "Accounting and reporting practices of long term insurance institutions" obviously applies only to those rather specialised institutions and will not be discussed further here.

7. The future of GAAP in South Africa

There is pressure on the South African profession, both internally and externally, to adopt the GAAP of the IASC. This will certainly happen at some time in the future, and could be adopted now with possibly beneficial results for the local profession. There is little doubt that the work done here does duplicate or at least overlap with the process of development of standards elsewhere.

Adopting the international GAAP could not only lead to cost savings for the local profession but also lead to wider acceptance of South African reporting internationally. It will almost certainly be necessary, though, to adapt some of the standards to take account of local conditions.

Key words
Accounting practices
Accounting Practices Board
Accounting Practices Committee
Exposure draft
Statement of generally accepted accounting practice
Accounting guideline
International Accounting Standards Committee
Technical reports
International Accounting Standards

Chapter 4

The legal environment: Forms of organisation

Many laws and regulations apply to all businesses, such as the various tax laws, and many more to all businesses of a particular type, such as the industrial council regulations. Municipal regulations affect all businesses operating within a defined area regardless of the legal form of the undertaking. However, there are many laws and regulations which apply only to one or other particular type of organisation, and this chapter concentrates on the characteristics of each of the major forms of organisation.

1. **Sole traders or one-man businesses**

2. **Partnerships**

3. **Close corporations**

4. **Companies**

5. **Co-operatives**

6. **Sundry other matters**

1. Sole traders or one-man businesses

Most small businesses start out in this form. It has advantages in respect of cost in that it is not necessary to incur any registration costs and in respect of simplicity since there are no formal laws of organisation regulating the undertaking. The entrepreneur simply finds premises and a product and starts business. Sometimes he even foregoes the premises and simply becomes a hawker, selling his goods from door to door or on the street, or a self-employed taxi driver.

The advantages of this form of organisation are legion. As mentioned above, there is no public register of such businesses which means that the businessman has a great deal of freedom in which to manoeuver. He is solely responsible for deciding the policies to be followed by the firm and is responsible for seeing that those policies are actually carried out. He can therefore change his policies at a moments notice, without reference to anyone else, if he feels that circumstances have so changed as to warrant a change in policy or management style. All profits made by the undertaking belong to him alone, to deal with as he sees fit.

Naturally, there are disadvantages to counterbalance this freedom of action. These are generally financial by nature. Since all profits are the owner's to deal with as he sees fit, all losses are also his to deal with as he is able. Since he is answerable to no one, he is also unable to depend on anyone else's financial assistance and must rely on his own financial resources. This is by far the greatest problem faced by the one man business, since it is very seldom that a person goes into business with sufficient cash to carry the business through all its teething troubles and then through its later expansion. Most small businesses fail within three years, and usually because of lack of sufficient initial capital to carry them through this first period.

Failure, of course, brings to light the other great drawback of this form of organisation. While the accountant makes a distinction between the business and its owner for his financial records, the law makes no such distinction and regards the business and its owner as one entity. Failure of a business therefore exposes the owner to the risk of losing all his personal possessions as the creditors of the business take his house and car and whatever else they can lay their hands on in order to meet their claims against the business. This is seldom in the mind of the entrepreneur, of course, because he does not seriously consider the risk of failure when he sets out on a new business venture.

Summary

Who is served?	The consumer
Who decides on policy?	The owner
Who manages?	The owner
Who owns the business?	The owner
How is voting done?	None necessary
How may profits be applied?	As the owner wishes
What is personal liability?	Total—all the assets of the owner
Audit required?	No

2. Partnerships

2.1 Ordinary partnerships

Most one-man businesses struggle because of lack of capital, and the most obvious way of overcoming this lack is to look for a partner, or partners, who can put extra capital into the undertaking. The partner can also share some of the burdens of the business by undertaking certain of the tasks required of the owner/manager. Members of those professions which do not permit of incorporation usually expand in this way, but so do many trading firms. In terms of a provision of the Companies Act of 1973 no trading partnership may have more than twenty partners, but this does not apply to professional partnerships. Most of our partnership law is similarly indirect. There is no South African Partnership Act, as there is in so many other countries, and partnerships are regulated in terms of common law, case law and certain references in acts such as the Companies Act.

In terms of our law, as confirmed in *Joubert v Tarry & Co* 1915 TPD 277, the requirements for a valid partnership are very simple:
(a) there must be two or more people who
(b) operate a lawful business together, each contributing something
(c) for the purpose of making a profit
(d) which they will share among themselves.

As soon as these conditions exist there is a partnership. No registration is necessary and no documents need to be drawn up. If people act in such a way that a reasonable person would infer from their actions that the necessary conditions were being met, the courts would hold that a partnership existed even if this was not the intention of the parties, or some of the parties, concerned (see *Fink v Fink,* 1945 W.L.D. 226 and *Annabhay v Ramlall and Others* 1960 (3) S.A. 802 (D)). Further, if one of the parties finds that he has been induced to enter into a partnership by misrepresentation he is only entitled to claim rescission of the partnership. It is voidable, not void, and the ordinary consequences of partnership such as liability for debts incurred prior to the rescission will remain (*Farmer's Co-operative v Wrightson*, 1928 S.R. 10).

The partnership is still a very informal arrangement unless an agreement is drawn up imposing a series of restrictions on the various partners and on the partnership as a whole. This informality, and its concomittant anonymity, appeals to a great many people who shrink from the more rigid requirements imposed by the various types of incorporation. Since it is not incorporated, the partnership does not have a legal personality. It exists only in the persons of the individual partners who comprise it, and ceases to exist as soon as there is a change in the members of the partnership, whether by admission of a new partner or by the withdrawal of one of the existing partners. For some purposes it is what has been called a quasi-legal personality (*Potchefstroom Dairies v Standard Milk Supply Co* 1913 TPD 317). The partnership can be sued in terms of the Insolvency Act, for instance, with the implication that all the partners are being sued even though their names do not appear in the application to the Court. The partnership must register in respect of various tax acts and other acts relating to employers, but the partnership is simply the vehicle which the individual partners use, primarily for administrative convenience.

Since it does not have a legal personality the partnership cannot own fixed property in terms of the Deeds Registries Act, and any fixed property acquired by the partnership will be registered jointly in the names of the partners. A change of partners will require a new registration in the names of the new partners.

Administratively the partnership differs from the one-man business mainly in that the right of the entrepreneur to act as he feels best is restricted. He is no longer able to change policies and management style as he sees fit, but is forced to discuss the matter with his partners. Partnership means that an agreement demanding the utmost good faith exists between the partners, and no partner is entitled to enter into any acts contrary to the expressed wishes of the others. Any changes can only be effected if the partners have jointly agreed to them. Policy and management decisions are therefore the result of agreement between the partners.

In the absence of any agreement to the contrary, all partners are entitled to share in the day-to-day management of the partnership. Each partner is required to exercise due diligence in the carrying out of his duties and is obliged, as well as entitled, to put forth his best efforts in the interest of the undertaking. Sharing in the management of the undertaking means that each partner is in a position to bind the partnership in respect of any acts which are part of the normal business of the undertaking. Signature by any one of the partners to a contract which is in the normal course of the partnership's business will mean that the partnership can be compelled to carry out the terms of the contract.

Of course, a partnership agreement can be drawn up which could limit the power of any one of the partners or delegate all signing powers in respect of certain contracts to one of the partners. This partnership agreement would be binding on all members of the partnership, but would not be valid against third parties. The reason for this is that such a partnership agreement is not registered in any public registry but is purely an internal document regulating the relationships of the partners with each other. Outside parties can therefore not be presumed to carry constructive knowledge of such agreement and are therefore not bound by it. The partnership would be bound by a contract signed on its behalf by a member not entitled to sign such contracts in terms of a partnership agreement, but the other partners would be entitled to recover from the offending partner any monetary losses suffered as a result of his delinquent action. This, of course, presumes that he is able to bear the costs of making any reparation.

If the partnership activities result in the making of a profit, this will be divided among the partners. Profit here has been held to be net profit after the deduction of all expenses so that an agreement whereby one person receives a proportion of the gross income of any undertaking, such as a commission on sales, is not an agreement of partnership (*Blumberg & Sulski v Brown & Freitas*, 1922 T.P.D. 130). In the absence of any agreement the division will be in the same proportion as the proportion of capital contributed by each of the partners or, in cases where this is not possible to determine, equally. The most common case in which the proportion is not determinable is where one of the partners contributes money and the other skills or know how necessary to the successful running of the undertaking. A partnership agreement can specify any proportion for sharing of the profits and can even provide for such matters as the payment of a salary to a partner before the determination of distributable profit or payment of interest on the various capital accounts.

Variations can also be made when dealing with losses incurred by the partnership, though losses will normally be shared in the same proportion as profits. One partner, for instance, may share only in profits but bear no share of any losses incurred. This has been held to mean the net loss or profit over a period and not to mean that one person will share only in the results of profitable transactions and not in those of unprofitable ones (*Dickinson & Brown v Fisher's Executors*, 1916 A.D. 374).

An agreement to exempt a partner from any losses is again only valid within the partnership, and creditors of the partnership are able to attach the assets of the protected partner. He may then proceed against the other partners for recovery of the losses which he may have sustained (*Joubert v Tarry & Co.*, 1915 T.P.D. 277).

The greatest problem of the partnership again lies in the fact that the liability of the partners for the debts of the partnership business is unlimited. The liability of partners is joint and several, so that any one partner can be called upon to settle the total debts of the partnership once a partnership is insolvent. He can of course then proceed against his partners for recovery of their proportionate part of the debt.

It is important to note that proceedings can only be instituted against individual partners once the partnership has ceased to exist. While the partnership is in existence proceedings can only be instituted against the partnership as a whole, despite the fact that the partnership has no legal personality. If a creditor obtains a judgement against the partnership and the assets of the partnership are insufficient to settle his claim he can proceed against the assets of the individual partners.

A complicating factor is the position of the partnership in cases where one of the partners has a judgement taken against him in his personal capacity. If judgement is obtained in a magistrate's court the partner's creditors can attach his individual share in the partnership and sell this for the satisfaction of the judgement, which can obviously have a detrimental effect on the firm as a whole. The position is even worse where one of the partners is declared bankrupt in his personal capacity. This insolvency immediately leads to the dissolution of the partnership and calls for the distribution of the assets among the partners so that the creditors of the insolvent partner may attach his share of the partnership assets. To prevent this attachment, which may result in serious financial loss to the remaining partners, they may undertake to settle the insolvent partner's share of the undertaking out of their personal estates.

Should the partnership be declared insolvent, the personal estates of each of the partners will also be sequestrated unless one (or more) of the partners undertakes to pay the debts of the partnership and provides satisfactory surety within a time stipulated by the court.

2.1 Extraordinary partnerships

There are certain types of partnership in which some of the members of the partnership are protected in respect of partnership debts. The distinction between these types is a fine one, since both involve silent or sleeping partners with a limited liability for partnership debts as far as outside creditors are concerned. A specific partnership agreement setting out the position of the various partners, or classes of partners, vis-à-vis one another is required. Once again this document is not registered in any public registry.

The anonymous partnership is one in which two or more persons agree to carry on a business in the name of one of them, the others not participating in any way in the management of the undertaking nor holding themselves out generally to be partners. No outsider is to be aware that a partnership even exists. Creditors of the partnership are not able to proceed against the sleeping partner, though he is liable to the active partner for his proportion of the debts of the partnership. He cannot be called on to settle the debts of the partnership in the case of insolvency as can an ordinary partner.

The *en commandite* partnership is one in which two or more persons agree to carry on a business in the name of one or more of them, the others not participating in any way in the management of the undertaking nor holding themselves out generally to be partners. The *en commandite* partner is in a similar position to the anonymous partner, but is liable to his partners only to the extent of the money he has contributed to the undertaking and cannot be called on to make up any deficit incurred.

The logic behind this provision of protection is simple. A person entering into any contract with a partnership is aware that in the case of default by the partnership he can rely on the private estates of the individual partners and may rely on this to the extent that he would not have entered into the agreement if he had not had this assurance of security. If he enters into an agreement with a partnership and is not aware of the existence of the silent partners, he is obviously not relying on the private estates of those partners at the time of entering into the agreement and can therefore not claim against those estates later on. It follows that the silent partner must take every care not to allow himself to be seen as a partner by his actions or words; his name must not appear on any documents such as letterheads which are available for general perusal and he must not participate in the management of the business. The courts are not generally over-sympathetic to agreements of partnership which limit the liability of any of the partners, and where any doubts exist in the wording of such an agreement will always interpret the agreement to indicate that an ordinary partnership exists (*Barker & Co v Blore*, 1908 T.S. 1156).

Where a person enters into an agreement with one of the partners of an *ordinary partnership acting on behalf of that partnership*, it is not necessary that he be aware of the identity of all the partners in order to be able to rely on all their estates. It is sufficient that the partners acted as partners in the conduct of the business (*Eaton & Louw v Arcade Properties (Pty) Ltd*, 1961 (4) S.A. 233 (T)).

A point to be borne in mind is that the tax authorities have recently begun investigating certain tax avoidance schemes involving *en commandite* partnerships and seem determined to show that there is not a true partnership in such cases since this partner's property is not really at risk except to a possibly very limited extent. It may well be that such partnerships will be made invalid from the point of view of income tax law, and this may have a follow-on effect on the common law position of such partnerships.

2.3 Points affecting partnerships generally

The partnership must maintain financial records and each partner is entitled to full information regarding partnership affairs, though in terms of Roman-Dutch law no partner may demand a full account from his partners unless he has already given a full account of his own activities on behalf of the partnership or has at least offered to do so. Any partner appointed managing partner has as one of his duties the maintenance of such records, but is not required to give an accounting on demand at any time. He must give an accounting at the termination of the partnership and, during its existence, on an annual basis unless the partnership agreement stipulates more frequent reports. Any partner is, however, entitled to inspect the partnership books at all reasonable times.

Where one partner commits a criminal act in the furtherance of the partnership business, all the partners are deemed guilty of that act in terms of the Criminal Procedure Act. This is a deviation from the common law, and the partner who is innocent today must prove that he was unaware of the criminal act and could not have prevented it from taking place in order to be in the same position as he would have been before the passing of the legislation.

A partnership is dissolved under the following circumstances:

(a) Lapse of time where the partnership has been entered into for a specified period;

(b) Termination of the partnership business where the partnership was formed to perform a specific task such as the erection of a building;

(c) Mutual agreement or notice by one of the parties that he intends dissolving the partnership;

(d) Changes in the membership of the firm whether by admission of a new partner or the withdrawal, retirement or death of one of the existing partners;

(e) Insolvency of the partnership or of any one of its members; and

(f) Order of the Court where, for instance, one of the partners is declared mentally incompetent or where one of the partners has disappeared but has not been away long enough for presumption of death. It has also been held that where on outbreak of war one of the partners is in enemy territory, either of his own free will or because of being repatriated, the partnership is dissolved.

While the law does not require a written partnership agreement it is advisable that such a document be drawn up. This document should specify the method of division of profits and losses, provide for the carrying on of the business of the partnership in the case of the death of one of the partners, provide for the carrying of insurance policies on the lives of the partners to enable surviving partners to have the cash available to settle claims by the deceased estate, provide a mechanism for the easy dissolution of the partnership and distribution of the assets, include any limitations on the powers to act of any of the partners and any other matters which are relevant to the particular partnership concerned.

Summary

Who is served?	The consumer
How many people can participate?	Two to twenty, more for professional partnerships
Who decides on policy?	The partners agree
Who manages?	All the partners or as agreed
Who owns the business?	The partners
How is voting done?	The partners agree
How may profits be applied?	As the partners agree
What is personal liability?	Total—all the assets of the partners (but see extraordinary partnerships)
Audit required?	No, except if partners agree to it

3. Close corporations

Partnerships have two major drawbacks: they do not have perpetual succession, which means that they exist only as long as the original partners remain in the business, and the liability of the partners is unlimited. Both of these drawbacks can be overcome by incorporation, and the simplest method of incorporation is to form a Close Corporation in terms of the Close Corporations Act (Act 69 of 1984).

The Close Corporation is really a simplified form of limited company, with many of the characteristics of a partnership. Administratively it differs from the partnership in that certain documents in connection with the corporation are on public register and are available for inspection by members of the public, which includes people with whom the corporation wishes to transact business. It is a fairly recent innovation, brought into existance to meet the need of small undertakings to incorporate without forcing them to comply with all the rigid requirements which apply to a larger company.

In concept, the Close Corporation is a legal personality with perpetual succession and with all the legal capacity and powers of a natural person. It has its own assets and its own liabilities distinct from those of its members. It consists of from one to ten members, all of whom must be natural persons. These persons, like partners in an ordinary partnership, are deemed to be fully involved in the business of the corporation and to participate in the management and policy-making of the corporation. Like partners, they have a duty of utmost good faith to the close corporation and to their fellow members. While there is a limit on the number of members, there is no limit on the size of the business which may be operated in this form whether in terms of assets, turnover or number of employees. Generally, the members of the corporation have their liability in respect of the debts of the corporation limited to the amount of the contribution which they have made to the corporation as set out in the founding statement, but in some circumstances they can incur unlimited liability if the various provisions of the Act are not complied with.

It is a very simple procedure to form a Close Corporation. All that is necessary is to lodge a Founding Statement (Form CK 1) in triplicate (carbon copies are acceptable) with the Registrar of Close Corporations. This form contains details of the name of the corporation, a short description of its principal business, the date on which its financial year ends, its postal and registered address and the name, address and professional qualification of its accounting officer. In addition, the names, addresses and identity numbers of each of the members is required together with details of the amount and nature of the contribution made by each. It must also be stated what percentage of the total capital is contributed by each member, who must sign in the space provided just below the enumeration of his own particulars. The last page of the form is a Certificate of Incorporation which the Registrar signs and stamps as proof of the incorporation of the Close Corporation. One of the three copies is returned to the members, one is retained by the Registrar and the third is sent to the Receiver of Revenue.

It is advisable to enquire first about the acceptability of the proposed name of the corporation, since there may already be one with the same name or one very similar, but once the name is accepted the registration takes literally minutes. No other documents are registered on incorporation, so that a member of the public cannot be presumed to have knowledge of any internal arrangements between the members of the corporation such as the limitation of the powers of any of the members to act on behalf of the corporation.

The only time other documents have to be lodged with the Registrar is when there are changes to the original founding statement (Form CK2), while the other forms prescribed by the Act deal with Court orders, application for the restoration of registration and conversion from a company to a close corporation. As far as the relationship of the members of the corporation with each other is concerned, any corporation having more than one member may at any time draw up an Association Agreement regulating the internal affairs of the corporation. A new member joining the corporation is bound by such agreement as though he had signed it, but this document is purely an internal one and is not registered. In the absence of such an association agreement, sections 46 to 52 of the Act effectively provide the rules for the internal relationships of the members with one another. Amongst other things, provision is made for all members to share in the management of the business and for voting to take place on the basis that each member has voting power corresponding to the percentage of his interest in the total capital of the corporation.

While it is not subject to audit, a Close Corporation must appoint an accounting officer who is charged with determining whether the annual financial statements are in accordance with the financial records, determining the accounting policies applied in the preparation of the financial statements and reporting to the members on these matters. He also has certain other duties, which are detailed in Section 62 of the Act, concerning the reporting of irregularities to the Registrar. The accounting officer may be a member of the Close Corporation, and must have a professional accounting qualification which the Minister has accepted as being adequate for the purpose acting as accounting officer. At the time of writing, the members of the following professions were accepted as qualified to act as accounting officers:

(a) The South African Institute of Chartered Accounts;

(b) Accountants and auditors registered under the Public Accountants and Auditors Act 51 of 1951;

(c) The South African Institute of Chartered Secretaries and Administrators;

(d) Chartered Institute of Management Accountants;

(e) The Association of Commercial and Financial Technicians of Southern Africa; and

(f) Some members of the Institute of Administration and Commerce of Southern Africa who have passed certain named examinations in some of the variations of this diploma.

Other qualifications may from time to time be accepted by the Minister and notice of such acceptance will be published in the Government Gazette.

The personal liabilities of the members is normally limited to the amount of their contribution, but the Act provides for exceptions to this. A member will generally only be liable to outside parties if the business is conducted with gross negligence, or if certain actions constitute a gross abuse of the juristic personality of the corporation, but there are some transgressions of the Act which render the members liable to fines in their personal capacity. Members are also liable to their fellow members and to the corporation for losses suffered as a result of a breach of their fiduciary duty, and in some specified circumstances members can become liable in their personal capacity in respect of certain specified liabilities of the corporation.

Summary

Who is served?	The consumer
How many people can participate?	One to ten natural persons
Who decides on policy?	The members agree
Who manages?	All the members or as agreed
Who owns the business?	The close corporation, which is owned by the members
How is voting done?	As the members agree
How may profits be applied?	As the members agree
What is personal liability?	Limited to the amount of the contribution but there are exceptions
Audit required?	No, but a qualified accounting officer must be appointed

4. Companies

For most of commercial history there were no undertakings which required very large amounts of capital for extended periods of time. The start of the age of European exploration changed this, with government charters being granted to various groups of people to manage large areas of the world. A prime example is the Dutch East India Company. The commercial development of the company only came later, however, as the Industrial Revolution gathered steam. The economic expansion which resulted meant that for the first time there were commercial enterprises which required amounts of capital so large and for so long a time that they could not be accommodated under the form of a partnership.

The first companies were effectively large *en commandite* partnerships, with a small number of active partners and a large number of investors who were at risk only to the extent of their original contribution. There was thus a distinct separation between the investors and the management of the company, which is still a major feature of the company form of organisation and is responsible for the way in which most Companies Acts, including the South African one, are constructed.

Because of the problems inherent in the fact that partnerships had no perpetual succession, these corporations or companies soon gained juristic personality and from there to the company as we know it today was but a short step. The early companies differed from *en commandite* partnerships only in the fact of juristic personality. The active partners, who became known as directors, were still fully liable for the debts of what was then known as a "joint stock company", but the development of the theory of juristic personality soon led to the acceptance of the company as having its own assets and debts, which meant that the directors were treated in the same manner as ordinary shareholders and had their personal liability limited, usually to the contribution they had made in the form of share capital. The first companies were all large undertakings but as the advantages of perpetual succession and particularly of limited liability became more obvious, small companies also came into being and company law was adapted to allow such smaller companies.

The company as it exists today has a juristic personality distinct from that of its shareholders (*Dadoo Ltd and others v Krugersdorp Municipal Council* 1920 AD), whose personal liability for the liabilities of the company is limited. The limit of their liability is usually the amount they have paid for their shares, but there are exceptions such as the company limited by guarantee, which is discussed below, and the company which has partly paid shares. While the Companies Act only allows shares to be issued as fully paid shares, the previous Act allowed shares to be issued as partly paid. A shareholder could then purchase, say, a one Rand share and only pay ten cents on allotment of the share. As the company required more capital it could call upon the shareholder to pay in the outstanding amount up to the face value of the share. In the case of the insolvency of the company the shareholder would immediately become liable for all amounts outstanding on his shares. Such shares which were in existence when the current Act came into force are still regulated in terms of the old Act, and the purchaser of a partly paid share would find that he is liable not only for the amount he has paid for the share but also the amount required to make the share fully paid up.

The shareholders do not have the power to bind the company and are not presumed to be involved in the management of the company. These tasks are delegated by the shareholders to the directors of the company. Usually the directors are shareholders of the company, but a company can permit non-shareholders to act as directors if it so wishes. Directors are elected by the shareholders in accordance with the company's own rules, and stand in a position of utmost good faith towards the company and the shareholders. It is their responsibility to put forward their best efforts on behalf of the company and to report to the shareholders on their actions on behalf of those who elected them. In larger companies the directors are often not involved in the day to day management of the company, but they are responsible for the appointment of people to perform this task.

The company has its own assets and liabilities, its own profits (on which it pays its own income taxes) and its own losses. In South Africa companies are controlled by the Companies Act, Act 61 of 1973. This act is the culmination of developments over the last few centuries, and will obviously continue to be amended to take new developments and changes in the commercial world into account. The act is largely concerned with the protection of shareholders. It recognises that most shareholders have no intimate contact with the companies in which they have invested, and seeks to prevent directors from concealing information about the companies and from performing any acts which might affect the value of the shareholder's investment without first informing the shareholder and, in many cases, obtaining his permission. It is thus primarily aimed at large companies and not at those with only a few shareholders who are involved in the management of the business, but it does make a few concessions to these smaller companies since, before the Close Corporations Act, small businesses could only incorporate in terms of the Companies Act.

The formation of a company is a more complex affair than that of a close corporation. Firstly, formal acceptance of the proposed name of the company must be received from the Registrar of Companies; this is applied for on form CM5. Once the name has been approved three sets of documents are prepared in triplicate, and it is necessary to obtain a notarial certificate that the three copies are identical. The first document is the Certificate of Incorporation (form CM1), which is very similar to the last page of the founding statement of the Close Corporation. This is signed and stamped by the Registrar as proof of incorporation. Next is the Memorandum of Association of the company, which is equivalent to the founding statement of the Close Corporation. It consists of forms CM2A, CM2B and either CM2C (where more than one person signs the memorandum) or CM2D (where only one person signs the memorandum), and contains the name of the company, the main object for which the company is formed, special powers or exclusions of powers, details of pre-incorporation contracts and details of the share capital. The third document to be prepared is the Articles of Association, which regulates the internal relationships between the company and its members, between the directors and the members and between the members themselves. This is a major difference between the company and the close corporation, for this document is placed on register and is available for inspection by any member of the public. Limitations on the borrowing powers of directors, for instance, will be contained in this document and anyone dealing with the company is deemed to have constructive knowledge of such limitation since the information is freely available to him. However, if the directors, in terms of the Articles, are empowered to perform certain acts after certain preliminaries have been completed, the outside party is not required to ensure that such preliminary acts have in fact been performed (first stated in the British case of *Royal British Bank v Turquand* 1868 LR5 EQ316 and confirmed in the South African courts in *The Mine Workers Union v J P Prinsloo* 1948 (3) SA (AD)). Two model sets of Articles of Association are contained in the First Schedule to the Companies Act, Table A for a public company having a share capital and Table B for a private company. A company is entitled to adopt one of these, with or without modification, or to draw up its own set of Articles.

The Memorandum and Articles of Association have both to be signed by the persons forming the company, each of whom has to state the number of shares he is taking up. The signatories to the Memorandum are then not only the first shareholders of the company, they are also the first directors until a meeting of shareholders has taken place at which directors are appointed. Other documents which have to be lodged when registering a company include the notice of approval of the name, a notice of the address of the registered office of the company, a statement by each signatory that the share capital will be sufficient for the purposes of the company or, if not, how the company will raise the extra funds necessary, details of all the directors and officers of the company and a Certificate to Commence Business, which must be signed and stamped by the Registrar before the company can start operating.

A final document which is necessary is an agreement by an auditor to accept appointment, since a company must have an auditor who is registered with the Public Accountants and Auditors Board. The auditor is appointed by the shareholders of the company, not by the directors, and it is his duty to report to the shareholders on the acceptability or otherwise of the reports sent to them by the directors.

Any changes to any of the above must be notified to the Registrar so that an up to date record is always on file. All of this applies to any company, whether it has one shareholder or several thousands.

There are certain differences between these companies, however, and the nature of the various types of companies will be discussed below.

4.1 Public companies

These are the companies for which the Companies Act largely caters and can be identified by the fact that the word "Limited" is added at the end of the name of the company. The Companies Act is a voluminous one, with 443 sections and 4 schedules to follow. It is divided into seventeen chapters dealing with everything from registration of a company to the winding up of a company, but chapters V to XI, comprising sections 74 to 310, make up the bulk of the Act. These deal with the offering of shares, the administration of companies, directors, the ways in which shareholders can proceed against the company to obtain remedy for perceived unfair treatment by the company or the directors, with auditors and with the requirements for accounting and disclosure to members.

A public company must have a minimum of seven shareholders and two directors. No maxima are laid down in the Act. It has the right to issue a prospectus inviting members of the public to subscribe for shares in the company. Such a prospectus must comply with the requirements of Schedule 3 of the Act, giving sufficient information to enable the prospective investor to evaluate the risk and reward of investment in the company. If it does allot shares after registration, whether as a result of the issue of a prospectus or otherwise, it must inform the Registrar of this fact.

It may apply for a listing on a stock exchange, in which case it will have to comply with the rules of that stock exchange as well as with the Companies Act. It will normally have no restrictions on the transferability of its shares in any case, but this will definitely be required before any listing on a stock exchange is granted.

There is a further type of public company which should be noted. A company can be registered where the liability of the members is limited, not by the amount they have paid for their shares, but by guarantee. Each shareholder guarantees to contribute a certain amount in the event of the company being wound up, and his liability is limited to the amount of his guarantee. All such companies are regarded as public companies and can be identified by the words "Limited by Guarantee" as the last part of the name.

Summary

Who is served?	The consumer
How many people can participate?	From seven upwards
Who decides on policy?	The directors
Who manages?	Professional managers appointed by the directors
Who owns the business?	The company, which is owned by the shareholders
How is voting done?	One vote per share
How may profits be applied?	Dividends to shareholders, retained for expansion
What is personal liability?	Limited to the amount paid for the shares or to amount guaranteed
Audit required?	Yes

4.2 Private companies

Private companies are generally smaller business and can be identified by the words "(Proprietary) Limited" at the end of the name. They are exempted from some sections of the Companies Act: there can be variations in the voting rights of shares of the same class, for instance, and the auditor of the company may also perform some or all of the duties of the bookkeeper of the company. They are also exempted from requirements in respect of half-yearly interim reports and have different requirements regarding quorums at meetings.

In return for these exemptions certain restrictions are imposed on them. They may not approach the public to subscribe for shares. They may not have more than fifty members, though employees and former employees who became shareholders while they were employees are not included in this total. Finally, they must impose restrictions on the transferability of their shares. This is usually done by requiring that a shareholder wishing to dispose of his shares must first offer them to other existing shareholders and that such existing shareholders can have the right to refuse to register the transfer of shares to a person of whom they do not approve.

Summary

Who is served?	The consumer
How many people can participate?	One to fifty
Who decides on policy?	The directors
Who manages?	Professional managers who may be the directors
Who owns the business?	The company, which is owned by the shareholders
How is voting done?	One vote per share, but this can be varied
How may profits be applied?	Dividends to shareholders, retained for expansion
What is personal liability?	Limited to the amount paid for the shares
Audit required?	Yes

4.3 Incorporated companies

Reference was made above to the fact that limited liability is not a characteristic of all companies registered under the Companies Act. The previous Companies Act permitted the registration of companies with unlimited liability, and the current Act provides that companies so registered under that Act can retain their status, but there is no provision for unlimited companies except for the special case of the incorporated company.

This form of company was introduced especially to meet the desire of professional people for the privilege of incorporation and perpetual succession. Not all professional bodies have modified their rules to allow their members to incorporate. The incorporated company is essentially a private company with a provision in its articles that the directors and past directors are jointly and severally liable with the company for its debts, provided that these were contracted during their period of office. Such a company has as the last word of its name the word "Incorporated". (This word has different meanings in different countries. In the United States of America, for instance, the word Incorporated is generally used instead of the word Limited.)

The Articles of Association of an incorporated company often provide that only people qualified to practice the relevant profession may hold shares in the company, though this depends on the rules of professional conduct of the profession concerned.

Summary

Who is served?	The client
How many people can participate?	One to fifty
Who decides on policy?	The directors
Who manages?	The directors or professional managers who are appointed by them
Who owns the business?	The company, which is owned by the shareholders
How is voting done?	Usually one vote per share, but can be varied
How may profits be applied?	Dividends to shareholders, retained for expansion
What is personal liability?	Unlimited under certain conditions for directors and ex-directors
Audit required?	Yes

4.4 Section 21 companies

A company may be incorporated not for commercial purposes but for purposes of promoting religion, art, science, charity, recreation or other social or communal or group interests. Such a company, which must be a company limited by guarantee, is known as an association not for gain, and may use its profits only in the promotion of its main object. No dividends may be paid. The last words of its name will be "Association incorporated under section 21", though if it was incorporated before June 1980 it may use the words "Incorporated Association not for gain" instead.

Such a company has no share capital and the way in which people can become members and the determination of their voting power will be set out in the Articles of Association.

Summary

Who is served?	The community or a specified part of it
How many people can participate?	From seven upwards
Who decides on policy?	The directors
Who manages?	Professional managers appointed by the directors
Who owns the business?	The company, which is owned by the members
How is voting done?	In terms of the Articles of Association
How may profits be applied?	Promotion of the objectives of the company

What is personal liability?   Limited to the amount guaranteed
Audit required?   Yes

5. Co-operatives

Co-operatives are generally found in one of three forms in South Africa. They are either the giant agricultural co-operatives (and some estimates have put the share of South African commercial activity transacted by these co-operatives at as high as thirty per cent of the total), special farmer's co-operatives or trading co-operatives, most of the last being the small home produce co-operatives which are quite common nowadays.

In all cases the controlling Act is the Co-operatives Act, Act 91 of 1981, which appoints a Registrar of co-operatives to administer it.

A co-operative is a juristic person, just like a company, but it differs from a company in several important respects. The first of these is the objective for which it is formed.

The co-operative is formed for the benefit of its members acting in concert. A trading co-operative may have any objective, while an agricultural co-operative may be formed to market agricultural products or products derived from agricultural products, to acquire and sell requisites or facilities necessary for, or used in, farming activities, to render farming services, to carry on farming operations, to undertake insurance business on a pool basis and to act as agents for an agricultural marketing board. A special farmer co-operative may be formed for any of the same objectives as an agricultural co-operative and may in addition carry on business as a dealer in agricultural products or anything derived from agricultural products.

The controlling document of a co-operative is the Statute of that co-operative, which is akin to the Memorandum and Articles of Association of a company. It contains details of the name of the co-operative, the kind and form of co-operative it is, its objectives, the address where its main business is situated and where it may establish depots and a set of rules governing the various internal affairs.

Co-operatives are generally given much the same powers as companies, but have certain restrictions placed upon their activities. These include restrictions on borrowing and lending and on transactions with non-members. These last effectively state that agricultural co-operatives may not transact more than five per cent of their business with non-members and special farmer co-operatives not more than fifty per cent, though these can be adjusted by the Minister in respect of any particular co-operative. Restrictions are also placed on the membership of these two types of co-operative, effectively barring persons or bodies not carrying on farming operations from membership. Membership is evidenced by the holding of shares, which can be cancelled upon cessation of membership.

A co-operative can be classed as a closed co-operative if the Registrar is satisfied that its transactions were all with members, or that transactions with non-members were limited to a volume necessary for the attainment of the objectives of the co-operative. This has benefits from an income tax point of view, since a closed trading co-operative is entitled, in terms of section 27(1) of the Income Tax Act, to deduct from its taxable profit the amount of any bonus distributed to members up to 10% of the value of business transacted with members during the tax year. A similar provision in section 27(2)*(a)* allows all agricultural or special farmer co-operatives to deduct bonuses from their taxable income, subject to certain restrictions.

All other co-operatives are taxed in the same way as companies, but there are certain special allowances available to them.

Summary

Who is served?	(1) Members of the co-operative
	(2) Other consumers to a limited extent
How many people can participate?	Seven upward, except in the case of a primary trading co-operative where the minimum is normally twenty-five
Who decides on policy?	The directors, who must be members
Who manages?	The directors or professional managers who are appointed by them
Who owns the business?	The co-operative, which is owned by the members
How is voting done?	One vote per member, but up to four additional votes can be granted to a member on the basis of business done
How may profits be applied?	Bonuses to members, dividends to shareholders, retained for expansion. Maximum dividend is 15%
What is personal liability?	Limited to the amount paid for shares
Audit required?	Yes

6. Trusts

Trusts have been used for some time as vehicles for commercial transactions, though there is little doubt that this is not the purpose for which they were designed. Trusts originated for the purpose of preserving some property or source of income for the benefit of certain nominated people such as the wife or children of the person forming the trust.

The essence of a trust is that the person forming the trust passes ownership of certain property to that trust, either by donating it or by selling it to the trust, in the case of what is called an *inter vivos* trust, or by bequeathing it to the trust in the case of a testamentary trust. The first of these, which is formed while the founder of the trust is still alive, is the type of trust which is relevant here, and one which has played a prominent part in planning for the minimisation of estate duty.

The trust is formed by the founder and takes over full title to the various assets which are donated or sold to it. The people for whose benefit the trust is created are called beneficiaries, and it is administered on their behalf by one or more trustees.

Most trusts are formed for the benefit of the dependants or the descendants of the founder, who generally appoints the first trustees, naming himself as one of them. The assets of the trust are distributed to the beneficiaries on the happening of a certain event, such as the coming of age of the youngest beneficiary, or on a specified date. Until the date of distribution the income arising from the activities of the trust may be paid out wholly or in part to the beneficiaries, or it may be re-invested for them depending on the terms of the trust.

An analysis of the composition of the trust will reveal that it differs very little in its essence from a company. The company also owns its own assets independently of the shareholders, is administered by a group of people (trustees v directors) for the benefit of another group of people (beneficiaries v shareholders). The profits made can be distributed to this second group or re-invested on their behalf. The difference firstly lies in the fact that the directors of a company are appointed by the shareholders, whereas the trustees of the trust are appointed by the founder, who normally makes provision for the procedure whereby future trustees will be appointed. One of the trustees is normally a body corporate, such as a bank, to ensure that there will be continuity of trusteeship. The other major difference is that company law is codified in terms of a body corporate formed for purposes of trading, whereas trust law is still an amalgam of legislation and common law, with some aspects having been granted the sanctity of court rulings. All companies are bound by the same Act, but the nature of a trust can be largely determined by the founder in terms of the Trust Deed whereby he founds the trust.

Certain people examined these structures and decided that the differences between a company and a trust could be overcome if the founders, the trustees and the beneficiaries could be the same, or substantially the same, group of people and promptly set out to test whether this could be done, since the law was understandably vague on this point. A landmark decision in this respect was that in *Goodricke & Son (Pty) Ltd v Registrar of Deeds*, 1974 (1) SA 404 (N), wherein it was held that the essentials of a trust were that the founder or settlor had to forego ownership of the assets concerned and that these had to be administered other than purely for the benefit of the administrator. In this case there were four settlors, who were also the sole beneficiaries. They were also trustees, but had taken the precaution of appointing a fifth, corporate, trustee. Even though the four could dismiss this trustee, there was not complete identity between the individuals making up the three interested groups, settlors, trustees and beneficiaries. The courts therefore held that the essentials of a trust existed and that a valid trust existed. This trust could then be used as a vehicle for the commercial activities of the people concerned.

The advantages of a trust as compared to a company can be shortly given as follows:

1. The trust is not taxed on any income which it distributes to its beneficiaries, who are taxed in their own right on this income. Even if the trust does not distribute the income but the beneficiaries are fixed and determined they will be taxed on the income which is re-invested for them. Where the beneficiaries are not

determined the trust will be taxed on the undistributed income as though it were an unmarried person rather than on a flat rate as in the case of a company.

The beneficiaries are regarded as not being determinable when a trust is set up for, say, the benefit of all grandchildren of the founder who are alive on a certain date in the future. This may mean that some of the beneficiaries are not yet born, so that it would be unreasonable to tax the known beneficiaries on income which may eventually accrue to someone else.

2. The trustees have the benefit of limited liability except in cases of fraud (see *Magnum Financial Holdings (in liquidation) v Summerley* 1984 (1) SA 160 (W)).
3. The trust does not have a full corporate personality. It is therefore not geographically bound as is a company, but has its being wherever the trustees are. If the trustees decide to leave the country, therefore, the trust moves with them. The assets then belong to a foreign trust, even if they cannot at this stage actually be moved out of the country.

Summary

Who is served?	The beneficiaries
How many people can participate?	No limits
Who decides on policy?	The trustees
Who manages?	The trustees or professional managers who are appointed by them
Who owns the business?	The trust
How is voting done?	As specified in the trust deed
How may profits be applied?	Distributions to beneficiaries, retained for re-investment
What is personal liability?	None
Audit required?	If specified by the trust deed or called for by the Master.

7. Other forms of organisation

Most other forms of organisation are variations of the above. Various corporations have been called into being by specific acts of Parliament, but these generally follow the pattern of the Companies Act. Certain specific types of business also have their own governing Act, such as building societies, insurance companies and mutual insurance associations. These do not differ in principle from companies but have certain extra requirements or are exempted from certain requirements due to their specialised nature.

Another term which one comes across is joint venture, which is essentially a partnership formed for the performance of a specific task and applies only to that task. Commonly one finds this when a large construction contract is awarded to two or more companies who have tendered jointly because of the size of the contract, but who do not otherwise operate together.

Syndicates are also normally formed for a specific venture, and may operate as joint ventures or may operate in the form of a company or close corporation formed for the purpose.

Key words

Sole trader
Partnership
En commandite partner
Limited liability
Private company
Public company
Co-operative

Proprietorship
Silent partner
Legal persona or juristic person
Close corporation
Incorporated company
Section 21 company
Trust

Chapter 5

The legal environment: Taxation

This chapter gives an overview of the South African tax system, concentrating largely on Income Tax.

Other aspects which receive attention are the disclosure of taxation in the financial statements of companies and the elements of tax planning for minimisation of tax liability.

1. **The background of the tax system**

2. **Types of taxation**

3. **Indirect taxes**

4. **Direct taxes**

5. **Tax planning**

6. **Taxation in financial statements**

1. The background to the tax system

Governments, despite talk of improvements in the productivity of the public sector, are not in themselves directly productive. They may provide services which indirectly assist productivity such as security services, health services and education, and are often intimately involved in the provision of transport and communication infrastructure for use by the productive parts of the economy. Since these and other government expenditures do not produce any product which may be sold, the government is forced to levy taxes on the users of the services so as to be able to finance them.

If this were the only purpose of taxation the financing of government expenditure would be a relatively simple task of persuading the productive sector to pay what the government wants to spend on its services, but unfortunately the tax system has been corrupted by many other considerations. Tax has become part of the arsenal of social engineering and is used to distribute wealth (from the rich to the poor) and to pay for various ideologies which employ a large proportion of the population in non-productive capacities. To assist in the implementation of these ideologies various tax concessions are given to those who fit into the ideological pattern, while those who do not fit the pattern are taxed more heavily to compensate for the cost of those concessions. The tax system becomes more and more complex, and in many countries the tax laws are complex virtually beyond human understanding.

South Africa has suffered as much as most countries in this respect, but the whole thrust of the government's financial planning is now, officially at any rate, towards the purification of the tax system by eliminating the various concessions, possibly substituting a system of subsidies which will have to be paid for out of tax receipts but which will allow of a simpler tax system.

2. Types of taxation

There are two broad categories of taxation: direct and indirect taxes. Direct taxes are those which are levied directly on the taxpayer such as income taxes and wealth taxes, while indirect taxes are levied on transactions and only paid indirectly by the taxpayer such as sales taxes, customs duties and value added taxes. Before the development of the economy to a level sophisticated enough to permit income taxes most governments relied on indirect taxes or on wealth taxes, but direct taxes have become more and more important during the course of this century. The pendulum is now beginning to swing the other way, however, since income taxes have become so confiscatory that there are strong signs of taxpayer (ie voter) revolt. Governments have therefore been looking for ways to introduce more and more indirect taxes which can be more easily hidden so that the taxpayer is less aware of how much he is actually paying.

3. Indirect taxes

The indirect taxes most applicable to South Africa are the Value Added Tax

(VAT) and a range of import duties, excise duties, stamp duties, transfer duties and levies on fuel and a range of other commodities.

Most of these are not directly subject to any discretion on the part of the taxpayer. The only way to avoid the stamp duty on debit entries in bank accounts, for instance, is not to have a bank account; the only way to avoid transfer on property is not to buy property, and so on for the other taxes mentioned. As soon as any action is taken, the taxes become payable.

4. Direct taxes

South Africa's direct taxes are levied in terms of the Income Tax Act 1962, as amended annually. This Act was a revision and consolidation of the previous income tax acts and was based on the same principles. The Margo Commission on Taxation presented a comprehensive report which, when it first appeared, would lead to the introduction of another new Act. However, so many of the key recommendations of the commission were not accepted by the Government that it now appears that we may simply have a few years of more than usually comprehensive amendment Acts further confusing the original Act. A new Act must, however, be expected in the not too distant future.

4.1 Gross income

The principles of our tax system, which have not been attacked by the commission, are that all income earned during a tax year is subject to Income Tax in that year as soon as it meets the following criteria for gross income laid down in section 1 of the Act:

4.1.1 It must be received or accrued during the tax year;

4.1.2 It can be in cash or otherwise;

4.1.3 It must be from a South African source or a source deemed to be South African; and

4.1.4 It must not be income of a capital nature.

Section 10 of the Act lays down that certain specified types of income, such as certain amounts paid to the State President and certain investment income, are exempt from income tax even though they fit within the above definition.

4.1.5 *Amounts received by or accrued to the taxpayer during the course of the tax year*

The time unit for payment of income tax is one year. In the case of an individual the tax year will end on the last day of February each year except in the case of certain farmers, fishermen and diamond diggers whose tax year ends on 30 June as a result of their election in 1962 to be taxed on what is essentially the pre-1962 system.

In the case of incorporated bodies there is no problem in obtaining permission to use another date, since the Act specifies that the tax year of a company is the financial year of that company. Most companies, however, are also registered with financial years ending on the last day of February.

All income to which a taxpayer becomes entitled during the tax year is taxable during that year (*CIR v Lategan*, 1926 CPD 203 at 209, 2 SATC 16 at 20), whether it has actually been received or merely accrued. Doubts were expressed about this interpretation of the meaning of the Act in *CIR v Delfos* (1931 AD 215, 5 SATC 93), though no conclusion was reached as it was not germane to the decision. A majority of the bench in this case held that accrued amounts should only be those which were due and payable, which would exclude amounts which, while accrued to the taxpayer, were not yet due and payable. In practice there are many cases where people are taxed on a receipts basis.

A typical instance is the taxation of interest in the hands of an individual who may have lent money to another party in September of a particular tax year, the loan being repayable, along with interest, in August of the following year. Instead of declaring the interest accrued in February the individual would usually declare the full amount of interest in the tax year when the loan is repaid. Strictly speaking, this does not comply with the definition in Lategan's case, but for purposes of convenience for all parties concerned the practice of the tax authorities is to permit it, thus tacitly accepting the validity of the view of the judges in the Delfos case.

There are also people who are still specifically taxed on a receipts basis, since for certain taxpayers, primarily professional people, this option did exist in former times. A careful reading of the definition shows that the tax authorities do have the option of taxing on a receipts basis, since any income received in a tax year which had accrued in the previous tax year could be taxed in the year in which it is received provided it had not already been taxed in the year in which it accrued (*CIR v Delfos*). However, the tax authorities do not permit taxpayers to make this election any longer.

4.1.6 *Amounts received in cash or otherwise*

Tax is not levied on cash received but on value received. All receipts, whether in cash or in kind, are subject to income tax. The problems which exist in applying this lie largely in the cash equivalent valuation of benefits received in a form other than cash. These problems will continue forever in certain cases such as barter transactions, but many of the problems have been eliminated for all practical purposes by the seventh schedule to the Act. When the "fringe benefits" taxation provisions were adopted in the Income Tax Act, 96 of 1985, this schedule, titled "Benefits or advantages derived by Reason of Employment or Holding of any Office", came into being. It contains various administrative regulations and also lays down certain fixed rules according to which the value of fringe benefits is to be determined. In order to avoid too many objections these rules are fairly generous in their treatment of the taxpayer and in the majority of cases it remains preferable from a tax point of view to obtain income in the form of fringe benefits rather than in cash.

4.1.7 *Amounts received from a South African source*

There are two possible bases of income taxation. A majority of countries around the world tax on the basis of residence. This means that any person who is a resident of that country for tax purposes will be taxed there on all income earned anywhere in the world. South Africa is one of the minority of countries which has chosen to tax on a source basis whereby all income earned in South Africa is taxed in the hands of the recipient, regardless of where this recipient may be resident.

The corollary to this, of course is that income earned outside of South Africa by someone resident in South Africa is not liable to South African Income Tax. This has led to a number of abuses, particularly while the TBVC countries were tax levying jurisdictions.

Besides this, certain income has always been deemed to be South African income, primarily investment income from other countries. The rationale behind this has been that such income is earned by South African capital. Naturally, if the income is not earned by South African capital it will not be taxed here. Examples of this include investment income received by immigrants on investments which they held before first coming to settle in South Africa or on investments inherited by a South African resident from someone living abroad and not subject to South African tax on the income, or various other similar cases.

The fact that South Africa taxes on a source base and other countries on a residence base means that there must be times when certain receipts are taxable in two or more jurisdictions. A foreigner, resident in his own country for tax purposes, may earn money in South Africa. He is taxable in both jurisdictions unless there is an agreement between the various jurisdictions involved on the taxation of such amounts. These agreements are known as double taxation agreements and they regulate various tax matters between the countries.

Some of the agreements which South Africa has with other countries are very comprehensive, covering all aspects of income earned by the residents of the two tax jurisdictions. Typical of these agreements is the one South Africa has with the United Kingdom. Other agreements are very limited in scope, such as the one with Denmark which covers only profits derived from the business of sea or air transport between the two countries.

4.1.8 *Amounts not of a capital nature*

This is the most contentious aspect of income taxation. The Act states that amounts of a capital nature are not taxable, but does not define what such amounts are. There are a great many cases in this respect which shows that there are many perceptions of what constitutes a capital amount, and no precise way of defining it.

In a broad economic sense ". . . 'Income' is what 'capital' produces, or is something in the nature of interest or fruit as opposed to principal or tree. This economic distinction is a useful guide in matters of income tax, but its application is often a matter of very great difficulty, for what is principal or tree in the hands of one man may be interest or fruit in the hands of another." (*CIR v Visser*, 1937 TPD 77, 8 SATC 271 at 276.)

There are several tests which the courts will apply in determining whether a receipt is capital or taxable income. The most important of these is the determination of the intention with which the taxpayer acquired or held the asset. If the intention was to make a profit from acquiring or holding the asset, the profit is taxable. If the intention was to hold the asset for income producing purposes or expense saving purposes, any profit made will be incidental and will not be subject to tax.

Note that intentions may change over a period of time. A building may be purchased with the intention of letting it and receiving rental income, so that any sale would be regarded as incidental to the intention with which the asset was acquired. However, if the taxpayer undertook extensive renovation of the building after a few years and then sold it, the question would arise of whether or not he had changed his intention and undertaken the refurbishing with the intention of selling at a profit. If so, he would be taxable on the profit. (*Natal Estates v SIR* 1975 (4) SA 177 (A) 37 SATC 193.)

There is also the possibility of mixed motive. A share could be purchased with the idea of holding it for a while to obtain dividend income and then selling it at a profit. In a case like this the court would have to decide on the dominant motive. (*African Life Investment Corporation (Pty) Ltd v SIR* 1969 (4) SA 259 (A) SATC 163 at 175.)

Most of the other tests which the courts apply in deciding on the question of capital or revenue are actually derived from this one of intention. The courts will look at the length of time the asset has been held, the circumstance of the sale, the way in which the transaction was financed, the previous history and activities of the taxpayer and, in the case of a company, at the objects for which the company was formed. In the case of a company, which obviously cannot have intentions of its own, the intentions of the directors or dominant shareholders will be examined to determine whether or not an amount is taxable. (*Elandsheuwel Farming (Edms) Bpk v SBI* 1978 (1) SA 101 (A) 39 SATC 163 at 175.)

4.2 Expenses which can be deducted from income in the determination of taxable income

The Act also lays down the general nature of the expenses which may be claimed against gross income before determining the amount which is subject to income tax, and who is liable for payment of the tax.

The general deduction formula is laid down in section 11(*a*) of the Act. All expenditure and losses incurred in the Republic in the production of income, provided that such expenses or losses are not of a capital nature, are allowable as deductions. Without limiting this definition, section 11 then carries on to list a number of specific expenses which are deductible, and the limitations on these expenses.

4.3 The taxable unit

Taxes are levied on:
1. Incorporated bodies such as companies, co-operatives and close corporations;

2. Single persons
3. Married men and women
4. Some trusts

4.3.1 *Taxation of companies*

Companies and close corporations are taxed in exactly the same way as far as income tax is concerned. From gross income they can deduct all allowable deductions and all exempt income and they are taxed at a flat rate, currently 40 %, on all taxable income.

The Act does distinguish between private companies and public companies. For tax purposes the definitions of the two differ slightly from those of the Companies Act. Public companies, for tax purposes, must not merely be public companies but must have a satisfactory spread of shareholders as well. For a company quoted on a stock exchange this means that at least 40 % of the shares must be held by the general public, and the percentage rises to 50 % if the company does not have its shares quoted on a stock exchange. The general public is so defined as to exclude the directors of the company or their immediate families as well as other family units (husband, wife and minor children) which hold more than 15 % of the shares. Any company unable to meet these criteria is a private company for tax purposes. The public company has certain benefits such as exemption from donations tax. All companies are exempted from income tax on dividend income.

One point worth noting in the taxation of companies is the treatment of assessed losses carried forward. If a company incurs a loss in any one trading year it may carry that loss forward to write off against future profits subject to certain limitations. It loses the benefit of the loss if it ceases to trade for one full tax year, if it substantially changes the nature of its business or if there is a major change in shareholding. This last is not very well defined and care must therefore be taken in admitting a new shareholder to a company with an assessed loss to ensure that the benefit of the loss is not foregone.

4.3.2 *Taxation of close corporations*

Close corporations are treated as private companies for income tax purposes.

4.3.3 *Taxation of co-operatives*

Co-operatives are taxed as companies except for certain exemptions in respect of bonuses paid to members. Agricultural co-operatives are also entitled to special allowances in respect of buildings and machinery.

4.3.4 *Taxation of single people*

A single person for tax purposes is one who has never been married or one who is divorced, not remarried, and does not have the burden of supporting the children of the marriage. A divorced person supporting the children is taxed as a married person until the last of the children no longer qualifies for the child rebate. The child must be supported out of own resources and not out of alimony or maintenance payments received from a former spouse.

Single people are taxed on their gross income less various deductions. Specific deductions allowed include allowances in respect of physical disabilities and medical costs in excess of 5 % of the taxable income, current and arrear payments to pension funds and retirement annuity funds, certain donations to specified educational institutions, a nominal tool allowance for artisans and certain entertainment and travelling expenses.

On the taxable income so determined income tax is payable on a sliding scale.

From the tax certain rebates are deducted. These are currently a primary rebate of R1 100, a rebate in respect of each of the first five children of R100, a rebate in respect of each child in excess of five of R150 (illegitimate children qualify for these rebates) and special rebates in respect of the aged. People over 65 may claim an extra R500.

4.3.5 *Taxation of married people*

Levying of income tax has gradually moved over the last few years from joint taxation of husband and wife towards separate taxation of spouses. At present husband and wife are taxed separately on income earned from employment or the carrying on of a trade or profession, even where the wife is working in her husband's business or vice versa. The only place where taxation is not yet completely separate is in the area of investment income. In the case of people married out of community of property, investment income earned by each spouse is taxed in the hands of that spouse, but in the case of people married in community of property each is taxed on half of the total joint investment income. Taxation is on a sliding scale where higher incomes are taxed more heavily than lower ones. Only one spouse, normally the husband, can claim in respect of allowances for children.

The rates of tax differ for married men and married women, with the current position being that the maximum marginal rate for married women is lower than that for married men, but the maximum is reached at a lower level.

4.3.6 *Taxation of trusts*

While RDJ, writing in the Income Tax Reporter,[1] questions the validity of the taxation of trusts, it has long been the practice of the tax authorities to tax trusts as though they were unmarried persons without the right to any rebates. Broadly speaking, trusts are taxed on the income which they receive and hold in trust for the beneficiaries. Income paid out to the beneficiaries or expended on their behalf is taxed in their hands and not in the hands of the trust itself.

Where income is not paid out but merely accrues to the beneficiaries the taxable entity will depend on the terms of the trust deed. Where the beneficiary has an absolute right to the income he is taxed upon it. Where the right is contingent, the trust will be taxed on it. A simple example of this is a trust which is created for the benefit of a specified person and all income accrues to that person. He will be taxed on the income, even if he is only entitled to draw it at a later time. On the other hand, if the income from the trust is to be accrued for the benefit of a person if he is still alive on a particular date and will otherwise be paid out to, say, his descendants, the trust will be taxed on the income which is not paid out.

Trusts used as a vehicle for carrying on a trade are now being taxed on the same basis as companies.

4.4 The payment of tax

The payment of income tax is becoming increasingly complex, with a number of parties being responsible for ensuring that the tax is actually paid.

4.4.1 *Employees' tax—PAYE and SITE*

Any employer is compelled to deduct from the earnings of his employees certain taxes in accordance with tables published by the Department of Finance and to pay these over to the department by the seventh day of the month following that in which the taxes are deducted. There are different classes of employees who are taxed differently. Firstly, twenty-five per cent must be deducted from the earnings of part time employees.

For full time employees a distinction has to be made between those who are liable for Standard Income Tax on Employees (SITE) and those who have deductions made in accordance with Pay As You Earn (PAYE) tables.

The intention is that all salary payments should eventually be liable to SITE, and only those who are in possession of non-salary income will then be liable to fill in income tax returns. Currently the upper limit of the earnings subject to SITE is set by Parliament each year. Under the provisions for SITE, the deductions are regarded as the final deduction for the year. There will be no refunds for overpayments nor will there be extra assessments in respect of short payments. The full liability for collecting and paying the tax therefore rests with the employer.

If deductions are made according to the SITE tables for part of the year and the employee then moves out of that category into the PAYE category, payments of SITE up to the date of the change will be regarded as PAYE payments and will be included in the tax certificate issued by the employer.

All employees whose income is too high for them to be treated as SITE employees will have PAYE deducted from them. Those paying PAYE are obliged to complete a tax return at the end of each tax year.

The liability for the collection and payment of this tax is also that of the employer. He is also obliged to give his employee a tax certificate after the end of February of each year specifying the amount of earnings, of tax deducted and of certain other matters in accordance with the requirements of Schedule 4 of the Income Tax Act. If the employee leaves his service during the course of a tax year he is obliged to present him with such a certificate within two weeks of the cessation of employment.

4.4.2 *Provisional tax*

All taxpayers who derive more than R1 000 per year in a form other than remuneration from which tax is deducted and all directors of private companies are regarded as provisional taxpayers, as are all companies and close corporations. A provisional taxpayer is required to make a payment in respect of his total tax liability for a tax year by not later than the end of the sixth month of that year (in the case of natural persons by the end of August each year) and another payment by the end of that year (in the case of natural persons by the end of February). These payments are calculated on the basis of the last assessment issued for the taxpayer since it is accepted that it is impossible to estimate accurately the income to be earned in a particular year. Effectively, the system presumes that the taxpayer's income in one year will be the same as in the previous year.

The actual amount of provisional tax paid is an amount read off from the tax tables less the total of employees tax deducted for the year to date. If there is an assessed credit balance outstanding, this will also be deducted from the amount payable.

A further payment has now been added to the requirements for companies earning more than R20 000 per year and individuals earning more than R50 000 per year. By the end of six months after the end of the tax year (in the case of natural persons by the end of August each year) a third payment must be made. The total of the three payments and any PAYE paid must be sufficient to settle the total tax liability in respect of the tax year. Underpayment will result in severe penalties in the form of interest from the first of September up to the date on which the assessment is actually paid.

4.4.3 *Assessments*

Each taxpayer who is not subject only to SITE must complete a return of taxable income each year. On the basis of this return an assessment is issued showing the total amount of tax payable in respect of the year and the total amounts already paid in respect of PAYE and provisional tax. The difference between the tax payable and the tax paid is either payable by the taxpayer or refundable by the department.

4.5 Taxation of specific types of income

Certain types of income are taxed in specific ways. The most important of these are discussed below.

4.5.1 *Investment income*

Investment income is income from interest or from dividends. Interest income is treated as ordinary income except that there is a specific deduction in respect of interest available to individuals in that the first R2 000 of interest earned in a year is exempted from tax.

Dividends and distributions from a close corporation are currently exempt from tax.

4.5.2 *Farming income*

It is not true that farmers are exempted from income tax, but they have been given very special treatment. It is generally accepted that their treatment in the past has been over-favourable, but there are political difficulties involved in taking away this type of favouritism. Among the preferences given to farmers are the right to write off capital expenditure in the year in which it is incurred or, in some cases, as soon as the farmer has a tax liability arising from farming activities. He is also given rules regarding the valuation of his livestock which are very favourable when compared to the rules applying to the valuation of trading stock. A third benefit given the farmer, but not others such as professional sportsmen and authors who also have a fluctuating income, is the right to average income. The full amount of the taxable income will be taxed in any one year, but at the average rate applicable to the last three years.

Most of the problems concerning farmers have been concerned with the activities of part-time farmers, some of whom farm with the intention of making a loss which they can write off against other income.

To counter this type of activity, the tax authorities have placed more and more emphasis on the separate taxation of various aspects of an individual's income, despite the statement that the unit for taxation is the individual. The Margo commission supported this practice and suggested several modifications to the law governing farming income. The most important modification is that losses on livestock should now only be deductible from farming income and not from other income. This would mean the end of a number of tax avoidance schemes currently in vogue. It was further proposed that standard livestock values be adopted for all tax purposes. This type of separation of the various types of income is called "ring-fencing".

Margo's proposal that farming capital expenditure be written off on a 50:30:20 basis rather than in full in the year of purchase has been accepted by the government, but subject to the report of a technical working group. It is unlikely to be implemented. There are also proposals regarding an objective test for part-time farmers, but this is so hedged about with qualifications that it is likely to be full of possible loopholes if it is introduced. Farming losses for part-time farmers would also only be deductible from farming income which is departmental practice already.

4.5.3 *Mining income*

Mining income is also taxed on a special basis. The most important deviation from the taxation of other income is again that capital expenditure can be written off in full in the year of purchase. Gold mines are taxed at rate calculated in accordance with a formula, the effect of which is to tax rich mines at a high rate and poorer mines at a lower rate. Diamond mines are also taxed at a different rate which is determined annually.

The proposals of the Margo Commission regarding mining have virtually all been referred to a technical working group. Some have been accepted subject to the report of this group while no position has been taken on others at this stage. Among those which have been accepted are those relating to the rates of tax which suggest that the various surcharges paid by the mines be scrapped and that direct payments rather than capital allowances be given to new and ultra deep mines.

4.6 Other taxes

The Income Tax imposes a donations tax. Donors are liable to tax on donations made by them on a sliding scale which is a lifetime scale rather than an annual scale. This tax, together with estate duty, was due to be phased out and replaced by a capital transfer tax at some time in the near future, but the change of government may lead to its being retained.

5. Tax planning

By tax planning is meant arranging transactions in such a manner that they do not attract any more tax than is necessary. With the very high tax rates in this country and elsewhere a whole tax planning industry has arisen in order to exploit loopholes in tax systems for the benefit of the taxpayer. This has often meant developing plans which violate the very spirit of the law, thereby calling forth responses from the tax authorities to close the various loopholes so exposed. As is usual in such cases, the authorities have totally overreacted. In South Africa we have now had a deputy minister claiming that planning transactions in such a way as to avoid paying tax is no different from dishonestly or immorally evading payment of taxes which should be paid. The long accepted difference between legal tax avoidance and illegal tax evasion has been blurred by the coining of the word "avoision", which is apparently government's way of telling us that it does not only want its pound of flesh but the taxpayer's as well. We have also been subjected to a totally indefensible spate of retroactive legislation leading to people being taxed on amounts which were previously not taxed in terms of the legislation existing at the time when the transaction was entered into.

5.1 The various parties for whom planning should be done

There are various aspects to tax planning. Anyone looking at tax planning should realise that it is only a part of overall financial planning, and that overall objectives have to be set before the tax aspects are taken into account. After all, if tax were the sole criterion it could be avoided simply by not earning any income.

Tax planning should be done for:

5.1.1 *Your company*

As a manager responsible for the profits generated by your company or by any section or division of it you should be aware of the fact that there are different ways to structure many transactions and that it is your responsibility to ensure that the most tax-efficient method consistent with your overall objective is employed.

5.1.2 *Your company's employees*

An important resource of the undertaking is its employees. An undertaking which is interested in its employees' welfare should take care to ensure that employees obtain the maximum after tax remuneration consistent with the employee's own objectives and the total cost of the financial package which the undertaking is prepared to pay. The most important aspect of this is fast becoming the preparation of the employment contract, which defines the employees responsibilities so that he may deduct relevant expenses which would probably not be allowable if he could not prove that they were part of his laid down responsibilities *(CIR v van der Walt 1986 TPD 48 SATC 104)*. The other aspect receiving a great deal of attention is the cafeteria approach to the structuring of remuneration packages whereby the employee is able to choose which particular combination of cash and fringe benefits he would like from a range of options offered by the employer.

5.1.3 *Yourself*

Last but certainly not least. Personal financial planning should involve lifetime objectives, including retirement objectives. Within this framework tax planning can play a major part in ensuring that you have the maximum amounts available at the appropriate times to finance retirement, children's education or whatever else is of importance to you. Again, this involves your employment contract and the structuring of your remuneration package if you are an employee, and matters such as your insurance portfolio whether you are an employee or not.

5.2 The objectives of tax planning

Tax planning has as its main objectives, firstly, the minimisation of tax agony and, secondly, the maximisation of after tax profit or after tax cash flow or both of these, within the overall strategy of the undertaking.

In order to achieve this it is necessary to analyse the overall objective, to break it down into a number of sub-objectives. The sub-objectives which have to be considered for a tax plan include:

5.2.1 *Flexibility for protection against adverse circumstances and for taking advantage of opportunities*

Tax law is obviously a shifting minefield laid in a swamp of uncertainties. Under such circumstances the taxpayer has to be prepared to alter his course at any time and with a minimum of notice, either to take advantage of new allowances or to protect himself against new attacks. Specific points which should also be borne in mind concerning flexibility are the possibility of new taxes being introduced and changes in the rates of existing taxes.

It is always a worthwhile exercise to look at factors which could have some effect on the taxes we pay, such as foreign political actions which make some of our previous planning obsolete. An ongoing review of our tax planning is necessary, but currently, in the light of the Margo report and of the Government's response in the form of a White Paper, it is necessary to look at those aspects which have as a result become more important or applicable, and those which have become less so, and to concentrate on improving our tax planning systems in order to accommodate the changes.

5.2.2 *Minimisation of income taxes*

Income tax is the tax which offers probably the most opportunities for tax planning, so that it is normally the focus of most tax planning.

5.2.3 *Minimisation of other taxes*

While other taxes may offer less opportunity for planning they must not be ignored, especially in the planning of individual transactions.

5.2.4 *Provision for liquidity to pay taxes*

This is of cardinal importance. Failure to pay taxes as required will result in heavy penalties in the form of interest which is not deductible for tax purposes plus possibly penalties for non-payment. It also leads to your file being flagged for possible future investigation, which is a calamity. Even if you have nothing to hide the cost, in time and money, of satisfying all the queries which are likely to be raised means that such an investigation is usually a further financial burden added to the taxpayer.

5.2.5 *Adequate but straightforward administration procedures to minimise compliance costs and to ensure victory in disputed matters*

This has become particularly important since the publication of the Margo Report and the subsequent irresponsible actions of the tax authorities and, particularly, of the politicians. Margo set as a goal a vast improvement in the rate of collection of tax. His investigations indicated that the fiscus suffered a great deal of loss due to errors and fraud, either on the part of the taxpayer or on the part of the tax collectors. For the many cases where there are errors or fraud, Margo particularly saw a need for an improvement in the following:

● Desk audits of returns;

● VAT inspections;

● PAYE and SITE inspections;

● Fringe benefits tax inspections; and

● Controls over investment income.

This means a massive increase in the cost of administering the tax system, not only in the form of more civil servants to be paid, but also of higher costs of administration within the private sector. It is typical of the pattern of historical development of tax systems throughout the world that this should be one of the key recommendations of the Margo Commission. As governments require more and more money to finance their ever-increasing interference in the economic activities of the country they look for more and more tax. They normally start off by increasing rates of personal tax, either directly or, rather dishonestly, by making use of "bracket creep" or "fiscal drag". When resistance to personal tax becomes so high that it carries a political risk new taxes, generally indirect ones such as VAT, are introduced, and are also subject to increasing rates. In this country personal tax rates have long since reached levels where tax morality has been undermined, and this has carried over into the field of other taxes. Very few people even feel guilty about cheating the taxman. All that is left, then, is for an improvement in the rate of collection, since the other alternative, a real reduction in government expenditure, can only be implemented at the cost of a great sacrifice in government power, which is obviously not part of the planning of any government.

It must be accepted without any reservation that existing tax administration systems within an undertaking, whether in respect of income tax or in respect of the other taxes for which the employer acts as unpaid tax collector, must be subjected to a very particular scrutiny. This must be done bearing in mind Revenue's stated intention of cracking down on certain as yet unspecified sensitive areas where tax avoidance procedures and schemes are more easily instituted. These will no doubt include foreign transactions, including losses and profits on foreign exchange and the fixing of transfer prices. It can be accepted that Revenue will seek to appoint specialists in these areas in order to crack down on any suspected tax avoidance schemes. In all other areas we can expect to see a great many extra inspectors appointed so that the risk of detection of any errors made by the undertaking will increase tremendously. Most of these inspectors will, of course, be inexperienced. There will be training programmes within the department but it will be some time before they are really competent at their jobs. This does not mean that there is less pressure on the undertaking to review its tax administration programme immediately. On the contrary, experience indicates that there will be a great many more queries than one would expect later on when they have learned something about their jobs. These queries are often minor, but answering them is time consuming unless the tax administration is adequate.

The penalties for being caught not complying with all requirements of the legislation can be very stiff. Margo has proposed retention of the two hundred per cent penalty for fraudulent evasion of tax, and added a suggestion of a one hundred per cent penalty for negligence, though he does not want any penalty for genuine error. It is not too clear just how the authorities will differentiate between genuine error and negligence, so it is as well not to commit any errors even though the authorities will have the right to reduce or eliminate the penalties. To cut down on the risk of incurring penalties, the undertaking should compile and study its own tax profile:

● It must have full knowledge of the tax burden which it bears in the form of income tax *and* other taxes, and of the indirect liability it bears in the collection of taxes such as employees tax deductions (PAYE and SITE);
● It must be aware of areas in its own operation which are possibly suspect since non-compliance due to ignorance can be a very serious matter;
● It must also be aware of those areas of its operations where there may be possibilities for lightening the overall tax burden.

Having developed and studied his tax profile, the taxpayer can then proceed to improve his system of tax administration. Knowing the full spectrum of taxes for which he is liable he can institute a system which will enable him to control all the taxes, including those which have usually received scant attention such as the various customs and excise duties. Many taxpayers who are responsible for the payment of these taxes do not even understand them, never mind control them. Awareness of such a lack means that the manager can develop a tax team within his organisation: people who are deemed to require knowledge of a particular range of taxes can be trained to a satisfactory level of expertise for the internal administration of those taxes. The expenditure incurred in this training can be regarded as an investment which can render returns in two possible ways. Firstly, ignorance of the taxes means that the firm is as likely to be overpaying as it is to be underpaying on that particular tax, and any such errors in the favour of the fiscus can be eliminated. Secondly, a satisfactory level of administration of that tax means that the undertaking is likely to comply with all the requirements of the Revenue and thus not to be subjected to any penalties.

This tax profile must be constantly updated. The tax acts will be modified considerably in the years that lie ahead and provisions that have been instituted will be modified as they are found wanting in any respect. There will inevitably be a great deal of new case law and the revenue authorities will develop new departmental practices. All of these changes will have to be assimilated into the tax profile in order to give the undertaking the opportunity to deal with problems before they arise.

5.3 The tools the tax planner uses to meet the objective of minimisation of the tax burden

The above are general objectives for a tax planning system at any time, and the tools which the tax planner has at his disposal are also pretty general. It is not possible to lay down a specific course of action for a particular taxpayer in an overview such as this, but the tools generally available include:

5.3.1 *The sourcing of capital and revenue flows and the use of double taxation agreements*

A great deal of tax planning in South Africa in recent years has involved the sourcing of income in the TBVC states, all of which also taxed on a source base. A South African resident who was able to do so could pay income tax on a part of his income in South Africa and on another part in, say, Bophuthatswana. While this would not reduce the total amount of his taxable income it could have a dramatic impact on the total tax paid since he would be able to pay on lower marginal rates in two jurisdictions rather than pay at a maximum rate in one or other of the jurisdictions. The re-incorporation of these states means that similar schemes are now being applied in neighbouring countries, such as Swaziland.

Double tax agreements also present opportunities for tax planning. This is a highly specialised field, since making the optimum use of such agreements involves not only a study of the agreements which South Africa has with other countries but also the agreements between other states since it might be possible to make use of a two stage plan to gain advantages offered to another country but not to South Africa.

5.3.1.1 *Double tax agreements*

Essentially, double tax agreements are straightforward. The purposes of double tax agreements are generally agreed to be the following:

1. Avoidance of double taxation

2. Prevention of tax evasion
3. Exchange of information between the tax authorities of the contracting states.
   The agreements all contain clauses dealing with the operation of the agreement.

   Relevant points in most of them include:
1. A definition of a resident of each of the contracting states.
2. A definition of what constitutes a permanent establishment in each of the states, which may render the undertaking liable to tax even if it is not actually resident.
3. A schedule of withholding taxes on income earned in the one jurisdiction but being paid in the other.

5.3.2 *The timing of capital and revenue flows*

Tax is levied on an annual basis. Sometimes it is possible to delay or to speed up receipts or expenses so as to obtain the benefits in a particular tax year. With the phasing out of investment allowances on plant and machinery, for instance, it became of prime importance that certain items of capital equipment were brought into use in time to claim the benefits. In other cases it may be advisable to postpone a receipt until a future year by careful wording of the contract in terms of which the amount is to be paid.

5.3.3 *Changing the nature of capital and revenue flows*

Capital receipts are not taxable. Revenue expenses are allowable as deductions. It is therefore obviously in the taxpayer's interest to so structure a deal that receipts will not be regarded as revenue while expenses will not be regarded as capital. An elementary example of this is the leasing of an asset rather than the purchase of it, the lease payments being revenue but the purchase of a car being capital.

5.3.4 *The use of various taxable entities*

In many cases it is advisable to split income among several entities. Income receivable by a taxpayer may therefore be so split that part of it is payable to a company or close corporation or a trust, all of which may have tax benefits in a particular set of circumstances.

5.3.5 *The use of tax allowances*

The word allowances should be interpreted as broadly as possible to include all allowable deductions from income. General deductions in terms of section 11(*a*) should be maximised, but special attention should be paid to the various specific allowances which are given from time to time.

This is probably the area in which there is going to be the greatest change in tax planning following the Margo proposals. The commission has stated unequivocally that the tax system is not the best home for the various economic incentives which have been included in the specific tax allowances. It proposed that all tax incentives which currently exist be phased out over a period of time and be replaced by a system of cash grants. The actual effect this will have will of course depend on the period of phasing out and the conditions of the new incentives which are to be granted.

The Government has accepted the commission's proposals fully in respect of certain allowances such as the export marketing allowance but has not accepted the recommendation in respect of sports sponsorships, which will continue to be allowable. It has expressed reservations about the housing allowances and the depreciation allowances.

5.4 Tax planning overall

Since taxes are so complex nowadays it requires a specialist in the field to do any tax planning. No person without that sort of knowledge is going to be capable of the task, but any manager should have an outline available within which he can appoint specialists to do the work. The foregoing section is an attempt to provide the basis for such an outline which can be applied to virtually any type of undertaking.

6. Taxation in financial statements

Taxation is only relevant for financial statements of those entities which are liable for tax in their own right. There would be no mention of tax in the financial statements of a business run by a sole trader since the owner would be liable for tax on his total income and there would be no tax payable by the business as such. The same applies to a partnership, where each partner is liable for tax on his share of the profits but the partnership itself does not pay profits. While there should be some reference to tax in personal financial statements, reference to taxes only really becomes relevant in the case of incorporated bodies such as companies, building societies and close corporations. The requirements will be discussed below.

6.1 Requirements of the Companies Act

The Companies Act requires that the company disclose in its income statement the amount provided for taxation, specifying the nature and origin of the various taxes for the relevant financial year and for any previous year. (*Schedule 4, paragraph 36(g)*.) There is no particular requirement for the disclosure of the liability for tax in the balance sheet beyond the requirements of paragraph 9 regarding the disclosure of liabilities under appropriate headings.

6.2 Requirements of the Close Corporations Act

The Close Corporations Act only gives a very general guide to the requirements for the financial statements of a close corporation in paragraph 58. The most relevant section is paragraph 58(b) which requires that the statements are prepared in conformity with generally accepted accounting practice.

6.3 Generally accepted accounting practice

The current GAAP statement AC102 deals with Taxation in the Financial Statements of Companies. This statement was originally issued to take effect from

1 January 1976, but a drastically revised AC102 was issued to take effect from 1 July 1989.

The statement does not attempt to deal with particular types of companies, but seeks to cover the majority of situations normally experienced. It deals purely with income tax.

Most of the problems arising from the disclosure of tax liabilities lie in the fact that taxable income is not necessarily the same as the accounting income shown. This can be due to two different classes of reasons:

6.3.1 *Timing differences*

Timing differences arise when the tax charge is levied in a period different from that in which the accounting charge or income is raised. These differences arise largely because of provisions in tax law allowing some form of accelerated depreciation for tax purposes compared to that used for accounting purposes or to losses or provisions charged in the income statement but not allowed for tax purposes until some later date. The effect is that the accounting and tax incomes will tend to be the same over an extended period of time but will differ in any one year.

6.3.2 *Permanent differences*

Permanent differences arise where certain expenses deducted in arriving at the accounting income are not allowable for determination of the taxable income, or where certain accounting income is exempt from tax. In either case the tax will differ from the amount that would result from applying the income rate to the accounting income.

6.3.3 *Deferred tax*

In order to comply with the accounting concepts of matching and prudence it is necessary to match the tax charge in an accounting period to the accounting income in that period whether or not the tax is immediately payable or only payable in some future period. If only permanent differences have occurred in that period, the lower (or higher) tax charge will represent the full charge for the period. No adjustment is therefore necessary in respect of such differences. In the case of timing differences it is necessary to calculate the tax payable immediately on the taxable income and also to provide for any further tax the payment of which is deferred to some future period because of the workings of the tax law. The amount of the provision for such deferred tax should be shown in the balance sheet of the company as a separate item and not as part of shareholders equity. Everingham and Hopkins believe that it should be shown immediately after long term liabilities, while there are others who classify it as a long term liability.

This statement introduces the concept of partial deferment of tax, which is designed to give a more accurate picture of those firms which have no intention of scaling down their activities and have as a result a "hard core" of deferred tax which will keep being renewed. The statement then accepts that deferred taxation need only be provided in any year when it is probable that tax will become payable as a result of the future reversal of existing timing differences. In other cases the comprehensive method of providing fully for deferred tax in each tax year will have to be adopted.

6.3.3.1 *The liability method*

This method of providing deferred tax regards a deferred tax balance as representing a future liability. This means that the balances have to be constantly maintained at current tax rates since the liability can only exist at current rates, necessitating an adjustment every time there is a change to the companies tax rate.

6.3.4 *Arguments against providing for deferred tax*

Many people claim that provision for deferred tax is a waste of time. Some of them base this on a belief that the tax paid represents the full liability and that the provision for deferred tax is merely an accounting exercise which does not affect economic reality. However, this argument ignores the matching concept and can lead to an unrealistically high expectation of future after tax earnings. A second, and more powerful argument, is that a deferred tax balance tends to remain on the balance sheet forever since the amounts included tend to revolve. As the amounts in respect of one asset are reversed, new amounts have to be added in respect of new assets and the balance tends to remain the same or even increase in times of inflation.

6.3.5 *Wider application of AC102*

There can be little doubt that the whole question of deferred taxation will be reviewed and developed in the future. A great deal of attention is being paid to the matter overseas, and the question is one which is enjoying some discussion in South Africa at present as well. In the meantime, the statement does attempt to show a more realistic picture of the financial position of the company as far as its tax transactions are concerned. It is logical that the same statement should apply to the financial statements of close corporations and to bodies such as co-operatives and mutual building societies. It probably also has application in the field of personal financial statements, which is rapidly gaining recognition as one area where it is necessary to rethink the whole question of presentation.

Key words

Direct taxes
Gross income
Residence
Capital or revenue
Value added tax
SITE
Tax avoidance
Deferred tax

Indirect taxes
Source
Income tax
PAYE
Provisional tax
Tax evasion
Tax evasion

Questions and exercises on Part One

Chapters 1–3

1. Name the three types of accounting information as identified by Horngren.
2. The holder of the C A (S A) qualification is not entitled to
   (a) Serve as the accounting officer of a close corporation
   (b) Serve as the financial director of a public company
   (c) Carry out audits of public companies
   (d) All of the above
3. The body which prepares the statement of GAAP released in South Africa is
   (a) The PAAB
   (b) The SAICA
   (c) The IASC
   (d) The APB
4. For which of the following qualifications is a formal period of practical training required?
   (a) CFA
   (b) C A (S A)
   (c) CIMA
   (d) All of the above
5. Which of the following qualifications are recognised for purpose of serving as accounting officer of a close corporation?
   (a) C A (S A)
   (b) CFA
   (c) CIMA
   (d) ACCA
6. In order to be classified as an extraordinary item in the income statement an event or transaction should be
   (a) Infrequent and material but not necessarily unusual in nature
   (b) Infrequent in nature but not necessarily material
   (c) Infrequent and material and unusual in nature
   (d) Material and unusual but not necessarily infrequent
7. Changes in accounting practice are often made and the monetary impact of this recorded in the financial statements even though, in theory, this may be in violation of the convention of
   (a) Materiality
   (b) Consistency
   (c) Conservatism
   (d) Objectivity
8. Depreciation is defined in AC106 as
   (a) A fund built up for the replacement of assets at the end of their useful life
   (b) An attempt to show assets at a fair value on the face of the balance sheet by showing the decrease in value through use

      (c) The allocation of the cost of an asset over its useful life

      (d) A method of decreasing taxable income without laying out any cash

9. For purposes of financial reporting, AC115 defines a segment as

      (a) A geographical segment (separating operations in different countries)

      (b) An industrial segment (separating different types of operations)

      (c) Neither of the above

      (d) Both of the above

10. Statements of Generally Accepted Accounting Practice issued in South Africa

      (a) Must, in terms of the Companies Act, be applied to every set of company financial statements

      (b) Can be applied at the option of the company

      (c) Must be applied unless the company and the auditor agree that a different method of presentation is applicable

      (d) Can be ignored provided full disclosure of this fact is given in the financial statements

Chapter 4: Forms of organisation

1. Essentials for the formation of a partnership include

      (a) A written partnership agreement

      (b) The objective of making a profit

      (c) Both of the above

      (d) Neither of the above

2. The major difference between a company and a close corporation is

      (a) The documents relating to the relationship between a close corporation and its members is not kept on public register

      (b) The liability of members of a close corporation is not limited

      (c) Dividends are not deducted in the determination of a company's taxable income, but distributions by a close corporation are deducted

      (d) A company may hold shares in another company, but a close corporation may not hold shares in a company.

3. An ordinary shareholder of a company has the following rights

      (a) The right to a dividend whenever the company makes a profit

      (b) The right to vote at any general meeting of the company in proportion to his shareholding

      (c) The right of access to the company's financial records

      (d) All of the above

4. Differences between a private company and a public company include

      (a) The private company has a limit to the number of members it may have

      (b) The private company limits the transferability of its shares

      (c) Both of the above

      (d) Neither of the above

5. A partnership is

      (a) A legal entity

      (b) An accounting entity

      (c) Both of the above

      (d) Neither of the above

6. The differences between a public company and a co-operative include
   (a) A co-operative may freely repurchase its own shares, while a company may not
   (b) Voting in a company takes place on one vote per member basis and in a co-operative on a one vote per share basis
   (c) A company may sell its shares to anyone while a co-operative may only sell shares to certain classes of people e g an agricultural co-operative may only sell shares to farmers.
   (d) All of the above
7. A partnership is a quasi-legal persona for purposes of
   (a) V A T
   (b) Ownership of fixed property
   (c) Income tax
   (d) All of the above
8. Which of the following are not legal entities?
   (a) A close corporation
   (b) A co-operative
   (c) A sole trader
   (d) All of the above
9. Which of the following statements is true?
   (a) A close corporation may be converted into a company
   (b) A private company may be converted into a close corporation
   (c) Neither of the above
   (d) Both of the above
10. Ordinary partners in a business
   (a) Are liable for the debts of the partnership in proportion to their interest in the partnership
   (b) Are each liable for all the debts of the partnership
   (c) Are liable for all the debts of the partnership in respect of transactions which they approved
   (d) Are each liable for all the debts of the partnership up to the amount of their interest in the partnership

Chapter 5: Taxation

1. Income tax is levied on
   (a) Partnerships
   (b) Incorporated bodies such as companies
   (c) Sole traders
   (d) All of the above
2. Which of the following will not be subject to income tax in the hands of a South African resident?
   (a) Dividends received on shares inherited from a grandfather who never visited South Africa
   (b) Royalties received from a foreign publisher on foreign sales of a book written in South Africa

(c) Interest from a fixed deposit held with a bank in Botswana
(d) None of the above

3. Which of the following may lead to a private company losing the benefit of an assessed loss?
 (a) A major change in the shareholders
 (b) Ceasing to trade for a full tax year
 (c) Changing the nature of the company's business
 (d) All or any of the above

4. John Doe purchased an old house for R100 000. He lived in the house for two years, during which time he spent R80 000 renovating it. He then sold the house for R250 000 and bought another old house for R120 000, which he promptly started renovating. He could be subject to income tax on:
 (a) R70 000
 (b) R150 000
 (c) R30 000
 (d) R130 000

5. A woman, married in community of property, works for her husband and draws a salary; this salary will be taxed
 (a) In her husband's hands
 (b) In her own hands
 (c) Half in her husband's hands and half in her own
 (d) In any one of the above ways at the discretion of the Receiver of Revenue.

6. A person becomes liable for registration as a provisional taxpayer if
 (a) He earns interest of R1 000 per year
 (b) He earns dividends of R3 000 per year
 (c) He has his own business which generates income of R2 000 per year
 (d) None of the above

7. The income of a trust is taxed
 (a) In the hands of the trust
 (b) In the hands of the beneficiaries to the extent that they have received payments from the trust
 (c) At company rates where the trust is running a business
 (d) All of the above

8. Betty Bubbly sells goods on commission. She is paid commission two months after the sale and only on those sales where the customers have not returned the goods or made a claim against the sellers. During January and February 1994 she earned commission of R5 000 per month, which would be paid out at the end of March and at the end of April. The amount of R10 000 should be taxed
 (a) In the tax year ended February 1994
 (b) In the tax year ended February 1995
 (c) Partly in the 1994 tax year and partly in the 1995 tax year to allow for returns by customers
 (d) On any one of the above bases at the discretion of the Receiver of Revenue.

9. A South African resident would be liable for income tax on
   (a) Winnings from a casino
   (b) The profit on the sale of a private residence
   (c) The profit on the sale of shares inherited from a relative overseas
   (d) The profit on the sale of Krugerrands
10 The amount on which tax must be paid in respect of fringe benefits is based on
   (a) The financial benefit or saving received by the employee
   (b) The cost to the employer
   (c) A value agreed by the employer and the employee
   (d) An arbitrary amount laid down by the Receiver of Revenue

Questions and exercises

1.1 Discuss the differences between "extraordinary items" and "abnormal items" as they may appear in the income statement of an undertaking.
1.2 Discuss the process whereby Statements of Generally Accepted Accounting Practice are brought into being.
1.3 Discuss the differences between the following qualifications
   Chartered Accountant (S A)
   ACMA
   CFA
   CIS
1.4 In each of the following cases indicate in which tax year the amount in question should be taxed and, where more than one taxpayer is involved, which one will be taxable. Support your view in each case with a brief discussion.
   1. Scrooge had money on deposit at a bank. The full interest of R1 500 was payable on 30 June 1995, which was the last day of a two year deposit period.
   2. Wilmot let his house on a two year lease from 1 March 1995 at a rental of R1 000 per month. He owed Rochester R24 000 in respect of an interest free loan and in repayment thereof he ceded the lease agreement to Rochester, who accepted the cession in full settlement of the loan. Ignore any possible fringe benefit implications of the interest free loan.
   3. Would it have made any difference to the problem if, instead of ceding the loan, Wilmot had undertaken to use the monthly rental receipts to repay the loan to Rochester?
   4. John Brown accepted an appointment as a security officer at a large estate while the owner was overseas on holiday for the period 1 February 1995 to 15 March 1995. He was to be paid at the rate of R3 000 per month, which would amount to R4 500 for the entire period. The total amount was to be paid to him in one lump sum on 15 March 1995, but only if there had been no theft from the property during the entire period. If there had been thefts the owner could reduce the amount at his discretion. There were no thefts and the full amount was paid to John.

1.5 A private company operated two farms known as Welbekend and Onbekend. the manager, a one-third shareholder, decided to retire and handed everything over to his two sons, who had no real interest in farming themselves and decided to sell the farms. These sons held the rest of the shares. Since land prices were low at the time they decided to hold on and continue farming until prices rose. When they did, Welbekend was sold off at a very good price. The brothers had in the meantime been told that they could improve their profits by converting Onbekend into a township and selling off the township plots. They did this and did generate for higher profits than they would have if they had simply sold off the land.

Required:

Discuss whether the profits in each of the above cases are revenue profits or capital profits.

Cases

1.1 The following information applies to Mars Limited for the year ended 30 June 1989.

Income statement

Net operating income after charging depreciation of R23 000	60 000
Tax—South African normal and deferred	30 000
Net income after taxation	30 000
Dividends	12 000
Retained income for the year	18 000
Retained income at the start of the year	56 000
Retained income at the end of the year	74 000

Balance sheet

Capital employed		
Ordinary share capital		120 000
Non-distributable reserve		51 000
Distributable reserve		74 000
		245 000
Long term liability		62 000
Deferred tax		7 500
		314 500
Land and buildings at valuation		85 000
Plant and machinery at cost	230 000	
Accumulated depreciation	57 500	172 500
		257 500
Net current assets		59 000

Current assets		
Stock	68 000	
Debtors	79 000	149 000
Current liabilities		
Creditors	34 000	
Bank overdraft	56 000	90 000
		314 500

Additional information:

1. All plant and machinery was bought on the same day. Depreciation is provided at 10% per annum on cost.

   The gross current replacement cost of the plant and machinery is as follows:

30 June 1988	R260 000
30 June 1989	R280 000

2. No depreciation is provided on land and buildings. The valuation took place three years ago, but the directors estimate that current market value is R110 200.

3. Cost of sales were determined as follows:

Opening stock	48 000
Purchases	305 000
	353 000
Closing stock	68 000
	285 000

4. The following indices are available:

	Consumer price index	Index for goods sold
Beginning of the year	198	185
During the year		
when opening stock was bought	195	182
when closing stock was bought	220	205
End of year	227	210
Average	212	198

5. Interest on the long term liability amounted to R6 000.

6. The financial structure of the company remained fairly constant during the year.

Required:

Prepare the supplementary current cost income statement for the year ended 30 June 1989.

1.2 A builder named Stuart purchased three sites in the name of a company, Midas (Pty) Ltd. The main objective of this company was to speculate in fixed property, but it had as ancillary objective the holding of property as an income producing asset. On one of the sites he erected a building and sold the improved property. The other two sites were separated by another one on which a block of flats had been erected by the owner.

About two years after Midas (Pty) Ltd had purchased the properties, a partnership consisting of three men purchased this block of flats through a nominee. One of the partners, Mohammed, was of the opinion that the property was to be developed by the erection thereon of a petrol station and testified to this effect in court, but the other two, Mustapha and Ali, stated that, while the idea had been mentioned, the estate agent handling the sale had pointed out that the property was too small for this purpose and that the flats had therefore been purchased as an income producing asset. The estate agent did suggest that the partnership acquire the two properties from Midas (Pty) Ltd so as to obtain a large enough site for development purposes. Mohammed withdrew from the partnership at this point.

The remaining partners did approach Stuart to form a new partnership involving all three sites, but he refused. The partners then got another person, a certain Brown, to purchase the shares in Midas (Pty) Ltd, so obtaining the properties, and the two partners plus Brown became the directors of the company. By this time some eight years had elapsed since the purchase of the properties by Midas (Pty) Ltd.

The partners looked at, and quickly abandoned, ideas of developing the site as a petrol station or shopping centre, before finding another more suitable site on which they subsequently erected a petrol station. At no stage did they consolidate the sites, nor did they change the ownership of the sites. They then sold all three properties to a single purchaser at a very good price, some ten years after the original purchase. The price was apportioned over the three properties, resulting in a profit of over R51 000 to the company.

They claimed this as a capital profit, claiming that there had been a distinct change of intention from holding the properties as stock in trade to holding the properties as capital assets after the change in ownership of the shares, with the profit arising only because of the chance appearance of a more suitable site for development purposes. They appealed against the Commissioner's decision to assess it as taxable income.

Required:

State whether you feel that the appeal is justified on the basis of the facts. Mention the tests that the court would apply in coming to its decision.

1.3 A medical practitioner practising in Durban had, in each of five tax years, deducted an amount from his taxable income for "replacement of white safari suits used exclusively for medical practice". This claim was disallowed and the tax payer objected.

In court it was admitted that the tax payer and his partners had agreed that they should wear white safari suits for work. It was contended that in Durban's hot climate such dress had become associated with medical practitioners and other associated with the medical profession such as pharmacists, but no evidence was led to support this.

Previous judgements which were referred to in the judgement included the one from which this statement is taken:

"The truth is that the employee has to wear something, and the nature of his job determines what that something will be."

A second case, a British one, to which reference was made concerned a female barrister who purchased "dark clothing of a sober kind" specifically to conform to the rules of her Bar Council. Since she led evidence to indicate that she did not normally wear that type of clothing, her claim that this was a legitimate deduction was upheld.

Required:

On the basis of the facts given, should the doctor be allowed to deduct the cost of his safari suits?

Part two

Financial records and reports

This section explains the double entry system of accounting and then looks at the way in which accounting practices and form of accounting reports are prescribed or influenced by the various forms of organisation. It also looks at some of the new directions in which accounting is developing as a result of socio-political and economic pressures.

Chapter 6

The elements of financial accounting

This chapter is designed to give an understanding of what assistance a financial accounting system can give to a manager, and to give an understanding of how the double entry system works.

1. The objectives of a financial accounting system

2. The double entry bookkeeping system

3. An elementary example of how the double entry system works

4. An example of a more complex business

5. A few extra points

1. The objectives of a financial accounting system

A financial accounting system is designed to provide the owners or managers of an entity with information concerning its finances. An entity is a separate, identifiable financial unit such as a business, a part of a business, a non-profit organisation (such as a church), a government or an individual person. Any of these is at some time involved in transactions involving money, and the accounting system is there to provide information concerning money. Specifically, the accounting system provides two key sets of financial information:

1. The financial position of the entity at any *point in time*; and
2. The changes in the financial position over any *period of time*.

The financial position of the entity is just how rich or poor the entity actually is: What it owns, and what it owes to others. The changes in financial position reflect whether the entity has become richer or poorer over the period at which one is looking. Stated differently, the accounting system keeps a record of how much money has been received by an undertaking and of how this money has been spent.

In order to provide this information, a great many data have to be collected and processed by the accounting system. The collection of the data and control procedures to ensure that all data are actually processed are the preserve of the accountant and will not be dealt with in this book. Those who are studying accounting for purposes of becoming accountants should study one of the many excellent texts on the market already. This book will deal only with the actual processing system whereby all the raw data are transformed into information which can be used by management, and will deal with that only to an extent which will enable the aspiring manager to understand how the system works, what its limitations are and what information the accountant is capable of supplying to him. To put it a different way, the *objective* of this part of the book is to *make the accounting system* and, hopefully, the accountant *accessible* to the manager or prospective manager.

The first step in this process of making accounting accessible is to explain how the basic bookkeeping system operates.

2. The double entry bookkeeping system

This is the system whereby financial records are maintained throughout the whole western world and most of the rest of the world as well. It is essentially a very simple system based on the rather obvious concept that every time one spends or receives money at least two aspects of one's life are affected. For instance, if you spend ten Rand on food, the two aspects which would be affected are cash and food:

1. you would now have ten Rand less cash; and
2. you would now have ten Rand worth of food which you did not have before.

The same would apply to any other transaction involving money. If you buy a car and pay cash for it, you have less cash than before but you now have a car which you did not have before. If you should buy that same car on credit your actual cash would not change, but:

1. you would now have a car that you did not have before; and
2. you would also owe money that you did not owe before.

The double entry system is designed to take account of both aspects that change. The *double entry* arises because you enter the *same amount twice*, once in respect of each aspect. For example, the ten Rand mentioned in the first example above would be deducted from cash and also entered as an addition to food.

3. An elementary example of how the double entry system works

From an economic and accounting point of view the simplest undertakings are those in the service sector. The process is straightforward: the undertaking renders a service for which it gets paid, and the amount received is used to pay the expenses of the business and to provide the owner with an income. There may be many personnel or customer relations problems but these are not the concern of the accountant. The complications from an accountant's point of view begin when the undertaking starts trading or manufacturing and there are stocks of goods to be sold.

For this reason a simple service business, without any of the accounting complications caused by buying and selling goods or by manufacturing, will be used to illustrate how the accounting process works.

The business which has been chosen is the estate agency business run by Martin Mahvel. The background to this business is that, after working for other people for several years and, by dint of studying hard, passing all his estate agent's examinations, Martin has decided to open his own estate agency. To get the business going he has a motor car which he values at R40 000 and which is fully paid and has R10 000 in the bank. The financial position of his business at the opening on 1 March 1994 will be reflected in a *balance sheet* which looks like this:

MARTIN MAHVEL
Balance sheet at 1 March 1994
Assets

Motor vehicle	40 000
Cash in bank	10 000
	50 000

Liabilities

None	0

Capital

(Assets—Liabilities)	50 000
	50 000

Figure 6.1

The three headings have the following meanings:
Assets are items which Martin owns, regardless of whether or not he has paid for them;
Liabilities are amounts owed; and
Capital is simply the difference between the assets and the liabilities. It is also known as net worth or owners equity or shareholders equity.

From this balance sheet his starting financial position can be seen, but in order to get his accounting system started he has to bring these figures into his financial records. To do this he has to buy two basic accounting books: the *journal* and the *ledger*.

The journal is the book in which all financial transactions are first recorded. It is the financial diary, listing all transactions day by day as they take place. All transactions could be recorded in one basic journal, particularly in a small business such as this.There are various different journals in most businesses, though, each dealing with a certain type of transaction such as credit sales or credit purchases or cash payments. These separate journals exist because there are so many transactions of these particular types that it makes sense to deal with them in one book.

The ruling of the pages in the basic journal look like this (the headings don't normally appear but have been placed there so that you know what each column is for):

Mth	Day	Particulars	Ref	Rand	c	Rand	c

Figure 6.2

The first two columns are obviously for the date of the transaction and the third for particulars of the transaction. The fourth column is a reference column which will be used later in the process and then there are two sets of money columns. The left hand one is known as the *debit* column and the right hand one as the *credit* column, but these names are not important to an understanding of how the process works.

There are certain basic rules for the way in which money amounts are entered into these columns, rules which a bookkeeper *must* know. The following table shows in which column the various different types of transaction are entered:

	Increase	*Decrease*
Assets	Debit (left)	Credit (right)
Liabilities	Credit (right)	Debit (left)
Capital	Credit (right)	Debit (left)
Income	Credit (right)	Debit (left)
Expenses	Debit (left)	Credit (right)

Applying these rules to Martin's opening financial position gives the following entry in the financial records of his business:

Mch	1	Motor vehicle			40 000	00		
		Cash in bank			10 000	00		
		Capital					50 000	00
		Opening Entry						

Figure 6.3

The motor vehicle represents an increase in the assets of the business since it had no assets beforehand. In terms of the table of rules it is then entered in the debit or left column. The same argument applies to the cash in the bank.

A look at the rules will show that, since the capital of the business has increased from nil to R50 000, the amount of this increase must be entered in the credit or right column. The journal entry is completed by adding an explanatory note, called a narration, and ruling off the entry by drawing a line across the particulars column.

The first amounts have now been entered in the financial records of the undertaking, but the process is not yet complete. A moment's thought will make it clear that the information in the journal is simply a list of transactions which will not mean very much unless the items in the list are sorted and classified into different categories.

In order to do this sorting and classifying, the next step is to transfer the amounts in the journal to the ledger, which is a book in which we sort out our transactions and list similar items together. This process of transferring the amounts is known as posting to the ledger.

A page in the ledger usually looks like this:

DEBIT				CREDIT			

Figure 6.4

While the ruling looks different, one still finds that there are two sets of money columns which are used in exactly the same way as those in the journal. As a matter of fact, items in the left hand column of the journal are simply transferred to the left hand column of the appropriate page of the ledger, and similarly with items in the right hand column of the journal.

One page of the ledger is reserved for each type of transaction. This page is known as the *account* for that particular type of transaction and all transactions of that type will be transferred from the journal into the account for that type of transaction. In this case three accounts will be opened immediately: one for cash in bank, one for motor vehicle and one for capital. All subsequent transactions dealing with cash in bank, for instance, will be transferred to the cash in bank account. This account will then be a record of all the bank transactions.

To summarise: the journal is used to record all transactions as they take place without any attempt to sort them out. These unsorted amounts are then transferred to the ledger where they are sorted according to their nature so that all similar transactions are now kept together which makes the total importance of any type of transaction clearer.

The story of Martin Mahvel continues. In order to start his business he needed premises, so he rented a small office in a busy shopping centre some way out of the centre of the city. He paid R800 on 1 March to cover the first month's rent. He also bought some furniture for a total of R4 500. Half of this he paid in cash and agreed to pay the other half in equal instalments over the next six months. His cash account would now appear as follows:

Cash in bank

Mch	1	O/bal	1	10 000	00	Mch	1	Rent	1	800	00
							1	Furn	1	2 250	00

Figure 6.5

These amounts would all have been entered in the journal first, of course. The figures in the reference column (also called the folio column) refer to the page of the journal on which the original entry is to be found just as the numbers in the reference column of the journal refer to the pages of the ledger:

Mch	1	Rent	4	800	00		
		Cash in bank	1			800	00
		Rent for March					
	1	Furniture	5	4 500	00		
		Cash in bank	1			2 250	00
		Furnmart	6			2 250	00
		Office furniture, balance to be paid over 6 months					

Figure 6.6

The transactions for the rest of the first month were as follows:
- Purchased stationery for R200 and paid cash.
- Paid R200 for the installation of a telephone.

									2
Mch	1	Stationery	7	200	00				
		Cash	1				200	00	
		Stationery purchased							
	1	Telephone costs	8	200	00				
		Cash	1				200	00	
		Installation							
	10	Cash	1	4 000	00				
		Commission	9				4 000	00	
		Commission on sale of Mr X's home							
	31	Advertising	10	800	00				
		Northside News	11				800	00	
		Account to be paid by 15/4							
	31	Cleaning	12	400	00				
		Cash	1				400	00	
		Office cleaning							
	31	Petrol deposit	13	500	00				
		Cash	1				500	00	
		Sols Service Centre							
	31	Petrol	14	350	00				
		Sols Service	15				350	00	
		Mch petrol account							
	31	Telephone	8	400	00				
		Postmaster	16				400	00	
		Mch phone account							

Figure 6.7

- Sold a property for Mr X and received commission of R4 000 paid over immediately in cash
- Advertised in the local newspaper to a value of R800 on account to be paid by the fifteenth of April.
- Paid R400 for office cleaning.
- Paid R500 for a petrol account deposit.
- Received accounts for R400 in respect of telephone and R350 in respect of petrol.

The journal entries would be as shown above.

There would be far more transactions than these in most businesses, but they would be entered in exactly the same way as those shown above and the journal at the end of the month would be exactly like the one above except for the number of entries. All these entries would now have to be transferred or *posted* to the ledger. After this exercise the ledger accounts would be as follows:

Capital 1

								Mch	1	O/bal	1	50 000	00

Motor car 2

Mch	1	O/bal	1	40 000	00								

Cash in bank 3

Mch	1	O/bal	1	10 000	00	Mch	1	Rent	1		800	00
	10	Comm	2	4 000	00		1	Furn	1		2 250	00
							1	Stat	2		200	00
							1	Phone	2		200	00
							31	Clean	2		400	00
							31	Deposit	2		500	00
								Balance			9 650	00
				14 000	00						14 000	00
Apl	1	Balance		9 650	00							

Rent 4

Mch	1	Cash	1	800	00						

Furniture 5

Mch	1	Sundries	1	4 500	00						

							Mch	1	Furniture	1	2 250	00

Furnmart   6

Mch	1	Cash	2	200	00						

Stationery   7

Mch	1	Cash	2	200	00						
	31	P O	2	400	00						

Telephone   8

							Mch	10	Cash	2	4 000	00

Commission   9

Mch	31	N/News	2	800	00						

Advertising   10

							Mch	31	Advert	2	800	00

Northside News   11

Mch	31	Cash	2	400	00						

Cleaning   12

Mch	31	Cash	2	500	00						

Petrol deposit   13

Mch	31	Sols	2	350	00						

Petrol   14

Sols Service Centre												15
							Mch	31	Petrol	2	350	00

Postmaster												16
							Mch	31	Phone	2	400	00

Figure 6.8

A quick look at these accounts will show that all the rules regarding debit and credit have been observed. All assets, such as cash, the motor car and the petrol deposit, have debit balances (the amounts on the left side of the ledger total to more than the amounts on the right side); all liabilities, such as Sols Service Centre and the Postmaster, have credit balances; all expenses, such as petrol and telephone, have debit balances and all income items, the only one here being commission, have credit balances, as does the capital account.

Other points to note are that the ledger does not give very much detail about the various transactions. If one were to look at the commission account, for instance, one would simply see that cash had been received in respect of commissions. To get the detail one would go back to the book of first entry, the journal. The ledger gives a reference number for the page of the journal and one can easily go back to the first entry and see what commission it is that has been paid. The overall position for an account is given in the ledger, however. One would go to the ledger to see what the cash balance is, but for the detail of each transaction one would go back to the journal.

The ledger account for cash in bank has been *ruled off* at the end of the month and the *balance carried down* to the start of the next month. This little exercise is generally performed for active accounts so that one has a clear picture of what is happening at present without the view being cluttered by all the previous transactions. Without this one would have an account going on forever, while this effectively breaks the account into more easily grasped periodic sections.

Once all the transactions for a period have been entered it is necessary to do a check to see whether there are any errors. There is a standard test for this which is known as a *trial balance*. The trial balance is not actually a part of the bookkeeping system. It is a partial test of the correctness of the entries and is used as part of the working papers for the preparation of the various accounting reports. It is very simple in structure since it is simply a list of the ledger accounts with their balances and is prepared on a sheet of journal paper:

		Trial balance at 31 March 1994					
1	Capital					50 000	00
2	Motor car		40 000	00			
3	Cash in bank		9 650	00			
4	Rent		800	00			
5	Furniture		4 500	00			
6	Furnmart					2 250	00
7	Stationery		200	00			
8	Telephone		600	00			
9	Commission					4 000	00
10	Advertising		800	00			
11	Northside News					800	00
12	Cleaning		400	00			
13	Petrol deposit		500	00			
14	Petrol		350	00			
15	Sols Service Centre					350	00
16	Postmaster					400	00
			57 800	00		57 800	00

Figure 6.9

The important point about the trial balance is that the totals of the debit and credit columns must agree. The logic behind this is simple: in every individual journal entry the total amount on the left hand side equals the total amount on the right hand side. This means that the total of all the entries in the left hand column of the journal must equal the total of all the entries on the right hand side of the journal. Therefore, if all the amounts have been transferred to the ledger, if no mistakes have been made in transferring the amounts across to the ledger and if no errors have been made in adding up the ledger accounts, the total of all the balances on the left hand side of the ledger will equal the total on the right hand side of the ledger. If the trial balance does not balance, if the left hand total is not equal to the right hand total, then an error has been made and will have to be found and rectified.

This trial balance does balance, but it should still be checked carefully to see that everything does look reasonable since it is quite possible that a transaction may have been left out completely or that a correct amount has been posted to the wrong account. In this case there is no problem, so the next step can be taken if so desired.

While a trial balance should be extracted regularly to check on the correctness of work done it is not necessary to prepare financial reports every time. They must be prepared at least once a year, but outside of that they are prepared for the benefit of the owner or manager of the undertaking and are only prepared as often as he wants them.

There are two basic financial reports: an *income statement*, giving details of the profit or loss for the period, and a *balance sheet* which shows the financial position at the end of the period. These can be prepared directly from the ledger, but it is more usual to prepare them from working papers. The first of these working papers is the trial balance, such as the one prepared above, and the other working papers are usually simply lists of adjustments made to the trial balance to bring into account any items not reflected there. An example in the above case might be a receipt for interest on the balance in the bank account, the details of which would only be known a week or so after the end of the month when the bank statements are received.

After the adjustments have been finalised, an amended trial balance is drawn up and the financial reports prepared from that.

The first report to be prepared is the income statement. This is simply a list of all the accounts in the ledger representing income, then a list of all the accounts representing expenses and finally the determination of the difference between the totals of these two lists, which is the net income or net profit of the undertaking. Of course, if the expenses are greater than the income then this difference is the net loss of the undertaking. In Martin's case income exceeds expenses, so that there is a small profit for the period:

MARTIN MAHVEL ESTATE AGENCY
Income Statement for March 1994
Income

Commission received		4 000,00
Expenses		3 150,00
Rent	800,00	
Stationery	200,00	
Telephone	600,00	
Advertising	800.00	
Cleaning	400,00	
Petrol	350,00	
Net income for the period		850,00

Figure 6.10

The net income or net profit at the end of the income statement is the amount by which the capital of the business has increased over the period.

All the items which are expenses have been listed in the income statement. It is important to note that the payment on the furniture is not an expense and nor is the petrol deposit. They are cash outlays, but in respect of assets. The petrol deposit can be claimed back, and you have the furniture in return for the cash laid out. In the case of expenses the money is gone and you have nothing concrete to show for it. The R400 in respect of cleaning, for instance, is represented by a cleaner office but the money is gone.

It is because of the difference between expenses and cash outlays that businesses are often unable to meet their commitments even though they are showing a profit. Money may have been spent on various assets such as machinery or stock for resale, items which are not expenses, and there is no money available for the running of the undertaking. The opposite can also happen, of course. The undertaking may have purchased goods on credit which will be reflected as expenses but the money may not yet have been paid to the creditor. In this case the undertaking will have more cash than one would expect from the profit figure!

The money spent on assets must be reflected somewhere, of course. The obvious place is on the balance sheet at the end of the period, which is simply a listing of all the items on the trial balance not listed in the income statement: the assets, the liabilities and the capital.

MARTIN MAHVEL ESTATE AGENCY
Balance Sheet at 31 March 1994

Assets		54 650,00
Motor car	40 000,00	
Cash in bank	9 650,00	
Furniture	4 500,00	
Petrol deposit	500,00	
		54 650.00
Liabilities		3 800.00
Furnmart	2 250,00	
Northside News	800,00	
Sols Service Centre	350,00	
Postmaster	400,00	
Capital		50 850,00
Opening balance	50 000,00	
Add net income	850,00	
		54 650,00

Figure 6.11

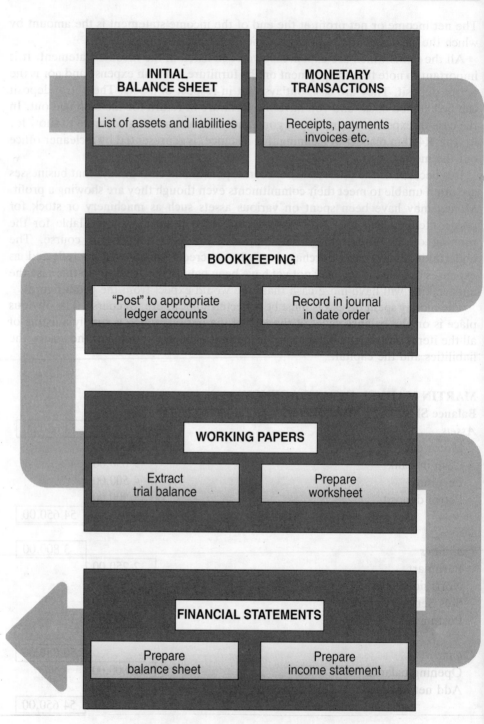

Figure 6.12   The Accounting Cycle

Once again the total of the assets is equal to the total of the liabilities and the capital. The capital has now increased to reflect the fact that the business made a small profit during the month which has so far been left in the business and not withdrawn for use by the owner.

Money spent on such items as furniture and the petrol deposit are shown here under assets to reflect the fact that, although the money has been spent, there is still an asset representing the value of that money.

All accounting systems work in exactly the same way as in this simple example. In a large business the only difference in principle is that there would be a great many more transactions. Often the bookkeeping system is computerised, in which case the computer performs many of the tasks, such as posting from the journal to the ledger and extracting a trial balance, which were done manually in our example. The whole process can be shown graphically as in figure 6.12 on the opposite page.

4 An example of a more complex business—PennyBee Boutique

A service undertaking such as that used in the previous example is the simplest type of business undertaking from an accounting point of view. As soon as a business starts trading, which is the buying and selling of goods, the accounting records and, particularly, the financial reports, become more complex. This complexity increases as the business adds functions: manufacturing, mining or farming in addition to the trading activities will require more records of more types and also more financial reports. This can be illustrated by looking at the story of Penny Banner. Penny had saved some money over the years that she had been working and decided to use this to start a small shop of her own. She intended selling sports clothes and equipment for women, since she had been active in sport all her life and knew how often she had struggled to find the clothes and equipment she had needed.

After settling on the name "PennyBee Boutique" she went out and found suitable premises. She then spent some time deciding just which manufacturers' goods she would stock. By 1 March 1999 she was ready to start and moved into her shop. It took a few days to sort things out, but by 6 March she had opened her doors to the public. The women of the city did not exactly overrun her shop but she felt fairly satisfied with the first month's operations. At the end of the month she sat down to write up her financial records so that she could see just what her position actually was.

The following transactions had taken place during the month:

1. She had opened a bank account in the name of her business into which she deposited R8 000 of her savings.
2. On the first of the month she had paid rent of R500 and had also paid a rental deposit of a further R500. She had also purchased certain shop fittings and equipment at a cost of R4 000. On these she had paid a deposit of R1 400 and had signed a suspensive sale agreement with Shark Investments Limited for the balance. This would be payable over three years and the finance charges involved amounted to R1 000.

3. Her initial purchase of goods for resale on the first of the month amounted to R5 000 of which she paid R2 000 by cheque. The balance was to be paid within thirty days from date of statement. Subsequent purchases of R6 500 on the thirteenth of the month and R3 500 on the twenty-seventh were all on credit with the same credit terms applicable.

4. The other payments made were for wages of R500 at the end of the month and for sundry petty cash expenditure: R50 up to the tenth of the month, R100 from then until the seventeenth, R150 from then until the twenty-fourth and a further R100 up to the end of the month.

5. Cash sales up to the tenth of the month came to R800; up to the seventeenth another R1 000; up to the twenty-fourth a further R1 500 and up to the end of the month again R1 500.

6. Credit sales to the tenth of the month came to R1 200; up to the seventeenth another R2 000; up to the twenty-fourth a further R2 500 and up to the end of the month another R3 500.

7. After closing shop on the thirty-first Penny listed the stock of goods still unsold in the shop. She went back to the purchase invoices to find the cost of these items and found that the total cost of merchandise for resale in stock came to R5 350.

These transactions would obviously have to be entered in the journal as the book of prime entry:

1

March	1	Bank		1	8 000	00		
		Capital		2			8 000	00
		Cash paid in by Penny Banner						
	1	Rent		3	500	00		
		Rental deposit		4	500	00		
		Bank—cheque 0001		1			1 000	00
		Rent March + 1 month deposit						
March	1	Shop fittings		5	4 000	00		
		Finance charges		6	1 000	00		
		Bank—cheque 0002		1			1 400	00
		Shark Investments Ltd		7			3 600	00
		Suspensive sale over 2 years at R150 pm—contract in file						

1

March	1	Purchases	8	5 000	00		
		Bank—cheque 0003	1			2 000	00
		Accounts payable	9			3 000	00
		Payment in 30 days					
	10	Petty cash expenditure	10	50	00		
		Bank—cheque 0004	1			50	00
		Expenditure to 10th March					
	10	Bank	1	800	00		
		Cash sales	11			800	00
		Sales to 10th, inv 1–9					
	10	Accounts receivable	12	1 200	00		
		Credit sales	13			1 200	00
		Sales to 10th, inv 1–6					
	13	Purchases	8	6 500	00		
		Accounts payable	9			6 500	00
		Payment in 30 days					
	17	Petty cash expenditure	10	100	00		
		Bank	1			100	00
		Expenditure 11–17 March					
	17	Bank	1	1 000	00		
		Cash sales	11			1 000	00
		Sales 11–17 March, inv 10–19					
	17	Accounts receivable	12	2 000	00		
		Credit sales	13			2 000	00
		Sales 11–17 March, inv 7–14					

					2		
March	24	Petty cash expenditure	10	150	00		
		Bank	1			150	00
		Expenditure to 18–24 March					
	24	Bank	1	1 500	00		
		Cash sales	11			1 500	00
		Sales 18–24 March, inv 20–30					
	24	Accounts receivable	12	2 500	00		
		Credit sales	13			2 500	00
		Sales 18–24 March, inv 15–23					
	27	Purchases	8	3 500	00		
		Accounts payable	9			3 500	00
		Payable 30 days					
	31	Petty cash expenditure	10	100	00		
		Bank	1			100	00
		Expenditure 25–31 March					
	31	Bank	1	1 500	00		
		Cash sales	11			1 500	00
		Sales 25–31 March, inv 31–37					
	31	Accounts receivable	12	3 500	00		
		Credit sales	13			3 500	00
		Sales 25–31 March, inv 24–34					
	31	Wages	14	500	00		
		Bank	1			500	00
		Wages for March					

Figure 6.13

Once all these transactions have been entered in the book of prime entry, the journal, they have to be *posted* to the accounts in the ledger, as described above:

			Bank								1
Mch	1	Capital	J1	8 000	00	Mch	1	Sundries	J1	1 000	00
	10	Sales	J1	800	00		1	Sundries	J1	1 400	00
	17	Sales	J1	1 000	00		1	Purchases	J1	2 000	00
	24	Sales	J2	1 500	00		10	Petty cash	J1	50	00
	31	Sales	J2	1 500	00		17	Petty cash	J1	100	00
							24	Petty cash	J2	150	00
							31	Petty cash	J2	100	00
							31	Wages	J2	500	00
							31	Balance	c/d	7 500	00
				12 800	00					12 800	00
Mch	31	Balance	b/d	7 500	00						

			Capital								2
						Mch	1	Bank	J1	8 000	00

			Rent								3
Mch	1	Bank	J1	500	00						

			Deposits								4
Mch	1	Bank	J1	500	00						

			Shop fittings								5
Mch	1	Sundries	J1	4 000	00						

			Finance charges								6
Mch	1	Shark Inv	J1	1 000	00						

			Shark Investments Ltd								7
						Mch	1	Sundries	J1	3 600	00

Purchases   8

Mch	1	Sundries	J1	5 000	00					
	13	Sundries	J1	6 500	00					
	27	Sundries	J2	3 500	00					

Accounts payable   9

						Mch	1	Sundries	J1	3 000	00
							13	Sundries	J1	6 500	00
							27	Sundries	J2	3 500	00

Petty cash expenditure   10

Mch	10	Sundries	J1	50	00					
	17	Sundries	J1	100	00					
	24	Sundries	J2	150	00					
	31	Sundries	J2	100	00					

Cash sales   11

						Mch	10	Inv 1–9	J1	800	00
							17	Inv 10–19	J1	1 000	00
							24	Inv 20–30	J2	1 000	00
							31	Inv 31–37	J2	1 500	00

Accounts receivable   12

Mch	10	Inv 1–6	J1	1 200	00					
	17	Inv 7–14	J2	2 000	00					
	24	Inv 15–23	J2	2 500	00					
	31	Inv 24–34	J2	3 500	00					

Credit sales   13

						Mch	10	Inv 1–6	J1	1 200	00
							17	Inv 7–14	J2	2 000	00
							24	Inv 15–23	J2	2 500	00
							31	Inv 24–34	J2	3 500	00

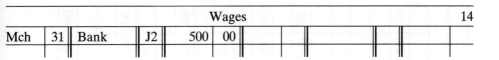

				Wages									14
Mch	31	Bank	J2	500	00								

Figure 6.14

The bank account has been balanced at the end of the month just to illustrate the process. The two sides of the ledger account are totalled, a balance inserted on the smaller side to make the two sides balance, both sides are then added up to the same total and the balance is carried down to the start of the next month. This will be done with all accounts with multiple transactions in order to show one total figure for the balance on each of those accounts.

There are also several simplifications. In real life the petty cash expenditure would be shown in detail, as would the names of those involved in the credit purchases and sales.

At this stage Penny decided that she would like to see the results of her first month of trading. Her first step was to check the accuracy of the accounting records which she had maintained. This she did by extracting a trial balance. The first two money columns of the worksheet in figure 6.15 below represent the original trial balance.

Penny realised that it would be necessary to make some adjusting entries. After all, she could not charge the entire amount of the finance charges against the income for the first month since these charges would only be incurred as the suspensive sale agreement continued. She therefore phoned the finance company for a settlement figure at the end of March and used this to apportion the finance charges. She also realised that she should write off depreciation to reflect the fact that her shop fittings were being used up. She decided that these would last ten years and would still have a value of R1 000 at the end of that time. This meant that she should write off R300 per year, or R25 per month. The journal entries to give effect to her calculations were entered in the adjustments columns of the worksheet.

There was one further adjustment to make. The stock on hand at the end of the year had to be brought to account, and this is also done in the adjustments columns.

The entries in the adjustments columns serve as pro forma journal entries. At the year end entries such as these would be entered in the journal and posted to the ledger but the accounting records are not normally closed off every month.

Depreciation entries, for instance, would usually only be put through once a year and the closing stock would certainly only go through once per year.

PENNYBEE BOUTIQUE—Trial balance at 31 March

	Original		Adjustment		Final	
	Dr	Cr	Dr	Cr	Dr	Cr
Bank	7 500 00				7 500 00	
Capital		8 000 00				8 000 00
Rent	500 00				500 00	
Deposits	500 00				500 00	
Shop fittings	4 000 00				4 000 00	
Finance charges	1 000 00			945 00	55 00	
Shark Investments		3 600 00				3 600 00
Purchases	15 000 00			5 350 00	9 650 00	
Accounts payable		13 000 00				13 000 00
Petty cash expenditure	400 00				400 00	
Cash sales		4 800 00				4 800 00
Accounts receivable	9 200 00				9 200 00	
Credit sales		9 200 00				9 200 00
Wages	500 00				500 00	
Depreciation			25 00		25 00	
Provision for depreciation				25 00		25 00
Finance charges not due			945 00		945 00	
Stock on hand			5 350 00		5 350 00	
	38 600 00	38 600 00	6 320 00	6 320 00	38 625 00	38 625 00

Figure 6.15

From the final trial balance, which is the last two columns of the worksheet, the two basic financial statements can now be prepared. The income statement is now a little more complex than before in that the two aspects of the business are separated:
1. the first aspect is the actual trading, or buying and selling of goods, and is dealt with in the first section of the income statement. This is known, appropriately enough, as the trading account; and
2. the second aspect, known as the profit and loss account, is the rest of the undertaking's activities, which in the case of PennyBee Boutique consists of the support activities for the trading.

If the undertaking had a variety of activities these should each be represented by a separate part of the income statement or by separate income statements which could later be combined. There could be, say, a manufacturing section for a manufacturer or an investment or rental section for any undertaking involved in activities of this type.

The financial statements for Penny's business after one month of operations are shown in figures 6.16 to 6.18 below:

PENNYBEE BOUTIQUE
Trading account for March 1999

Sales		14 000
Cash sales	4 800	
Credit sales	9 200	
Deduct cost of goods sold		9 650
Purchases	15 000	
Deduct closing stock	5 350	
Gross profit (45 % of cost of goods sold)		4 350

Figure 6.16

Gross profit is one of the first control points in the preparation of financial statements. If gross profit is expressed as a percentage of cost of sales it is known as the mark up (mark up percentage, mark up margin). This is the percentage which is added to the cost price of goods to arrive at the selling price. In this case, Penny marks her goods up by 45 %.

If she knows that in actual fact she marks up by 50 % then she will immediately be able to see that there is a problem in her business. Either there is a problem with her records or she has calculated the value of her closing stock incorrectly, or else there is theft of either money or goods. If there is a shortage of money the amount can be determined by adding fifty per cent to the value of cost of sales and deducting from this the amount of sales recorded (R9 650 × 1,5 = R14 475 − R14 000 = R475). If the problem lies with stock shortages, determine what the cost of sales should have been and deduct this from the cost of sales shown. Cost of sales at a 50 % mark up should be 66,66 % of sales, so (R14 000 × 2/3 = R9 333; R9 650 − R9 333 = R317).

PENNYBEE BOUTIQUE
Profit and loss account for March

Gross profit	4 350
Expenses	1 480
Depreciation	25
Finance charges	55
Rent	500
Sundry expenses	400
Wages	500
Net profit for the month	2 870

The trading account (or trading statement) and profit and loss account (or profit and loss statement) are combined to produce the income statement.

In future periods the cost of goods sold, or cost of sales, will be determined by taking into account the opening stock (which is the closing stock at the end of the previous month) as well as purchases and closing stock. Say that Penny purchased goods for resale for R12 000 during April and that her closing stock at the end of that time was R4 350. Cost of goods sold would be determined as follows:

Cost of sales for April:	
Opening stock (Closing stock at end March)	5 350
Purchases for the month	12 000
Cost of goods available for sale	17 350
Deduct closing stock	4 350
Cost of sales	13 000

Penny's balance sheet can now be prepared. It is prepared in a more acceptable manner than that of Martin Mahvel above, with assets and liabilities being sorted into two groups each: long term or fixed and short term or current. These terms are discussed in more detail in chapter 8.

PENNYBEE BOUTIQUE
Balance Sheet at 31 March

Capital		10 870
Amount paid in	8 000	
Net profit for the month	2 870	
Long term liabilities		2 655
Suspensive sale payable	3 600	
Deduct finance charges not due	945	
Current liabilities		
Accounts payable		13 000
		26 525
Fixed assets		3 975
Shop fittings at cost	4 000	
Deduct provision for depreciation	25	
Current assets		22 550
Bank balance	7 500	
Accounts receivable	9 200	
Deposit	500	
Stock on hand	5 350	
		26 525

Figure 6.18

There is only one aspect of this balance sheet which may not be clear: Long term liabilities, where the final amount shown is the amount Penny would have had to pay to settle the account at the end of March. The finance charges not due relate to future periods, since she will only be charged the full amount of this interest if she pays strictly in terms of the agreement. Settling the outstanding amount earlier will result in a reduction of the total finance charges bill. Every other item on the face of the balance sheet should be clear by now.

While these financial statements are not subject to any particular legal requirements, they are subject to all the accounting conventions referred to in chapter 3:

1. The going concern convention is obviously applied. The balance sheet reflects a business which is operating, and the valuations on the balance sheet reflect this. Stock, for instance, is not reflected at the price it would fetch on a forced sale but at the cost price of goods which are intended for resale.
2. The matching convention is applied in the adjustment to the finance charges. While one may query the way in which Penny arrived at the amount to bring to account in the current period, she did relate the charges for the period to the use of the assets during the period.
3. The convention of consistency cannot apply since this is the first set of financial statements. Similarly the convention of prudence could scarcely apply as yet.

4. The realisation convention applies in that all transactions leading to a profit or loss have been included, even where there has not yet been any cash flow e g credit sales.
5. The conventions of disclosure and materiality apply. All transactions are fully disclosed, but the small amounts of petty cash expenditure are simply lumped together. The only material expense item, wages, is disclosed separately.
6. The conventions of objectivity and verifiability have been adhered to in that anyone else working from the same source documents should arrive at an identical set of financial statements, except possibly that the deferred finance charges and depreciation may be calculated at different rates. However, the rates and methods used by Penny are verifiable.
7. The other conventions such as historical cost also have no real significance at this early stage of the undertaking's existence, but they have been applied anyway.

While this introduction to the double entry accounting system has been very superficial it does cover the entire process and anyone who understands the examples in this chapter should have no trouble in understanding how the system works. From the point of view of the manager it should clarify why the accountants are always looking for the vouchers and other bits of paper showing what other people have been doing in the undertaking: they need them in order to do their job. Their job is to process all the data contained in those bits of paper to provide managers with the financial reports which managers need in order to determine just how well the undertaking is faring.

5 A few extra points worth mentioning

5.1 The cash book

Accountants in the English speaking countries have generally used a short cut in dealing with cash or, more usually, bank entries. Instead of journalising these entries they have made use of a "cash book". This book is in reality the cash or bank account in the general ledger, and transactions are entered directly into it. All amounts on the debit side of the cash book are then posted to the credit side of another ledger account and vice versa. The cash book has therefore performed a function very similar to that of a journal, but generations of accountants-to-be have struggled with the concept that items from the journal are posted to the same side of the relevant ledger account, but that entries from the cash book are posted to the opposite side of the relevant account.

This practice is actually illegal in some countries, particularly in continental Europe. It is now gradually dying out for two major reasons:
1. There is a movement towards the international standardisation of accounting practice, and if one is standardising one may as well do it correctly; and
2. Far more importantly, most computerised accounting systems are based on the use of a journal system, and nearly everyone is either using or intending to use a computer based accounting package.

PENNYBEE BOUTIQUE

Sales journal

1

Date	Inv no	Customer	Fol	Total	Shoes	Tennis racquets	Skirts	Tops	Accessories	Track suits	Sundries
Mar 1	1	M B Simmes		100 00					100 00		
3	2	R Blair		250 00			250 00				
4	3	M van der Westhuizen		200 00	200 00						
5	4	N Stewart		250 00				250 00			
7	5	C Livingstone		150 00		150 00					
9	6	L Kai		250 00						250 00	0
				1 200 00	200 00	150 00	250 00	250 00	100 00	250 00	0

Figure 6.19

5.2 Journals and journal entries

Every transaction which takes place must be recorded. The first place in which it is recorded, the book of prime entry, is a journal. In the simple examples above use was made of only one journal. In reality, the volume of transactions in a normal business leads to the use of a number of journals, each having a specific purpose. Penny Banner, for instance would probably have maintained a sales journal for recording credit sales. This journal could have been used as an analysis book to give her more detail of the transactions.

The sales journal for PennyBee Boutique could have looked much like figure 6.19. Instead of merely keeping a record of sales in total, this book could give details of the type of merchandise being sold and Penny could have this information at her fingertips. She could keep separate ledger accounts showing the sales of each type of merchandise to help her in her planning decisions. Only the total of each column would be posted to the general ledger, while the details of each customers' purchases would be posted to her individual account in the accounts receivable ledger. The accounts receivable account in the general ledger would then show the total amounts owing to PennyBee, but there would be no detail whatever. The total of the accounts in the accounts receivable ledger would total to the balance on the accounts receivable account in the general ledger at all times when postings for a period have been completed.

An account such as this in the general ledger is known as a *control account* since it provides a control total against which the total of a list of balances extracted from the accounts receivable ledger can be balanced or controlled.

Similar control accounts can be maintained for accounts payable, contracts in progress and trust accounts maintained by attorneys, for example.

Key words

Double entry	Journal
Ledger	Income statement
Balance sheet	Trading account
Cost of sales	Gross profit
Trial balance	

Chapter 7

Computerised accounting and accounting information systems

This chapter has two distinct sections, the first of which simply uses the Pennybee case from the last chapter. The transactions from that chapter are shown on a computerised system to show some of the advantages of a computerised system.

The second part of the chapter discusses some aspects of accounting as an information system within the undertaking and develops a framework for the development of such a system.

1. **Computers and data processing**

2. **Business data processing**

3. **An illustrative example**

4. **Management information systems**
   Accounting information systems in management planning and control

1. Computers

Computers as we know them are of comparatively recent origin. There were no computers whatever as little as fifty years ago, and even as late as the nineteen fifties there was so little appreciation of their possible uses that a commission appointed by the British Government saw little chance of the world ever needing more than about three computers. The commission therefore recommended that no British funds be invested in the development of such machines. By the nineteen sixties the price of computers had dropped to levels where they could be commercially applied, but they were still cantankerous machines which needed special care in the form of temperature and humidity control, could only be tended by specialists who developed a mystique which led to a great deal of computer phobia and took up a great deal of space. Rapid developments in the electronics field quickly led to miniaturisation as valves were replaced by transistors, which were also less temperamental and did not need such special care. Printed circuitry followed, and the silicon chip, which is essentially a highly sophisticated printed circuit, allowed computers to become smaller still while constantly improving their reliability. Some of the more complex chips developed for use in control equipment were capable of being programmed to hold a set of instructions, but some electronics hobbyists realised the potential of such a chip and developed complete computers using these chips, the favourites for this purpose being the Intel Z-80, used on the Radio Shack TRS-80 microcomputer introduced in about 1977, and the MOS Technology 6502 as used on the Apple II, introduced at roughly the same time. The Z-80 came to dominate the micro computer market, with an industry standard operating system known as CP/M becoming so well known that it was used as the basis for MS-DOS, which became the standard operating system for the next generation of microcomputers introduced by IBM in the early 1980's. By this time computing power which had not even been dreamed of twenty years before was available to even the smallest business, and a typical desktop micro-computer nowadays would be an IBM or IBM-compatible computer with at least 640 kilobytes of memory on board and a hard disk storage system with a capacity of up to a thousand megabytes, with prices running under R5 000 for a system with software.

This has led to a revolution in the accounting field, with accountants now able to use fewer staff members to process more data than before and to supply information both more relevant and more timeous than could ever be possible using a manual system.

2. Business data processing

Computerised data processing systems have the following advantages over manual or mechanised systems:

2.1 Speed

By human standards, computers are incredibly fast. They can calculate far faster than any alternative processing method, and programming can lead to standardised decisions being treated as calculations. They can also produce the results of their calculations at the same type of speed, with only the mechanical slowness of the printers available slowing them down when producing hard copies.

2.2 Reliability

The computer is the perfect slave. It is incapable of reasoning and will always do exactly as it is told, no matter how boring the task may be. It cannot make a mistake on its own: all mistakes are due to inexpert programming, operator error or mechanical failure of some sort.

2.3 Memory

The computer can store incredible amounts of information and always be able to retrieve it without error.

These aspects make it ideal for processing information under certain types of circumstances, specifically where there are large amounts of transactions which are repetitive by nature.

The transactions of even a small business comply with these requirements. A sizeable number of transactions will take place when buying and selling goods or when selling services, and there will be a very small variety of types of transactions. There may be several hundred sales on credit to various different customers, but the nature of the transaction will be the same in every case.

The major requirement for a computerised business data processing system is therefore that it be capable of handling a large number of simple data processing transactions (simple from the point of view of the computers processing ability). Since the computer itself can do this very quickly it is obvious that a system must be designed whereby the information can be quickly and easily be verified and supplied to the computer, and also designed so that the output devices such as printers are free of bottlenecks so as to be able to produce the required output as quickly as possible.

2.4 Schematics of a computer system

There are two basic approaches to the design of computer systems for business data processing, batch processing systems and interactive systems.

2.4.1 *Batch processing systems*

Batch processing systems were the first type of business data processing systems to be developed. The relevant data, say credit sales invoices, are collected and stored for processing at a later time. These will normally be collected in batches, possibly of pre-determined size, which will be coded and subjected to some sort of numerical control. The simplest type of control is to total the invoices in the batch and to use this total as a control measure to ensure that all the invoices have been processed, but there have been many more sophisticated methods developed where the security of the information is of paramount importance.

These batches can then be processed at any time, which can be of great use in a system where the computer is at times fully loaded. The banks still use this type of processing for cheques, for instance: they can be processed at night, when there are few interruptions from outside, leaving the computer free for enquiries and control of ATM machines during the day.

People making use of computer bureaus for data processing are nearly always on a batch processing system, usually with manual delivery of input data to the bureau, although some of the bureaus now have facilities whereby the user can collect data and transfer it electronically to the bureau's computer at predetermined times.

The disadvantages of such a system lie in the fact that information is not always up to date. Smaller applications may transfer their input to the bureau or even an in-house computer at intervals of a week or even a month, and output would correspondingly only be available at intervals as large as these.

Since the input data is sorted before being processed in a batch system it is possible to make use of sequential storage materials for the data. Magnetic tapes are therefore commonly used in batch processing systems to store input and even output data.

2.4.2 *Interactive systems*

Interactive systems are those in which data is processed as the transaction takes place. A typical example would be the use of a computer terminal to produce invoices for credit sales. These invoices would be produced and, upon verification, would be posted immediately to the debtors account the moment the sale is complete. Access to the account would at any time give up to the minute information.

Such systems are becoming more common as more businesses obtain their own computer systems. One very popular system currently in use has been designed for pharmacies and makes use of varied input media including real time invoicing machines with light pens which enable them to maintain their stock records by the simple reading of a bar code. A system such as this may have only one access point or may have several terminals with access to the system. For various reasons some of these terminals may only have enquiry access to the data stored in the computer and will not be able to enter data.

In view of the fact that there is no pre-sorting of the input data it is essential that use be made of random access storage media when using an interactive system. This is one reason for the fact that these systems are only now becoming available. Until the development of low cost, high capacity hard disk drives real time systems were just too expensive to contemplate for any but the largest undertakings.

2.4.3 *Distributed data processing*

Microcomputers nowadays perform many tasks which would have been entrusted to a mainframe only a few years ago. The result of this is that many small sub-operations of larger organisations now possess their own data processing capability. This has in some cases meant that there has been duplication of data processing work, with the main computer processing data at corporate level, often on a batch processing basis, and the microcomputers processing the same data at branch level on an interactive basis. Many of these cowboy systems at branch or department level have now been tamed, however, and brought into the mainstream of the organisations data processing by the use of some form of direct electronic communication.

The actual processes have not changed. All that has happened is that the duplication has to a large extent been eliminated by using the microcomputer to supply up to the minute information at the sub-level and then to periodically dump the processed data onto the memory of the main computer, where it is processed further for purposes of corporate reporting. This further processing could involve the consolidation of the results of the various branches into a summary report, for instance. One still finds the combination of interactive and batch processing, but each is appropriate to the particular application and duplication of processing is avoided.

The mainframe computer has several advantages over the microcomputer operating in its own environment. The first of these is that it is normally much faster when it comes to processing or retrieving data, and consequently usually more cost effective. It also has far more memory space, and can store data bases which would be far beyond the capacity of the microcomputer. For this reason it is vital that the entire computer system be carefully planned to determine just what information the microcomputers will dump onto the mainframe and what types of communications systems will be installed to enable the microcomputer to withdraw information from the mainframe as required.

The microcomputer gives local management the opportunity to utilise computer power in the running of the local operation, but if it can be connected to the mainframe, allow the mainframe to perform the more complex functions and keep itself free to collect information which it can dump and to perform local functions, such as branch budgets and "what if" calculations which may assist in decision making, then it can truly come into its own as an essential part of the management information system.

3. An illustrative example

The financial records of PennyBee Boutique used in the previous chapter will be set up using a computerised system, and transactions for the following month will be shown as well in order to illustrate the value of computerisation. The system utilised is of the type described above: a Mecer IBM compatible, locally assembled, with a 4 Mb memory and 210 Mb hard disk. The accounting system used here is called NewViews, a Canadian developed system which is extremely flexible, allowing the user to define his accounting system in accordance with his own requirements. It is a complete system, allowing general ledgers, accounts payable and accounts receivable with as many accounts as you have capacity to handle within the constraints of your storage media. Due to the flexible reporting formats systems can be set up to handle costing systems, time reporting systems and even wage systems, though these last are usually better handled by specialist packages with automatic adjustments for changes in rates of deductions for tax and

```
                Ledger: Cash at bank                         03 Jul 88
!================================================================!
! Name         BANK              ! Reconcile                     !
! Description  Cash at bank      ! Date               00,000.00  !
! Normal Bal   D                 ! Balance                 0.00  !
!--------------------------------!-------------------------------!
! Next Ref#    0                 ! Closing Bal         7,500.00  !
! # of Items   14                ! Opening Bal             0.00  !
!================================================================!
! Date    ! Ref# !    Description       ! Amount  ! Balance ! Account !R!
!---------!------!----------------------!---------!---------!---------!-!
! 01 Mar 89!   0! Savings paid in        ! 8,000.00 ! 8,000.00 ! CAPP  ! !
! 01 Mar 89!   1! Rent paid to           !  500.00- ! 7,500.00 ! RENT  ! !
! 01 Mar 89!   1! Rent deposit paid to   !  500.00- ! 7,000.00 ! DEPS  ! !
! 01 Mar 89!   2! Shark Investments      ! 1,400.00-! 5,600.00 ! SHRK  ! !
! 01 Mar 89!   3! Purchases of merchandise! 2,000.00-! 3,600.00 ! PURC ! !
! 10 Mar 89!   4! Petty cash reimbursement!   50.00-! 3,550.00 ! PCASH ! !
! 10 Mar 89!   0! Cash sales to date     !  800.00  ! 4,350.00 ! SALC  ! !
! 17 Mar 89!   5! Petty cash reimbursement!  100.00-! 4,250.00 ! PCASH ! !
! 17 Mar 89!   0! Cash sales to date     ! 1,000.00 ! 5,250.00 ! SALC  ! !
! 24 Mar 89!   6! Petty cash reimbursement!  150.00-! 5,100.00 ! PCASH ! !
! 24 Mar 89!   0! Cash sales to date     ! 1,500.00 ! 6,600.00 ! SALC  ! !
! 31 Mar 89!   7! Petty cash reimbursement!  100.00-! 6,500.00 ! PCASH ! !
! 31 Mar 89!   8! Wages for the month    !  500.00- ! 6,000.00 ! WAGE  ! !
! 31 Mar 89!   0! Cash sales to date     ! 1,500.00 ! 7,500.00 ! SALC  ! !
!         !     !                        !         !         !         ! !
!================================================================!
! Date    ! Ref# !    Description       ! Amount  ! Balance ! Account !R!
!================================================================!
```

```
  Setup: Balance Sheet                          03 Jul 88
|=====================================================================================+======|
|  Balance Sheet      |Beg:01 Mar 89 |End:31 Mar 89 |  Type: A  |C|U|  Name  |B| Total to | Total to |T| Report |
|---------------------+--------------+--------------+-----------+-+-+--------+-+----------+----------+-+--------|
| S CAPITAL           |              |              |           | | |        | |          |          | |BS      |
| t brought forward   |       0.00   |              |           |1| |CAPS    |C|CAPA      |          | |BS      |
| t paid in           |   8,000.00   |              |           |1| |CAPP    |C|CAPA      |          | |BS      |
|                     |------------- |              |           |1|S|        | |          |          | |BS      |
|                     |              |   8,000.00   |           |2| |CAPA    |C|CAPB      |          |T|BS      |
| ncome for the period|              |   2,370.00   |           |2| |CAPI    |C|CAPB      |          |T|BS      |
|                     |              |------------- |           |2|S|        | |          |          | |BS      |
|                     |              |              | 10,370.00 |3| |CAPB    |C|CAPC      |          |T|BS      |
| s drawings          |              |              |     0.00  |3| |DWGS    |D|CAPC      |          | |BS      |
|                     |              |              |-----------|3|S|        | | .        |          | |BS      |
| ce on capital account|             |              | 10,370.00 |3| |CAPC    |C|TOTL      |          |T|BS      |
|                     |              |              |           | | |        | |          |          | |BS      |
| TERM LIABILITIES    |              |              |           | | |        | |          |          | |BS      |
| purchase creditor   |              |   3,600.00   |           |2| |HPCR    |C|LTLI      |          |T|BS      |
|   Finance charges not due |        |     945.00   |           |2| |FCND    |D|LTLI      |          | |BS      |
|                     |              |------------- |           |2|S|        | |          |          | |BS      |
|                     |              |              |  2,655.00 |3| |LTLI    |C|TOTL      |          |T|BS      |
|                     |              |              |-----------| | |        | |          |          | |BS      |
|                     |              |              | 13,025.00 |3| |TOTL    |C|          |          |T|BS      |
|                     |              |              |===========|3|D|        | |          |          | |BS      |
|  ASSETS             |              |              |           | | |        | |          |          | |BS      |
| ture and fittings   |              |   4,000.00   |           |2| |FURN    |D|TOTF      |          | |BS      |
|  Depreciation provision |          |      25.00   |           |2| |DEPF    |C|TOTF      |          | |BS      |
|                     |              |------------- |           |2|S|        | |          |          | |BS      |
|                     |              |              |  3,975.00 |3| |TOTF    |D|TOTA      |          |T|BS      |
| WORKING CAPITAL     |              |              |           | | |        | |          |          | |BS      |
| nt assets           |              |              |           | | |        | |          |          | |BS      |
|   at bank           |   7,500.00   |              |           |1| |BANK    |D|CASS      |          | |BS      |
|   on hand           |       0.00   |              |           |1| |PCASH   |D|CASS      |          | |BS      |
| ors                 |   8,700.00   |              |           |1| |AR      |D|CASS      |          |T|BS      |
| its                 |     500.00   |              |           |1| |DEPS    |D|CASS      |          | |BS      |
| k                   |   5,350.00   |              |           |1| |STCK    |D|CASS      |          | |BS      |
|                     |------------- |              |           |1|S|        | |          |          | |BS      |
|                     |              |              | 22,050.00 |2| |CASS    |D|WCAP      |          |T|BS      |
| nt liabilities      |              |              |           | | |        | |          |          | |BS      |
| tors                |              |              | 13,000.00 |2| |APR     |C|WCAP      |          |T|BS      |
|                     |              |------------- |           |2|S|        | |          |          | |BS      |
|                     |              |              |  9050.00  |3| |WCAP    |D|TOTA      |          |T|BS      |
|                     |              |              |-----------|3|S|        | |          |          | |BS      |
|                     |              |              | 13,025.00 |3| |TOTA    |D|          |          |T|BS      |
|                     |              |              |===========|3|D|        | |          |          | |BS      |
|---------------------+--------------+--------------+-----------+-+-+--------+-+----------+----------+-+--------|
|   Description       |Beg:01 Mar 89 |End:31 Mar 89 |  Type: A  |C|U|  Name  |B| Total to | Total to |T| Report |
|=====================================================================================+======|
```

```
    Setup: Income statement                    03 Jul 88
|=============================================================================================
|   Income statement    |Beg:01 Mar 89 |End:28 Feb 90 |  Type: A    |C|U|  Name  |B| Total to | Total to |T| Re
|-----------------------+--------------+--------------+-------------+-+-+--------+---------+----------+-+----
|Credit sales           |              |    8,700.00  |             |2| |SALA    |C|SALT    |         |  |IS
|Cash sales             |              |    4,800.00  |             |2| |SALC    |C|SALT    |         |  |IS
|                       |              |  ------------ |             |2|S|        | |       |         |  |IS
|Total sales            |              |              |  13,500.00  |3| |SALT    |C|GRPR    |         |  |T|IS
|Less: Cost of sales    |              |              |             | | |        | |       |         |  |IS
|Opening stock          |     0.00     |              |             |1| |OSTK    |D|COGA    |         |  |IS
|Purchases              |  15,000.00   |              |             |1| |PURC    |D|COGA    |         |  |IS
|                       |  ----------- |              |             |1|S|        | |       |         |  |IS
|Goods available for sale|             |   15,000.00  |             |2| |COGA    |D|COGS    |         |  |T|IS
|Closing stock          |              |    5,350.00  |             |2| |CSTK    |C|COGS    |         |  |IS
|                       |              |  ------------ |             |2|S|        | |       |         |  |IS
|Cost of goods sold     |              |              |   9,650.00  |3| |COGS    |D|GRPR    |         |  |T|IS
|                       |              |              | ------------|3|S|        | |       |         |  |IS
|Gross profit           |              |              |   3,850.00  |3| |GRPR    |C|NINC    |         |  |T|IS
|                       |              |              |             | | |        | |       |         |  |IS
|Expenses               |              |              |             | | |        | |       |         |  |IS
|Depreciation           |              |      25.00   |             |2| |DEPR    |D|TOTX    |         |  |IS
|Finance charges        |              |      55.00   |             |2| |FINC    |D|TOTX    |         |  |IS
|Rent                   |              |     500.00   |             |2| |RENT    |D|TOTX    |         |  |IS
|Sundry expenses        |              |     400.00   |             |2| |SUNX    |D|TOTX    |         |  |IS
|Wages                  |              |     500.00   |             |2| |WAGE    |D|TOTX    |         |  |IS
|                       |              |  ------------ |             |2|S|        | |       |         |  |IS
|                       |              |              |   1,480.00  |3| |TOTX    |D|NINC    |         |  |T|IS
|                       |              |              | ------------|3|S|        | |       |         |  |IS
|Net income for the period|            |              |   2,370.00  |3| |NINC    |C|CAPI    |         |  |T|IS
|                       |              |              |=============|3|D|        | |       |         |  |IS
```

Setup: Accounts payable   03 Jul 88

Accounts payable	Beg:01 Mar 89	End:28 Feb 90	Type: A	C	U	Name	B	Total to	Total to	T	Report
Investments Limited			3,600.00		2	SHRK	C	LPAY			AP
					2	S					AP
			3,600.00	3		LPAY	C	TOTP	HPCR	T	AP
wear Limited			2,500.00		2	DELS	C	APAY			AP
Fashions Limited			2,500.00		2	FOLF	C	APAY			AP
n Reef Sportswear Limited			2,000.00		2	GRSW	C	APAY			AP
nwheels Bodyshop			2,000.00		2	HWBS	C	APAY			AP
swear Limited			2,500.00		2	SPWR	C	APAY			AP
a Shoes Limited			1,500.00		2	VICT	C	APAY			AP
					2	S					AP
			13,000.00	3		APAY	C	TOTP		T	AP
					3	S					AP
ACCOUNTS PAYABLE			16,600.00	3		TOTP	C			T	AP
					3	D					AP

Description	Beg:01 Mar 89	End:28 Feb 90	Type: A	C	U	Name	B	Total to	Total to	T	Report

```
                     Ledger: Healthwheels Bodyshop                    03 Jul 88
 !=================================================================================!
 ! Name        HWBS                          ! Reconcile                 !
 ! Description Healthwheels Bodyshop          ! Date            00,000.00 !
 ! Normal Bal. C                             ! Balance              0.00 !
 !--------------------------------------------+------------------------------------!
 ! Next Ref#     0                            ! Closing Bal     2,000.00 !
 ! # of Items    2                            ! Opening Bal         0.00 !
 !=================================================================================!
 ! Date  ! Ref# !         Description         !  Amount  ! Balance  ! Account !R!
 !-------+------+----------------------------+----------+----------+---------+-!
 !01 Mar 89!    0!Exercise equipment          ! 1,000.00 ! 1,000.00 !PURC     ! !
 !27 Mar 89!    0!Exercise equipment          ! 1,000.00 ! 2,000.00 !PURC     ! !
 !       !      !                             !          !          !         ! !
 !       !      !                             !          !          !         ! !
 !       !      !                             !          !          !         ! !
 !       !      !                             !          !          !         ! !
 !       !      !                             !          !          !         ! !
 !       !      !                             !          !          !         ! !
 !       !      !                             !          !          !         ! !
 !       !      !                             !          !          !         ! !
 !       !      !                             !          !          !         ! !
 !       !      !                             !          !          !         ! !
 !       !      !                             !          !          !         ! !
 !       !      !                             !          !          !         ! !
 !       !      !                             !          !          !         ! !
 !       !      !                             !          !          !         ! !
 !       !      !                             !          !          !         ! !
 !       !      !                             !          !          !         ! !
 !       !      !                             !          !          !         ! !
 !       !      !                             !          !          !         ! !
 !       !      !                             !          !          !         ! !
 !       !      !                             !          !          !         ! !
 !       !      !                             !          !          !         ! !
 !-------+------+----------------------------+----------+----------+---------+-!
 ! Date  ! Ref# !         Description         !  Amount  ! Balance  ! Account !R!
 !=================================================================================!
```

```
         Analysis: Accounts receivable                    03 Jul 88
|==========================================================================================|
Accounts receivable      |   (1)    |   (2)    |   (3)    |   (4)    |   (5)    |   (6)     |
         |--- Begin      | 00 000 00| 01 Mar 89| 01 Feb 89| 01 Jan 89| 00 000 00| 00 000 00 |
Period 1: -| End         | 31 Mar 89| 31 Mar 89| 28 Feb 89| 31 Jan 89| 28 Feb 90| 28 Feb 90 |
         |--- Type       | A        | 0        | 0        | A        | B        | B         |
         |--- Begin      | 00 000 00| 00 000 00| 00 000 00| 00 000 00| 00 000 00| 00 000 00 |
Period 2: -| End         | 00 000 00| 00 000 00| 00 000 00| 00 000 00| 00 000 00| 31 Mar 89 |
         |--- Type       |          |          |          |          |          | A         |
Ratios:  % of Account    |          |          |          |          |          |           |
Graphs:  # of Columns,Scale | 0    0 | 0     0  | 0     0  | 0     0  | 0     0  | 0      0  |
|==========================================================================================|
   Description       |  Total  |  Current  |  30 Days  |  60 Days  | Credit limit |Over limit (-)|
-------------------+---------+-----------+-----------+-----------+--------------+--------------
lair R             |  250.00 |   250.00  |    0.00   |    0.00   |    500.00    |    250.00
urke M             |  700.00 |   700.00  |    0.00   |    0.00   |    500.00    |    200.00-
yers J             |  800.00 |   800.00  |    0.00   |    0.00   |  1,000.00    |    200.00
asey A             |  750.00 |   750.00  |    0.00   |    0.00   |  1,000.00    |    250.00
ortez R            |  500.00 |   500.00  |    0.00   |    0.00   |    500.00    |      0.00
rable J            |  450.00 |   450.00  |    0.00   |    0.00   |    500.00    |     50.00
ai L               |  250.00 |   250.00  |    0.00   |    0.00   |    250.00    |      0.00
ivingstone C       |  150.00 |   150.00  |    0.00   |    0.00   |    250.00    |    100.00
artel S            |  400.00 |   400.00  |    0.00   |    0.00   |    500.00    |    100.00
iceli M            |  400.00 |   400.00  |    0.00   |    0.00   |    500.00    |    100.00
oolah F            |  450.00 |   450.00  |    0.00   |    0.00   |    500.00    |     50.00
ortensen C         |  500.00 |   500.00  |    0.00   |    0.00   |    500.00    |      0.00
gunlana B          |  300.00 |   300.00  |    0.00   |    0.00   |    500.00    |    200.00
ay V               |  400.00 |   400.00  |    0.00   |    0.00   |    500.00    |    100.00
ichter W           |  500.00 |   500.00  |    0.00   |    0.00   |    750.00    |    250.00
ose T              |  350.00 |   350.00  |    0.00   |    0.00   |  1,000.00    |    650.00
immes M B          |  100.00 |   100.00  |    0.00   |    0.00   |    250.00    |    150.00
tewart N           |  350.00 |   350.00  |    0.00   |    0.00   |    500.00    |    150.00
an der Westhuizen M|  600.00 |   600.00  |    0.00   |    0.00   |    500.00    |    100.00-
oges S             |  500.00 |   500.00  |    0.00   |    0.00   |    500.00    |      0.00
                   |---------|-----------|-----------|-----------|--------------|--------------
OTAL ACCOUNTS RECEIVABLE | 8,700.00 | 8,700.00 |   0.00   |    0.00   | 11,000.00   |  2,300.00
                   |=========|===========|===========|===========|==============|==============
```

```
   Description       |  Total  |  Current  |  30 Days  |  60 Days  | Credit limit |Over limit (-)|
|==========================================================================================|
```

other items. Provision is also made for interaction with various spreadsheet packages such as Lotus 1-2-3.

For particular businesses there are specialised packages which have been developed, ranging from very elementary systems to highly complex ones which incorporate items like full stock control systems, but there are also a number of generalised packages on the market. Most of these packages do not have the flexibility offered by NewViews, but for most single application users this will not be particularly important.

Only some of the computer printouts concerning the transactions of PennyBee Boutique are given here. The others are very similar and have been fully dealt with in the discussion of the manual system in the previous chapter. The bank account, as the ledger account with the most transactions, is shown as an example of a ledger account. The account has a full description of Cash at bank but is coded BANK for posting purposes. The code for each account can be from one to ten letters. The system allows automatic reconciliation with bank statements, but since no reconciliation has been performed at this time the reconcile block is vacant. If you wish, you can automatically number transactions such as cheques so that it becomes unnecessary to enter the reference number each time. A count is also kept of all transactions entered.

Entry takes the form of entering the date, which can also be· programmed for automatic entry, a reference number if applicable, a description of the transaction and the amount. A balance is then automatically calculated and the code of the cross account to which the amount is to be posted must be entered. This other account is then automatically updated at the same time before the system will permit any further entries.

The system does not therefore make use of journals in the form used for the· manual system. Amounts are entered into one account and posted directly to another. For audit purposes, however, it is essential that a system of filed journal vouchers be used so that it is possible to determine the details of any transaction by reference to the vouchers on file.

Since it is an asset account the destination of the cash at bank account is the balance sheet. The full balance sheet setup is given here to show how the user can determine the appearance of the balance sheet. There are three columns in which amounts can be entered, and the entry in the column headed C determines in which particular column a particular amount will appear. The column headed U, permits underlining, either S(ingle) or D(ouble). The name of the account is its alphabetical code. The column headed B requires a statement of whether the balance will normally be a D(ebit) or C(redit) one. The arrangement of totals and sub-totals is determined by the Total to columns. Normally, the first of these will apply to the document being set out and the second will apply to another document such as a funds statement. The T column requires identification of those amounts which are totals or sub-totals.

This balance sheet, once set up, is maintained as entries are made. At the conclusion of a set of postings the balance sheet can be examined to determine the current position. This one, it can be seen, is identical to the earlier balance sheet prepared manually for PennyBee, and the same applies to the income statement. The final figure on the income statement, the net income for the period, is instructed to total to CAPI, which appears on the balance sheet.

In addition to the general ledger, the system can maintain other records such as accounts receivable and accounts payable.

The accounts payable report gives details of the various firms to which PennyBee owes money and makes use of the double Total to facility to maintain a separate record of hire purchase creditors as a memorandum which does not appear on the balance sheet. An age analysis could also be prepared here, as it is for the accounts receivable report.

The accounts receivable report has six columns which can be utilised as the user wishes. It has been set up here to show an age analysis of the total for current, 30 days and 60 days and then has two credit control columns, one showing the credit limit allowed each customer and the other the extent of unused credit or the amount by which the limit has been exceeded. It can be seen at a glance that two customers have already exceeded their limits.

As the business grows it will require increasingly sophisticated management information and the system can be adapted to provide this on virtually a real time basis, but at this stage the control of credit is probably the most important. The next major application would be to add stock control to the debtors control so that it can be seen at any time what is in stock and how well the various items are selling. This can assist in making purchasing decisions so as to ensure that there is no over investment in items which are not selling and that orders are always placed for items selling well so that there is never a shortage of these.

Stock and debtors are normally the two critical areas for management of a trading undertaking and are therefore the two aspects which are first to be computerised. There are also probably more packages available for these two than for any other accounting application, with the possible exception of wages.

4. Management information systems

The total management information system (MIS) within the undertaking consists of two distinct sections: a formal system and an informal system. This last may in many organisations itself be split into two parts: an official informal system and an unofficial informal system. The formal system is structured to deliver certain pre-determined information to certain pre-determined destinations for the purpose of supplying management with information perceived to be necessary for the performance of its task. This information is normally quantitative by nature, either in terms of money or in terms of units of production, of persons employed, of distances travelled or of any other measurable dimension of the undertaking. The qualitative aspects are usually delivered by the informal system, since the formalisation of dimensions which are not objectively measurable usually leads to dissension within the organisation. This is not to say that dimensions such as employee job satisfaction are not capable of being verified, but this normally is not part of an ongoing formalised information system which produces regular periodic reports.

5. Accounting information systems in management planning and control

The accounting information system (AIS) is normally a subset of the management information system within the undertaking. As such it provides some of the input for the planning process and for the control process. The information which it provides is internally generated information concerning the financial performance and financial position of the undertaking. The financial planning process usually relies on information provided by the AIS in respect of past performance and limitations on future expenditure to develop its end products, normally budgets of various types. The financial control process relies on the AIS to provide information concerning the achievements of the undertaking in relation to the plans in order to determine whether the plans are being met or whether corrective action is necessary in order to ensure compliance with these plans.

The critical factors in the provision of such information are those of timeousness and relevance. In the past, accounting systems have tended to fall down on the first of these simply because of the time-consuming nature of the accounting process. Modern computer based accounting systems have solved this problem, however, and the focus has now shifted to the one of relevance. The very fact that the computer is capable of processing so much data and producing so much information means that it is necessary to design the AIS very carefully. It does not help to produce such volumes of documentation that the reader is overwhelmed to the extent of not being able to find the necessary detail which he requires.

The design of an AIS involves a careful analysis of the nature of the work performed at each level within the organisation. Once the nature of each person's work has been defined it is possible to determine what information each person requires in order to perform his task. What control information is required at each level, for instance, and at what levels is there a need for overall planning information?

Once the information requirements have been determined the format of the reports to each person can be designed, and the accounting information system can then be designed around these reports. While the design must be capable of being modified as the organisation changes, an AIS designed on this basis will provide each person with all the information which he requires, and only that information, on a regular basis. He will therefore, from an information point of view, be in a position to perform this task within the organisation without a great deal of the static which can be generated by excessive and unnecessary computer printouts.

The actual nature of the reports produced by the AIS will obviously vary tremendously according to the nature of the operations of the undertaking, the organisational structure and the degree of sophistication of the users of the system. It is scarcely the task of this book to examine all the various possibilities.

A rough outline of the process to be followed in introducing an accounting information system is quite a reasonable task, however. This process can usually be split into seven steps.

1. Although the power of the computer is so great that merely converting manual systems to computerised systems doing the same work is usually a waste of potential, the first step must be a *systems analysis* which begins with a look at the existing systems within an organisation. This helps the analyst to determine how the undertaking functions which will help when he comes to design the new system.

   Matters which have to be taken into account in this analysis include a look at the general background of the undertaking. The organisation structure and job descriptions within it must be examined. Current documentation and procedures must be analysed in order to determine where the deficiencies of the present system lie, and after that recommendations can be made.

2. This analysis must lead to a *statement of objectives*. This will clarify the purpose and overall objectives of the proposed system which will give the analyst the opportunity to determine the outputs necessary to achieve these objectives and therefore the data base necessary.

   This step would involve looking at the overall purposes and also specific objectives at various levels in the undertaking. The determination of objectives allows the determination of the required output and therefore of the data required to present this output. It will also be necessary to consider any controls which may be necessary in terms of verification of input and output and of restriction of access to information.

   It would also be necessary to make an evaluation of the effect of the implementation of a new system on the organisation. At times the management of the organisation would feel that the impact of the new system would be so drastic as to negate the improvement in the information availability. This is important since it is necessary to obtain management approval by this stage before proceeding with the whole process.

3. This must now be refined into a *system design* in which the analyst must specify where the data must be captured, the type of processing and the application of the output. This will normally be done on a modular basis where there are several aspects to the system, and the modules must then be combined into a functional whole.

4. Once the system has been broadly designed it must be specified in detail. The exact hardware and software, the exact appearance of input and output documentation, the program flow charts and details of the files to be maintained as well as details of any manual procedures must form part of this *system specification*.

5. With this done, *programming* can start. This step will involve writing programs to perform the tasks specified, developing test data, testing the programs and preparing program and operator documentation.

6. *Implementation* will follow. This consists of replacing the old system with the new. It may involve parallel running of the two systems until such time as the

operators are familiar with the new system, it will involve training and conversion of files to the new system. It will probably also involve the physical installation of new computer equipment.

7. After the system has been installed it is necessary for *evaluation* of it. This should be done by an independent party who can clinically evaluate the performance of the system and the acceptance of it by the personnel of the undertaking.

All the computer technical aspects mentioned in the last five points above are best covered in detail by specialist books so no attempt will be made here to discuss them. The broad process as set out here will, however, be sufficient to give an idea of how the AIS must be developed.

Key words
Computer
Electronic data processing
Accounting information system (AIS)
Management planning
Management control

Chapter 8

Financial reporting for companies

The most powerful single influence on the format of financial statements in this country is the Companies Act of 1973. This Act lays down minimum requirements for the financial reports which companies prepare for shareholders. Public companies have certain extra requirements in terms of the Act and listed companies are also subject to the disclosure requirements of the Johannesburg Stock Exchange. Statements of Generally Accepted Accounting Practice also impose certain requirements.

This chapter sets out the more important aspects of the requirements in terms of these laws and regulations for companies and for groups of companies.

1. The reasons why companies have such strict requirements

2. The requirements of the Companies Act

3. Financial reporting for groups of companies and for associated companies

4. The requirements of the Johannesburg Stock Exchange and GAAP

1 The reasons why companies have strict reporting requirements

Companies differ from virtually all other forms of commercial organisation in at least one of two aspects. The first of these is the aspect of limited liability, which means that people dealing with companies must rely solely on the assets of the undertaking for settlement of any liabilities which the company has incurred toward them. The financial report of the company provides information about the financial position and financial performance of the company, and people dealing with the company must be able to rely on this information in order to do business with the company.

The second aspect is that the company can have a multitude of shareholders scattered all over the world, people who have invested their money in the company but have no direct contact with its daily operations. Such people must also rely on the financial report in order to make investment decisions.

In order to provide these groups of people, both of which are essentially outsiders to the operations of the company, with reliable information the Companies Act has laid down very comprehensive regulations about the content and format of the financial reports which companies have to send to all shareholders and which, by implication if not by law, will also be available to those creditors who require information about the financial performance of the company. These statements have to be available to the shareholders within six months of the end of the company's financial year.

2 The requirements of the Companies Act

2.1 Where to find the reporting requirements

Chapter XI of the Companies Act, No 61 of 1973, deals with the requirements in respect of accounting and disclosure. Briefly, the act requires that the company maintain accounting records meeting certain requirements and that it prepare annual financial statements and, in the case of holding companies, group annual financial statements which must be laid before the annual general meeting and copies of which must be sent to every shareholder.

These financial statements are to consist of a balance sheet, an income statement, a directors' report and an auditors' report. Section 286 gives the overriding provision in respect of these financial statements: in conformity with generally accepted accounting practices, the financial statements must fairly present the state of affairs of the company at the end of its financial year and the profit or loss of the company for that financial year. Certain requirements in respect of disclosure of loans and directors' emoluments are contained in sections 295 to 297 and the duties of the auditor are set out in sections 300 and 301.

Section 303 requires public companies having a share capital to send an interim report to shareholders after six months of operation and section 304 requires that any such company which has not sent final financial statements within three months of the end of its financial year must send provisional financial statements to its shareholders. Such provisional statements do not have to be audited.

For the actual contents of the financial statements, though, the section 286 of this chapter refers one to Schedule 4 to the Act. Paragraph 44 of this schedule requires a cash flow statement in addition to the reports required by section 286.

Schedule 4 is divided into four parts dealing with:
 I The contents of the financial statements of a company
 II The contents of the financial statements of a group of companies
 III The contents of the directors report
 IV Interim and provisional financial statements

2.2 A summary of the more important requirements for disclosure

Regulations for disclosure will never satisfy all the interested parties. Companies obviously do not want to disclose all details of their transactions for their competitors to see but financial analysts do want to see full disclosure. The guideline generally followed around the world by regulatory agencies is to require full disclosure of all information which would assist the investor in coming to a decision about the company, but to allow the company to withhold information about the details of its operations. There are many arguments about just where the line should be drawn between investor-valuable information and competitor-valuable information but the usual argument is that full disclosure must be given of all assets and liabilities of the company (these disclose the potential of the undertaking) but that most details of income and expenditure do not have to be disclosed (since these give details of how that potential is being used).

The prescribed method of disclosure is best illustrated by means of an example, firstly for the balance sheet:

PARADIGM PRODUCERS (LIMITED)		*Comparative figures*[1]	
Balance sheet at 28 February 1999	*Ref*	*1999*	*1998*
Capital employed			
Share capital	2	500 000	500 000
Non-distributable reserves	3	200 000	200 000
Distributable reserves	4	300 000	200 000
Shareholders equity		1 000 000	900 000
Long term liabilities	5	250 000	200 000
		1 250 000	1 100 000
Employment of capital			
Fixed assets	6	800 000	600 000
Investments	7	200 000	200 000
Net current assets		450 000	500 000
Current assets		850 000	900 000
Stock	8	350 000	325 000
Debtors	9	450 000	500 000
Cash on hand and in bank		50 000	75 000
Current liabilities		400 000	450 000
Creditors		200 000	250 000
Bank overdraft	10	150 000	100 000
Tax payable	11	50 000	100 000
		1 250 000	1 100 000

Figure 8.1

The first point to note is the general layout of the balance sheet. The Act does not prescribe the vertical form shown here and a balance sheet drawn up in the horizontal format with assets on one side and liabilities and capital items on the other would meet all its requirements. What the Act does require is the grouping of assets and liabilities into categories. Assets must be split into at least two groups. Current assets are those which are used up in the operations of the company and are loosely defined as those which are already cash or equivalent and those which will in the normal course of operations be turned into cash within the next year. All other assets can be regarded as fixed assets, but the overriding provision that the financial statements must reasonably present the affairs of the company sometimes leads to other categories being introduced. In this case investments are shown separately, though in some cases they may actually be fixed or current assets.

Liabilities must similarly be grouped into long term and current liabilities, with those due for payment within one year being regarded as current liabilities.

The various items require some explanation. The numbers here are the reference numbers in the above balance sheet.

1. The Act requires that comparative figures must be shown for all items for at least the preceding year. This is simply because it is very difficult to judge the performance or position of an undertaking purely on the figures for one year. Comparative figures give the opportunity to judge the undertaking's performance in the light of what has gone before to determine whether matters are improving or deteriorating.

2. Full details must be given of all aspects of share capital. The following information must be given in respect of each class of shares:

Authorised
    5 000 000 ordinary shares of R1 each   R5 000 000
Issued
    3 000 000 ordinary shares of R1 each   R3 000 000

The authorised share capital is the amount which the company is authorised to issue in terms of its Memorandum of Association. This amount can be increased by special resolution. The issued share capital represents the shares actually issued and paid for. Full details must be given by way of note of the conditions under which the unissued shares may be issued. Normally the shares could only be issued by the company in general meeting but the shareholders often delegate this power to the directors.

Most companies have only one class of shares but sometimes there are different classes which have different rights. The commonest variation is that some companies have preference shares which have some preferential rights vis-a-vis the ordinary shares. They usually have a preferential right to dividends at a predetermined rate before the ordinary shareholders are entitled to any dividend, but sometimes also have preferential rights to capital repayment in the case of the company being wound up. Preferential shares can be made redeemable, and are the only shares which a company is allowed to redeem freely.

Note that shares do not need to have a par value (or face value). The Companies Act makes provision for a company to issue shares of No Par Value. In this case a company simply reflects the entire amount received from the issue of shares as 'Stated Capital'. An example of this can be found in the balance sheet of Magrad Limited on page 234.

If the shares are preference shares then details must be given of their special rights, such as the percentage to which they are entitled. If such shares are redeemable or convertible details of the conditions of such redemption or conversion must be given. If there are arrear dividends in respect of cumulative preference shares the fact must be stated by way of note. Such dividends, while the company is obliged to pay them, do not actually become liabilities until the dividend has been formally declared.

3. Non-distributable reserves are those reserves which may not be used for the payment of dividends. They are normally not built up out of normal operating profit but arise because of certain special transactions or actions. Examples are the premium received on the sale of shares at a price higher than face value and the amount of the increase in the monetary value of assets because of inflation:

Property at revaluation	R800 000
Property at cost	R300 000
Non distributable reserve arising on revaluation	R500 000

If the property is now reflected on the balance sheet at its adjusted value of R800 000, there will also be a non-distributable reserve of R500 000 shown.

It is perfectly logical that this should be non-distributable since there has been no real profit. The adjustment simply means that the value of the money invested in the property has declined to such an extent that it now takes R800 000 to buy what could at some earlier time be bought for R300 000.

4. Distributable reserves are those built up out of the profits of the company. The commonest such reserve is simply undistributed profits, more commonly known nowadays as retained earnings.

5. Full details of long term liabilities must be given including terms of repayment with the relevant dates, rates of interest and details of the assets used as security for the loan. Any portion of a long term liability which is payable within one year must be shown as a current liability.

6. The part of the balance sheet dealing with fixed assets is covered at some length in chapter 11. It is the part which contains the most problem areas. Because of the effects of inflation the figures on the balance sheet often become totally unrepresentative of the actual value of the assets concerned

within a few years. There are proposals for making adjustments to take into account the effects of inflation, but there is no really satisfactory solution to the problem of values, since there are many factors other than inflation which affect assets. These would include the fact that most assets wear out over a period of time and, more important, that assets have different values for different purposes. An example would be that of a desktop computer. An IBM 8086 PC would have virtually no commercial value at this time, but if it were still doing the work required of it then its value in use would be the same as that of a brand new computer with many times its capacity and many times its speed of operation. Which value would be the one which should be shown on the face of the balance sheet, since both can be regarded as realistic depending on one's purpose in doing the valuation?

The Act does not attempt to force anyone to value any fixed asset. It simply requires full disclosure of actual information concerning assets and leaves the user of the statements to determine a value for his own purposes. Any of these assets may be shown at a value based either on cost or on a valuation, provided all the relevant information is given.

In respect of land and buildings the original cost has to be shown together with the date of purchase. The cost of any improvements must also be shown together with the relevant dates. Details must be given of the size and situation of the property, whether it has improvements on it or not and whether it is encumbered in any way by mortgage bonds or otherwise. Companies owning more than five pieces of fixed property do not have to give this information with the balance sheet but may inform members of the whereabouts of a register of fixed property so that they may obtain the relevant information if they wish to do so.

Where the property is shown at a valuation the same information must still be given and, in addition, details of the valuation must be given. These would include the date of valuation, the method of valuation and the qualifications of the person doing the valuation.

The manner of disclosure in respect of depreciable assets is also clearly laid down. The total cost price in respect of each class of assets must be stated, together with the accumulated depreciation and the net book value. The idea of this is to give an indication of the average age of the assets in each group, since those which have been written down to a very low value compared to original cost are obviously old assets.

In addition to fixed property and depreciable assets, intangible assets are also treated as fixed assets. Details of the basis of valuation for such assets must also be given, and again the matter is discussed in chapter 11.

7. Investments are generally reflected at cost unless there has been a change in the value of such investments, either up or down, which in the opinion of the directors is likely to be permanent and not simply as a result of temporary movements in the market. In addition, the aggregate market value of listed investments must be given. A valuation of unlisted investments must also be given, though in practice this is usually simply an estimate by the directors of the current value of the asset.

8. The whole question of disclosure in respect of stock is covered in some detail in chapter 11. The Companies Act requires that the different categories of stock be shown separately, that there must be a statement of whether the basis of valuation is consistent with that of the previous year and broad details of the method of valuation.

9. If the whole amount represents trading debtors there are no specific requirements. However, if the amount includes some short term loans then the amounts of these must be stated separately and if they are loans to directors or managers then full details of the loans must be given including the security provided.

10. Details must be given of the security offered for the bank overdraft.

11. A company must calculate its own tax liability and provide in the financial statements for the full amount of such tax less any provisional payments made.

In addition to the assets and liabilities shown on the face of the balance sheet there are other matters which must be disclosed by way of note. The most important of these are contingent liabilities, those which will only come into existence on the occurrence of a certain event. An example of this would be standing surety for someone else. The liability is that other person's, but if he should fail to meet his obligations the holder of the company's surety will turn to the company and demand payment, at which stage it will become a liability of the company balanced by an asset of a claim against the defaulter.

A note must also be made of any commitments which will eventually lead to the creation of liabilities such as contracts signed for work to be done in the future. An important commitment in many cases is in respect of leases. The lease payments to be made in terms of the lease agreement only become liabilities as they fall due periodically, but the commitment is there and must be reflected

There are more detailed requirements regarding less frequently encountered items but this review of the more important provisions should be enough to show that full disclosure is required in respect of the balance sheet, even if in some cases it is simply disclosure of information which can assist the user in formulating his own opinions as to value. The requirements in respect of the income statement are very different. Only a select few items have to be disclosed, the argument being that the balance sheet simply shows the potential of the company by showing what it has at its disposal while the income statement shows just how that potential is being used. A complete income statement reveals exactly how a company is being run, and no business would like to supply its competitors with this information. An example will again show the elements of the requirements in respect of the income statement:

PARADIGM PRODUCERS (LIMITED)
Income statement for the year ended 28 February 1999

	Ref	1999	1998
Turnover	1	4 500 000	4 000 000
Net operating income	2	330 000	280 000
Investment income	3	20 000	15 000
Net interest paid	4	50 000	35 000
Net income before taxation and extraordinary items		300 000	260 000
Taxation	5	100 000	90 000
Net income after tax		200 000	170 000
Extraordinary items	6	50 000	0
Net income for the year attributable to share-holders		150 000	170 000
Dividends declared	7	50 000	50 000
Increase in retained earnings for the year		100 000	120 000
Retained earnings at the beginning of the year		200 000	80 000
Retained earnings at the end of the year		300 000	200 000

Figure 8.2

It should be immediately obvious that there is actually very little detailed information on the face of this income statement. There are some further disclosure requirements which will be mentioned in a moment but the fact remains that only a very small percentage of the total expenses of the company will be detailed. The two major items which do not have to be disclosed, purchases and remuneration of employees, make up at least eighty per cent of the expenses of most undertakings and operating expenses generally make up a large part of the rest. The major items which do have to be disclosed, going by the reference numbers above, are:

1. Turnover must be disclosed, and the company's definition of turnover must be given.
2. Net operating income will be taken from the complete income statement prepared for internal use by the company. Certain of the expenses on that income statement have to be disclosed and these are usually simply listed in a note to the financial statements. They include the following:

   The auditors' remuneration must be shown, specifying the amount paid for the audit and any amounts paid for other services.

   The amount charged to depreciation must be shown, as well as any profits or losses on the disposal of fixed assets. In the case of depreciable assets, such profits or losses are, at least in part, adjustments to depreciation.

   The aggregate remuneration paid to directors must be shown, broken down into amounts paid for services as directors (directors fees), amounts paid for other services within the company and any other amounts paid by way of, for example, consultancy fees.

   Leasing charges must be reflected in full in respect of all items which would have been subject to depreciation if they were owned by the company.

Amounts paid in respect of managerial, technical, administrative or secretarial services must be stated in full except where these services were performed by employees of the company.

Disclosure must also be made by way of note (if not reflected in the income statement) of changes in the basis of accounting and of charges in diminution of the value of assets other than by way of depreciation.

3. Investment income must be reflected, and a distinction must be drawn between income received from listed investments and that from unlisted investments.
4. The aggregate amount of interest paid must be reflected.
5. The amount of tax calculated as being payable in respect of the income for the year must be reflected, and if no tax is provided the reason for this fact must be stated.
6. Transactions of a sort not usually undertaken by the company or any other transactions which by virtue of circumstances are deemed unusual must be reflected separately whether these are items of income or expenditure.
7. Full particulars are required in respect of all dividends declared.

While this information may appear very sketchy when one looks at how little is actually revealed, an income statement such as this does give the basic information necessary for investment decisions in providing turnover, profits and dividends. It also provides information of direct interest to the shareholders such as details of how much the directors are paying themselves (they work for the shareholders, remember) and of the amounts paid to the auditors, who are also responsible to the shareholders.

The requirements in respect of the cash flow statement are covered fully in chapter 16 and will not be discussed at any length here.

The directors' report has to be in narrative form and must discuss not only the prescribed matters but also any other matters material for an appreciation of the state of affairs of the company and its operating results.

It must review the operations generally and include a statement of the profits or losses from each of'the classes of operations of the company. Specifically, it must review the nature of the company's business or businesses and of any material change in this during the year. It must give particulars of changes in the share capital and fixed assets. Dividends paid or proposed must be specified as well as the names of the directors and the secretary of the company, as well as their nationality. A very important provision is the one which requires that any material fact or circumstance which has occurred between the date of the financial statements and the date of the report must be dealt with.

The requirements in respect of interim financial reports to be sent out after the first half of the company's financial year are not very onerous. There must be a narrative which covers effectively those parts of the directors' report relating to the operations of the company and a statement giving the profit or loss and any dividends paid or proposed. Comparative figures must also be given of the previous interim period.

The provisional financial statements must give essentially the same information but in respect of the full year.

3 Financial reporting for groups of companies and for associated companies

3.1 Definitions

The Companies Act lays down extra requirements in respect of groups of companies in Part II of Schedule 4. In order to apply these provisions it is first necessary to define the concept of a group of companies. A group of companies consists of a holding company and one or more subsidiary companies. A company is defined in Section 1(3) of the Act as a subsidiary company of another company if that other company:

1. is a member of it and controls the composition of its board of directors; or
2. owns more than 50 % of its share capital; or, a company is a subsidiary of another company
3. if it is a subsidiary of yet another company which is a subsidiary of the other company; or
4. if subsidiaries of the other company hold more than 50 % of its equity share capital among them
5. if the other company and its subsidiaries together hold more than 50 % of its equity share capital.

A careful look will show that the key factor is one of control. As soon as a company can control the composition of the board of directors of another company, whether by holding, directly or indirectly through other subsidiaries, more than 50 % of the equity share capital or by some other means, then that other company becomes a subsidiary. The definition goes on to discuss the effect of shares held in a fiduciary capacity rather than in a personal capacity (they are not taken into account in the determination of the 50 % holding), control of bodies corporate other than companies (they are treated as companies for purposes of group statements) and a few other minor matters.

Associated companies are not defined in the Act. The concept is actually a fairly recent one in South Africa, though this is one of those countries where it is probably most applicable. Until 1983 investment in a company other than a subsidiary was simply reflected as an investment as described above, usually at cost price with a note concerning current market value or estimated value. Since then, however, certain investments in other companies, known as associated companies, have had to accounted for under the equity method described below.

An associated company, in terms of statement AC 110 (see chapter 3) is one:

1. in which the investor company holds more than 20 % of the equity share capital; or
2. in which the investor holds enough of the equity share capital to have the power to exercise significant influence over the financial and operating policies of that company, known as the investee company.

The investor company can decide which of the two definitions it would prefer to use and must then must apply this definition to all its investments in other companies for purposes of financial reporting.

3.2 Companies Act requirements in respect of groups of companies

The same basic provisions apply to group financial statements as apply to single company financial statements, with the proviso that any intra group profits or losses must be excluded in determining group profits and losses and amounts owing must be excluded in determining the assets and liabilities of the group.

Section 289 of the Act requires consolidated financial statements but lays down that where consolidated statements are not prepared the financial report must present, as far as practicable, the same or equivalent information. It allows for the presentation of separate financial statements dealing with each of the subsidiaries, several separate sets of consolidated statements dealing with different groups of subsidiaries or statements annexed to the company's own financial statements giving the required information about the subsidiaries.

The directors' report in respect of a group of companies must contain complete information about the percentage holding in respect of each class of share in each subsidiary, the names and, if they are not South African, the places of incorporation of each subsidiary. There are other detailed requirements, but the most important one is the overriding requirement that there must be a group review and that it must deal with every material fact or circumstance necessary for an appreciation of the financial statements.

3.3 The mechanics of consolidation

Consolidation of the financial statements of a group of companies can become very involved, particularly when the group structure involves subsidiaries of subsidiaries and when there are companies which are subsidiaries by virtue of the fact that several of the subsidiaries of a company hold, among them, more than 50 % of the equity share capital. The principles of consolidation, however, are very simple: simply eliminate all items which represent intragroup assets or liabilities and intragroup profits or losses, then add together all the remaining items. For instance, if one of the current assets of the holding company is an ordinary debtors account of a subsidiary, this asset must be eliminated as must the creditor account in the records of the subsidiary. The remaining debtors of the holding company and the subsidiary will be added together to get the total debtors of the group, and the remaining creditors will be added together to get the total creditors of the group. This can be illustrated by means of a few simple examples:

Abridged balance sheet of Mother Limited

Share capital—ordinary R1 shares	1 000 000
Distributable reserves	1 500 000
Shareholders equity	2 500 000
Liabilities	500 000
	3 000 000
Fixed assets	1 500 000
Investment in subsidiary—Daughter Limited	500 000
200 000 R1 ordinary shares	[1]200 000
Current account	[2]300 000
Current assets	1 000 000
	3 000 000

Abridged balance sheet of Daughter Limited

Share capital—ordinary R1 shares	(1)200 000
Distributable reserves	500 000
Shareholders equity	700 000
Liabilities	(2) 500 000
	1 200 000
Fixed assets	500 000
Current assets	700 000
	1 200 000

Abridged consolidated balance sheet of Mother Limited and its subsidiary

Share capital (See below)	1 000 000
Distributable reserves (1 500 000 + 500 000)	2 000 000
Shareholders equity	3 000 000
Liabilities (See below)	700 000
	3 700 000
Fixed assets (1 500 000 + 500 000)	2 000 000
Current assets (1 000 000 + 700 000)	1 700 000
	3 700 000

Figure 8.3

The items in common between the balance sheets of the holding company, Mother Limited, and the subsidiary, Daughter Limited, are:

1. the share capital. Mother Limited obviously bought 100 % of the shares in Daughter Limited when that company was formed; and
2. the current account. Daughter Limited must be disclosing this as part of the liabilities, so that liabilities for the group amount to R(500 000 + 500 000 − 300 000) = R700 000.

Note that the share capital on the consolidated balance sheet is the same as the share capital for the holding company. This will always hold true, even when the holding company does not hold all the shares in the subsidiary. A slightly more complex, but more realistic, example should serve to show how this comes about. High Limited purchased sixty per cent of the shares in Low Limited on 1 March 1998. The balance sheet of Low Limited on 28 February 1998, which can be regarded as identical to that at the start of business on 1 March 1998 is given below as well as the income statements of both companies for the following year and the balance sheets at the end of February 1999.

Abridged income statements for the year ended 28 February 1999

	High Ltd	Low Ltd
Sales	9 600 000	3 500 000
Cost of sales	7 680 000	2 800 000
Gross profit	1 920 000	700 000
Other income		
Administration fees received	100 000	
Dividends received	75 000	
	2 095 000	700 000
Administration fee paid		100 000
Other expenses	1 520 000	350 000
Net income before tax	575 000	250 000
Tax	275 000	100 000
Net income after tax	300 000	150 000
Dividends	150 000	100 000
Increase in retained earnings	150 000	50 000

Figure 8.3

Included in the sales of High Limited are goods sold to Low Limited at normal commercial prices which included a markup of 20 % At the end of February 1999 Low Limited still had in stock goods purchased from High Limited to a value of R60 000. This meant that the stock of Low Limited included an amount of R10 000 which represented profit made by High Limited. This amount will form part of the reported profit of High Limited, but it must be eliminated in the consolidated financial statements since the group as a whole does not make a profit until the goods have been sold to someone outside the group.

Abridged balance sheets at 28 February 1999

	High Ltd	Low Ltd
Share capital	1 000 000	250 000
Distributable reserves	875 000	350 000
Shareholders equity	1 875 000	600 000
Loan to Low Ltd	100 000	
Current liabilities	1 200 000	120 000
	3 175 000	720 000
Fixed assets	2 000 000	250 000
Shares in Low Ltd	350 000	
Loan from High Ltd		100 000
Stock on hand	450 000	160 000
Other current assets	375 000	210 000
	3 175 000	720 000

Figure 8.4

Certain of the common items can be eliminated directly, such as the administration fees paid and received and the loan from High to Low. Beyond that point it is clear that one cannot do the same straightforward type of elimination which was done in the first example of Mother and Daughter. Not only does High Ltd not own all the shares in Low Ltd, it did not pay face value for the shares which it does have. The fact that it does not own all the shares means that it also did not receive the whole of the dividend paid out, so that can also not be cancelled out directly. The method adopted is to analyse the equity of Low Ltd at the time of acquisition and at the time of the preparation of the group financial statements a year later.

Abridged balance sheet of Low Ltd at 28 February 1998

Share capital	250 000
Distributable reserves	300 000
Shareholders equity	550 000
Current liabilities	150 000
	700 000
Fixed assets	240 000
Stock on hand	150 000
Other current assets	310 000
	700 000

Figure 8.5

The balance sheet shows the financial position of Low Ltd at the time of the acquisition of sixty per cent of the share capital. Since the company had built up reserves before the date of purchase, High effectively bought not only sixty per cent of the share capital but also sixty per cent of the reserves. The analysis is used firstly to determine the value which High Ltd purchased. The difference between the value purchased and the price paid is known as *goodwill arising on consolidation* or premium paid on acquisition where, in case like this the price paid exceeds the tangible value purchased. Where the price is less than the tangible value purchased the difference is known as a *non-distributable reserve arising on consolidation*.

Analysis of the equity of Low Ltd

At acquisition	High Ltd (60%)	Minority (40%)	Total
Share capital	150 000	100 000	250 000
Reserves	180 000	120 000	300 000
	330 000	220 000	550 000
Paid by High Ltd	350 000		
Goodwill	20 000		
Since acquisition			
Net earnings	90 000	60 000	150 000
Dividend paid	60 000	40 000	100 000
	30 000	20 000	50 000
Total minority interest		240 000	

Figure 8.6

The second calculation in the analysis is to determine the value of the section of the company still owned by the *minority shareholders* or outside shareholders. As can be seen in the above analysis, the value of their shareholding at the time of acquisition was R220 000, but this is not where the story ends. Forty per cent of the earnings since the date of acquisition belong to them, and the value of their share of the company has increased by this amount less the forty per cent of the total dividends which were paid out to them.

The third part of the calculation is to determine the value of the increase in the retained earnings of the group as a result of the earnings of the subsidiary since the date of acquisition. This is clearly sixty per cent of the net income of the subsidiary less the sixty per cent of the total dividends which have been received.

With this analysis done the consolidation of the financial statements can now proceed. The trading account of the group is not simply the sum of the two trading accounts, since the sale to Low Ltd of goods which are still in stock must be totally eliminated. This would mean reducing the combined sales by the amount of the sale, reducing cost of sales by the cost price of R50 000 and reducing gross profit by the markup of R10 000. Dividends received by High Ltd must also be reduced by the R60 000 received from Low Ltd, leaving an amount of R15 000 received from outside the group.

The consolidated income statement should then look like this:

Consolidated income statement of High Limited and its subsidiary at 28 February 1999

Sales (9 600 000 + 3 500 000 − 60 000)	13 040 000
Cost of sales (7 680 000 + 2 800 000 − 50 000)	10 430 000
Gross profit (1 920 000 + 700 000 − 10 000)	2 610 000
Other income	
Dividends received (75 000 − 60 000)	15 000
	2 625 000
Other expenses (1 520 000 + 350 000)	1 870 000
Net income before tax (575 000 + 250 000 − 10 000 − 60 000)	755 000
Tax (275 000 + 100 000)	375 000
Net income after tax (300 000 + 150 000 − 10 000 − 60 000)	380 000
Deduct minority share of income of subsidiary	60 000
Net income attributable to the shareholders of High Ltd	320 000
Dividends	150 000
Increase in group retained earnings	170 000

Figure 8.7

A consolidation journal could be prepared which would look something like this:

Feb	28	Consolidated sales		60 000	00		
		Consolidated C O S				50 000	00
		Consolidated stock				10 000	00
		Elimination of unrealised profit					
		Cons divs received		60 000	00		
		Cons divs paid				60 000	00
		Elimination of intra-group dividends					
		Minority interest		40 000	00		
		Cons divs paid				40 000	00
		Divs paid to minority					

Figure 8.8

Sales are reduced by R60 000, cost of sales by R50 000 and gross profit by R10 000. The dividends received from the subsidiary are eliminated, leaving only R15 000 which must have been received elsewhere (presumably the investments are included under fixed assets). The share of income belonging to the minorities as calculated above is deducted to obtain the net income attributable to the shareholders of High Limited and, after the dividends paid by High Limited have been deducted the final figure is the increase in the consolidated retained income. This is equal to the income for the year retained by the holding company (R150 000) plus the share of the income of the subsidiary calculated in the analysis of equity above (R30 000) minus the R10 000 written back on the elimination of intragroup sales which have not yet been finalised with an out of the group transaction.

The consolidated balance sheet as shown below has as its first item the share capital of the holding company, the share capital of the subsidiary having been taken care of in the analysis of equity: 60 % of it is written off against the purchase price of the shares paid by High Limited and the remaining 40 % is included in the minority interest.

The next item is the consolidated retained earnings. This consists of the retained earnings of the holding company (R875 000) plus the 60 % share of the earnings for the year of the subsidiary calculated above (R30 000) minus the R10 000 write back of profit on intragroup transactions. The retained earnings of the subsidiary company prior to becoming a subsidiary are either written off against the purchase price paid by High Limited (60 %) or included in the minority interest (40 %).

Current liabilities, fixed assets and other current assets are simply the sum of the amounts on the balance sheets of the holding company and the subsidiary, while goodwill arising on consolidation is the amount calculated above in the analysis of equity. Stock is the sum of the two amounts on the balance sheets, again adjusted for the unrealised profit on intragroup transactions.

Consolidated balance sheet of High Limited and its subsidiary at 28 February 1999

Share capital	1 000 000
Distributable reserves	895 000
Shareholders equity	1 895 000
Current liabilities	1 320 000
	3 215 000
Fixed assets	2 250 000
Goodwill arising on consolidation	20 000
Stock on hand	600 000
Other current assets	585 000
	3 455 000
Deduct minority interest in the assets of the group	240 000
	3 215 000

Figure 8.10

While the complexity of the consolidation process increases as groups of companies become more complex, the results will remain the same. When the process has been completed there will be consolidated financial statements in which intragroup transactions and balances have been eliminated, there will be minority interests and there will usually be goodwill or non-distributable reserves arising on consolidation. Some groups eliminate the goodwill arising on consolidation by writing such amounts off against group retained earnings.

The treatment of associated companies is in effect like a mini-consolidation. The investment in the associated company is brought into account at the cost of the acquisition of the shares but this amount is increased each year by the holding company's share of the profit of the associated company less any dividends received. Effectively, the calculation is exactly the same as that done in the analysis of equity calculation for the period after acquisition. In each year the value of the investor company's asset is increased, this being balanced by an increase in the reserves. If the investee company should make a loss, of course, both the value of the investment and the reserves will be written down by the investor company's share of that loss.

Accounting by the equity method does not free a company from giving full details of income received from the associated company in the form of dividends or otherwise.

4 The requirements of the Johannesburg Stock Exchange and GAAP

The Companies Act specifically requires that company financial statements not only comply with the specific requirements laid down in the Act and Schedule 4 to the Act, but also to Generally accepted accounting practice. The South African statements of GAAP are summarised in chapter 3 of this book, but it must be emphasised that the local statements may soon be replaced by the international ones. This should not affect most companies, but could have some effect on matters like reporting for associated companies.

The Johannesburg Stock Exchange lays down certain extra requirements in respect of companies which are listed on that exchange. The most important of these is the shortening of the reporting period of grace to three months. Any company which has not submitted to the JSE and sent to its shareholders at least provisional financial statements within three months of the end of its financial year will automatically have its listing terminated. The other requirements are generally not applicable to the financial statements as such but to the narrative information which has to accompany it. This information could be carried in an expanded directors' report but is generally contained in a separate report going by a name like chairman's report or chairman's review or management review. The JSE is currently seeking to expand its requirements in order to obtain better reporting standards and has for some time been working on a requirement that companies should report on the effects of inflation on their financial results and position. It is to be expected that South Africa's re-entry into the world will bring with it a tightening of reporting standards for listed companies and the JSE will be working on this.

Key words

Companies Act	Schedule 4
Audit report	Directors' report
Fixed assets	Current assets
Long term liabilities	Current liabilities
Reserves	Group of companies
Subsidiary company	Consolidated financial statements
Minority interest	Goodwill arising on consolidation
Associated company	

Chapter 9

Financial reporting for close corporations

Close corporations are intimate businesses, with only a few members who are usually directly concerned with the business. Because of this, the regulating act sets out fairly elementary accounting requirements. It has been left to the professional accounting bodies to set out the formal accounting requirements for the close corporation.

1. Annual financial statements
2. General accounting requirements
3. Accounting officer
4. Timing and relevance of financial statements
5. Guide on close corporations
6. An illustration of the financial statements of a close corporation

1. Annual financial statements

In terms of section 58 of the Close Corporations Act (referred to as "the Act" in the rest of this chapter), members of close corporations are required to "make out" financial reports not more than nine months after the end of each financial year. These reports must consist of a balance sheet and an income statement (or other similar statement which may be more appropriate), together with any explanatory notes, and must be accompanied by a report by the accounting officer as defined in section 62(1)(c). Sufficient information must be given in these statements to determine the aggregate amounts at the end of the year and the movements during the year in respect of the following:

● Contributions by members;
● Undrawn profits;
● Revaluations of fixed assets; and
● Amounts of loans to or by members.

There is no equivalent to the fourth schedule to the Companies Act which gives detailed information disclosure requirements. This is regarded as not being necessary since all members of close corporations are presumed to have intimate knowledge of the affairs of the corporation and to be actively involved in the management of it. While this may not always be true, it is certainly true that there is no necessity for the elaborate disclosure requirements needed to inform widely distributed and often uninvolved shareholders about the activities of a company.

2. General accounting requirements

Broadly speaking, close corporations have accounting requirements somewhat similar to those of companies. Section 56 of the act lays down the records that must be maintained. These include accounting records showing assets (and revaluations of fixed assets), liabilities, members' contributions and loans to or by members. A comprehensive fixed assets register must also be maintained, plus records of the day to day transactions whether cash or credit. Records of the annual stocktaking and the determination of the value of such stock are necessary and vouchers in support of the entries in all these records must be kept.

The act further lays down that there must be adequate safeguards against falsification of the records, which have to be kept at the place(s) of business or the registered office of the corporation where they must be available for inspection by members during all reasonable times.

3. Accounting officer

Section 59 of the act requires that every close corporation shall appoint an accounting officer who has been deemed to qualify for this position in terms of section 60. In terms of section 62(1) this officer has the duty, within three months after the completion of the annual financial statements:

3.1 of determining whether these are in agreement with the accounting records of the corporation;

3.2 of determining the accounting policies applied in preparing the annual financial statements; and

3.3 reporting on the above matters to the members.

3.4 If he should find that the corporation is not carrying on business and has no intention of carrying on business or if its assets exceed its liabilities (whether this is reflected in the financial statements or whether his investigation gives him reason to believe that this is the true state of affairs) or that there are changes in the founding statement which have not been registered, he has to notify the Registrar of the relevant fact by registered post.

4. Timing and relevance of financial statements

The wording of the act is a little ambiguous, but it seems that the members must prepare the financial statements not more than six months after the end of the financial year if the accounting officer is to have the full three month period for preparation of his report. In most cases, of course, the accounting officer is going to be a professional accountant who will also be responsible for the preparation of the financial statements.

In any case, the accounting officer has three months from the date on which the statements are completed to prepare his report in terms of the act, so that the close corporation seeking timeous financial reporting for management purposes is going to have to come to an agreement concerning timing with the accounting officer. This agreement is normally going to be part of the contract entered into when he is appointed.

5. Guide on close corporations

In view of the fact that the act does not lay down a specific form of presentation for the financial statements of a close corporation the professional accounting bodies co-operated in setting out a guide for their members to use in the preparation of such financial statements. Each of these bodies presented a guide for the benefit of their own members, but there is very little difference in the various guides. An Accounting and Audit Guide was issued in January 1985 which was "developed by the South African Institute of Chartered Accountants to give guidance to members on the accounting and reporting requirements of the Close Corporations Act". While it obviously does not have the force of law, this Guide forms the basis of most financial statements prepared for close corporations.

5.1 The Guide gives a brief summary of the most important provisions of the Close Corporations Act and then gets down to the financial statements which "should be prepared in a manner which enables the affairs of the corporation to be readily understood by the members, and to this end they should be presented as simply and logically as possible, bearing in mind the overriding requirement of fair presentation".

A short summary of the accounting requirements of the Act is given, followed by a discussion of the desirable features of the financial statements of a close corporation. In addition to the balance sheet and income statement required by the Act, the guideline recommends a cash flow statement, a member's net investment statement analysed by member and a description of the transactions with members which have been included in arriving at net income. There is also some discussion of the exact meaning of the requirements for the report of the accounting officer and a summary of legal opinions on this and other ambiguously worded sections of the Act. The uncertainty concerning the duties of the accounting officer led to the inclusion of a Notice to Readers which points out that representations have been made to amend the wording of the Act to remove this uncertainty, but that until this amendment is passed all reports should be very specific as to the extent of work performed so as not to create the impression that a total audit has been performed.

5.2 Other matters discussed in the Guide include discussions of the broad outlines of taxation which is specific to close corporations, certain matters of professional conduct and problems and benefits of converting a company to a close corporation.

5.3 The engagement letter

The guide notes that the duties of a Chartered Accountant appointed by a close corporation to act as accounting officer may find that more is expected of him than just those duties laid down by the Act. To prevent any misunderstanding he should issue an engagement letter to the corporation setting out precisely what his duties are and what he expects from the client. Depending on his agreement with the client, the duties may be confined to those specified by the act or may be far more comprehensive. It should also specify the basis on which his remuneration is to be determined as well as such matters as the date on which he would be expected to report to the members on the annual financial statements or any other reports prepared in terms of the contract.

6. An illustration of the financial statements of a close corporation

Report of the accounting officer to the members of Dube Furnishers CC

I have performed the duties of the accounting officer of the above corporation for the year ended 28 February 1987 in accordance with the guide established by the South African Institute of Chartered Accountants. No audit has been carried out and no opinion is expressed as to fair presentation in the financial statements.

Based on the performance of my duties, I report that the financial statements set out on pages 1 to 5 hereafter and initialled for purposes of identification are in agreement with the accounting records at 28 February 1987 and have been prepared in accordance with the accounting policies set out in note 1 to the financial statements.

T Bird
Chartered Accountant (SA)
27 May 1987

POINTS TO NOTE:
1. If T Bird were a member of the close corporation a paragraph such as the following would be inserted:
   "I am a member of Dube Furnishers CC and all the other members have consented in writing to my appointment as accounting officer."
2. The professional qualification of the accounting officer should be stated.
3. The date should not be earlier than the date on which the financial statements are approved.

1

DUBE FURNISHERS CC

Balance sheet at 28 February (R 000)

	Note	1987	1986
Capital Employed			
Members' contributions		2 280	2 280
Undrawn profits		3 660	3 655
Members interest		5 940	5 935
Long term loan	2	2 850	3 540
		8 790	9 475
Employment of Capital			
Leasehold improvements	3	2 310	2 425
Other fixed assets	4	910	990
		3 220	3 415
Investments	5	220	225
Loans to members		90	45
Net current assets		5 260	5 790
Current assets			
Stock	1	3 285	3 580
Debtors		3 635	3 640
Cash and bank balances		315	495
Prepayments		105	95
		7 340	7 810
Current liabilities			
Creditors		1 775	1 625
Accrued expenses		305	395
		2 080	2 020
		8 790	9 475

The accounting officer's report and the notes to the financial statements should be read in conjunction with this balance sheet.

POINTS TO NOTE:
1. The Close Corporation has "Members' Contributions", not share capital or member's capital. This amount is the one shown in the founding statement.

2. The term "Undrawn Profits" (Close Corporations Act) or "Undrawn Income" (Guide) is used instead of the better known "Retained Earnings" or "Undistributed Profits" used in the case of companies.
3. The Act does not require comparative figures for the previous year. This is a requirement of the Guide.
4. The Act requires that the financial statements be signed by or on behalf of members holding more than 50% of the voting power of the close corporation. There is no specific requirement as to where these signatures should appear in either the Act or the Guide.

2

DUBE FURNISHERS CC

Income statement for years ended 28 February (R 000)

	Note	1987	1986
Net sales		17 835	18 930
Opening stock		3 640	3 535
Purchases		12 265	12 005
Closing stock		(3 635)	(3 640)
Cost of sales		12 270	11 900
Gross profit		5 565	7 030
Operating expenses	6	5 730	5 365
Operating profit (loss)		(165)	1 665
Interest		635	635
Income before extraordinary items		(800)	1 030
Extraordinary items			
Provisions written back			
—stock obsolescence		690	0
—bad debts		120	0
Profit after extraordinary items		10	1 030
Tax		0	440
Profit after tax		10	590
Undrawn profits at the beginning of the year		3 655	3 465
		3 665	4 055
Distributions during the year		5	400
Undrawn profits at the end of the year		3 660	3 655

The accounting officer's report and the notes to the financial statements should be read in conjunction with this income statement.

POINTS TO NOTE:

1. This is a complete trading and profit and loss account. It does not, like the income statement required by the Companies Act, give minimum disclosure.

Since there is no audit requirement in this case the accounting officer will also not insist on an abbreviated statement which he can certify.
2. While the structure is very similar to that which would be used by a company giving full disclosure, the terminology is different. "Undrawn profits" is used instead of retained earnings and "distributions" rather than dividends.
3. The operating expenses could of course be shown in full on the face of the income statement rather than being shown here in total with the details being shown in the notes.

3

DUBE FURNISHERS CC

Cash flow statement for the years ended 28 February (R 000)

	1987	1986
Operating income after extraordinary items	645	1 665
Depreciation	295	305
	940	1 970
Changes in working capital:		
Stock	295	50
Debtors	5	(105)
Prepayments	(10)	(5)
Creditors	150	80
Accruals	(90)	105
Cash generated by operations	1 290	2 095
Interest paid	(635)	(635)
Taxation paid	0	(405)
Distributions to members	(5)	(440)
	650	615
Long term loans repaid	(690)	(40)
Members loans repaid/(advanced)	(45)	25
Cash available for investment/(cash deficit)	(85)	600
Fixed assets purchased	(100)	(485)
Other investments	5	5
Change in cash and bank	(180)	120

POINTS TO NOTE:
1. This statement has been prepared in accordance with the Guide. No attempt has been made to modify the layout or to comply with any of the formats suggested in the various exposure drafts on cash flow statements.
2. The Act does not prescribe any funds flow or cash flow statement. The guideline implies that comments received indicated that this format would be easily understood and would thus be the most acceptable type of flow statement for a close corporation.

4

DUBE FURNISHERS CC

Members' net investment statement for the year ended 28 February 1987

Members' interests	A M Dube	P M Dube	Total
	80%	20%	100%
	R 000	R 000	R 000
Balance at beginning of year	4 703	1 187	5 890
Movements for the year:			
Contributions introduced	0	0	0
Contributions repaid	0	0	0
Revaluations	0	0	0
Net income	8	2	10
Distributions	(4)	(1)	(5)
Loans from members	0	0	0
Loans to members	(45)	0	(45)
Balance at end of year	4 662	1 188	5 850
Represented by:			
Members' contributions	1 824	456	2 280
Revaluations	0	0	0
Undrawn profits	2 928	732	3 660
Loans from members	0	0	0
Loans to members	(90)	0	(90)
	4 662	1 188	5 850

POINTS TO NOTICE:

1. The whole outline of this statement as laid out in the Guide has been shown above. Obviously the zero items would not be included in practice.

2. Members' interests are given as percentages to start off with before going into the financial section. The Rand amounts of the net income and such items as revaluations are apportioned according to this percentage interest in the first section of the statement, as are undrawn profits and revaluations in the second part.

3. The term "Net income" has been used here rather than net profit to indicate the fact that the figure being used is after interest, taxes and extraordinary items.

5

DUBE FURNISHERS CC

Notes to the financial statements at 28 February 1987

1. Accounting policies

   1.1 The financial statements are prepared in accordance with generally accepted accounting practice on the historical cost basis. The following policies, all of which are consistent with those of previous years, have been specifically applied:

1.2 Fixed assets are depreciated on the reducing balance basis at appropriate rates which agree with those allowed for tax purposes.

1.3 Stock is valued at the lower of market value and cost on a first in, first out basis.

2. The long term loan is from the Kwazulu Development Corporation. It is repayable over a ten year period at fluctuating interest rates.

3. Leasehold improvements represent buildings erected on property occupied in terms of a ninety-nine year lease which was entered into in 1984. It is the intention of the corporation to purchase this property if legislation is so amended as to allow this.

4. Fixed assets (R 000)	Cost	Depreciation	Net book value
Furniture, fittings and equipment	625	145	480
Computer system	188	94	94
Motor vehicles	421	85	336
	1 234	324	910

5. Investments are shares in the following quoted and unquoted companies:

	Cost	Market price or valuation
A full list should be given here	—	—
	220	296

6. Operating expenses
   A full list should be given here

POINTS TO NOTE:
1. The Act does not lay down precisely what notes should be given, nor does the Guide. It should be borne in mind that the financial statements are being prepared for the benefit of the members, and the extent of the notes will depend largely on their requirements.
2. There may be other interested parties such as the corporation's bank. The requirements of such parties should also be met by the notes.
3. It is likely that these statements are also, in all probability, prepared for tax purposes. It may be useful to give details of tax calculations as part of the notes.

Key words

Accounting officer
Distribution to members
Guide to CCs

Undrawn profits
Members' net investment statement

Chapter 10

Financial reporting for partnerships

Partnership accounting is more complex than that of sole traders or incorporated bodies in several respects. Firstly there is the necessity for maintaining separate accounts for the contributions and drawings of each of the partners and for apportioning to each of them the amount of profit or loss attributable to them over a period.

Secondly, there are various problems which arise with the admission or retirement of a partner. These of course lead to a dissolution of the old partnership and the creation of a new one. The assets and liabilities of the old partnership are usually carried over to the new one, and this has to be accounted for. If they are not carried over they still have to be accounted for.

1. **The partnership income statement and balance sheet**

2. **Admission of a new partner**

3. **Retirement of a partner**

4. **Dissolution of a partnership**

1. The financial statements of a partnership

Before examining the accounting peculiarities of a partnership it is necessary to have an understanding of the nature of a partnership. A discussion of the partnership as a form of business organisation will be found in chapter seventeen and it is advisable to read this through before going any further.

The very simplest form of partnership from an accounting point of view is one where two people have contributed equal amounts to the partnership business and share equally in all profits or losses, without paying themselves any salaries or interest on capital or on loan or drawings accounts.

The whole bookkeeping process will be precisely the same as in the financial records of a sole trader except for the fact that there will be two separate capital accounts and two separate drawings accounts.

The financial statements will be the same up to a point. The net income for the period is determined exactly as for the sole trader, but it is then necessary to prepare a separate statement, known as an appropriation statement or division of profits statement, in order to show how the profits are divided between the partners. The balance sheet will contain two separate capital accounts showing the exact position of each of the partners.

The following is a simplified example of the financial statements of such a straightforward partnership.

Example 1

ARNOLD BENNETT AND CHARLES DICKENS
Trial balance at 28 February 1989

Capital account—A Bennett		50 000
Capital account—C Dickens		50 000
Drawings—A Bennett	30 000	
Drawings—C Dickens	30 000	
Fixed assets	55 000	
Fixed assets—provision for depreciation		5 000
Stock on hand—1 March 1988	100 000	
Debtors	25 000	
Cash on hand and in bank	6 000	
Creditors		40 000
Sales		600 000
Purchases	400 000	
Administrative expenses	24 000	
Selling expenses	72 000	
Depreciation for the year	3 000	
	745 000	745 000

Stock at 28 February 1988 was R110 000.

Bennett and Dickens do not pay interest on capital accounts or charge interest on drawings. They also do not pay themselves any salaries. All profits are shared equally between them.

Required:
Prepare the financial statements at 28 February 1988.

Answer:

Arnold Bennett and Charles Dickens

Income statement for the year ended 28 February 1988

Sales		600 000
Less: Cost of sales		
Opening stock	100 000	
Purchases	400 000	
	500 000	
Less: Closing stock	110 000	390 000
Gross profit		210 000
Less: Expenses		
Administrative expenses	24 000	
Selling expenses	72 000	
Depreciation for the year	3 000	99 000
Net income for the year		111 000

Arnold Bennett and Charles Dickens

Appropriation statement for the year ended 28 February 1988

Net income per income statement		111 000
Transfer to capital account—A Bennett	55 500	
Transfer to capital account—C Dickens	55 500	111 000

Arnold Bennett and Charles Dickens

Balance sheet at 28 February 1988

Equities		
Capital account—A Bennett	50 000	
Add share of net income	55 500	
	105 500	
Deduct drawings	30 000	75 500
Capital account—C Dickens	50 000	
Add share of net income	55 500	
	105 500	
Deduct drawings	30 000	75 500
Partner's equity		151 000
Creditors		40 000
		191 000
Assets		
Fixed assets at cost	55 000	
Less: provision for depreciation	5 000	50 000
Current assets		
Stock	110 000	
Debtors	25 000	
Cash on hand and in bank	6 000	141 000
		191 000

In practice it is found often enough that the appropriation statement is not prepared as a separate statement but is simply shown as a part of the income statement.

Partnerships are often far more complex than this. Partners may contribute different amounts to the partnership as capital and therefore either want profits to be shared in the ratio of the capital accounts or want interest to be paid on the capital accounts before the profits are shared out. Certain partners may play a far more active part in the partnership affairs than others and may consequently feel entitled to be remunerated for the extra effort. Whatever the reason, partnership agreements often specify profit sharing ratios and make arrangements for salaries to be paid to the active partners and interest to be paid on a mutually agreed basis to the various partners and to be charged to the partners on their drawings during the year.

Example 2

Aphra Behn and Jane Austen run a travel agency on a partnership basis. Behn, lacking funds but with an extensive knowledge of the Americas and continental Europe, does most of the actual work while Austen has contributed the necessary capital. The partnership agreement states that each partner may draw up to R2 000 per month for personal use and that interest at the rate of 15% per annum will be charged on those drawings. Behn receives a salary of R2 000 per month for her efforts and interest is paid or charged at the rate of 12% per annum on the opening balance on capital accounts. Profits or losses after taking these into account are shared equally. The following trial balance was extracted after the agency had been operating for two years:

B & A TRAVEL AGENCY
Trial balance at 28 February 1989

Capital account—Jane Austen		100 000
Capital account—Aphra Behn		10 000
Drawings—Jane Austen	24 000	
Drawings—Aphra Behn	24 000	
Salary—Aphra Behn	24 000	
Fixed assets	40 000	
Fixed assets—provision for depreciation		6 000
Debtors	20 000	
Cash on hand and in bank	25 000	
Commissions received		250 000
Depreciation	4 000	
Administrative expenses	141 000	
Marketing expenses	64 000	
	366 000	366 000

Drawings by each partner were taken out in amounts of R2 000 at the end of each month.

Required:

Using the above trial balance and information on the partnership agreement, prepare financial statements for the partnership at 28 February 1989.

Answer:

B & A TRAVEL AGENCY

Income statement at 28 February 1989

Commissions received		250 000
Expenses		
Administrative expenses	141 000	
Depreciation	4 000	
Marketing expenses	64 000	209 000
Net income before partnership adjustments		41 000
Partnership adjustments		
Salary—A Behn	24 000	
Interest on capital—J Austen	12 000	
Interest on capital—A Behn	1 200	37 200
		3 800
Interest charged on drawings—A Behn	1 650	
Interest charged on drawings—J Austen	1 650	3 300
Net income after partnership adjustments		7 100
Transfer to capital account—A Behn	3 550	
Transfer to capital account—J Austen	3 550	7 100

B & A TRAVEL AGENCY

Balance sheet at 28 February 1989

Equities

Capital account—J Austen	100 000	
Add: Interest	12 000	
Share of net income	3 550	
	115 550	
Deduct: Drawings	24 000	
Interest	1 650	89 900
Capital account—A Behn	10 000	
Add: Interest	1 200	
Share of net income	3 550	
	14 750	
Deduct: Drawings	24 000	
Interest	1 650	−10 900
Net partners' equity		79 000

Assets

Fixed assets	40 000	
Deduct: Provision for depreciation	6 000	34 000
Current assets		
Debtors	20 000	
Cash on hand and in bank	25 000	45 000
		79 000

Workings:

Interest paid to Jane Austen:
12% pa of R100 000 (opening balance)
= 12/100 × R100 000
= R12 000

Interest paid to Aphra Behn:
12% pa of R10 000 (opening balance)
= 12/100 × R100 000
= R1 200

Interest charged to each of the partners

15% pa of R2 000 for 11 months, 10 months . . . 1 month
= 15% pa of R2 000 for 66 months
= 15/100 × R2 000 × 5,5 years
=R1 650

Note that Behn is now overdrawn on her capital account, but that the partnership as a whole is solvent. The layout of the income statement is acceptable, but could be improved by separating the finance aspects from the operating aspects. The last part of the income statement would then be as follows:

Net income before partnership adjustments		41 000
Partnership adjustments		
Salary—A Behn		24 000
Net operating income after partnership adjustments		17 000
Interest on capital—J Austen	12 000	
Interest on capital—A Behn	1 200	13 200
		3 800
Interest charged on drawings—A Behn	1 650	
Interest charged on drawings—J Austen	1 650	3 300
Net income after partnership adjustments		7 100
Transfer to capital account—A Behn	3 550	
Transfer to capital account—J Austen	3 550	7 100

This would, of course, only be a reasonable layout if the salary paid to Behn were a realistic one. If it were too low or too high in terms of the market value of her services this refinement would not add to the value of the statements in any way.

It is also fairly common practice for salaries paid to partners simply to be included in the operating expenses, but for the sake of full disclosure it is advisable to show such payments separately while partnership financial statements are not published, they are used in negotiations for loans or overdrafts. The goal should therefore be full reasonable disclosure.

2. Admission of a new partner

There are two possible ways in which a new partner can be brought into the partnership. He can either purchase an interest directly from one of the existing partners, which means that there is no payment into the partnership but only directly to one of the partners as in example 3, or he can contribute directly to the capital of the partnership, which means that the total capital of the partnership is increased.

Example 3

Shelley and Keats were in partnership, sharing profits on a 60:40 basis. They admitted Byron to the partnership by allowing him to purchase 50% of Shelley's share of the business for an amount of R25 000, payable directly to Shelley. Shelley's capital account stood at R40 000 at the time of the transaction.

Required:
Prepare the necessary journal entries to show the effect on the financial records of the partnership.

Answer:

Capital Shelley	20 000	
Capital Byron		20 000

Adjustment to record Byron's admission as a
partner following his direct purchase of 50% of
Shelley's interest.

No other entries are necessary in the books of the partnership at this stage. At the end of the year the appropriation statement will be different to the extent that the profit sharing ratio has changed. While the new profit sharing ratio will be a matter for agreement between the partners, it is likely that it will be adjusted on the basis of the old ratio and that Keats, Shelley and Byron will share profits in the ratio of 4:3:3. The goodwill paid by Byron is not reflected in the records of the partnership since it was paid to Shelley.

If the new partner makes a direct contribution to the partnership the bookkeeping entries can be more complex depending on whether there is any payment for goodwill. If there is no payment for goodwill the entry is also straightforward.

Example 4

Andrew Marvell and John Donne are in partnership. They decide to admit Richard Crashaw as a third partner on payment to the partnership of R25 000.

Required:
Prepare the necessary journal entries to show the effect on the financial records of the partnership.

Answer:

Cash	25 000	
Capital account R Crashaw		25 000

Capital introduced by Crashaw on his
admission as a partner

No other entry is necessary in the books of the partnership at this stage. The financial statements at the end of the year will reflect the new division of profits in accordance with what the partners have agreed.

If there is a question of goodwill to be paid by the new partner then the entries must reflect this. There are two possibilities as far as goodwill is concerned. It can be reflected in the records of the partnership or it can be a payment made outside the partnership directly to the existing partners. In either case the first task of the accountant must be to determine whether or not there is any goodwill being paid, since agreements usually simply state that a certain amount is to be paid for a share in the partnership without specifying whether or not there is a payment for goodwill.

Example 5

Beaumont and Fletcher were in partnership. The balances on their capital accounts stood at R50 000 each. They decided to admit Marlowe as an equal partner on payment of the sum of R75 000 to the partnership.

Required:

Prepare the necessary journal entries to show the effect on the financial records of the partnership. Show all calculations.

Answer:

Cash	75 000	
Capital Marlowe		75 000
Cash contribution by Marlowe on		
admission to partnership		

Goodwill	50 000	
Capital—Beaumont		25 000
Capital—Fletcher		25 000
Goodwill recorded following		
admission of Marlowe to partnership		

Calculation of goodwill:

Total assets will equal 3 × 75 000 since Marlowe		
paid R75 000 for a 1/3 share		225 000
Total capital after admission of Marlowe:		
Beaumont	50 000	
Fletcher	50 000	
Marlowe	75 000	175 000
Goodwill		50 000

The goodwill belongs to the old partners and Marlowe's payment for goodwill must be divided between them. This increases their capital accounts and all three partners now have equal capital accounts.

Since goodwill is highly subjective and is often regarded as purely a piece of window dressing aimed at increasing the totals of the balance sheet, many partnerships choose not to reflect it on the face of the balance sheet even though they charge it when admitting a new partner. While it is possible simply to pay each partner an amount outside of the partnership so that the goodwill never appears in any of the records of the partnership, the cash paid for the goodwill is usually required for the operations of the partnership and a way then has to be found of reflecting the payment without showing goodwill. This is achieved by creating the goodwill account and then writing it off against the partners' capital accounts in the proportion of the new profit sharing ratio.

Example 6

Laurel and Hardy were in partnership. The balances on their capital accounts stood at R60 000 and R80 000 respectively. They decided to admit Keaton as an equal partner on payment of the sum of R100 000 to the partnership, but not show goodwill in the financial statements of the partnership.

Required:

Prepare the necessary journal entries to show the effect on the financial records of the partnership.

Answer:

Cash	100 000	
Capital Keaton		100 000
Cash contribution by Keaton on		
admission to partnership		

Goodwill	60 000	
Capital—Laurel		30 000
Capital—Hardy		30 000
Goodwill recorded following		
admission of Keaton to partnership		

Capital—Laurel	20 000	
Capital—Hardy	20 000	
Capital—Keaton	20 000	
Goodwill		60 000
Goodwill written off		

Calculation of goodwill:
Total assets will equal 3 × 100 000 since
Keaton

paid R100 000 for a 1/3 share		300 000
Total capital after admission of Marlowe:		
Laurel	60 000	
Hardy	80 000	
Keaton	100 000	240 000
Goodwill		60 000

The only difference between the solution to this problem and the solution to the previous one lies in the last entry which eliminates the goodwill created on admission.

3. Retirement of a partner

There is very little difference in the accounting procedures for the retirement of a partner and the admission of a new partner. In some cases the whole process is exactly the same. If a partner wishing to retire sells his interest to someone wishing to enter the partnership, one finds admission and retirement in the same transaction. No entries would be made in the records of the partnership other than to note that the composition of the partnership has changed. Any goodwill paid is for the benefit of the retiring partner and is not included in the records of the partnership.

In cases where there is no simultaneous admission and retirement the accounting treatment again depends on whether or not there is goodwill to be taken into account.

Example 7

Horatius, Spurius and Herminius were partners who shared profits in the ratio 4:3:3 respectively. The balances on their capital accounts were R80 000, R60 000 and R60 000 respectively. Horatius decided to retire on the following terms:

1. R20 000 should be paid out to him immediately on retirement; and

2. The remainder should be treated as a loan to the partnership, and interest at 20% would be charged on it. The full balance would be paid out within five years.

Required:
Prepare the necessary journal entries to show the effect on the financial records of the partnership.

Answer:

Capital—Horatius	80 000	
Loan—Horatius		80 000
Capital balance transferred to loan account in terms of retirement agreement		

Loan—Horatius	20 000	
Cash		20 000
First payment in terms of retirement agreement		

No adjustments need to be made to the capital accounts of the other partners, and there is no change in total assets other than the fact that cash has been paid out.

If there is a question of goodwill having to be paid to the retiring partner it is necessary to determine the amount of this and the amount due to the retiring partner and to enter these amounts in the records.

Example 8

Athos, Porthos and Aramis are in partnership sharing profits in the ratio 9:6:5. The balances on their capital accounts were R180 000, R120 000 and R100 000 respectively when Athos decided that he wanted to retire. He wanted twenty per cent of the amount due to him paid out immediately and the balance over five years with interest at three per cent above prime overdraft rate. He also wanted to be paid out for goodwill, which the partners agreed was worth R100 000.

Required:
Prepare the necessary journal entries to show the effect on the financial records of the partnership.

Answer:

Goodwill	100 000	
Capital—Athos		45 000
Capital—Porthos		30 000
Capital—Aramis		25 000
Recording of goodwill on retirement of Athos		

Capital—Athos	225 000	
Loan—Athos		225 000
Capital balance transferred to loan account in terms of retirement agreement		

Loan—Athos	45 000	
Cash		45 000
First payment in terms of retirement agreement		

If the new partners decided that they did not want to show goodwill on the financial statements of the partnership there would have to be a further journal entry:

Capital—Porthos (6/11)	54 445	
Capital—Aramis (5/11)	45 555	
Goodwill		100 000
Goodwill written off		

4. Dissolution of a partnership

In addition to the cases mentioned above of admission of a partner or retirement of a partner, dissolution of a partnership occurs when one of the partners dies or goes insolvent or when the task for which the partnership was formed is completed. The accounting entries are much the same as those which are prepared in the case of an ordinary retirement but the exact accounting treatment in each of these cases is usually dependent on the terms of the partnership agreement, which will specify the way in which the assets have to be distributed or the conditions under which the remaining partners will continue with the business.

Provision is usually made for one or more of the remaining partners to purchase the share of the deceased or defaulting partner, often from the proceeds of an insurance policy taken out for just that contingency.

General points to be remembered in the case of partnership accounting are that the proportion of the profit accruing to any partner is agreed among the partners. Common law principles decree that in the absence of agreement the profits be split equally.

Key words

Admission   Retirement
Profit-sharing ratio   Goodwill
Appropriation statement

Chapter 11

Reporting on specific assets and liabilities

The previous chapters briefly covered the reporting requirements of various types of business entities. This chapter gives a little more depth to certain aspects of financial reporting and analysis.

1. Fixed assets and depreciation
2. The valuation of trading stock
3. Investments
4. Long term liabilities and lease commitments
5. Intangible assets

1. Fixed assets and depreciation

Fixed assets can either be tangible or intangible.

Intangible assets are such assets as goodwill or development expenditure which have a value in that they can contribute to income of the organisation concerned. This value is usually subjective to some degree and difficult to verify. As this value declines over a period of time the assets are normally written off. This process of writing off an intangible asset is known as amortisation.

Tangible fixed assets fall into one of three groups:
- Assets which do not wear out, such as industrial land;
- Assets which wear out and are replaced, such as plant and machinery; and
- Assets which are depleted in the course of their useful life, such as the ore body of a mine.

Accounting practice has always been to show all three of these at cost, less an allowance for depreciation in the case of assets which would wear out. Depreciation is the process of allocating the cost of a tangible fixed asset to the accounting periods covering its useful life; it is not an attempt to indicate a diminution in value of the asset or an attempt to determine the true residual economic value of the asset.

Since the asset is depreciated over its useful life, it follows that the process of writing off depreciation cannot begin before estimating the useful life of the asset. This is obviously a technical matter, and beyond the competence of the accountant. Certain guidelines have been developed over the years, however. A motor vehicle is generally regarded as having an economic life of five years, light machinery from four years if used on a twenty-four hours per day basis to ten years if used on a single shift basis and office furniture about fifteen years, and most depreciation calculations are based on these guidelines. In exceptional cases an estimate may be made of the useful life of a particular asset, and some undertakings use a single conventional economic life which is applied to all fixed assets.

1.1 The depreciable cost of an asset

The other matter which has to be determined is the cost which is to be depreciated over the useful life of the asset. This is not always a straightforward matter. A motor vehicle may cost a certain amount including all the extras and this amount may be used as the depreciable base, but what of the cases where a particular piece of equipment is purchased from an overseas supplier, various shipping charges and import duties are payable, special modifications have to be made to the plant to accommodate the machine and the installation and commissioning costs are fairly substantial. There are also test runs during the commissioning process, which obviously cost money. Should all of these be included in the cost of the machine for purpose of determining the depreciable base? What of those cases where a machine is rebuilt extensively at the end of, say, five years? Is this a repair cost or should the cost of such a rebuild be regarded as a capitalisable outlay to be depreciated over the remainder of the useful life of the asset? What of those cases where a piece of equipment is actually manufactured by the undertaking itself?

Obviously a certain amount of judgement has to be exercised in deciding just what amount should be capitalised in order to reflect the most appropriate depreciable base. Most undertakings have a convention whereby all amounts under a certain limit, be it R500 or R25 000, are written off as expenses and no arguments arise. For amounts over this limit, the general rule is that the cost of a purchased asset together with any costs incidental to its erection, testing and commissioning should be capitalised.

In the case of rebuilding of an asset it should first be determined to what extent the rebuilding has contributed to the future economic usefulness of the asset. Has the productive capacity of the asset been raised? Has the remaining economic life been extended? or has the machine simply been put back into the state that was first assumed when predicting the economically useful life? On the basis of the answers to these questions a decision will be made as to whether the cost of the rebuilding should be capitalised.

If such rebuilding was originally envisaged when the machine was purchased or built then prudent practice would be to build up a provision as the machine is used and to write off the costs of such rebuilding against this provision. Where the rebuilding is unplanned, however, it will be necessary to examine the effect of the rebuilding and capitalise an appropriate amount if necessary.

When an undertaking has manufactured an asset for its own use some judgement is again required. There can be no doubt that the costs of material, sub-contracted work and direct labour should be charged to the asset, but there are various arguments concerning the costs of indirect labour and various overheads. The arguments firstly concern the extent to which the capacity of the undertaking is being utilised. When the firm is operating at or near maximum capacity then the use of what are then scarce productive resources for the production of an asset means that the undertaking has an opportunity cost of overheads and indirect labour which should be charged to the asset. On the other hand, if the undertaking is operating well below capacity it is merely utilising idle capacity and there is no opportunity cost. Arguments rage in favour of and against capitalising overhead costs in a case like this, one side of the argument being that no cost was incurred which was not already there and so no cost should be charged to the asset and the other being that all work performed should bear some part of the general overhead cost.

A factor which can assist in the settling of this argument in any particular case is the market cost of a similar piece of equipment. If this is higher than the direct costs it is difficult not to argue that at least some of the indirect costs should be capitalised. If it is lower than the direct cost it is obvious that the undertaking was merely using idle capacity and there is little point in capitalising the cost of this. Generally speaking, whichever method is used, the capitalised cost should not exceed the purchase value of similar equipment. The cost should not be written up to purchase value, however, if it is in actual fact lower than this. The "profit" on such an asset should only be taken into account when the asset is actually sold.

A further factor which in practice affects the way in which undertakings pass judgement on whether or not to capitalise is the tax effect of the decision. Since the tax laws permit writing off of expenses immediately and of capital outlays only over a period of time the pressure is always on the decision maker to write off costs immediately and so gain tax benefits. Unfortunately, this sometimes leads to unsatisfactory financial reporting practices.

1.2 The cost of non-depreciable assets

Land is a non-depreciable asset. The cost of the land is the amount paid for it plus any costs incurred such as transfer duties plus the cost of bringing the land into a condition suitable for its planned use. This may include clearing costs when bush land is turned into farming land, costs of landscaping or of laying out of gardens and the cost of demolition of existing structures on the land where there are no plans for erecting new buildings.

Buildings, other than industrial and hotel buildings, are generally not depreciated in South Africa. This practice can again be traced to the influence of the tax laws which only grant allowances in respect of those two types of building. The cost of buildings is the actual cost of planning and erecting the building and of such charges as assessment rates up to the time of completion of the building. This can include such costs as demolition of existing structures on the land to be used for the building.

1.3 Assets subject to depletion

The prime example of this type of asset is a mine. The property of which the mine is part is purchased, or the mineral rights are purchased, or some sort of mineral lease is entered into and the cost of this is capitalised. In addition, the cost of developing the property for mining is capitalised. This includes the cost of mining exploration and preliminary development work prior to the start of production.

Problems arise when the cost of development exceeds the expected production value of the mine. In a case like this the capitalised costs should be written down to a value representative of the amount which is likely to be realised from the exploitation of the ore body.

The capitalised amount, less the expected recovery of costs from the sale of the property, should then be amortised over the period of the expected life of the mine or at a rate in accordance with the annual production of the mine in mineral units compared with the total expected total production of those mineral units.

1.4 Depreciation

There are several methods used in the computing of depreciation charges for a particular period. The simplest of these is the straight line method. The depreciable amount is simply written off in equal instalments over the estimated useful life of the asset. The depreciable amount is defined as the total cost of the asset less any amount which it is expected may be recovered at the end of the asset's useful life in the form of scrap or trade in allowances.

> *Example:* An asset costing R10 000 is estimated to have an economic life
> of 5 years with no residual value. What would be the annual
> depreciation charge if a straight line basis were to be used?

> *Answer:* R10 000/5 = R2 000 per year.

Another commonly used method, is the declining balance or reducing balance method. The asset is written off over an infinitely long period, but most of the depreciable value is written off fairly quickly.

Example: An asset costing R10 000 is to be written off at 20% per annum on the reducing balance basis. Show the annual charge and the depreciated value for the first five years.

Answer:

Cost	10 000
Charge year 1	2 000
Balance at end year 1	8 000
Charge year 2	1 600
Balance at end year 2	6 400
Charge year 3	1 280
Balance at end year 3	5 120
Charge year 4	1 024
Balance at end year 4	4 096
Charge year 5	819
Balance at end year 5	3 277

The charge each year represents not 20% of the original value, but 20% of the reduced value reflected as the balance at the end of the previous year. The depreciation charge will thus become smaller each year.

A third method which has been little used in this country but which has found strong support overseas is the sum of the years digits method, which accelerates the writing off of the asset. This had some theoretical support in earlier years when people were trying to argue that the depreciated value of an asset should reflect the actual monetary value of that asset, but this argument has little support nowadays. An argument which is still used in favour of both this method and the reducing balance method is that the machine makes the greatest contribution to income when it is new and operating smoothly, so that it is only logical that it should bear a greater part of the costs when it is contributing more to income.

Example: An asset costing R6 000 was expected to last for three years and to have no residual value at the end of that time. Show the annual depreciation charges and the book values for the three year period.

Answer: Years which the machine will last: 1 + 2 + 3 = 6
Charge for the first year is therefore 3/6 × cost

Cost	6 000
Charge year 1	3 000
Balance at end year 1	3 000
Charge year 2	2 000
Balance at end year 2	1 000
Charge year 3	1 000
Balance at end year 3	0

The machine is written off to zero over the three year period, with the larger charges taking place in the first part of the life of the machine. A general formula for determining the sum of the digits is

$$SYD = n \frac{(n + 1)}{2}$$

where n is the number of years the asset is expected to last.

A fourth method is the units of production method, which is similar to the production method of writing off wasting assets. Rather than writing off depreciation based on a time scale, depreciation is written off in terms of units of output or operating hours.

> *Example:* A machine costing R55 000 is expected to be able to produce 500 000 units of a product before being sold for R5 000 as scrap. In the first year of production 60 000 units are manufactured. Show the depreciation charge if the units of production method is used.
>
> *Answer:* Amount to be depreciated   R50 000
> Number of units to be produced   500 000
> Depreciation charge per unit   R0,10
> Depreciation charge per 60 000 units   R6 000

Exactly the same approach would be used if hours of production rather than units of production were the measure to be used.

1.5 Revaluations of depreciable assets and provisions for increased replacement cost of fixed assets

Economic theory holds that depreciation represents a fund being held in the undertaking for the purpose of financing the replacement cost of assets at the end of their useful life. Accounting theory holds a simpler view of depreciation, but acknowledges the necessity of providing for the replacement of assets. During times of stable prices the accounting theory and the economic theory coincide, since the expensing of the asset automatically provides the fund for replacement. However, in times of rising prices the accounting depreciation only provides for the funding of the original cost of the asset, which may be considerably lower than the replacement cost. The only way to provide for this increased replacement cost is to constantly revalue replaceable assets and to provide an extra depreciation charge based on this replacement value. This charge will affect both the current year and previous years since the amount charged in previous years will obviously be inadequate to meet the requirements of current inflated prices.

1.6 Financial disclosure of fixed assets

In terms of the Companies Act, financial statements should reflect in respect of all fixed assets the original cost, the accumulated depreciation or amortisation and the net book value, with the assets being grouped in appropriate major categories such as land and buildings, plant and machinery or goodwill. Alternatively, the assets can be shown at a valuation rather than cost price, with the accumulated depreciation and net book value again being reflected. Details of the valuation, including the date of the most recent valuation, the basis of the valuation, the names and qualifications of the valuers and whether they were independent valuers or employees of the undertaking, should be shown. Items which should be shown by way of note include the depreciation policy followed and the particulars of the undertaking's policy in respect of capitalisation of expenditure.

1.7 The importance of fixed asset reporting for financial analysis

Fixed assets form a large part of the asset structure of manufacturing undertakings and even for other types of undertaking. The analyst must therefore have a thorough grasp of the implications of the reporting on fixed assets and depreciation.

The three figures of cost or valuation, accumulated depreciation and net book value are used together with the depreciation charge in the income statement to determine various important aspects including the following:

The gross depreciable base, cost or valuation, is divided by the appropriate depreciation charge to determine the average depreciable life of the undertaking's assets. A lengthening of this life over time would suggest that the undertaking is deliberately lengthening the depreciable period, thereby reducing the annual depreciation charge, which could indicate problems with maintaining earnings. If such a trend is accompanied by income statement charges in respect of losses on disposal of fixed assets the analyst would have serious doubts about the quality of earnings of the undertaking;

The accumulated depreciation is divided by the appropriate depreciation charge to determine the average age of the undertaking's assets;

Capital expenditures, obtained from the director's report and the funds flow statement or from the notes to the financial statements, are compared with the annual depreciation charge to determine whether or not the firm is investing adequately in future production facilities. A continuing excess of annual depreciation charges over annual capital expenditure would indicate that the undertaking's assets are being allowed to age and become uncompetitive;

The depreciation charge affects the reported income and, in a manufacturing concern, the gross margins. Changes in depreciation policy should therefore be carefully monitored for the effect they may have on income. Careful note should also be made of gains or losses on disposal of fixed assets. This can be very tricky in times of inflation since assets may be sold at a price which, while representing a gain on their historical value, could still be a loss in terms of current cost.

2. The valuation of trading stock

Trading stock is the single largest asset in many trading concerns. Its valuation therefore determines the composition of the balance sheet and of course also determines the reported gross and net income for the period. The total value of the stock on hand is determined by multiplying the quantity on hand by the cost or value per unit. The quantity is determined either on a perpetual basis, with a record being kept of all stock movements, or on a periodic count basis. The latter is used ninety per cent of the time, but easy to use computer systems are making the former more accessible for an ever increasing number of undertakings. Whichever method is used, however, there should be periodic physical stock counts.

As far as cost goes, the general rule is that stock should be valued at the lower of cost or realisable value. This seems simple enough, but there are problems in evaluating cost of trading stock just as there were in evaluating the cost of fixed assets.

In certain cases there are no problems. A jeweller, for instance, maintains a careful record of all the quality items he has on hand and knows the cost of each one. Every diamond is separately identifiable and there are no problems of determining the cost of each one.

In most cases, however, the items are not individually identifiable and some sort of conventional system is applied in estimating the value of the trading stock on hand. In many cases stock is valued simply on the basis of the price paid for the last units received, but this method is dangerous in that it may include some holding profits in respect of older stock. It is, however, an approximation of the method favoured by the tax authorities and which is the first method to be discussed here.

The following table of physical quantities of stock will be used to illustrate the differences arising from the use of the different methods.

Date	Details	In	Out	Balance
Jan 10	Brought forward	0		0
Jan 12	Purchases @ R10 pu	10		10
Jan 15	Sales		5	5
Jan 20	Purchases @ R12 pu	10		15
Jan 22	Sales		10	5
Jan 25	Purchases @ R15 pu	10		15
Jan 30	Sales		5	10

2.1 The first-in, first-out method (FIFO)

The conventional methods ignore the actual physical units sold and make assumptions about the movement of stock. This method assumes that the items sold are the oldest ones in stock, even if they were taken from the most recently delivered batch.

A value table prepared in accordance with this method would look like this in respect of the above transactions:

Date	Details	In	Out	Balance
Jan 10	Brought forward	0		0
Jan 12	Purchased 10 @ R10 pu	100		100
Jan 15	Sold 5 @ R10 pu		50	50
Jan 20	Purchased 10 @ R12 pu	120		170
Jan 22	Sold 5 @ R10 pu		50	120
Jan 22	Sold 5 @ R12 pu		60	60
Jan 25	Purchased 10 @ R15 pu	150		210
Jan 30	Sold 5 @ R12 pu		60	150

The closing stock value represents the cost of the last shipment received, or 10 units at R15 per unit, irrespective of whether the ten left in stock actually came from this shipment or from an earlier one. In this particular case, valuing all the stock on hand at the last price paid would give the same result as the FIFO system at the end of January. If stock had been valued at 25 January, however, using the last value would have given a stock value of R225 rather than R210 shown by the FIFO method.

This method is generally regarded as giving the balance sheet value which is closest to actual cost of stock on hand, but it has some problems for profit determination. It is the method favoured above all others by the tax authorities, though they will accept some other methods.

2.2 The last-in, first-out method (LIFO)

This method is the exact opposite of FIFO. It presumes that items sold came out of the last batch received and that the remaining units are therefore from an older batch, and therefore cheaper in inflationary times. A value table would be as follows:

Date	Details	In	Out	Balance
Jan 10	Brought forward	0		0
Jan 12	Purchased 10 @ R10 pu	100		100
Jan 15	Sold 5 @ R10 pu		50	50
Jan 20	Purchased 10 @ R12 pu	120		170
Jan 22	Sold 10 @ R12 pu		120	50
Jan 25	Purchased 10 @ R15 pu	150		200
Jan 30	Sold 5 @ R15 pu		75	125

The units remaining in stock would then be 5 @ R10 per unit, or R50, and 5 @ R15 per unit, or R75, giving a total of R125.

This method understates balance sheet values and therefore shows a smaller gross profit and ultimately net profit. For this reason it has been banned by the income tax authorities even though it is the system which can reflect the truest picture of the undertaking's earnings. The reason for this is that, in times of rising prices, it writes off the increased cost of merchandise as the prices increase. Current costs are therefore written off against current income and the losses arising from increased cost of inputs are written off against the stock value.

This method therefore gives a more accurate picture of the periodic income, but gives a warped picture of the asset at the end of the period. The longer an item is held in stock the bigger its potential distorting effect. If the undertaking never lets its stock level of this item get below five it will always show that it has five at a cost of R10 in stock even if the current cost rises to a hundred times that amount.

Many undertakings in other countries are using both these methods. The income is determined using LIFO, but a balance sheet value based on FIFO is used. The difference between the two is shown as a reserve arising from the changing cost of stocks purchased or a so-called "holding profit".

2.3 The standard cost method

In terms of this method a standard or budgeted cost is applied to every unit of stock over the accounting period and any differences written off at the end of the period. A value table, assuming a standard value of R12, would look like this:

Date	Details	In	Out	Balance
Jan 10	Brought forward	0		0
Jan 12	Purchased 10 @ R12 pu	120		120
Jan 15	Sold 5 @ R12 pu		60	60
Jan 20	Purchased 10 @ R12 pu	120		180
Jan 22	Sold 10 @ R12 pu		120	60
Jan 25	Purchased 10 @ R12 pu	120		180
Jan 30	Sold 5 @ R12 pu		60	120

The closing stock would consist of 10 units at R12 each standard price. The difference between the actual purchase price and the standard purchase price, in this case a net of R10 unfavourable, would be written off against income for the period. At the start of the new year a new standard would be set and the opening stock revalued at this price.

2.4 The average cost method

This is the last method in common use. It has never been very popular because of the amount of calculation required, but computer systems have removed the drudgery from this and the system is being looked at again.

A value table using this system would look like this:

Date	Details	In	Out	Balance
Jan 10	Brought forward	0		0
Jan 12	Purchased 10 @ R10 pu	100		100
Jan 15	Sold 5 @ R10 pu		50	50
Jan 20	Purchased 10 @ R12 pu	120		170
Jan 22	Sold 10 @ R11,33 pu[1]		113,33	56,70
Jan 25	Purchased 10 @ R15 pu	150		206,70
Jan 30	Sold 5 @ R13,78 pu[2]		68,90	137,80

1.   5 @ R10 = R50

$$10 @ R12 = \frac{120}{170}$$

15 units cost R170 so that 1 unit must cost R11,33

2.   5 units @ R11,33 = R56,65

10 units @ R15   = $\frac{150,00}{206,65}$

15 units cost R206,65 so that one unit must cost R13,78

All purchases were booked in at actual cost, while all issues were booked out at the calculated value. The balance of stock on hand represents ten units at the calculated average price of R13,78.

2.5 The retail method

Another method which is used in some types of retail business is the valuation of stock at selling price. The method adopted is to add to the opening stock the total value of purchases to obtain value of goods available for sale, all at cost price, and then to do the same at selling price. The difference between these two values is then calculated as a percentage of cost to give the markup percentage. Sales at selling price are then deducted from cost of goods available for sale at selling price and the difference is stock on hand at period end at selling price. This is then adjusted by the markup percentage to get the cost of stock on hand. While this gives an approximation of stock value if there is no shrinkage of goods, it is obviously not adequate for all purposes and a physical count must be made at intervals. This method is widely used for interim profit determination, however.

2.6 The importance of stock reporting for financial analysis

The valuation of stock affects the determination of profit and the composition of the balance sheet. The management of stock is also one of the prime measures of management effectiveness. Any financial analysis must therefore take full note of all the information pertaining to stock which can be gleaned from the financial statements.

A preliminary to any calculations affecting stock would be to read the notes on valuation methods adopted and any other relevant matters. Where there are several classes of stock it is necessary to examine the particulars of each one separately as well as the whole lot collectively.

Changes in the composition of the total stock should be examined. If there is an increase in raw materials relative to other components of stock it may indicate poor purchasing management. Alternatively, it may represent intelligent stockpiling in the face of looming shortages or price increases. An increase in the work in process component may indicate problems with the manufacturing process, with factory throughput slowing down. Alternatively, in a contracting type of operation it may indicate that certain big contracts are nearing completion and that there will soon be large cash inflows. A build up of finished goods normally indicates problems with marketing of the goods, and is usually a sign of impending trouble.

The classical method of evaluating overall stock management is to calculate the stock turnover or the stock turnover period. A weakening in these ratios indicates management problems. At times an attempt is made to mask such problems by pushing deliveries out just before the financial year end, often by allowing debtors to purchase on extended credit terms. Such ploys can be picked up by examining the debtors collection period to see whether there are signs of a slackening in that area, for these two aspects of current assets normally relate very closely to each other.

3. Investments

Investments are held either as long term assets or as current assets. Long term investments are often referred to as trade investments and are often made for other than purely direct income reasons. A long term investment may have been made to ensure the co-operation of a supplier or of a customer, or even to ensure the survival of a valued supplier. In any case the financial statements should reflect the investment as a fixed asset at cost with a note stating the current value of the investment and the basis on which this valuation has been made. There is no problem with a quoted investment: the market value is available. Unquoted shares should be valued and the identity of the valuer revealed. Normally the investment will not be written up as the value rises, but any drop in value, which the undertaking is satisfied represents a permanent decrease in value, is taken into account and the value of the investment written down.

Short term investments are shown as current assets at cost, but a note must be given of the market value or realisable value at the reporting date.

4. Long term liabilities and lease commitments

An undertaking incurs long term debt to finance specific projects. This debt carries two obligations: to pay interest on the capital amount and to repay the capital amount on or by a specific date. It is the one aspect of the undertaking which is normally favourably influenced by inflation in that the debt will be repaid in full in monetary terms but with money which has lost a good deal of its value. No cognisance is taken of this in the financial statements, since the amount of the gain which the undertaking may achieve is undeterminable at the date of the statements and the convention of prudence prevents such a gain from being taken into account before it has been realised. It should nevertheless be considered when evaluating the company.

Long term debt can be in the form of debentures or of long term loans from one or more financial institutions. Factors to be noted include the term of the debt and the earliest dates on which redemption can be expected to take place, and the interest rate which is to be charged. If the debt is convertible into shares at any stage this must be noted, as must the terms of the conversion. Conversion could be compulsory or optional and the analyst must examine the current performance of the undertaking to estimate the likelihood of conversion and the effect that this is likely to have on the value of existing shares whose value is to be diluted by the issue of the new shares for the conversion.

Other factors which have to be taken into account when looking at long term debt include the issue of security. Where any assets of the undertaking are bound as security for its debt this must be disclosed. The analyst will then compare the value of the assets so bound and the amount of the debt in order to determine the company's future borrowing capacity.

Related to long term debt is the company's obligation in respect of leases. In terms of accounting practice as it is currently developing, the commitment in respect of leases will be disclosed as though it were a long term debt obligation, and the items leased will be disclosed as assets belonging to the company if the lease is of such a nature that ownership is to pass to the lessee at the conclusion of the lease. Full disclosure of the nature of this obligation will be made in the notes to the financial statements and must be considered in the evaluation of the total debt structure of the undertaking.

Where the lease is one in which the ownership of the asset will not pass to the lessee at the conclusion of the lease full details of future obligations in terms of the lease must be given in the notes to the financial statements. At present this is an optional treatment for all leases, but it can be expected that this option will be narrowed down, especially for listed companies, in the years ahead.

5. Intangible assets

As mentioned at the beginning of this chapter, intangible assets have a value which may be difficult to quantify. The general rule is that the asset is carried at cost and written off over a period. This would apply to such assets as the cost of purchasing a patent, goodwill arising on the purchase of a business and the cost of purchasing a franchise. All of these assets should contribute to the profits of an undertaking over time, but the question is over how much time? Sometimes the time may be stipulated, as in a franchise agreement, but the period during which goodwill makes a contribution to profits is a matter of judgement. The value at which goodwill is reflected in the balance sheet is dependent on the results of this judgement which determines the period of time over which it is written off.

Leasehold improvements are normally written off over the period of the lease and patents over the period until the patent expires so that there is not much doubt about how they should be disclosed. However, no attempt is made to determine a value for this type of asset. A patent could be worth a fortune, or it could be worth very little depending on the extent to which it provides the holder with a competitive advantage over his competitors.

Research and development costs are often capitalised and shown as assets on the face of the balance sheet. This is very common in the pharmaceutical industry where the costs of developing new drugs are carried as assets until the drug becomes marketable. The cost of development is then written off over a period not exceeding the expected useful product life cycle of the drug.

The great problem in recent years has been the topic of brand name accounting. It is held by some people that the brand names built up by a company have a value and that this value should be reflected in the balance sheet. Such a value is virtually impossible to quantify, however, and the exercise seems to many to be equivalent to creating goodwill in your own name.

Key words

Adequate disclosure

Intangible assets

Amortisation

Reducing or declining balance method

LIFO

Average cost

Tangible assets

Depreciation

Straight line method

Sum of the years digits

FIFO

Standard cost

Chapter 12

Developments in financial reporting

Accountants have been attacked as never before because their increasing stature in the business world has made them better targets. They have been attacked for presenting accurate but irrelevant information; for presenting inaccurate information; for ignoring the requirements of various interested parties and for a wide range of imperfections beside these.

The critics never seem to realise that the criticisms they offer are usually a parroting of the self-criticism of the professional accounting bodies, academic accountants and accounting practitioners and that this self-criticism is the basis for a great deal of research and experimentation. This chapter looks at some of this research and experimentation to show some of the directions in which financial reporting is moving.

1. **Introduction**

2. **Accounting for inflation**

3. **Human resources accounting**

4. **Reporting to newly important user groups**

5. **Conclusion**

1. Introduction

The accounting profession has grown in stature within the business community during the last half century because of its ability to supply the information without which no business can exist. Along with this increase in stature has come an increase in criticism. Some of this criticism is based on ignorance of what the accountant is actually trying to achieve and on the poor results obtained by using his information for purposes for which it was never designed, but some of it is valid. The accounting bodies are well aware of this and there is a great deal of research into ways of improving financial reporting. The two main areas in which this research is taking place are those of making the information more accurate and those of meeting the reporting requirements of those who have a stake in the business, albeit indirectly, but who were not previously regarded as requiring, or deserving, information. Under the first category must be mentioned the attempts to come to grips with the distortions caused by rising price levels so as to prepare reports which present the state of affairs more reasonably and the attempts to account for the investment which a business makes in its human resources. These are often the most valuable of its assets. Under the second category must come the special reports for employees of the undertaking and reports to the community in which the undertaking is operating, and these are all discussed briefly below.

2. Accounting for inflation

The western world has been beset with high levels of inflation on several occasions during the period which started just after the First World War. Price movements prior to this had generally been of a cyclical nature, with price rises and falls following each other. Information available in the United States, for instance, shows the prices of agricultural products to have been generally within 5% of the 1776 prices in 1920 despite high prices which had ruled at intervening times. Since then, however, prices have just moved upwards. This has naturally resulted in distortions in the economy as a whole, and financial reports based on the tried and tested system of historical costs have become inadequate for showing the financial position of a firm.

2.1 The ways in which inflation affects financial statements

2.1.1 Balance sheet values are always affected. Long-term assets reflected at historical cost, particularly land and buildings, are understated. With the high rates of inflation experienced since 1973 even short-term assets are shown at unrealistic values. Stocks are usually understated since their replacement cost is often considerably above historical cost, while debtors are often overstated in real terms since the real value of the payments received from the debtors will have decreased by the time the debts are paid. This is to some extent offset by the fact that the creditors are overstated for the same reason.

2.1.2 Profit figures are distorted because no provision is made for increased replacement costs of stock and fixed assets. This generally means that profits are overstated in real terms and that these "profits" are never translated into cash flows.

2.1.3 Cash flows are distorted because of the fact that cash holdings lose value. There is, therefore, a tendency to use debt to the greatest possible extent and to invest cash in some form of hard asset which should appreciate in monetary value. At the same time the increasing cost of replacing stock calls for higher monetary levels of working capital, so that the tendency is toward ever lower acid test ratios and liquidity generally.

2.2 Problems in adjusting figures shown in financial statements

2.2.1 The first problem which is always mentioned in any discussion of adjustments to financial statements is the one of subjectivity. Financial statements prepared on the historical cost basis are objective, but inaccurate. Is it better to have statements reflecting figures based on judgement, possibly accurate but not necessarily so and in any case difficult to verify?

2.2.2 Price movements are not uniform. There are indices which indicate the change in the purchasing power of money generally, such as the consumer price index, but in a particular industry these indices may be irrelevant. Machine tool prices have rocketed at a rate well in excess of the consumer price index, but many of the tools bought today are far more productive than those bought five or ten years ago. How does one go about valuing the machine tools of mixed ages held by a company? By application of an index or by the expensive method of revaluing at regular intervals?

2.2.3 There are obviously two components to changes in prices. One is the decline in the purchasing power of money, the second is the increase in the specific prices of certain assets. Is it desirable to separate these two components and show an adjustment in respect of general inflation and another in respect of specific price variations? For example, should one show that assets have increased in value from R10 000 to R16 000 of which R4 000 was due to the declining purchasing power of money and R2 000 due to wise investment in assets which increased in real value as well as in cost?

2.2.4 Lastly there is the thorny question of liabilities. Long-term liabilities on the face of the balance sheet are almost certainly overstated. The monetary value stated in the financial report is in terms of today's money, while payment will eventually be made in money which has considerably less real value than today's.

2.3 The approach of the accounting bodies to the problem of inflation

2.3.1 In the United States Financial Accounting Standard 33 lays down certain requirements which are applicable only to large companies (assets exceeding $1 billion or net assets exceeding $125 million). Historical cost statements are retained, but supplementary information is required giving changes due to general inflation and to specific price changes. In the United Kingdom SSAP 16 also requires historical cost statements as well as an income statement and balance sheet adjusted for inflation, though either set of statements can be presented as the prime set. South Africa does not as yet have a statement on inflation accounting. A guideline has been issued (4.003, now renumbered AC201) which will probably form the basis of an eventual statement, though it may be adjusted in the light of SSAP 16.

2.3.2 The South African guideline calls for a supplementary Current Cost Accounting (CCA) income statement. The assumption is made that all assets consumed will be replaced as necessary; where this is not so, allowance must be made for this fact. It explicitly recognises two types of CCA income which must be allowed for:

2.3.2.1 Entity operating income which is calculated in relation to the assets employed in the business; and

2.3.2.2 Owners' income, which is entity operating income adjusted for the effects of financial gearing and interest.

2.3.3 The presentation of a CCA income statement must give effect to three different adjustments. If all three are not made the information should not be presented as an income statement but should merely be supplementary information. The three adjustments are:

2.3.3.1 Depreciation adjustment

Depreciation should be calculated at standard rates on current cost of the equipment. The difference between depreciation calculated on this basis and that calculated on the historical cost basis will be the current cost depreciation adjustment. The guideline actually recommends using the average of original cost and current cost for this calculation, but the reasoning behind this is not very clear.

2.3.3.2 Cost of sales adjustment

This is an attempt to adjust for the effect of steadily increasing prices paid for trading stock during the year. The procedure is to calculate the average price for the year, using indices, then to convert the opening and closing stocks to this average price. A cost of sales figure is then calculated using opening and closing stocks at average price and purchases at actual cost. The difference between this cost of sales figure and the cost of sales calculated on the historical cost basis is then the CCA cost of sales adjustment.

2.3.3.3 Financial gearing adjustment

This is the most contentious of the three required adjustments. Entity operating income is not affected by it, but owners' equity is. It assumes that there will be no significant change in the financial gearing of the company and that any increases in cash required to maintain the current ratio will have to come from the shareholders' pockets. Any decrease in the monetary requirements will be for the benefit of the shareholders.

Where there is currently a net surplus of monetary assets over monetary liabilities the shareholders will therefore be charged with an amount representing this surplus multiplied by an appropriate index. This is justified by pointing out that the surplus means that a portion of the owners' equity is invested in monetary assets which will lose purchasing power.

Where there is a net surplus of monetary liabilities over monetary assets the credit to owners' income is rather more complex. It is based on the proportion of the first two adjustments which can be written back because they are financed by outside sources of funds, and accepts that some portion of the losses arising from higher depreciation and cost of sales is borne by outsiders.

The adjustment is calculated by multiplying the sum of the depreciation and cost of sales adjustments by the net monetary liabilities and dividing the answer by the sum of net monetary liabilities and other credit balances.

2.4 Probable changes to be expected in the standard when it appears

As mentioned above, it is likely that the South African standard will be strongly influenced by SSAP 16 in the United Kingdom. A current cost balance sheet may be required as well as an adjustment in respect of a loss on monetary assets in arriving at the entity income. IAS 15 "Information reflecting the effects of changing prices" should also have an influence on South African practice.

2.5 Revaluations of fixed assets

Guideline AC201 specifically acknowledges that the adjustments to the income statement mentioned above are not adequate to reflect all aspects of the effects of changing price levels. Guideline AC202 "Accounting for fixed asset revaluations" gives acknowledgement to the fact that fixed assets, particularly land and buildings, should be revalued at regular intervals so as to reflect a reasonable value on the face of the balance sheet, though the period is not specified and no method for revaluation is laid down.

2.6 Ratio analysis and inflation

Several ratios have been developed in response to the effects of inflation on an enterprise, particularly on the liquidity. The following is the only one which seems to have gained any general acceptance.

2.6.1 *New liquidity ratio*

This ratio has as its objective determining the extent of the pressure on an enterprise to raise new finance or retaining earnings during inflationary times. The numerator of the ratio is (stock + debtors − creditors), the three items which will automatically have to increase in monetary terms if the same level of activity is to be maintained. The smaller this figure the better off the company will obviously be, since the creditors will be bearing most of the effects of inflation. This figure is then divided by the total long-term funds in the business, whether owners' equity or long-term loans. The lower the ratio, the better off the firm will be; the higher the ratio, the greater will be the pressure to raise new finance to increase the monetary value of its activities.

2.7 An example of a supplementary inflation adjusted income statement

The following are the financial statements that have been prepared on a historical cost basis. No inflation adjusted statements have ever been prepared.

CROESUS LIMITED
Trading and profit and loss accounts for the year ended 30 June 1988

Sales		1 000 000
Cost of sales		800 000
Opening stock	100 000	
Purchases	820 000	
Closing stock	(120 000)	
Gross profit		200 000
Interest paid	15 000	
Depreciation (20% on cost)	24 000	
Other expenses	116 000	155 000
Net income for the period		45 000
Taxation		20 000
Net income after taxation		25 000
Retained earnings brought forward		75 000
		100 000
Dividends paid		15 000
Retained earnings carried forward		85 000

CROESUS LIMITED
Balance sheet at 30 June 1988
Equities

Share capital		25 000
Retained earnings		85 000
Shareholder's equity		110 000
Long-term liability		90 000
		200 000

Assets

Fixed assets		
Land and buildings		100 000
Plant and machinery at cost	120 000	
Deduct depreciation	60 000	60 000
		160 000
Net current assets		40 000
Current assets	120 000	
Stock	60 000	
Debtors	50 000	
Cash	10 000	
Current liabilities		80 000
Creditors	75 000	
Taxation	5 000	
		200 000

The land and buildings have recently been revalued by outside valuers who estimated its current value at R160 000.

The current replacement cost of the plant and machinery is R200 000.

The index applicable to the trading stocks reads as follows at the relevant times:

When the opening stock was bought	200
Average for the year	220
When the closing stock was bought	240
At the end of the financial year	250

Required: Prepare an inflation adjusted supplementary income statement.

Answer:

Workings:

1. Cost of sales adjustment

In order to eliminate the effects of inflation all three components of cost of sales must be reduced to average prices for the year by use of the index figures.

Opening stock adjustment: 220/200 × 100 000 = 110 000
Purchases: No adjustment since they were bought at the average price for the year.
Closing stock adjustment: 220/240 × 120 000 = 110 000

The adjusted cost of sales is therefore		820 000
Opening stock	110 000	
Purchases	820 000	
Closing stock	(110 000)	
Unadjusted cost of sales		800 000
Cost of sales adjustment is therefore		20 000

2. Depreciation adjustment

Depreciation on replacement value at 20%	40 000
Depreciation charged	24 000
Depreciation adjustment	16 000

3. Accumulated depreciation adjustment

Depreciation charged in previous years (60 000– 24 000)	36 000
This obviously represents depreciation for 1,5 years at R24 000 per year. Adjusted depreciation at R40 000 per year for 1,5 years is	60 000
The adjustment to accumulated depreciation is therefore	24 000

4. Gearing adjustment

Calculation of net monetary assets/liabilities position

Monetary liabilities

Long term liability	90 000
Creditors	75 000
Taxation	5 000
	170 000

Monetary assets		
Debtors	50 000	
Cash	10 000	60 000
Net monetary liabilities		110 000
Shareholders' interest in the company		
Shareholders' equity per balance sheet		110 000
Increases in value of assets		
Land and buildings	60 000	
Plant and machinery	40 000	
Stock ((250/240 × 120 000) − 120 000)	5 000	105 000
Total adjusted shareholders' investment		215 000
Net monetary liabilities		110 000
Total adjusted investment in the undertaking		325 000

The proportion of the loss due to inflation which is borne by the outside suppliers is therefore 110/325 = 33,85%.

CROESUS LIMITED

Supplementary current cost income statement for the year ended 30 June 1988

Turnover		1 000 000
Net operating income		60 000
Interest paid		15 000
Net income before taxation		45 000
Current cost adjustment in respect of cost of sales and depreciation		36 000
Net entity income		9 000
Gearing adjustment (33,85% of 36 000)		12 186
Net shareholder income		21 186
Taxation		20 000
Adjusted income after tax		1 186
Retained income brought forward	75 000	
Adjustment to accumulated depreciation	24 000	51 000
Amount available for distribution		52 186
Dividend paid		15 000
Adjusted retained earnings		37 186

This statement obviously paints a very different picture of the position of the company from the one we get from the unadjusted statements. It is clear that the company is actually paying dividends out of reserves and that what appeared to be a not too excessive dividend of sixty per cent of the profit for the year is actually far more than the company can afford to pay.

This is the major purpose of this statement. It must show the shareholders the extent to which the company is providing for its future by retaining an adequate part of its profits to finance replacement of assets and any planned expansion.

3. Human resource accounting

3.1 The complaint that accounting reports give dysfunctional information in the longer term

One complaint often made against accountants is that their reports concentrate too heavily on the short term. Income statements cover a period of one year, and companies are too often judged on the performance of that year only. This may sometimes lead to decisions being made which, while they could improve the profit in a particular year, could be dysfunctional in the longer term. One of the fields in which such decisions could be made is that of human resources.

All undertakings employ people; these people are often the most valuable resource that the enterprise has. Service organisations are obviously dependent on their personnel, but manufacturing, retailing and wholesaling and agriculture are just as dependent on their staff, even if they do have other important assets. In times of economic stress, however, many managements start cutting costs by getting rid of staff. Reducing the wage bill is certainly one way of cutting costs in the short term but there are doubts about its wisdom in the longer term. Japanese companies have made inroads into world markets by producing high quality products at low prices, but they have never cut costs by retrenching staff, and the question arises of whether there is not a lesson to be learnt here.

3.2 One attempt to incorporate a long term factor

From the accounting point of view there is an acceptance that most current accounting reports are short term in nature, though attempts are being made to incorporate longer term effects. One of the avenues being explored is that of accounting for the enterprise's investment in human resources. The idea first surfaced early in the 1960's that costs involved in training of staff were not actually costs which should be written off immediately. If the matching concept is to be consistently applied then the costs of training a man to do a job should be written off over the period that he uses the skills acquired by that training. After all, if he leaves the enterprise it will have to incur those costs again in training someone else, while if he stays those costs will not have to be re-incurred. Actual costs are more than just those of recruitment and training, of course. Employers incur costs in respect of employees other than these and wages for work performed. There are various welfare schemes, pension plans, recreational facilities and others whereby the employer strives to increase the employment satisfaction of the employee and thereby to win his loyalty and long service.

The use of an accounting system which capitalised the costs of recruiting and training employees would, it was postulated, give more relevant information for a decision on whether to lay off staff or not. If the amount of these capitalised costs were available management would be able to assess the future impact of a layoff by facing up to the fact that an asset worth a certain amount was being scrapped in order to cut costs in the short term and that it would cost a certain amount in recruitment, training and other costs to replace that asset when it was required during an economic upswing.

Human resource accounting (HRA) thus developed as a tool of management. It soon became apparent that it would also serve a purpose if it were to be incorporated into the published financial statements. One of the matters into which the analyst looks before passing judgement of the financial position of an enterprise is the question of human resources. There has always been an attempt to find out what the position is as regards staff turnover, efficiency, level of training achieved for the required tasks and so forth. These matters were never quantified, but human resource accounting provides a method for such quantification. The appearance of an amount in respect of human resources in the financial statements of an undertaking also gives an idea of the importance of these resources relative to the other assets of the undertaking.

3.3 Objections to human resource accounting

Objections have of course been raised to the concept. The most persistent of these is that workers are free, not slaves. They are not owned by the company and so should not appear as assets in the records of that company. They can leave at any time, so that the company does not possess any future economic benefit. As against this, proponents of the concept argue that while this is true of each individual employee, it is not true of the labour force as a whole. Recognising that the labour force plays a very important part in the economic future of an enterprise is only realistic, even if some of the individual members of that labour force will be leaving at some date in the near future.

3.4 Problems with human resource accounting

3.4.1 The greatest problem is that of measurement. How much of the expense incurred by a company in developing its human resources is actually capital expenditure and how much is just ordinary running cost? How should the capitalised amount be written off? There have not been satisfactory answers to these questions and this is what has prevented human resources accounting from being generally adopted. Several American companies have adopted some form of HRA, notably the R G Barry Corporation which has been extensively written up in the accounting literature.

Two measurement methods have been developed, both of which have adopted the individual employee as a starting point. The values of individual employees are then added together to obtain the total human resources value, but it has also been suggested that values could be determined for groups of employees rather than individuals. Both the methods try to assess the economic benefit which would accrue to the firm from the continued employment of that employee.

3.4.1.1 The first method is that which has been broadly described above. The costs involved in training and the rest are capitalised and written off over the expected employment period of the employee.

3.4.1.2 The second method looks at the matter from the other side altogether. The benefit of the employee to the enterprise is reflected in the salary he earns, goes this argument. His future value can therefore be determined by discounting the amounts which he is expected to earn over his working life at the enterprise. This amount would be reflected as an asset and written off over the expected working life of the employee.

3.5 Current reporting on human resources

Because many firms have experienced difficulty with the concept of HRA, most reporting on human resources is currently in non-financial terms. The financial statements of Anglo-Alpha in appendix 2 provide a good example. Full relevant particulars of the senior managers and the directors are given: position held, years of service and academic and other relevant qualifications. The rest of the personnel are dealt with in the statistics, the social report and the notes on staff turnover.

Whether the future holds improvements in HRA to the extent that it becomes generally acceptable or whether the type of reporting in the Anglo-Alpha statements is refined and expanded is anybody's guess at this stage. What is certain is that recognition has been granted to the importance of the labour force in evaluating the economic future of an undertaking and that this will lead to greater demands for reporting on human resources, their maintenance and their deployment.

4. Reporting to stakeholders

In recent years the claims of various user groups which were previously not recognised have been receiving increasing attention. The accounting profession has been trying to move with the times and to present information which is relevant to these groups who have a stake, no matter how indirect, in the future of the business under consideration.

4.1 Employees

Economic activity requires capital and labour. Both have a vested interest in the performance of any economic entity in which they invest, whether the investment is one of money or of time and effort. The supplier of capital wants information on which to base his investment policy, while the supplier of labour wants information on which to base his wage claims and his decision on whether to continue working for that employer. The investor of money has long been recognised as having a right to information relevant for his purposes and this right is enshrined in companies legislation, in most of the accounting standards which have been issued, and in all accounting texts. The right of employees or employee organisations to information has been completely ignored until very recently and there is still little clarity on what information is required by these people.

4.2 The value added statement

One early attempt to supply information relevant to employees was the development of a value added statement, which has been found generally useful when dealing with people of a non-financial background. The concept is relatively simple and can be explained as follows: if a firm purchases raw materials for R100 and, after processing, sells them for R200, it has added R100 in value to the raw materials. This R100 would then be split up to show how much of the added value was due to expenditure on wages, how much on overhead costs and how much was left as profit to the firm. While it is a concept which has been borrowed from the field of economics which attempts to work in real values, the accounting statement of added value is generally merely a rearrangement of the income statement. More and more companies are incorporating such a statement into their annual reports, but there is as yet no standard which defines the form of this statement. An example is the one by Anglo-Alpha in appendix 2. The primacy of employee interest in this report is emphasised by the fact that the notes to this statement contain the relevant information concerning staff turnover, absenteeism, retrenchments and absolute numbers of employees in various categories.

For Engineering Firm (Pty) Ltd the value added statement would appear as follows:

Value added statements for Engineering Firm (Proprietary) Limited

	Note	1985	1984	1983
Sales for the year		4 650 000	4 550 000	3 665 000
Amounts paid to outsiders for goods and services	1	2 535 000	2 542 500	1 918 500
Value added		2 115 000	2 007 500	1 746 500
Investment income		24 500	3 000	0
Total value added		2 139 500	2 010 500	1 746 500

	1985	1984	1983
Distributed as follows:			
Employees			
Salaries, wages and benefits	1 910 000	1 718 000	1 439 000
Providers of finance: Interest	4 500	31 000	13 000
Providers of capital: Dividends	0	0	0
Government: Taxes	0	58 000	28 000
Replacement of assets: Depreciation	103 000	105 500	125 500
Expansion and growth: Retained income	122 000	98 000	142 000
	2 139 500	2 010 500	1 746 500

This statement, prepared from the information in the financial statements, is not wholly accurate. In actual fact the share of government is far larger, since there is an element of taxation in most purchases in the form of VAT input taxes and various levies and duties and the amounts paid to employees are shown inclusive of the PAYE tax deductions which were paid. Overall, though, it gives a good picture of what happened to the wealth created. There is just one point which is of concern to private companies generally: should the remuneration paid to the director/shareholders be shown as payment to suppliers of capital? Or should it possibly be shown separately? This is a major problem of this type of statement, with workers often wanting a split between the different classes of employees in order to satisfy themselves of the relative amount coming to their own class. The calculation of the amount paid to outsiders is given below:

Note 1:	1985	1984	1983
Amounts paid to outsiders			
Sales	4 650 000	4 550 000	3 665 000
Operating income	102 000	184 000	183 000
Total expenses	4 548 000	4 366 000	3 482 000
Not paid outside	2 013 000	1 821 000	1 563 500
Direct wages	1 475 000	1 400 000	1 150 000
Salaries—factory	165 000	145 000	120 000
Salaries	90 000	65 000	69 000
Directors' salaries	180 000	108 000	99 000
Depreciation	103 000	105 00	125 500
	2 535 000	2 542 500	1 918 500

4.3 The employees' report

South Africa can expect this subject to become important in the near future with the rapidly developing sophistication of the various trade unions. In the United Kingdom the matter has been considered relevant for many years and has been included in various bits and pieces of legislature, but there has never been any complete survey of what should be reported to employees, nor is there any standard in sight which may clarify the matter. Many companies, however, have been providing employees with special reports for a number of years.

These reports generally contain an abridged version of the financial statements presented to shareholders, often presented graphically rather than in tabular form, plus information relating specifically to employees. The following are samples of the information currently presented:

4.3.1 Details of manpower, broken down by categories, of absenteeism, of turnover and retrenchments and of any planned changes in work methods or other factors which may influence the levels of manpower or the composition of the labour force.

4.3.2 Manpower performance details such as sales per employee, assets per employee and details of productivity increases and how they were accomplished.

4.3.3 Rates of pay, pay policy, pensions, sick benefits and other benefits to which employees are entitled. The Trade Union Congress asked in 1970 that full details of directors' remuneration also be included but later dropped this when some companies not only did this but also gave details of the remuneration of leading trade union members. The current policy requested by this body is for details of remuneration in the value added statement to be split between management/ supervisory remuneration and other remuneration.

4.3.4 Conditions of service including policies on recruitment, promotion, redundancy and redeployment.

4.4 No request for any of the above information can be construed as being unreasonable for the employee (or employee organisation) wishing to evaluate the position of the undertaking from his point of view. Most of the information mentioned above is actually contained in the annual financial statements of Anglo-Alpha in appendix 2, but it is not in a concise form which could be readily understood by the employees of the company. There will undoubtedly be calls for such concise employees' annual reports as time goes on, but just how much information will be required in these and the form which they will take is anyone's guess.

A British survey conducted by Paul Norkett found that 43,3% of respondent companies presented special employees' reports and that 39,3% published relevant information in the company magazine. Whatever the method used, employers were presenting information to employees largely to improve industrial relations, but many (67,3%) had fears that the information would be misinterpreted by employees who had no training whatever to assist them in their understanding of the matters reported to them.

4.5 Social reporting

Large companies exist in a community which they influence. Mining companies ruin areas of the countryside, industrial companies pollute the water and air resources of the country and ethical drug companies produce medicines which sometimes have undesirable side-effects. These and other types of operation exist by using the resources of the community and by selling to the community. They modify the community by these actions, sometimes in undesirable ways, so that the community at large must have some right to information concerning the activities of these companies.

The concept of the social responsibility of business is not a new one. Classical economic theory held that profit maximisation was the goal of a business and that in order to maximise profit it was necessary for the business to form a symbiotic relationship with its community, a relationship whereby the community would benefit as well as the business. Any other type of relationship would result in the business making only short-term profits since the impoverishment of the community would destroy the business. This approach was developed in the 1970's, but another view developed at the same time that business existed for the community and that profit maximisation by the business should not be regarded as the major objective. Profits should only be at a satisfactory level concomitant with community objectives. Proponents of this approach failed to state how a satisfactory profit was to be defined or how anyone would be encouraged to accept the risks of a business venture if his level of profit was to be kept to what some bureaucrat felt was "satisfactory".

However, it is now widely accepted that large companies do have responsibilities to their communities and it will be seen that many companies are starting to include information on such matters as the following in their financial reports:

4.5.1 Environmental matters, such as pollution control and reclamation of land used for mining and conservation activities, whether of own accord or by support of public conservation bodies.

4.5.2 Product quality maintenance, guarantees, advertising policies and product research.

4.5.3 General community activities such as support for charitable institutions, general involvement in community affairs and policies regarding recruitment of employees in relation to local communities.

5 International accounting standardisation

Since the end of the second world war there has been a tremendous increase in international trade, which sparked some interest in international accounting practices and the differences between the way in which the accounting profession operated in different countries. This remained a fairly academic interest until the 1980's however, when the growing international trade was followed by a dramatic surge in over the border investment. There had always been investment in other countries, of course. Britain and France had invested extensively in their colonies and dominions and in the United States, while the United States had invested in Europe and to a lesser extent in Latin America. All these investments, however, were direct, in that a company in one of the investor countries would set up a wholly owned subsidiary in the other country and have no need for interpreting the financial statements which would be drawn up to meet the needs of head office. Of course, there would be statutory accounts to meet the local legal requirements but these would simply be one of the necessary costs of doing business abroad. As increasing market efficiencies world-wide, partly due to the electronic revolution, and greater competition within the financial services industry forced investors to look beyond individual markets to enhance returns and to spread portfolio risk, however, there came a tremendous surge in cross-border equity investment. This meant that fund managers and individual investors started looking at financial statements prepared in other countries and according to different requirements. The difficulties created by this led to calls for international standardisation. Companies which started to list their shares in stock exchanges in more than one country also found that they were having to prepare several different sets of financial statements to meet the requirements of the different stock exchanges.

At present the moves towards standardisation have been very tentative, with the general movement being to accept that local circumstances may prevent the profession from standardising world-wide until the politicians see some benefits in the move and change their legislative requirements, but that it may be possible to devise a formula that will satisfy all stock exchange requirements and that a supplementary set of statements may be required from every company which is listed anywhere. The company would then prepare a set of statements to meet local legislative requirements, but also a set to meet investor requirements. This set may be produced in a number of languages, with European companies now quite commonly presenting statements in their own language, together with a set in English and a set in French or German.

There are two major problems facing the investor looking at the financial statements of a company in another country. The first is that of language which, as mentioned above, has to some extent been tackled by the larger European companies. However, attempts to overcome this problem sometimes lead to problems of misinterpretation. Anyone who has tried to follow the assembly instructions written in English for a product manufactured in Taiwan or Korea should be able to appreciate the problems which can be caused by translation.

The second problem is far more serious. Financial statements are prepared in different countries for different purposes and for different audiences, and have therefore been developed along different lines. There are several different models for accounting reports, of which the major ones are

1. The Anglo-American model, which is also used throughout the Commonwealth.

   This model tries to present a fair view of the company's performance and financial position from the point of view of the equity investor, both for investment decisions and for protection of the shareholder. It requires extensive disclosure of assets and liabilities and rather more limited disclosure of operating incomes and expenditures. Independent audits are compulsory and disclosure of such matters as directors and management remuneration are generally required. Stock exchanges in these countries are a prime source of equity finance, with strong participation in equities by individual investors. Accounting practices in Britain and the United States, which were virtually identical earlier in the century, have diverged somewhat in recent years as Britain has moved closer to European practice in many ways.

2. The South American model, which has its roots in the Anglo-American model but which has had to contend with volatile and highly inflationary economic circumstances. The emphasis in this model has moved to accounting for the effects of inflation and hyperinflation, but techniques have not yet been standardised with the result that financial statements prepared in different Latin American countries are not all comparable.

3. The European model is not really a single model, since each country in Europe has its own requirements, but the European system can be logically grouped within one model because of certain similarities. Also, it is in Europe where the greatest degree of standardisation is taking place as a result of European economic integration. Companies in continental Europe have traditionally been financed not by individual investors but by large institutions, particularly the banks. Financial statements have therefore generally been drawn up to meet the requirements of the banks, which usually have direct access to the financial records of the company anyway. The requirements for independent audit have therefore not been regarded as of

great importance and, until the EC's Fourth Directive in 1986, only the largest of companies were subject to audit. Each country has its own reporting requirements brought about by its own historical circumstances. France is in the worst position, since it has for some reason retained the compulsory method of accounting introduced by the Nazi regime. This system was introduced in order to enable the occupying forces to plan the direction of the captive economy, and all companies were forced to present their statements in identical format to simplify planning. The documents produced are very much of the same calibre as those prepared for the Department of Statistics in this country, and have about as much relevance to the fair presentation of financial position. German financial statements, on the other hand, are prepared for purposes of tax determination and have no interest whatever in fair presentation.

It should be noted that the Netherlands is an exception to the general European model. Historically, the Netherlands is the home of the joint stock company, with shares being sold by public subscription for all the large ventures of the colonial period. Widespread public ownership of shares has continued to be a feature of the economic scene there, with the result that accounting practice is far more like the Anglo-American model. The Dutch have also been pioneers in the application of techniques to account for the effects of inflation.

4. The Japanese model, which is unique but of great importance because of Japan's great economic power. The model has elements of the Anglo-American model and elements of the European model. It is largely influenced by tax regulations and has no pretensions to fairness of presentation. Only historical costs are used, depreciation is in accordance with tax allowable rates and a uniform format is laid down for the presentation of the financial statements. It does require consolidation of the results of publicly traded groups, but does not require this from other groups. It also has the unique feature of using historical exchange rates when accounting for foreign investments rather than showing these at a current conversion rate.

There are many obstacles to standardisation, and it is more likely that some sort of harmonisation can be achieved with different countries still producing financial statements for the particular group which may be important in that country, whether banks or individual investors or government agencies, but taking into account the general requirements of true and fair presentation. Most of the important regulatory agencies world wide have now joined the consultative committee of the International Accounting Standards Committee (IASC), with the main exception being the governmental agencies in France. Hopefully, these bodies can now work together in order to produce an internationally acceptable way of presenting financial reports.

6. Conclusion

Accounting will never be perfect. However, it can be improved and there are many people working on the problem areas which exist if accounting, and specifically reporting, is to be improved. There is also constant monitoring of changes in technology, economic circumstances, laws and social behaviour patterns since these can bring new requirements to and place new pressures on the accountant and his profession. The above are a few of the areas under investigation at present, but there are others which may be of greater importance. Whatever, accounting is not stagnant but is doing its best to meet the challenges posed by the changes taking place in our society.

Questions and exercises on Part Two

Test-yourself questions

Circle T or F to indicate your answer

1. The total amount of an undertaking's assets would not be affected by a cash purchase of office equipment   T   F
2. A one man business is an accounting entity   T   F
3. The capital of a business should be shown as an asset on the balance sheet   T   F
4. Total capital minus liabilities equals assets   T   F
5. Expenses include depreciation and cost of goods sold   T   F
6. The ledger is a book in which all the transactions of an undertaking are classified according to their nature   T   F
7. An increase in expenses can be balanced by a decrease in liabilities   T   F
8. Source documents are used to make entries directly into the ledger   T   F
9. Money drawn out of a business by the owner is an expense of the business   T   F
10. Payment of an account for goods purchased two months ago is an expense   T   F

Assignment material

Question 2.1: Multiple choice questions

Mark the correct answer by entering the appropriate number on your answer sheet.

1.1 When a business receives money from a debtor (a person who has bought on credit), the effect on the balance sheet is
   (a) An increase in capital
   (b) An increase in assets
   (c) No change in capital
   (d) A decrease in liabilities

1.2 A company's total capital would be increased by
   (a) Issuing shares to pay for a new building
   (b) Collecting money from a debtor
   (c) Selling a building at its value as shown on the balance sheet
   (d) All three of the above

1.3 A company purchased goods for resale for R100 000 on credit. The result was
   (a) An increase in its assets
   (b) No change in its assets
   (c) No change in its liabilities
   (d) A decrease in capital

1.4 A company made a cash purchase of goods for resale for R100 000. The result was
    (a) An increase in its assets
    (b) No change in its assets
    (c) An increase in its capital
    (d) A decrease in its capital

1.5 A company purchased a new computer system for R250 000. It paid a deposit of R50 000 and signed a suspensive sale agreement for the balance. The company's assets
    (a) Increased by R250 000
    (b) Increased by R200 000
    (c) Decreased by R100 000
    (d) Increased by R100 000

1.6 Joe Welsher borrowed R50 000, R40 000 of which he used to repay another loan. His total liabilities
    (a) Increased by R50 000
    (b) Decreased by R40 000
    (c) Increased by R10 000
    (d) Decreased by R10 000

1.7 Horatio Alger received R10 000 for a series of articles he had written.
    (a) His capital increased by R10 000
    (b) His assets increased by R10 000
    (c) Both of the above
    (d) Neither of the above

1.8 Which of the following would be regarded as a transaction
    (a) Sending a written order for goods to a supplier
    (b) Granting a discount to a customer when he settles his account
    (c) The death of the managing director due to a heart attack
    (d) Catching the cashier forging the managing director's signature on a cash cheque

1.9 A company's purchase of a new machine will increase its total assets if
    (a) The machine is bought for cash
    (b) The machine is bought on credit
    (c) Both of the above
    (d) Neither of the above

1.10 If a business settles its accounts payable by cash payments there will be no effect on
    (a) Assets
    (b) Liabilities
    (c) Capital
    (d) None of the above

Question 2.2

A list of transactions appears below. Fill in the amounts in the appropriate columns to show the effects of these transactions on the financial position of the undertakings concerned. Where a transaction involves a variety of amounts which could lead to both an increase and a decrease in a single block, enter *all* such amounts. Copy this table on to your answer sheet.

No	Transaction	Assets	Liabilities	Capital
1	Borrowed R100 000 cash on security of a mortgage bond			
2	Paid cash wages of R5 000			
3	Purchased a new car for R150 000 by paying a deposit of R50 000 and agreeing to pay off R100 000 over three years			
4	Made a cash purchase of R10 000 worth of goods for resale			
5	Bought R10 000 worth of goods for resale on credit			
6	Lost equipment worth R50 000 due to a fire and received an insurance payout of R40 000			
7	Returned unsatisfactory goods costing R10 000 to the supplier			
8	Sold goods which had cost R1 000 for R1 500			
9	Made a cash payment of an insurance premium of R1 000			
10	Received a payment of R1 500 on his overdue account from a customer			

Question 2.3

A list of possible ledger account categories appears below. Copy this table onto your answer sheet and place a cross in the appropriate column to show the category to which each of the items belongs.

No	Account name	Assets	Liabilities	Capital
1	Motor vehicles			
2	Patents owned			
3	Accounts payable			
4	Cash on hand			
5	Stock of goods for resale			
6	Net profit on a transaction			
7	Taxes payable			
8	Investment in another business			
9	Amount owing on suspensive sale			
10	Amount drawn out of business by owner			

Question 2.4

	Assets +	Liabilities −	Capital −	Expenses +	Income −
Assets−	1	2	3	4	5
Liabilities+	6	7	8	9	10
Capital+	11	12	13	14	15
Expenses−	16	17	18	19	20
Income+	21	22	23	24	25

State in which block of the matrix each of the following transactions should be placed. For example, the transaction "Paid cash wages" would appear in block 4 in the Assets − row and in the Expenses + column

1. Invoiced a client for professional services rendered.
2. Bought raw materials on credit.
3. Paid cash for office furniture.
4. Drew raw materials from store and used them for a contract.
5. Wrote off depreciation on fixed assets.
6. Revalued fixed assets upwards.
7. Paid cash wages.
8. Issued shares to pay for a new building.
9. Used money from a personal account to pay an account payable of a one man business.
10. Settled an account from a supplier.

Question 2.5

Copy the table below onto your answer sheet and fill in all the blank spaces using only +,– or 0 to indicate the net effect of these journal entries on the various aspects of a company's financial reports:

		Assets	Liabilities	Income	Expenses
1	Recording expenses which had been accidentally omitted				
2	Recording income which had been accidentally omitted				
3	Collecting cash from accounts receivable				
4	Providing for taxation to be paid				
5	Purchasing goods for resale on credit				

Question 2.6

Copy the table below onto your answer sheet and enter as many figures as necessary in each blank space to indicate all the effects of each transaction on the overall financial position of a company. Use pluses or minuses to indicate increases or decreases:

		Total assets	Total liabilities	Total capital
1	Issued shares for R100 000			
2	Borrowed R200 000 from the bank			
3	Purchased shop fittings on credit for R20 000			
4	Purchased factory machinery and equipment for R250 000. A deposit of R50 000 was paid, with the balance to be paid off			
5	Purchased raw materials on credit for R50 000			
6	Paid cash for factory operating expenses of R40 000			
7	Sold goods on credit for R50 000 (ignore cost of goods sold)			
8	Sold goods for cash for R50 000 (ignore cost of goods sold)			
9	Paid R20 000 on accounts payable			
10	Collected R25 000 from accounts receivable			

Question 2.7

The following types of transactions will maintain the balance of the accounting equation. The first two will also result in the totals of either side of the equation remaining unchanged:

1.   An increase and a decrease of an equal amount in assets, as when cash is decreased to purchase a fixed asset;
2.   An increase and a decrease of an equal amount in either liabilities or capital;
3.   An increase in an asset and an increase of an equal amount in liabilities or capital; and
4.   A decrease in assets and a decrease of an equal amount in capital or liabilities.

The following transactions, which are independent of each other, fall into one of the above categories. You are required to copy the table on to your answer sheet and to put a tick in one of the numbered columns (the numbers have the meaning accorded to the number above) and to put a figure in the last column to show the change in the total of the accounting equation in each case:

	1	2	3	4	Change in total of equation
1					
2					
3					
4					
5					
6					
7					
8					
9					
10					

1.   Shares were issued for R100 000.
2.   Goods for resale costing R20 000 were bought on credit.
3.   Machinery costing R20 000 was bought for cash.
4.   A loan of R250 000 was obtained on security of a first mortgage bond.
5.   A dividend of R100 000 was paid.
6.   Accounts payable of R20 000 were settled in cash.
7.   The owner of a one man business transferred his private car to the business. The car was valued at R100 000.
8.   Cash of R10 000 was received in respect of accounts receivable.
9.   Professional services were rendered and charged out to the client at R15 000.
10.   Operating expenses of R10 000 were paid in cash.

Question 2.8

Copy the tables below onto your answer sheet. Use the first table to trace the effect of the following transactions.

Enter the details of each transaction in the appropriate blocks with a + or − sign and determine the value of each block at the end of the period. Transfer these values to the appropriate space in the balance sheet which follows.

1. John Brown decided to start his own furniture manufacturing business. He drew R30 000 out of his lifetime savings and started a bank account for his business in the name of JB Furniture Factory.
2. He found a suitable building and purchased it for R150 000, obtaining a mortgage loan for the full amount.
3. He purchased some equipment for R50 000, paying a 10 % deposit and signing a suspensive sale agreement for the balance to be paid at R1 500 per month for the next five years.
4. He also put some machines that he owned into the business. These machines were valued at R80 000.
5. He purchased wood, glue, paint and varnish, nails, screws and other raw materials on credit for R45 000.
6. He employed several workers and paid wages of R15 000 in the first month of operations.
7. He used R25 000 of the raw materials during the first month of operations.
8. Other factory expenses, all on credit, were R10 000 for the first month.
9. There was no work in progress at the end of the first month, so that all the costs in 6, 7 and 8 above went into finished goods.

Assets	Liabilities
Bank (1)	Accounts payable (6)
Machinery and equipment (2)	Mortgage loan (7)
Land and buildings (3)	
Stock of raw materials (4)	**Capital**
	Owner's capital (8)
Stock of finished goods (5)	

JB FURNITURE FACTORY
Balance sheet after one month of operations

Capital—John Brown	9
Liabilities	10
Mortgage loan	11
Accounts payable	12
	13
Assets	
Land and buildings	14
Machinery and equipment	15
Stock of raw materials	16
Stock of finished goods	17
Bank	18
	19

Question 2.9

The first row across reflects the balances on the ledger accounts of D R Kwak, a surgeon who practices on his own, at the start of the month. The subsequent rows reflect the effects of transactions which took place during the month.

	Cash	Accounts receivable	Stock of medicines	Surgery equipment	Accounts payable	Capital D R Kwak
1	10 000	25 000	1 000	50 000	10 000	76 000
2	− 3 000				− 3 000	
3	− 1 000		+ 1 000			
4	+ 5 000	− 5 000				
5		+ 500	− 500			
6	− 3 000			+ 3 000		
7	− 1 000					− 1 000
8			+ 1 000		+ 1 000	
9		+ 10 000				+ 10 000
10				+ 2 000	+ 2 000	
11	+ 5 000					+ 5 000

You are required to describe the transaction which led to each of the above amounts being entered.

Question 2.10

Copy the following tables on to your answer sheet and enter the transactions in the appropriate block of the first table, then complete the income statement and balance sheet which follow:

1. Mary Muffet opened a bank account in the name of her new physiotherapy practice and deposited R10 000 of her own money.
2. She purchased R5 000 of equipment, paying half in cash and getting credit for the rest.
3. She also put some equipment valued at R20 000 into the business.
4. She paid R2 000 rent for one month in advance for her premises.
5. Her first client paid her R500 in cash.
6. The other clients for the first month were mainly medical aid patients. Her total accounts to the medical aid societies for the month were R15 000.
7. Other cash fees for the month amounted to R3 000.
8. She paid her receptionist her salary of R2 500.
9. The accounts which she received for sundry expenses such as telephone, water and electricity amounted to R1 000.
10. She paid the balance owing on the equipment purchased.

	Assets			Capital and liabilities		
	Cash	Equipment	Accounts Receivable	Capital	Income and expenses	Accounts payable
1	10000			10000		
2	(2500)	5000				2500
3		20000		20000		
4	(2000)		2000			
5	500				500	
6			15000		15000	
7	3000				3000	
8	(2500)				(2500)	
9					(1000)	1000
10	(2500)					(2500)
Total	4000	25000	17000	30000	15000	1000
		46000				

MARY MUFFET—PHYSIOTHERAPIST
Income statement for the first month

Fees received	18500
Expenses	5500
Net income	13000

MARY MUFFET—PHYSIOTHERAPIST
Balance sheet after one month

Assets

Equipment		25000
Accounts receivable		15000
Cash		4000
		44000

Liabilities

Accounts payable		1000
Capital		30000
Amounts contributed		
Net income	13000	13000
		44000

Question 2.11

Stewpot CC operates a retail store that sells gourmet cookware. The trial balance of the business at 28 February 1999 before making the year end adjustments is shown below:

Trial balance at 28 February 1999

Sales		285 600
Stock and purchases	188 400	
Insurance	1 800	
Wages	22 950	
Manager's salary	30 600	
Rent	8 100	
Water, electricity and sanitation	4 140	
Interest on loan now repaid	1 125	
Miscellaneous expenses	3 156	
Cash at bank	41 204	
Accounts receivable	25 000	
Furniture, fixtures and equipment	42 000	
Accumulated depreciation on furniture etc		12 600
Accounts payable		24 050
Members' contributions		28 000
Undrawn income		18 225
	368 475	368 475

Additional information:

1. The furniture, fixtures and equipment were purchased on 1 March 1995 and are estimated to have a useful life of ten years.
2. Stock at 28 February 1999 was valued at cost price of R23 000.
3. Insurance paid in advance at 28 February 1999 was R600.
4. Wages owing to employees at 28 February 1999 amounted R450.
5. Salary owing to the manager at 28 February 1999 amounted to R600.
6. Tax is payable on net income at a rate of 40%.

Required:

1. Prepare the adjusting entries required to take account of the above information either in journal form or in tabular form.
2. Prepare the complete income statement and balance sheet at 28 February 1999.

Question 2.12

Barney Google ran a business under the name of B Google and Company. The following trial balance was extracted from his books at 30 April, two months into his financial year:

Trial balance at 30 April

Advertising	10 716	
B Google—capital		30 000
B Google—drawings	2 500	
Bank overdraft		543
Cash on hand	100	
Furniture and fittings	1 200	
General expenses	1 766	
Insurance	326	
Loan at 12% per annum		5 000
Municipal charges	770	
Opening stock	7 834	
Plant and machinery	16 820	
Purchases	33 437	
Railage on purchases	952	
Sales		61 042
Sundry creditors		10 733
Sundry debtors	17 360	
Travelling and accommodation	3 862	
Wages and salaries	9 675	
	107 318	107 318

CLOSING STOCK 8431

Additional information:

1. Closing stock was valued at R8 931
2. Depreciation is to be provided at 10 % on plant and machinery and % on furniture.
3. Interest for a full year is due on the loan.

Required:

Prepare a trading and profit and loss account for the two months ended 30 April, and a balance sheet at that date.

Question 2.13

Towne and Suttee were in partnership as estate agents sharing profits in the ratios of 2:1 respectively. On 1 March 1988 they agreed to amalgamate their business with that of Field, who operated an estate agency in a different part of the district. The three agreed that the two offices would continue to be managed separately and set out the profit sharing ratios as follows:

	Towne	Suttee	Field
Towne and Suttee office	50 %	30 %	20 %
Field office	30 %	20 %	50 %

The balance sheets of the two firms prior to amalgamation are set out below. It was immediately evident that Field's accounting system would have to be modified, since he had maintained his records relating to property deals on a cash basis. In order to simplify the amalgamation it was agreed that commissions received in respect of unrecorded transactions for the previous year would be for Field's account.

Towne and Suttee

Capital—Towne	38 000
Capital—Suttee	26 000
Creditors—clients	22 000
Creditors—sundries	7 000
	93 000
Furniture	1 200
Debtors	38 500
Bank—current account	27 800
Bank—trust account	25 000
Cash on hand	500
	93 000

Field

Capital	26 500
Creditors—clients	16 000
Creditors—sundries	2 500
	45 000

Furniture	1 000
Debtors	8 200
Bank—current account	16 000
Bank—trust account	19 400
Cash on hand	400
	45 000

The following terms were agreed to by the partners:

1. Goodwill of Towne and Suttee was valued at R60 000 and of Field at R36 000. No goodwill was to be raised in the financial statements.
2. Furniture was revalued in both cases at half of the book value.
3. Interest on capital was to be allowed at 5% per annum.
4. Salaries of R8 000 for Towne and R6 000 for the other partners were to be paid.
5. Commission of R3 000 due by Towne and Suttee to Field was to be transferred to Field's capital account.

Relevant figures for the year ended 28 February 1989 were as follows:

	Towne and Suttee	Field
Commissions and fees	4 770	52 650
Commissions and fees—1988 year		6 200
Drawings—Towne	12 000	
Drawings—Suttee	10 000	
Drawings—Field		13 000
Salaries and expenses	58 200	35 400
Debtors	37 100	16 850
Creditors—clients	18 300	15 200
Creditors—other	4 500	2 300
Bank balances	43 670	19 600
Bank balances—trust accounts	21 900	16 600
Cash on hand	500	400

Required:

1. Make the necessary adjustments to reflect the amalgamation.
2. Prepare an income statement and balance sheet at 28 February 1989.

Question 2.14

Rose, Thorne and Budd are in partnership sharing profits in the ratio of 4:3:3 respectively. The following trial balance was extracted from the accounting records at 28 February 1989:

Accounting fees	1 000	
Bank overdraft		62 800
Bank charges	6 000	
Capital—Rose		82 000
Capital—Thorne		30 000
Capital—Budd		16 000

Creditors		64 100
Current account—Rose		8 200
Current account—Thorne		6 300
Current account—Budd	600	
Debtors	126 800	
General expenses	2 800	
Land and buildings	140 000	
Loan—Rose		76 000
Machinery at cost	162 000	
Office wages	4 200	
Purchases	345 000	
Provision for depreciation on machinery		65 000
Sales		543 400
Stock at 29 February 1988	79 200	
Telephone and insurances	4 400	
Wages	81 800	
	953 800	953 800

An examination of the records reveals the following:

1. Included in the item Machinery are the deposit and four monthly payments in respect of a machine purchased in November, 1988. The cash price of the machine was R16 000, a deposit of R1 600 was paid and the interest amounted to R1 800. The balance was to be settled by twelve equal monthly payments. The partners decided not to capitalise the interest but to apportion it equally over the term of the contract.

2. Debts totalling R940 are to be written off and the doubtful debts against which a provision is to be raised amounted to R4 500.

3. R1 680 was owing in respect of accounting fees.

4. R260 was owing in respect of telephone charges.

5. An annual insurance premium of R1 040, due on 30 November each year, had been paid early in December.

6. Budd was to be credited with R2 600 in respect of salary.

7. The loan from Rose was paid into the firm's bank account on 1 September 1988.

8. Depreciation is to be written off at the rate of 10% on cost.

9. Stock on hand at 28 February 1989 was R83 000.

Required:

Prepare the trading and profit and loss accounts of the partnership for the year and the balance sheet at 28 February 1989.

Question 2.15

At close of business on 28 February 1989 the trial balance of Marbar Limited was as follows:

Auditor's remuneration	7 000	
Bank	70 500	
Debentures		500 000
Debtors	178 000	
Directors' remuneration	158 000	
Discount on debentures	15 000	
Dividends received		30 000
Investments at cost	180 000	
Land and buildings at cost	800 000	
Marketing and administration expenses	337 500	
Motor vehicles at cost	134 000	
Motor vehicles—accumulated depreciation		40 000
Profit on sale of land		200 000
Purchases	1 320 000	
Retained income		20 000
Sales		2 000 000
Share capital—ordinary shares of R1 each		1 000 000
Stock	550 000	
Taxation	40 000	
	3 790 000	3 790 000

Investigation also brought the following to light:

1. On 1 March 1988 the company had issued 5 000 ten per cent convertible secured debentures of R100 each, to be converted into ordinary shares at par after five years. They were issued at a discount of 3%, this discount to be apportioned over the life of the debentures.
2. On 1 December 1988 a motor vehicle which had cost R60 000 on 1 March 1986 was traded in for R16 000 against a new vehicle costing R50 000. The cash payment of R34 000 was correctly posted, but the entry relating to the trade in has yet to be journalised.
3. Depreciation on motor vehicles is written off at 20% per annum on a straight line basis.
4. Bad debts of R9 000 were written off against the provision, which is to be increased to 5% of outstanding debtors.
5. The directors recommended a dividend of 10 cents per share, using capital profits if necessary.
6. Stock on hand at 28 February 1989 amounted to R47 000.
7. Directors' remuneration includes the following items:

Managing director's salary	120 000
Directors' fees	30 000
Entertainment allowances	8 000

Required:

1. Prepare a worksheet to bring the above information into account.
2. Prepare an income statement and balance sheet, together with any necessary notes, to 29 February 1988 to comply with the requirements of the Companies Act.

Question 2.16

Below are the balance sheets of Ubangi and Chari at 28 February 1989. Ubangi acquired 40 000 ordinary shares of R1 each in Chari on 1 March 1988, at which stage the balance of retained earnings of that company was R8 000.

	Ubangi Ltd	*Chari Ltd*
Capital employed		
Ordinary share capital	240 000	80 000
Share premium	24 000	
Retained earnings	44 000	28 000
	308 000	108 000
Current liabilities		
Trade creditors	36 000	30 000
Other creditors and accruals	16 000	11 600
Ubangi Limited		8 000
Shareholders for dividends	10 000	
	370 000	157 600
Represented by		
Fixed assets		
Land and buildings	150 000	50 000
Fixtures and equipment	20 000	12 000
Investment in Chari Ltd	82 000	
	252 000	62 000
Current assets		
Stock	38 000	21 000
Trade debtors	60 000	44 000
Chari Limited	8 000	
Cash and bank	12 000	30 600
	370 000	157 600

Required:

Presume that as a result of its shareholding Ubangi is entitled to appoint a majority of the members of the directorate of the company. Prepare a consolidated balance sheet at 28 February 1989.

Case studies

Case 2.1—Fanny Fastbuck

Fanny Fastbuck is an estate agent who also speculates in property for her own account. She has always worked for someone else in the past, but in the last week of February 1999 she set up business on her own as a sole proprietorship. The following statements apply to the position at the end of February 1999 or to transactions which took place during that month:

1. Fanny owed R100 000 on some undeveloped land which she had purchased some time previously at a cost of R160 000 for purposes of speculation. She used long term finance for this.
2. She also owed R120 000 on a mortgage loan on her own recently purchased home, which was transferred into her name in mid-February 1999. The house had cost her R170 000 in total.
3. She paid R15 000 for a Compuprop franchise. This was a computer network of independent estate agents, enabling them to pool information and so compete against the bigger operations.
4. She had R10 000 in her personal bank account and R14 500 in her business bank account before the transactions detailed below.
5. She owed R1 800 on her personal credit card.
6. On 26 February 1999 she employed Mark Ateer as an agent. He was very highly regarded in the industry, but was killed in a motor accident on 28 February.
7. On 27 February she purchased office furniture for R17 000. She paid R11 000 in cash and charged the rest to a current account. The next day she decided to take home a couch which had cost R1 500 to use in her TV room. On the same day she sold a chair costing R1 000 to the business next door at cost price.
8. On 28 February she purchased furniture costing R20 000 for her own home, paying a deposit of 25 % and signing a suspensive sale agreement for the balance.
9. She had personal assets of R30 500, consisting of shares and securities, in addition to the items mentioned above.

Required:

Prepare two balance sheets at the end of February 1999, one for the business and one for Fanny personally. Pay particular attention to the layout of the balance sheets.

Case 2.2—Lowveld Litho (Proprietary) Limited

Lowveld Litho (Proprietary) Limited was founded in 1980 as a speciality printing firm. Because of the high degree of technical proficiency shown by William Caxton, the owner, it grew very rapidly and was incorporated as a private company in 1984. Caxton held 55% of the shares and the rest were held by members of his family.

The company's only problem lay in the fact that its main market developed in the PWV area, about 300 to 400 kilometres away from the Eastern Transvaal town where it was situated. In order to overcome this problem Caxton decided in 1988 to uproot himself, his family and his business and to re-establish himself in his market area.

He found a site in Midrand which he could obtain at a very favourable price from the Town Council, which was trying hard to establish the area as a light industrial zone. The decision was made to move to Midrand, and to use the opportunity offered by the temporary halt in production to modernise the printing plant.

Exhibit 1 is a balance sheet of the company at the time the decision was made to move. Transactions arising from the move were as follows:

1. Land and buildings were sold for R67 400.
2. Certain equipment which appeared in the financial records at a cost price of R25 750 and a written down value of R11 450 was sold for R9 800 cash.
3. A new printing press with an invoice price of R39 200 was purchased subject to a cash discount of 2%. Delivery costs of R157 were paid to outside contractors but installation was done by the company's own employees in a time of 60 man-hours. These employees were normally charged out at R10 per hour, but were only paid R5 the balance was made up of an allowance for overhead of R3,90 and profit of R1,10.
4. The cost of the land was R30 000, but a valuation which Caxton commissioned gave a value of R49 000. The municipal valuation was R31 350.
5. There was an old farm building on the land and it cost Caxton R7 425 to have this demolished. The company also spent R4 750 on installing improved drainage facilities.
6. A reconditioned composing machine was purchased at a price of R9 800, of which R7 300 was paid in cash and the balance settled by a trade-in allowance against the old machine. This machine would have fetched a maximum of R2 100 in the open market, which was half of its cost price. Accumulated depreciation at the date of trade-in amounted to R1 800.
7. A new building was erected at a cost of R196 000, which was mainly financed by a mortgage loan of R147 000.
8. The fixed deposit matured and was redeemed.
9. A large paper cutter was subjected to extensive repairs at a cost of R1 950. In previous years no more than R140 had been spent on this machine.
10. Direct transportation and related costs of moving and re-installing the equipment amounted to R2 950 in addition to the estimated 125 hours spent by employees on this part of the move.
11. An accident during the move resulted in extensive damage to a piece of equipment costing R3 500. Costs of repair amounted to R950, but management felt that the damage had reduced the value to R490. Prior to the accident the equipment was depreciated at a rate of 10% per annum to an estimated salvage cost of R700. Accumulated depreciation at the date of the accident was R1 120.

Exhibit 1
LOWVELD LITHO (PROPRIETARY) LIMITED
Balance sheet at 28 February 1989

Capital employed:		
Share capital—ordinary shares of R1 each		154 000
Retained earnings		116 506
Shareholders equity		270 506
Represented by:		
Fixed assets		
Land and buildings at cost		64 700
Equipment at cost	62 690	
Less: accumulated depreciation	32 560	30 130
		94 830
Current assets		
Stock	26 534	
Debtors	61 504	
Fixed deposit	100 000	
Cash on hand and in bank	43 660	
	231 698	
Current liabilities		
Creditors and accruals	56 022	175 676
		270 506

Required:
1. Analyse each transaction in terms of its ultimate effect on the balance sheet and income statement. For those transactions that affect owner's equity distinguish between those that relate to the current year and those that do not.
2. Prepare a balance sheet showing the effect of these transactions. Assume a date of 1 March 1989.

Case 2.3—Overberg Optics Limited
While he was at university Tom Piper had had a dream of independence. He intended to achieve this by developing a smallish business which would specialise in a unique, highly technical product. When he set out to make this dream come true he moved into the field of optics. He knew that there was a high demand for certain optical equipment for both military and medical use, and decided to offer a service which would guarantee a quality higher than that offered by any of the possible competitors in the market place. He found that this was easier said than done, and went through a traumatic year of finding out just what was possible within the framework of the equipment and technical skills at his disposal, but eventually felt that he had sorted out his problems and was well on the way to achieving his dreams.

He started his business with R30 000 representing an inheritance. He also borrowed R12 000 from an uncle at 13% per annum. The uncle regarded this as a permanent investment and undertook not to call up the loan until Tom stated that he no longer had need of the money. In return for this Tom paid the first year's interest in advance. He used this money well and managed to keep his payment periods within reason so that he had no trouble with suppliers. Most of his purchases were for cash, though he did owe some amounts which are specified in *Exhibit 2*.

Some capital expenditure was necessary. Piper purchased some machines at a cost of R42 000, paying R6 000 down and agreeing to pay off the balance at R500 per month for four years plus interest at 15% on the outstanding balance. This equipment was purchased in September so that he had paid R3 000 plus interest of R1 744 by the end of the year. He also took out a single premium insurance policy in favour of the sellers at a cost of R1 200 to cover the outstanding balance for the four year period. His own estimate was that the equipment could last ten years, but he intended to sell it and upgrade within five years. He was sure that the equipment would have a trade in value of R3 000 in five years time.

By the end of the first year the staff complement consisted of Mary Muffet, who took care of the office work and assisted with packaging and shipping, Bobby Shaftoe and Jack Sprat who worked full time in the workshop and Tom himself. Tom spent about 20% of his time on administration and selling and the rest in the workshop. The earnings of these four are set out in *Exhibit 1* below:

Exhibit 1

Mary Muffet		7 200
Bobby Shaftoe		17 700
Jack Sprat		21 000
Tom Piper		36 000
		81 900

Of this total R54 030 had been paid to the employees, R19 050 had been paid over to the Receiver in the form of PAYE, R7 200 was due to the employees and R1 350 was due to the Receiver.

Most of Overberg's work was for the military. Some work for a private firm to the value of R2 250 earlier on had resulted in a bad debt for the total amount. An amount of R5 820 for work done on account of a military aircraft manufacturer had not yet been paid either.

Included in year end stock was an amount of R4 800 in respect of special items manufactured for an Armscor subsidiary but not yet shipped. Piper was worried about these since this represented the second half of an order and there had been quality problems with the first half of the order. No less than 20% of the items had been rejected by Armscor inspectors. This worried Piper, since he felt that he was producing a high quality product and had no idea why the products had been rejected. He was determined to appeal against this rejection since the items could not be reworked and had no value to anyone else in their present state. The invoiced amount in respect of these items is included in the debtors total in *Exhibit 2*.

Exhibit 2

Extracts from Overberg's financial records at 28 February:

Rent	12 000
Creditors for stock	30 780
Purchases paid for	36 360
Cash received from customers	117 750
Debtors	72 240
Spent on general expenses	1 200
Stock on hand at end of year	19 200
Administrative and selling expenses	16 380
Sundry production costs	2 580
Cash on hand	4 076

Required:

Prepare the company's income statement for the year and the balance sheet at that date. Show clearly how all figures were calculated or determined.

Case 2.4—Gratis Energy Company CC

John Graham was a research scientist who had developed some ideas concerning the use of solar energy while working for the CSIR. The idea had not been developed to the stage where it was commercially viable when that organisation started with a process of rationalisation which led to his being retrenched. He was allowed to take over the project since it had no commercial value for the CSIR and there was no one left there to develop it. Working full time on the idea he soon had it ready for the market but had a problem in financing the venture. A friend of his, Peter Tisent, was quite excited by the potential of John's ideas and offered to assist in getting the project going. He did not have much available in the way of ready cash, but did have a building which could be used as a factory. This building was valued at R200 000, and Peter felt that, if he used it as security, they could raise the necessary ready cash.

The two of them approached a bank for finance. They were given a warm reception, the manager being very keen on high technology products, but were told that they would have to provide certain information before the loan could be considered. They would have to decide on the form of organisation they were going to adopt for this business and then present forecast financial statements for the first year of operations: opening balance sheet, income statement and closing balance sheet.

After conferring with Peter Marwick, a friend who happened to be a Chartered Accountant, the two decided to form a close corporation. This CC would buy John's patent from him for R100 000 and buy Peter's property for R200 000. They would each put R5 000 of this into the CC as their contribution and the remainder would go on loan account. Expected costs to date of startup were as follows:

1. Costs of incorporation and fees in respect of the transfer of the property would be R5 000;

2. The cost of the necessary machines and equipment would be R50 000;
3. The initial purchase of raw material would be R5 000.

These costs would be financed by the bank. Financing for the machines would be through a suspensive sale agreement over three years, with repayments at the rate of R2 000 per month, while the rest would be financed by means of an overdraft. On the basis of this planning they prepared the following initial balance sheet:

GRATIS ENERGY CC
Balance sheet at start of operations

Members' contributions		10 000
Members' loans		290 000
Members' interest		300 000
Long term liability		
Suspensive sale agreement		50 000
		350 000
Fixed assets		
Property, plant and machinery		250 000
Legal costs		5 000
		255 000
Intangible assets—patent		100 000
		355 000
Net current liabilities		5 000
Current assets		
Raw materials	5 000	
Current liabilities		
Bank overdraft	10 000	
		350 000

The two then sat down to plan the operations for the year and concluded that the following represented a realisitc forecast of transactions:

1. Cash sales during the first year would be R350 000. There would be no credit sales.
2. Purchases, also on a cash basis, would amount to R100 000.
3. Direct labour expenses would be R96 000, and other selling and administrative expenses would be R24 000.
4. New equipment and tools would cost R10 000.
5. Closing stock of raw materials would be R10 000. Goods would only be produced to order and there would be no stock of finished goods.
6. Plant and machinery would be depreciated at 10 % per annum on a straight line basis.
7. The cost of the patent would be written off over its fourteen year remaining life.
8. Salaries would be paid to both of the members based on 20 % of turnover each.
9. No income taxes would be paid during the year.

Obviously, these transactions would affect one another throughout the course of the year and the members were not willing to estimate when each transaction would occur.

Required:
1. Analyse the effect of each of the above transactions on the initial balance sheet.
2. Prepare the projected income statement for the first year of operations and balance sheet at the end of the year based on the above estimates.

Case 2.5—Malgas Motors

Mandla and Marta Malgas purchased the total issued shares of a service station owning company from a development company known as Service Station Management (Pty) Ltd, and immediately changed the name of the company to Malgas Motors (Pty) Ltd. The story of the purchase of the company and the first six months of operations from 1 March 1999 to 31 August 1999 is related below.

The husband and wife partners bought the business for a price determined at R100 000 plus the book value of the net working capital at 28 February 1999. They each put in R20 000, most of which they had accumulated in various ways and the balance of which they had borrowed from friends or relatives. For the remaining R60 000 of the base payment they obtained a mortgage loan on their jointly owned house. The agreement allowed them to pay off the net value of stock and debtors minus creditors over the first three months of operations.

The audited closing balance sheet of the company at 28 February 1999 was as follows:

Capital employed
Share capital

Authorised and issued		4 000
Retained earnings		21 000
Shareholders equity		25 000
Shareholders loan		35 000
Loan from oil company		25 000
		85 000

Employment of capital
Fixed assets

Plant and equipment		65 000
Net current assets		20 000
Current assets	30 000	
Cash and bank balances	5 000	
Debtors	7 000	
Stock	18 000	
Current liabilities	10 000	
Creditors	9 000	
Accrued expenses	1 000	
		85 000

The garage building was a fairly new one and a valuer whom the partners brought in to look at the business though it would serve its purpose without any modifications for at least another ten years. The equipment, which he thought was fairly valued, was on average half depreciated. It was being written off on a ten per cent straight line basis to zero.

After one month of operations the partners had the following figures available:

Sales of petrol, oil etc		160 000
Purchases	132 000	
Wages and salaries	12 000	
Insurance	1 000	
Advertising	2 000	
Miscellaneous expenses	3 000	
Accounts payable		1 000
Stock on hand	22 000	
New equipment purchased	12 000	
Cash on hand	3 000	

The plant was purchased by paying a 10 % deposit, with balance payable over 36 months at R350 per month, and was to be used in the workshop which the partners intended opening on 1 April. They also intended dealing in second hand cars, but had made no moves in that direction as yet.

Required:
Prepare an income statement for the first month of operations and a balance sheet at the end of that month.

Part three

Financial analysis

With the background provided by the previous sections it is now possible to look at financial statements not simply from the point of view of records of historical financial transactions, but as vital documents containing information necessary to an understanding of the business. This section deals with the two basic tools of financial statements analysis, ratio analysis and cash flow analysis.

Chapter 13

Basic ratio analysis

Financial statements are only important because of their information content. While some of this information is obtained easily by just reading through the financial reports, much of it is only obtained after careful analysis of the statements.

One of the prime tools for analysis of financial statements is ratio analysis. It is a mathematically simple technique, but its application is complex. This chapter is designed to introduce the concept and methodology of ratio analysis.

1. Introduction

Financial statements are prepared in order to provide information about an entity. For many centuries the main purpose of financial reports was simply to provide stewardship information, or information about how an organisation (or a person) had used funds entrusted to it. Before the development of the double entry accounting system, accounting records were generally simply lists of money spent. This system brought new possibilities and for the first time allowed the construction of two primary reports, a static statement of financial position and a dynamic record of movements and changes in that position. In this way it made financial reports a source of information about all financially measurable aspects of the entity for those who had the skills to interpret all that appeared in the statements. The increasing complexity of business and the concomitant increase in the complexity of financial reports has made it ever more difficult to interpret these statements meaningfully, but this chapter provides an introduction to the most commonly used technique, that of ratio analysis.

2. Elementary ratio analysis

This is one of the primary tools of financial analysis. Intelligent use of so called financial ratios can assist the manager to understand the message of a set of financial statements. The concept of ratio analysis is very simple. One simply takes two figures from different parts of the financial statements, divides the one by the other and draws conclusions from the answer, which is known as a financial ratio. The questions which arise are obvious:
1. Which figures from which parts of the financial statements does one use?
2. How does one draw conclusions from the ratios?
A simple example should show just how straightforward an exercise in financial ratio analysis can be. To tell the truth, everyone does some sort of ratio analysis on his own financial position at some stage, and this situation can be used to illustrate the process.

Say that John Brown wants to borrow money from a bank. The banker will ask him to fill in a standard form giving details of his financial position, which may be something like this, ignoring those items for which he would enter a zero:

Assets
Fixed property
  House at 123 Archer Boulevard, Cape Town

Current market value		R200 000
Cost price	R140 000	
Date of purchase 1 July 1990		
Motor vehicles at current market value		
1993 Toyota Camry		100 000
1989 Volkswagen Golf		20 000
Household effects at current value		90 000
Investments (Give details on attached sheet)		40 000
Total assets		R450 000

Liabilities

Mortgage loans	R120 000
Institution: Allied Building Society	
Suspensive sale agreements	90 000
Loans	40 000
Current creditors	10 000
Total liabilities	R260 000

Income

Salary per month	Self	R10 000
	Spouse	4 000
Other income (Specify on attached sheet)		500
Total income		R 14 500

Expenditure

Income tax	R4 500
Bond repayments per month	2 000
Insurance and retirement funding	1 000
Medical expenses and insurance	400
Repayments on suspensive sales	2 900
Rates and taxes	500
Household expenses	2 000
Total committed expenditure	R 13 300

Figure 13.1

Put yourself in the bank manager's shoes and decide whether you would want to lend money to John. To make his decision the bank manager has to look at his objectives: a banker lends money in order to get it back with interest, which represents his profit. Before he lends money he must therefore decide whether the borrower can afford to pay the interest and repay the loan. Secondly, he needs some security for his loan in case something does go wrong and the borrower is not able to meet his commitments.

The first step would be to look at the ratio of income to expenditure. John spends a large proportion of his income every month. The ratio of expenditure is 13 300/14 500 or 91,7 % of income. This does not allow a large margin for error or for unexpected expenses such as major repairs to one of the cars. As a banker I would feel that John has very little scope for borrowing any more.

A look at his list of assets and liabilities (really a rough balance sheet) shows that he is apparently very solvent: the ratio of assets to liabilities is 450 000/260 000, or 1,73:1. He therefore appears to have enough security to cover a loan.

A deeper look at his balance sheet raises some queries, however. The house has a very large bond on it already, so that at best one could get a second bond. There is also the question of how much the house is actually worth since the value given on the balance sheet is probably simply John's own estimate.

The cars are apparently also subject to suspensive sale agreements, which means that they cannot be used as security for a loan, and household effects are normally very poor security since they usually realise very little on sale.

Amongst the liabilities there is also the matter of the loan of R40 000. John makes no provision in his monthly expenditure statement for repayment of this loan which means that he would have to give the bank some explanation.

All in all, John appears to be a very poor candidate for a loan. The ratio of expenditure is far too high and the ratio of assets to liabilities, while apparently quite high, is based on figures which do not stand up very well to an intelligent examination.

This is all that financial ratio analysis involves: simply finding two figures which are related to each other, such as income and expenditure or assets and liabilities, determining what the ratio is between the two and then deciding on whether this is a good ratio or a bad one. This last decision is the crux of the matter, since there are no hard and fast rules about when a ratio is bad or good. Everything depends on the circumstances of the case, and the ability to judge the significance of a ratio accurately under the relevant circumstances is the mark of a good financial manager.

To interpret the ratios of the financial statements of a business undertaking is a highly skilled task when done in depth, but a basic ratio analysis is essentially as straightforward as the above analysis of John Brown's financial position.

The first step in doing a ratio analysis is to decide what you want to know about the undertaking. Are you looking at it from the point of view of a banker who is considering lending money to the company, from the point of view of an investor who is considering a shareholding in a company, from the point of view of management, from the point of view of a trade union negotiator who is trying to determine just how much the company can afford or from some other point of view? And in each case, does your interest lie in the solvency and liquidity of the undertaking, its profitability or its management efficiency? The following example will show how a ratio analysis of a company can help all the parties interested in that company.

The financial statements of a company called Magrad, a manufacturer of pirate parts for the motor industry, are given as an example of the statements one could expect to see in practice. They are based on the actual financial statements of a group of listed companies, but the various written reports and the notes have been omitted. Where necessary for the purposes of the analysis extracts from the notes will be given.

The figures in the reference column do not form part of the financial statements. They have been placed there to assist in the explanations which follow.

Points to note before starting the ratio analysis are firstly that the heading specifies that this is an income statement for a group of companies (Magrad . . . and its subsidiaries) and not just the statement for a single company. The subsidiary companies are companies owned or controlled by Magrad, so that consolidated or combined statements are necessary to give a picture of the full range of activities.

Secondly, note that the statement gives figures for two years so that a comparison can be made to see if performance is improving or not. This is not only a legal requirement imposed by the Companies Act but is of vital importance for the analysis of the financial position of the undertaking. It is seldom possible to lay down a standard which will tell whether the performance is satisfactory. Usually one has to make do with comparisons—how does this undertaking compare with its competitors and how does current performance compare to that of the past? The figures for the previous year give a basis for evaluating current performance.

MAGRAD MOTOR COMPONENTS LIMITED and its subsidiaries
Consolidated income statement for the year ended 31 March 1993

	Ref	1993	1992
Turnover	1	21 909	24 703
Cost of sales	2	17 527	20 256
Gross profit	3	4 382	4 447
Operating expenses	4	2 176	1 763
Income before interest and taxation	5	2 206	2 684
Interest received (1992—paid)	6	7	290
Income before taxation	7	2 213	2 394
Taxation	8	246	123
Income before extraordinary item	9	1 967	2 271
Extraordinary item	10	0	461
Net income for the year	11	1 967	1 810
Ordinary dividend declared	12	554	498
Retained income for the year	13	1 413	1 312
Retained income at the beginning of the year	14	8 793	7 481
Retained income at the end of the year	15	10 206	8 793

Figure 13.2

Several points can be noted about this income statement before the formal analysis starts. The first is that the income statement is drawn up in very much the same way as the example in the previous chapter. It starts off with the determination of the gross profit (R4 382 in 1993), from which the operating expenses (R2 176) are deducted in order to arrive at the operating profit (R2 206), referred to here as "Income before interest and taxation", interest (R7) is brought into account and then taxation (R246) and finally the dividend for the year (R554) is shown in order to determine just how much of its profit the company is retaining (R1 413) for maintaining or expanding its operations. This amount is then added to the total of the retained earnings at the end of the previous year (R8 793) to obtain the total profits the company has retained since its formation (R10 206).

Extraordinary items and abnormal items

Included in the income statement of Magrad there is an "Extraordinary item" (item 10). An extraordinary item is defined in Statement of GAAP AC103 (see chapter 3) as a material item of income or expense arising from activities outside the ordinary activities of the enterprise. These must be reflected separately since any such item would distort the trend of the reported income if it were simply to be included without the user of the financial statements being aware of it.

Abnormal expenses are also reflected separately. These are items of income or expense within the normal activities of the undertaking but which are unusual because of their size in a particular year.

The second point to note is that the company's turnover has declined quite sharply from R24 703 in 1992 to R21 909 in 1993, a drop of 11,3 %, and the income before interest and taxation has fallen from R2 684 to R 2 206, a drop of no less than 17,8 %.

MAGRAD MOTOR COMPONENTS LIMITED and its subsidiaries
Consolidated balance sheet as at 31 March 1993

	Ref	1993	1992
Employment of capital	16		
Fixed assets	17	8 789	9 962
Net current assets	18	6 407	3 465
Current assets	19	12 053	8 154
Stock	20	2 480	1 986
Accounts receivable	21	4 050	4 057
Taxation	22	0	3
Bank and cash balances	23	5 523	2 108
Less: Current liabilities	24	5 646	4 689
Accounts payable	25	4 842	4 191
Taxation	26	250	0
Shareholders for dividend	27	554	498
	28	15 196	13 427
Capital employed	29		
Stated capital	30	3 428	3 428
Distributable reserves	31	10 206	8 793
Shareholders funds	32	13 634	12 221
Long term liabilities	33	1 493	1 131
Deferred taxation	34	69	75
	35	15 196	13 427

Figure 13.3

The above balance sheet is drawn up in accordance with the requirements of the Companies Act, but there are some terms which may require explanation.

The heading at reference 16 "*Employment of capital*" means "This is how we invested our money" and the heading at reference 29 "*Capital employed*" means "This is where we got the money to invest". "*Stated capital*" (Ref 30) is the amount paid in by shareholders when they bought their shares from the company, and "*Distributable reserves*" (Ref 31) represents the profits earned by the company over the years and retained for maintenance of the company's position or for expansion. A look back at the income statement will show that this is the same amount as the "Retained income at the end of the year" (ref 15). A critical point to note is that these reserves are not cash which can be paid out. They are part of the funding which the company has received and they have already been used to purchase the assets on the "Employment of Capital" part of the balance sheet.

Once the scrutiny of the financial statements has been completed the formal ratio analysis can start. A good starting point is to discuss the types of information which can be obtained from the financial statements.

The first point is to remember that the financial statements do not give all the information about a business. There are other sources of information such as general economic reports, economic reports specific to the particular type of industry and other published and unpublished information relating either to the company or to the industry in which it operates. All this information should be viewed together with the information obtained from the financial statements when analysing the company.

The aspects of the company about which the financial statements do provide information can be divided into the following groups:
1. Solvency and liquidity ratios
2. Profitability ratios
3. Activity or efficiency ratios
4. Debt or leverage ratios
An extra group which can be added in the case of companies quoted on the stock exchange is:
5. Investor or stock exchange ratios
Each of these groups of ratios provides some valuable information to the person analysing the financial statements and they will be discussed in some detail in the following pages.

There are other classifications of ratios used by various writers, but this classification is probably the most commonly used.

2.1 Solvency and liquidity ratios

Both of these concepts are measured by comparing certain specific amounts owned to amounts owed.

To measure *solvency* total amounts owned are compared to total amounts owed. Solvency simply means the ability to pay one's debts. In the case of a business this is normally taken to mean that the assets of the undertaking are greater than the liabilities. However, the mere fact that you own more than you owe does not necessarily mean that you are able to settle your debt. It is quite possible that your assets are in a form which is not readily available as cash. For instance, you may own a house which is worth far more than the total of the amounts which you owe. However, a house cannot be used to settle your account at the local chemist unless it is sold and converted into cash.

This is where the aspect of *liquidity* comes in: solvency simply means that your assets exceed your liabilities; liquidity means that you have assets in a form that can be used to settle your debt. Liquidity is measured by comparing the amount of readily available funds to the amounts which are due for payment. A liquid undertaking is one which has sufficient cash to meet its obligations, or sufficient assets which can be converted into cash quickly and without affecting the operations of the undertaking.

The measurement of solvency is one of the easiest and most understandable ratios: one simply compares the total assets to the total liabilities. In the case of Magrad this would mean adding the total of the fixed assets (item 17) to the total of the current assets (item 19) and comparing this to the total of the long term liabilities (item 33) and the current liabilities (item 24). For 1992 this would be (9 962 + 8 154)/ (1 131 + 4 689), which simplifies to 18 126/5 820, or 3,11:1. Obviously, the company is very solvent since the assets are more than three times as much as the liabilities. However, it is important to look at the position a year later and see whether the position is improving or deteriorating. For 1993 the solvency ratio is 2,91:1, showing a slight decline. While this decline is not serious it would become serious if the trend continued for several years.

While there is no doubt that the undertaking is solvent one does not know whether it is liquid enough to meet its current commitments. To determine this it is necessary to look at the *current ratio* and the *acid test ratio*, which is also known as the *quick ratio*.

The current ratio takes the total of the current assets and divides this amount by the total of the current liabilities. In the case of Magrad this would be the current assets of 8 154 (item 19) divided by 4 689 (item 24) in 1992, giving a current ratio of 1,74:1, and 12 053/5 646 in 1993, giving a current ratio of 2,13:1. The current ratio has improved considerably, indicating an improvement in liquidity over the period.

The current ratio has been refined to produce the acid test ratio by excluding stock from the calculation. The argument is that, while stock may be turned into cash fairly quickly, it is not available to settle debt until it has been sold. A more accurate measure of liquidity may therefore be to look only at those items which are certain to be available as cash. These would be cash itself and accounts receivable, which will normally be settled and therefore be turned into cash within a short period of time. In the case of Magrad this would be calculated by taking the current assets of 8 154 (item 19) and deducting the stock of 1 986 (item 20) to get a so-called "quick assets" total of 6 168 and dividing this by the current liabilities of 4 689 (item 24) in 1992, giving an acid test ratio of 1,32:1 in 1992, and (12 053 − 2 480)/5 646 in 1993, giving an acid test ratio of 1,70:1. This ratio has also improved considerably, and there is little doubt that Magrad is perfectly capable of settling all its short term debts without any problems whatever.

Certain desirable levels at which the liquidity ratios should stand were laid down in less complicated times. These standards or norms should be approached with care, since different types of businesses have different liquidity requirements and different economic circumstances also have an effect on them. However, for most types of business which do carry stocks for resale, having a current ratio of 2:1 is regarded as a good sign of liquidity, as is having an acid test ratio of 1:1.

To summarise the position we can say that Magrad is very comfortably solvent in that its assets are about three times its liabilities and that it seems to be fully liquid since its current ratio and acid test ratio both look high and have improved.

SUMMARY OF SOLVENCY AND LIQUIDITY RATIOS

	1993	1992	Comment*
Solvency ratio	2,91:1	3,11:1	Good
Current ratio	2,13:1	1,74:1	Good
Acid test (or Quick) ratio	1,70:1	1,32:1	Good

* Note that these comments are only basic indicators in this particular case. A constant increase in the current ratio would eventually be bad, so that the reasons why a ratio appears good must be given.

2.2 Profitability ratios

Profitability ratios measure the profit earned by the undertaking against a variety of other aspects of the undertaking. Different measures of profit, like gross profit and net profit after tax, are also used, depending on what is required from the ratio being calculated.

Typical measures of profitability include the following:

Gross (profit) margin, which is a comparison of gross profit with sales or turnover. In the case of Magrad this would be the gross profit of 4 447 (item 3) divided by the sales or turnover of 24 703 (item 1), giving a gross profit margin of 18,00 % in 1992. In 1993 this would be 4 382/21 909 or 20,00 %, a rise of 2 %. A rise in this figure indicates that margins have been increased. Since this is a manufacturing operation the assumption would be that there have been some improvements in productivity in the process. In a pure trading undertaking an increase would simply indicate that the undertaking had decided to increase the markup on goods sold, or possibly that there had been more efficient buying which had eliminated spoilage or that more effective security measures had lowered the rate of shrinkage (shrinkage is theft of stock by customers or employees).

Some people prefer to calculate the *markup percentage* rather than the gross margin. This is done by dividing gross profit by the *cost of sales* rather than by sales. In the case of Magrad this would be 4 447 (item 3) divided by 20 256 (item 2), giving a markup of 21,95 % and for 1993 the markup would be 4 382/17 527 or exactly 25,00 %. This gives exactly the same information as the gross margin, of course: there has been an improvement from 1992.

The *net (profit) margin* is calculated by dividing the net income before interest and taxation (PBIT) by the turnover. The reason why PBIT (otherwise known as operating income) is used rather than the final income after tax figure is simply that the interest factor has nothing to do with the operations. Interest is a factor of the way in which the business is financed. If you had two similar businesses with the only significant difference between them being that the one is financed largely by borrowed money and the other by the shareholders one could not determine which one was being operated more efficiently by looking at the final income figure. The manager of the one financed by interest may be operating his business far more efficiently even if the interest factor makes his final income smaller than that of his competitor. This greater efficiency would be shown by the operating income.

For the same reason, the fact that interest is a factor of how the assets were purchased rather than the effectiveness with which they are used, the *return on assets* is calculated by dividing the PBIT by the total of the assets of the undertaking. In the case of Magrad this would be 2 684 (item 5) divided by the total of the fixed assets of 9 962 (item 17) and of the current assets of 8 154 (item 19). This simplifies to 2 684/18 116, or 14,82 % in 1992. For 1993 the relevant figures would be 2 206/(8 789 + 12 054), or 10,58 %. This represents a sharp drop in profit in relation to assets used to generate the profit and must be a point of worry to the management and to the shareholders. The ratio tells us that assets have not been used as effectively to generate profits in 1993 as they were in 1992.

Operating income and operating assets

Magrad has only one business, with incidental interest income or earnings. Some undertakings have a variety of different businesses within one umbrella. An example would be a company which is basically a manufacturing company like Magrad but which also has a big investment income.

As far as possible the two aspects of the undertaking should be separated for analysis purposes. The investments should be excluded from the assets used in manufacturing process, which are known as the operating assets; in addition, the investment income, whether this consists of interest or dividends, should be separated from the income from manufacturing, known as the operating income. This operating income should be compared with the operating assets to determine the return on assets obtained from the manufacturing operation, while the investment income should be compared with the investment assets in order to determine the return on the investment assets. Mixing the two simply confuses the issue and makes it very difficult to come to a rational conclusion concerning either of the two operations.

As distinct from the above ratios which are concerned only with the effective utilisation of assets, the *return on equity* (or return on shareholders investment) is concerned not only with the operations of the undertaking, but with all aspects including the financing policies and the tax management. For this reason it is calculated using the *income after tax*, generally known as profit after tax or PAT. In the case of Magrad this would be 2 271 (item 9) divided by 12 221 (item 32), giving a return on equity of 14,81 % in 1992. For 1993 the figures would be 1 967 divided by 13 634, giving 14,43 %. In contrast to the return on assets ratio, this one shows only a small decline.

SUMMARY OF PROFITABILITY RATIOS

	1993	1992	Comments
Gross margin	20,00 %	18,00 %	Good increase
Net margin (PBIT)	10,07 %	10,87 %	Small drop—bad
Return on equity (PAT)	14,43 %	14,81 %	Small drop—bad
Return on total assets (PBIT)	10,58 %	14,82	Big drop—BAD

2.3 Activity or efficiency ratios

Efficiency ratios are ratios which help us to assess how effectively the assets of the business are being applied towards meeting the objectives of the undertaking. Assets are purchased with the intention of being used to make a contribution to income. If they are not put to use or if they are used ineffectively the undertaking will not generate the income it should. The basic way of evaluating whether an asset is generating an acceptable level of income is to compare the value of the assets to the turnover generated by the assets. This is done at different levels: for the total assets, for groups of assets and for individual types of assets. To start off, total assets are compared to sales to obtain what is known as the *asset turnover ratio*. For Magrad the ratio would be turnover of 24 703 (item 1) divided by fixed assets of 9 962 (item 17) plus current assets of 8 154 (item 19), which gives an asset turnover of 1,36 in 1992. Stated another way, for every Rand the company had invested in assets in 1992 it generated sales of R1,36. By 1993 this figure had weakened to 21 909/(8 789 + 12 053), which gives an asset turnover of only 1,05. This obviously represents a serious deterioration in the asset utilisation in the company.

To try to determine just why this has happened it is necessary to take a look at the asset turnover in more detail. The first step is to look at the *fixed asset turnover* to determine whether the deterioration took place because of inefficient use of fixed assets, and thereafter to take a look at the turnover ratios of the key current assets.

The fixed asset turnover for Magrad is 21 909 (item 1) divided by 9 962 (item 17), giving 2,48 in 1992. In 1993 the ratio is 21 909/8 789, or 2,49. There is hardly any change here, the fixed assets having decreased by as much as the sales. Since the problem does not lie here it must lie with the current assets.

The two key elements for analysis here are the accounts receivable and the stock. Cash also plays its part, but this will be examined later under the heading *cash flow analysis*.

Accounts receivable are evaluated by looking at the *collection period*. This is calculated by dividing the accounts receivable of 4 057 (item 21) by the turnover (item 1) and multiplying the answer of 0,164 2 by 365, the number of days in a year to get a figure of 60 days in 1992. In 1993 the figure was 4 050/21 909 × 365, or just over 67 days. This ratio reveals that it is taking longer to collect money after goods have been sold, a definite sign of decreasing efficiency in the credit collection department.

The effectiveness of stock control is measured by the *stock turn* or by the *stockholding period*. These ratios are properly measured by comparing cost of sales to stockholding, but often the cost of sales figure is not available to the outside analyst and the sales figure is used instead. This gives an inaccurate answer, but should still say whether stock control is being maintained or improved.

The stock turn for Magrad for 1992 is 20 256 (item 2) divided by 1 986 (item 20), which indicates that the business sells stock to 10,20 times the value of the closing stock per year. In 1993 this figure has deteriorated to 2 480/17 257, or 7,07 times per year.

While the stock turn is widely used in practice the stockholding period may be of more use in assessing the undertaking. It is calculated by dividing the number of days in the year (365) by the stock turn. For Magrad this would be 365/10,20 or about 36 days in 1992 and 365/7,07 or about 52 days in 1993. The lengthening of this period, or the decrease in the stock turn, both show that the business has more money tied up in stock than it had in the previous year. This is normally because of a deterioration in the stock management.

SUMMARY OF ACTIVITY OR EFFICIENCY RATIOS

	1993	1992	Comments
Asset turnover	1,05	1,36	Decline—bad
Fixed assets turnover	2,49	2,48	No change
Receivables collection period	67 days	60 days	Increase—bad
Stock turn	7 ×	10 ×	Decline—bad
Stockholding period	52 days	36 days	Increase—bad

2.4 Debt or gearing ratios

The final group of financial statement ratios is the one dealing with the financial structure of the undertaking. A business can get finance either from the owners (or shareholders) or by borrowing. Every undertaking has some owners finance and some debt. These ratios seek to determine the extent to which the undertaking is dependent on debt.

This is by far the most complex aspect of ratio analysis and is best left for a more advanced book. Only a few basic ratios will be discussed here, the first of which is the *debt/equity ratio*. This is determined by comparing the interest bearing debt to the shareholders interest in the company. These are the two aspects of financing which require payment for their use: Shareholders want dividends and the lenders ɔf such debt want interest. Non-interest-bearing debt is ignored because it does not require payment.

For Magrad the ratio would be calculated by looking at the only item of interest bearing debt, the long term liabilities and comparing this with shareholders funds. There could be other items of interest bearing debt such as a bank overdraft, which would appear as a current liability. If Magrad had an overdraft this would then have to be added to the long term liabilities. As it is, the ratio is long term liabilities of 1 131 (item 33) divided by shareholders funds of 12 221 (item 32), or 9,25 %. By 1993 this had increased to 1 493/13 634, or 10,95 %. While there is a slight increase, the figure is still extremely low with most people being quite happy with a ratio of 50 %.

The only other ratio which will be discussed here is the *interest cover*. (Some people put ratios like this one into a separate category called coverage ratios.) Interest cover simply tries to determine just how capable an undertaking is of meeting its obligations in respect of interest. This is done by comparing the income before interest and taxation to the interest paid for the year. For Magrad this is 2 684 (item 5) divided by 290 (item 6), giving a coverage ratio of 9,26. This is extremely good, since it says that even if the income declined to about one-ninth of its present level the company could still meet its interest obligation. In 1993 the position is even better since there is a net amount of interest received, which means that there is no question of interest cover.

SUMMARY OF DEBT OR LEVERAGE RATIOS

	1993	1992	Comments
Debt/equity ratio	10,95 %	9,25 %	No problem
Interest cover	—	9,35 %	Good

While there is obviously more to be learnt about this company, the basic ratio analysis done above reveals the following about the company
1. It is both solvent and liquid and would have no trouble in meeting its obligations;
2. There are problems with its profitability. While the gross margin has increased quite significantly, the net margin has dropped slightly. This indicates that operating expenses have not been brought down in line with the decrease in sales;
3. The activity ratios show where some of the problems lie. Asset turnover has declined as a whole. While fixed asset turnover has remained virtually steady both the receivables collection period and the stock turn have deteriorated, indicating that there has been a deterioration in the management of these aspects; and
4. The leverage ratios confirm what was seen when looking at the solvency and liquidity ratios. This company has very little interest bearing debt and is easily capable of servicing it.

Overall, then, the company is in a healthy position but a continued deterioration in the receivables and stock areas would eventually lead to problems.

3. Conclusion

This chapter introduced the concept of ratio analysis and showed how, even on an elementary level, it can provide information about an undertaking. The following chapters are intended to give a better idea of how the technique is used in practice, as well as the problems and limitations of ratio analysis.

Key words

Financial ratios   Ratio analysis
Solvency ratios   Liquidity ratios
Profitability ratios   Efficiency ratios
Debt ratios

Chapter 14

More about ratio analysis

Basic financial ratio analysis provides a number of figures relating to the performance and financial condition of an undertaking. The beginner usually does not know how to use these, nor what their limitations are nor what the major problems associated with ratio analysis actually are. This chapter discusses these factors in order to present a more coherent picture of the technique of ratio analysis.

1. The Du Pont cascade

2. An alternative cascade based on the Du Pont formulation

3. The analysis of service undertakings

4. Growth analysis

5. Factors specific to the analysis of listed companies

6. Problems and limitations of financial statement analysis

1. The Du Pont cascade

The previous chapter discussed certain groups of financial ratios, each of which was used in the analysis of a particular aspect of an undertaking or of its operations. No attempt was made to show the interrelationships which exist between these various ratios, or how each one could affect or be affected by others. In order to do a thorough analysis of an undertaking it is necessary to take these interrelationships into account. When one is examining an undertaking and tries to project the results of that examination into the future it is necessary to be able to assess the impact that changing circumstances will have on the performance of the undertaking. For instance, if an improved supply chain will enable the firm to maintain lower stock levels but that increased competition may lead to smaller gross margins, how is the overall performance of the undertaking likely to be affected?

One fairly simple way of examining the effect of changes in one area of operations on others or on the overall performance of the undertaking is by use of the cascade of ratios originally developed by the Du Pont Corporation in the United States during the 1920s and subsequently developed by a number of other people. This method of using ratio analysis is probably the most logical way for a person with a limited financial background to tackle the analysis of an undertaking. The logic of the Du Pont approach is that each of the ratios used is a synthesis of at least two other ratios, or that it is influenced by other ratios. In its original simple form, the Du Pont formulation simply looked at three ratios:

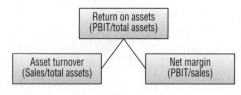

Figure 14.1

This triangle of ratios was used in evaluating firms for takeover purposes. The first ratio, the return on assets, would determine the overall efficiency of operations. If this was not satisfactory, an analysis of the secondary ratios would determine the area in which the undertaking was experiencing problems: insufficient sales or insufficient profit margins on sales. This secondary analysis would then allow an evaluation of whether it was possible to remedy the problem: was it possible to increase sales, or could margins be improved by raising prices or cutting costs?

It is easy to show that the primary ratio of Return on Total Assets is a synthesis of these secondary ratios. The formulae for the three ratios are as follows:

Return on total asset is:

$$\frac{\text{Profit before interest and tax (P)}}{\text{Total operating assets (A)}}$$

Asset turnover is:

$$\frac{\text{Total sales of products (S)}}{\text{Total operating assets (A)}}$$

Net margin is:

$$\frac{\text{Profit before interest and tax (P)}}{\text{Total sales of products (S)}}$$

Elementary algebra then shows that $(S/A) \times (P/S) = (P/A)$

The whole concept has been expanded considerably into a whole cascade of ratios and the following case study, Engineering Firm (Proprietary) Limited, will be used to demonstrate just how the ratio cascade is used.

1.1 Engineering Firm (Proprietary) Limited

Alan Baker, the senior director and major shareholder of Engineering Firm (Pty) Ltd (EF), is not quite happy with the current state of the company's affairs. It is profitable and is providing him with a good income but he cannot escape the feeling that there is some underlying cause for concern. The main reason for his worry, according to his co-director Colin Dover, is simply that the company appears to be doing so well during a period of general recession. Alan admits to feeling that the recession has to hit Engineering Firm (Pty) Ltd sooner or later and that this worries him, but insists that Colin is over-simplifying the matter. Much of their production is destined indirectly for the construction industry. Many long term contracts there are nearing completion and Alan feels that this will bring a drop in demand for their products. He has been monitoring building plans passed and construction contracts awarded and the constant downward tendency has given him sleepless nights. Colin, on the other hand, is confident that the drop in construction related work can be offset by new types of business.

A look at the history of the undertaking could explain the difference between the outlooks of the two men. Engineering Firm was founded in 1973 by Alan Baker to manufacture specialised sub-components. He had spotted a gap in the market and exploited it to the full, manufacturing to a very high standard certain goods which had previously been imported or else produced locally on a one-off basis at high cost . He soon built up an enviable reputation among the three undertakings which represented the total South African market for his product. He tried to build up an export market, but found that competition in Europe and the United States was so keen that the development of an overseas market would require a far greater investment of both time and money than what he had available at that stage. These considerations led him to take in a partner who could take care of the day to day management and free him to look at exports and any other promising developments. He eventually sold a substantial minority shareholding in the company to Colin Dover, putting the total amount paid by Colin into the business.

After a settling in period of about a year Colin started to spread his wings. Noting that the firm was dependent on just three customers (one of whom was in financial difficulties and was rumoured in the financial press as likely to fold or be taken over by one of the other two!), he set out to broaden the product base and, by implication, obtain a broader customer base. He felt that he was achieving some success, pointing out that the new products which he had introduced now accounted for twenty-eight per cent of total sales, although he admitted that the margins were probably not very big during what he referred to as a market penetration phase.

On the basis of the information available, particularly the financial statements below, Alan wants to know whether, at the end of 1985, he has any reason to be concerned and whether there are any danger signals in the medium to long term.

1.2 The analysis of Engineering Firm (Pty) Ltd

There are various reasons why one would analyse an undertaking like this: a bank manager would want an analysis before deciding on the granting of a loan, a potential purchaser would want to know what sort of return he could expect on his investment, analysts looking for weaknesses or problems and investigators looking for signs of misappropriations would all want to see what the financial statements could tell them. All of them, however, would start by looking at the profitability of the undertaking, which is also the point at which our cascade of ratios starts.

The ultimate measurement of profitability is the return which the owners get on the amounts which they have invested in the undertaking. This investment would be represented by the capital accounts in a sole trader's undertaking or a partnership, by the members' interest in a close corporation and by the shareholders' equity in a company.

The treatment of loans from shareholders in private companies and from members in close corporations

These should normally be treated as part of the equity. They are shown as loans rather than as equity to provide more flexibility to these (usually) smaller businesses.This is not an invariable rule. Sometimes the members or shareholders have advanced money to the entity on a purely commercial basis. Such loans are normally treated separately from the usual shareholders', directors' or members loans which are long term, interest free loans essential for the operations of the entity.

Since this is a private company and the loans are obviously long term and, in terms of note 4 to the financial statements, interest free, they will be treated as part of the equity. The equity at the end of 1983 then consists of:

Share capital	1 800
Retained earnings	320 000
Loans	183 200
	505 000

The income statement will show what return the shareholders are getting on their total equity. The figure to be used for evaluation of performance will depend on the purpose of the analysis. Those which could be used include dividends paid and operating profit, but only *Profit After Tax is used for the evaluation of Return on Equity*. This is logical, since this is the amount which actually accrues to the shareholders. It does not matter for an overall evaluation of the undertaking whether the profit is paid out to the shareholders in the form of a dividend or reinvested within the undertaking.

Exceptions to the profit after tax rule:

There are many variations on this rule for specific purposes. The *Financial Mail*, for instance, calculates a return on capital ratio by comparing income before interest and taxes with total funds employed. The term total funds employed is defined as being shareholders equity plus long term debt and is equal to net assets. The usual definition of net assets is total assets minus current liabilities.

The before tax profit would sometimes be used for purposes of comparison with other companies. Some companies could be sitting with an assessed loss for tax purposes, or may qualify for special tax rebates in certain years. In this case the taxes payable in the calculation of the after tax profit could obscure the comparative performance of the companies. The same would apply when comparing the trends of a company's performance over several years if the tax rates have varied during that time.

A problem which arises in the case of smaller undertakings is the amount which should be regarded as salary or remuneration to the owners or shareholders. The owners/partners of a small business or the working shareholder/director or member of a corporate entity should receive a market related remuneration for services performed. In the one man business this is normally ignored completely, but salaries paid to these people are reflected in the financial statements of partnerships or corporate entities. However, the salaries paid are often calculated in such a way as to minimise the total combined tax payable by the corporate entity and the shareholders. Before starting the analysis it is therefore necessary to determine the market related earnings of the people concerned and to adjust the profit figures accordingly for purposes of analysing the undertaking. The profit of a one man business should be reduced to the amount of the market related remuneration. In this case the payments to directors will be accepted as being realistically market related.

Using amounts determined in accordance with the above, the return on equity of
EF for the years 1983 to 1985, in what is known as time series analysis, would be
as follows:

	1985	1984	1983
Return (Profit after tax)	122 000	98 000	142 000
Equity (Including loans)	696 000	616 000	505 000
	17,53 %	15,91 %	28,12 %

This type of analysis is also known as dynamic analysis, while an analysis of the
figures of a single year is known as static analysis. There does not seem to be any
definite trend, a sharp drop being followed by a small rise. A glance at the income
statement, however, will show a dramatic drop in the effective rate of tax paid by
the company so that a better insight may be gained by looking at the pre-tax return:

	1985	1984	1983
Return (Profit before tax)	122 000	156 000	170 000
Equity (Including loans)	696 000	616 000	505 000
	17,53 %	25,32 %	33,66 %

For the sake of completeness this ratio can also be calculated on the basis of profit
before interest and tax (PBIT), which in this case represents the operating profit of
the company:

	1985	1984	1983
Profit before interest and tax	102 000	184 000	183 000
Equity (Including loans)	696 000	616 000	505 000
	14,66 %	29,87 %	36,24 %

Both of these ratios show a depressing picture and one which fully justifies Alan's
concern. The return is dropping sharply. The first picture of a drop and then a rise
is due entirely to the change in the effective tax rate. This drop in the tax rate was
due to tax concessions in respect of fixed assets for use in manufacturing,
concessions which were modified to a large extent shortly after the date of these
financial statements.

A further part of the analysis is to compare the results attained by this company
with those of its competitors, a process known as cross sectional analysis. As shown
graphically below in figure 14.2, this comparison further justifies Alan's doubts.
The whole industry has obviously felt the effects of the economic downturn, but EF
has fared worse than most. In 1983 it was one of the more profitable firms in the
industry, with ROE well above the industry average but by 1985 it had become one
of the laggards with ROE well below industry average.

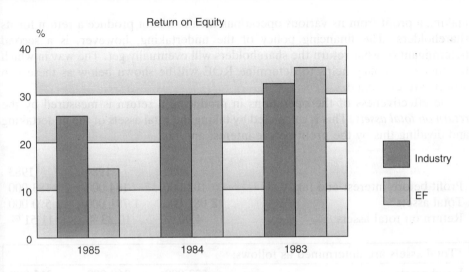

Figure 14.2

Industry averages

It is not easy to obtain industry averages in South Africa. There is no one body which collects this type of information and makes it available to the public. Several of the universities have databases, but these are inclined to be very limited in scope, while the more complete databases are not readily accessible. These include the databases of the commercial banks, the various development corporations and, of course, the database of Inland Revenue.

For practical purposes one is often forced to approximate an industry average by using figures for listed companies. The financial statements for these are readily available, but of course usually only contain the minimum information required. Figures such as cost of sales or details of expenses, for instance, are seldom published. The figures which are available usually provide a reasonable benchmark for comparison on the operations of a smaller undertaking, but larger companies are usually financed differently from smaller ones so that ratios involving debt and gearing are usually not reliable guidelines for what to expect in smaller companies.

It is also important that the companies used for comparison have the same financial year end, since using a company with a different year end will usually mean that the balance sheets are not comparable because of seasonal factors such as changes in stock levels.

The next step is to determine which aspect of the company's activities has been responsible for the drop in ROE. Broadly speaking, the first determinant of the ROE is the profit actually earned in the operating activities. If the company is not making a profit from its various operations then it cannot produce a return for its shareholders. The financing policy of the undertaking, however, is a second determinant of what return the shareholders will eventually get. The way in which the financing policy helps to determine ROE will be shown below as these two aspects are evaluated.

The effectiveness of the operations in producing a return is measured by the *return on total assets*. This is calculated by taking the total assets of the undertaking and dividing this by the profit before interest and tax:

	1985	1984	1983
Profit before interest and tax	102 000	184 000	183 000
Total assets*	2 081 000	1 781 000	1 590 000
Return on total assets	4,90 %	10,33 %	11,51 %

*Total assets are determined as follows:			
Fixed assets	572 000	360 000	315 000
Current assets	1 509 000	1 421 000	1 275 000
	2 081 000	1 781 000	1 590 000

Again there is a drop from 1983 to 1985, with ROTA falling to less than half of what it was. This leaves little doubt that a major part of the decline in ROE is due to the declining profitability of the operations, but there is still the aspect of financing to be considered.

A seldom used ratio will be calculated in order to show the effect of the financing policies on ROE. This is the ratio of total debt to total assets, which is the reverse of the solvency ratio calculated in the previous chapter. The ratio would normally be calculated by adding together the short term liabilities and the long term liabilities and dividing these by the total assets as calculated above. In this particular case there are no long term liabilities, so that short term liabilities represent the total liabilities:

	1985	1984	1983
Total debt	1 385 000	1 165 000	1 085 000
Total assets	2 081 000	1 781 000	1 590 000
Debt as a percentage of assets	66,55 %	65,41 %	68,24 %

The fluctuations are very small in themselves and also in relation to the industry average as can be seen in figure 14.3 below:

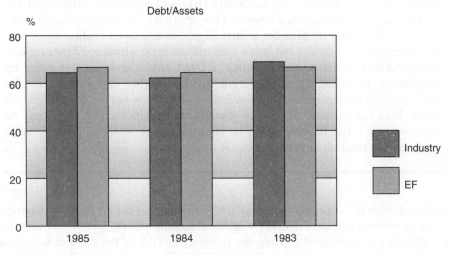

Figure 14.3

While the percentage does not vary enough to have a dramatic effect on the ROE, the small effect it has can be shown as follows:

	1985	1984	1983
ROE using PBIT	14,66 %	29,87 %	36,24 %
ROTA	4,90 %	10,33 %	11,51 %
ROE−ROTA	9,76 %	19,54 %	24,73 %
ROE−ROTA as a % of ROE	66,57 %	65,42 %	68,24 %

While there are small rounding off differences as a result of working to only two decimal places this last line is obviously the same as the debt/assets ratio calculated above. The relationship between these three ratios can be expressed as ROE = (Debt/assets)/(ROE−ROTA). Quite clearly, ROE is determined by the two subsidiary ratios of ROTA and Debt/assets and a change in either of these will effect a change in ROE. The fact that ROE and ROTA do not change at exactly the same rate in this case is due to the small changes in Debt/assets.

Return on net assets

Some firms use a return on *net* assets (RONA) approach rather than the ROTA approach described above. This approach is generally satisfactory when one is simply looking for a single figure to use as an evaluation of how well a company is doing, but it is a bastardised ratio which combines aspects of operations and aspects of finance. RONA could be improved either by improving the efficiency of operations (which is what one would normally desire) or by increasing current liabilities (which may not be desirable at all in the long run because of the way it could sour relations with suppliers). In the case of EF the RONA would be identical to the ROE on a PBIT basis, since equity (including loans) is equal to net assets.

The conclusion to be drawn from the above calculation is that ROE is dependent on the combined effect of ROTA and the financing policy, which was measured here in terms of debt:assets. A change in either ROTA or the ratio of borrowings will have a direct, proportional effect on ROE. The profits earned by operations (ROTA) are said to be geared up (or levered up) by the amount of borrowings and the greater the borrowings the larger will be the difference between ROE and ROTA.

The effect of gearing or financial leverage will increase both positive and negative operating results in exactly the same way. The more a company borrows, the greater will be the return to the shareholders in relation to the operating profit *and* the greater will be the percentage loss to the shareholders in relation to an operating loss.

Since the first step of the analysis indicated that the problems of the company lay on the operating side, it is on this side that the analysis must continue. This second triangle of ratios is the one first mentioned—the original Du Pont formulation shown in fig 14.1 above.

Since the superior ratio, return on total assets, has already been calculated it is only necessary to calculate the remaining two in order to determine where the fault lies. Asset turnover compares turnover and total assets to see how many times per year the company has "sold" the value of its assets. Problems encountered in practice with this ratio are those tied in with asset valuation, but if the values shown on the financial statements of Engineering Firm are accepted as being reasonable, the ratios for the three years would be as follows:

	1985	1984	1983
Sales for the year	4 650 000	4 550 000	3 665 000
Total assets	2 081 000	1 781 000	1 590 000
Asset turnover ratio	2,23 ×	2,55 ×	2,31 ×

This shows a sharp rise and then a fall back to below previous levels, this fall coinciding with a substantial increase in fixed assets. This occurs quite frequently, particularly when the new assets may have been bought towards the end of the year or possibly bought but not yet fully commissioned. A further possibility is that machinery has been bought in excess of current production requirements but in anticipation of a growing market in the near future. The answers to questions concerning these matters are not available in the information given, and could only be determined by enquiries on the spot. Examining Engineering Firm's performance in the light of that of the competition also does not tell one very much. It is slightly below industry average in 1983 and again in 1985, but slightly above in 1984, as shown in fig 14.4 below. The trends are much the same as for the average, but the changes are slightly bigger.

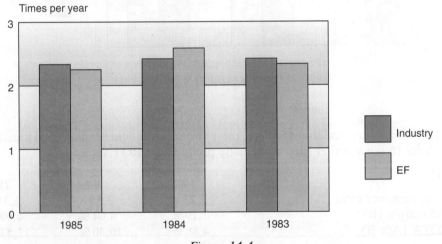

Figure 14.4

However, the fluctuations are not large enough to account for the drop in ROTA, and it is necessary to calculate the ratio on the other leg of this triangle, the net margin. This calculation is as follows:

	1985	1984	1983
Sales for the year	4 650 000	4 550 000	3 665 000
Net income (PBIT)	102 000	184 000	183 000
Net margin	2,19 %	4,04 %	4,99 %

In this case there is no need to agonise over the possible significance of small fluctuations. The sharp downward trend is quite apparent. What is more, there is a consistent downward trend as compared to the fluctuating trend of the industry average, and Engineering Firm has dropped from way above industry average to well below it as shown in fig 14.5.

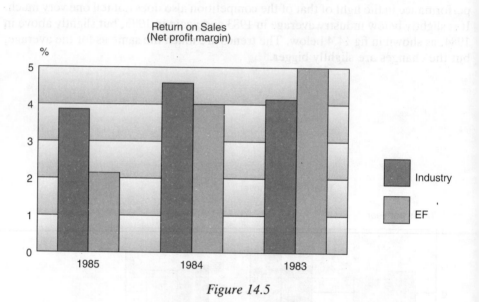

Figure 14.5

As a check on calculations to date, these two ratios should be multiplied together in order to see whether they do actually produce the ROTA:

	1985	1984	1983
Asset turnover ratio (A)	2,23 ×	2,55 ×	2,31 ×
Net margin (B)	2,19 %	4,04 %	4,99 %
ROTA (A × B)	4,88 %	10,30 %	11,53 %

Again there are small rounding off errors, but there can be little doubt that the ROTA of Engineering Firm has been dropping sharply and that the prime reason for this is the drop in net margin, compounded in 1985 by the sharp fall in assets turnover.

It might be as well at this stage to think about possible solutions to the problems which could cause either of the two ratios at the base of the original Du Pont approach to show deterioration. Since sales or turnover is the one factor common to both assets turnover and net margin, it forms a good starting point. An increase in sales would clearly have the effect of improving the asset turnover ratio if there were no corresponding increase in the assets base. What would be the effect of such an increase on the net profit margin? Simplistically, it might seem that such an increase might lead to a reduction in the net margin since increasing the denominator in a fraction gives an ever smaller fraction. In fact, this is unlikely to happen within normal operating ranges of production unless such sales have been achieved by cutting of margins. If the gross margin has remained constant an increase in sales will normally bring about an increase in net margin since the expenses of the undertaking tend to remain constant in total within specified ranges of activity. The gross profit will therefore tend to increase as sales increase, and an ever larger amount will be available to cover these relatively constant expenses. The result is that net profit tends to increase faster than sales, leading to an increase in net margin. This can be demonstrated by use of a simple breakeven graph as in fig 14.6. Fixed or non-variable expenses remain constant while direct costs, which in a pure trading concern equate to cost of sales, increase proportionately to sales. Once the margin on direct costs, or gross profit in the case of a trading concern, is big enough to cover the fixed costs, the net margin increases rapidly.

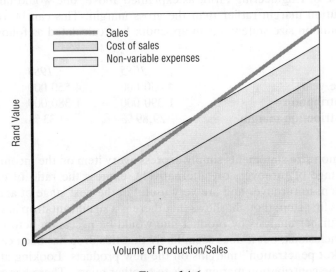

Figure 14.6

An analysis of the net margin (net profit over turnover) requires that the component parts of the net profit be broken down. Net operating profit is the difference between sales and expenses. If it is too small, the correction could come about either by increasing sales or decreasing expenses or some combination of these. Leaving the sales aside for the moment, the expenses can be split into two groups: those which vary directly with sales and those which do not vary with sales or do not vary directly with sales. In a trading concern items falling into the first category would be those which are normally included in cost of sales for purposes of determining gross profit; in a manufacturing concern there is not quite so absolute a relationship, but selling prices are normally based on direct production

costs with a pre-calculated contribution percentage added to cover overhead costs.
Such figures would not normally be available from the financial statements of listed
companies, and no effort has been made to try to determine an industry average for
gross profit or contribution margin. Fig. 14.7 shows the next triangle of ratios to be
calculated.

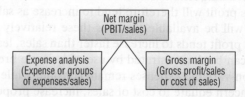

Figure 14.7

In the case of Engineering Firm, as explained above, one would take a look at
the contribution margin rather than the gross margin. This can be read directly
from the common size statements in appendix 1 or calculated as follows:

	1985	1984	1983
Sales for the year	4 650 000	4 550 000	3 665 000
Factory contribution	1 390 000	1 380 000	1 255 000
Factory contribution margin	29,89 %	30,33 %	34,24 %

The common size statements simply express every item on the income statement
as a percentage of turnover, or, alternatively, express the ratio of each income
statement item to turnover and are very useful in the next stage of analysis of net
margin. This first step, though, shows that there is a significant drop in contribution
margin. A further analysis by product line would be necessary before arriving at
any final conclusions, but it does seem likely that this drop has been caused by the
lower "market penetration" margins on the new products. Looking at the figures
making up the contribution margin leads to another query. There has been a slight
but persistent increase in design fees, which could tie in with the fact that new
products are being introduced, but there is a sudden large rise in subcontracted
work in 1985, which would have to be explained. It could be due to such factors as
a breakdown in the factory during the year forcing use of outside contractors or to
technical problems with the production of the new products which require specialist
contractors to make some parts.

The analysis to date has shown that the major problem lies in the net margin and
in the factors making up this net margin. No analysis could just be left there,
however. The other leg of the cascade was asset turnover, and it is possible that
there are problems hidden away in this leg as well. After all, fig 14.13 shows two
underlying ratios there and it is possible that one could be good and the other bad,
so giving an overall impression of average performance. As a matter of fact, there

are far more than just two, and one way of setting these out is the one shown in fig 14.8.

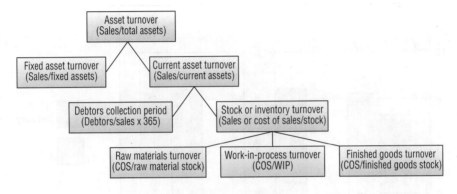

Figure 14.8

The first obvious subdivision of the ratios is that of splitting the assets into the major groupings of fixed and current assets. The other possibility would of course be to do a sales analysis to find out which products had fared well and which had not. While such an analysis would form part of any detailed analysis the information for this is not contained in the financial statements. An examination of the firm's management accounting records would be necessary. As far as information about the assets is concerned, however, there is no problem. The fixed assets turnover ratios for the three years are as follows:

	1985	1984	1983
Sales for the year	4 650 000	4 550 000	3 665 000
Fixed assets	572 000	360 000	315 000
	8,13	12,64	11,63

There is obviously a problem here, but as mentioned above it may be due to plant only being commissioned towards the end of the year or not fully productive during the year as new products are introduced and have to get up to scheduled production levels. This is a matter for investigation and further discussion with the company. When compared with the rest of the industry, Engineering Firm's fixed asset turnover looks very satisfactory. As shown in fig 14.9, it is consistently higher than that of its competitors. The only factor which has to be taken into account here is the possibility that Engineering Firm is making more extensive use of leased assets than its competitors, so that the figure is distorted by not bringing into account all the fixed assets in use. This is particularly pertinent in view of the requirements of AC105 which calls for capitalisation of assets used in terms of a financial lease. The notes to the financial statements of Engineering Firm specifically state that this policy has not been applied but that leased assets are only capitalised at the end of the lease period.

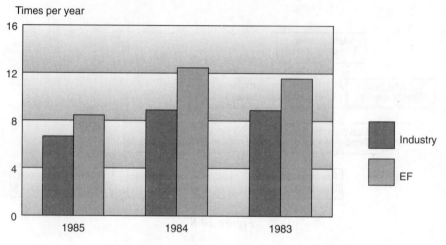

Figure 14.9

When it comes to current asset turnover, Engineering Firm does not look too bright. Fig 14.10 shows that its ratio is consistently well below that of its competitors. However, in practice one would not pay too much attention to this ratio. In fact, it would probably not even be calculated and is included here largely to show the cascade structure.

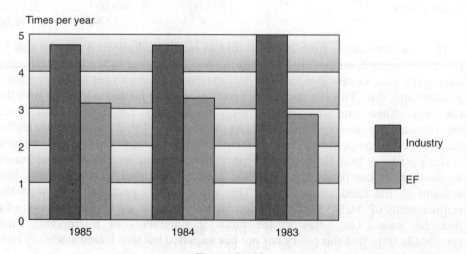

Figure 14.10

The fact of the matter is that this ratio is made up of underlying ratios which could so easily move in opposite directions that the overall trend in this ratio could serve to hide problems in the component ratios. It would be more usual to skip this "building block" step in the cascade and to go straight to the component ratios of stock and debtor turnover. It is also possible to calculate a cash turnover ratio, but since cash is so volatile, changing dramatically from day to day, this does not usually have much to say to the analyst who would obtain the required information about cash from the cash flow statement.

Debtors turnover can be calculated, but the ratio is usually inverted and instead of calculating turnover over debtors the debtors are calculated as a percentage of sales. This percentage is then applied to the accounting period of a year in order to obtain an indication of the percentage of a year which it takes to collect the amounts allowed in respect of sales on credit.

There are two calculations which can be made here. One could either calculate using total sales or using credit sales. The latter would be used to gain an indication of how efficiently debt collection procedures were being applied, while the former would be used in order to gain average cash flow information in respect of all sales. This ratio could be improved either by collecting outstanding debt more quickly or by improving the ratio of cash sales to credit sales.

In an undertaking such as Engineering Firm it would be a reasonable assumption that all sales would be on credit, so that there would only be one ratio to calculate in any case. This would be calculated as follows:

	1985	1984	1983
Debtors	1 300 000	1 210 000	1 064 000
Sales for the year	4 650 000	4 550 000	3 665 000
Debtors as % of sales (A)	27,96 %	26,59 %	29,03 %
A as % of 1 year (365 days)	102 days	97 days	106 days

While there was a slight overall improvement the period still seems very long. A comparison with the industry figures backs this up. Fig 14.11 clearly shows that Engineering Firm is taking far longer than its competitors to collect its debt, even though the industry figures have shown a marked deterioration over the three years. This is serious, since every day that the money is uncollected means that Engineering Firm has to finance its operations out of expensive sources such as the bank overdraft for an extra day.

The other aspect of current assets turnover is that of stockholding. This is one of those ratios which is very difficult to calculate accurately when one is working with financial statements of listed companies due to the lack of adequate information. Since stock, in all its manifestations, is valued at cost it is only logical to use cost of sales to determine stock turnover and stockholding period rather than to use sales. Cost of sales information is rarely published so that it is usually necessary to use sales figures to gain an approximate idea of stock movement. Any trends determined using sales must be based on the assumption that there have been no variations in markup over the period under review, since any such changes would introduce a distorting factor and possibly destroy the validity of the trends determined.

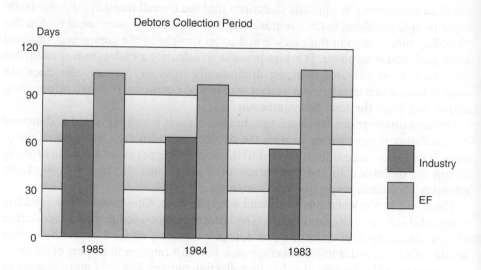

Figure 14.11

For purposes of comparison with the other companies sales have been used in the determination of a stock turnover period. However, for internal purposes it would be necessary to use a cost of sales figure, which could be based on the costs used to determine factory contribution

	1985	1984	1983
Stock	195 000	185 000	200 000
Sales for the year	4 650 000	4 550 000	3 665 000
Direct contribution	1 390 000	1 380 000	1 255 000
"Cost of sales"	3 260 000	3 170 000	2 410 000
Stock as % of COS (A)	5,98 %	5,84 %	8,30 %
A as % of 1 year (365 days)	22 days	21 days	30 days

These figures are reasonably accurate for use in a calculation about internal financing, but they cannot be used for comparison purposes. For these, a stock turnover figure based on sales is necessary:

	1985	1984	1983
Stock	195 000	185 000	200 000
Sales for the year	4 650 000	4 550 000	3 665 000
Stock as % of sales (A)	4,19 %	4,07 %	5,46 %
A as % of 1 year (365 days)	15 days	15 days	20 days

These figures can be compared with those for the industry as shown in fig. 14.12 and it can immediately be seen that Engineering Firm is far better than its competitors.

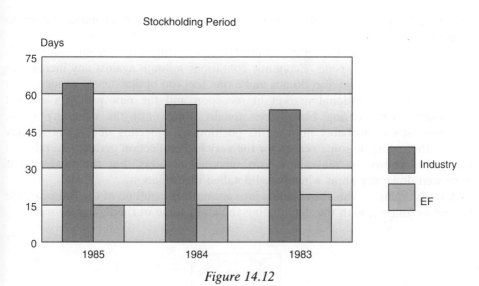

Figure 14.12

This is a typical example of what was mentioned above as a problem in the use of a composite current assets turnover figure. Debtors are much worse than industry average figures and show little improvement while stockholding figures are much better and show a distinct improvement and especially a relative improvement since the industry figure is deteriorating. The overall effect could be to show virtually no change in the composite ratio, which might hide from the casual observer the very real problem with debtors.

There could be several reasons for the relatively good stockholding figures. Larger firms possibly have larger contracts which take longer to complete; Engineering Firm and other smaller firms may be able to rely upon the stockholdings of their suppliers and keep very little stock on hand themselves or some of the firms may also manufacture sub-components which are held in stock until required for the main contracts. Whatever the reason (and it would have to be investigated), Engineering Firm has very little money tied up in stock on the dates of the balance sheets.

At this point it may be well to summarise. Using profits before interest and tax showed that there was indeed a worrying drop in profits. This was shown to be due largely to the poor return being obtained on assets, which was in turn due largely to the drop on net margin. This was largely due to the drop in contribution margin. A starting point in drawing up a list of problem areas to be sorted out would therefore be to investigate the reasons for this and to improve margins if possible, either by raising prices or cutting costs or both. It was also shown that an increase in the unit sales would lead to improved margins by reducing the non-varying or fixed costs per unit of product sold. An increase in sales could therefore overcome this problem as well.

Of course, there is seldom only one problem. Going back to the assets turnover path it was soon found that there was a major problem with the collection of debt.

This would naturally be another area for concern in the list of recommendations to Alan Baker.

The overall result of the analysis would be to confirm Alan's feeling that there is something seriously wrong. Economic conditions militate against any increase in prices at this point and also do not make one feel too optimistic about increasing sales. With its traditional market in recession and the new products not yet established, Engineering Firm faces tough riding until the economy turns. However, it can probably improve its position by collecting debt more quickly though there may be some reason for the very high collection period. Overall, not enough is known to make any firm recommendations, but the analysis has narrowed down the areas which need detailed investigation.

After bringing all the above ratios into account, the outline of the ratio cascade will be as follows, with the detail being shown in some of the figures above:

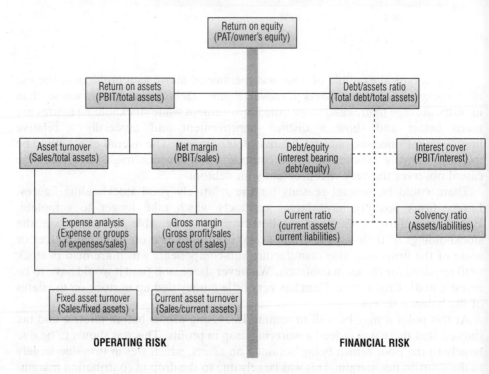

Figure 14.13

1.4 Ratios not discussed in the above analysis

The above analysis ignored the ratios dealing with the financial policies of EF after it was determined that these played little part in the drop in ROE. The important ones were discussed in the previous chapter under the headings "Solvency and liquidity ratios" and "Debt or gearing ratios", except for the so-called *leverage index* which is used to measure the overall effect of gearing. This is simply the ROE divided by the ROTA. In the case of EF this is as follows:

    1985   17,53/ 4,90 = 3,58
    1984   15,91/10,33 = 1,54
    1983   28,12/11,51 = 2,44

In each case the index is positive, indicating that the effect of gearing is positive for this company. As soon as the index becomes negative it indicates that the effect of gearing is negative. This would mean that the cost of borrowing the money (interest) is greater than the benefit received from the use of that borrowed money. This has happened on occasion when the rates of interest rise swiftly and undertakings with large borrowings suddenly find themselves in the position of carrying interest burdens so great as to wipe out their profits.

Another index figure which is used for year on year comparisons is the *liquidity index*. This is actually an alternative way of looking at the operating cycle, which is the subject of chapter 18. It simply looks at the elements of current assets and prepares an index showing the time taken to turn these assets into cash by multiplying these elements by the number of days it takes to turn them into cash (debtors collection period, stockholding period). It adds the products of these calculations together and divides the sum of the products by the total of the current assets as follows:

	1985			1984			1983		
	Amount	Days	Product	Amount	Days	Product	Amount	Days	Product
Cash	14	0	0	26	0	0	11	0	0
Debtors	1 300	102	132 600	1 210	97	117 370	1 064	105	111 720
Stock	195	15	2 925	185	15	2 775	200	20	4 000
	1 509		135 525	1 421		120 145	1 275		115 720
Index (Product/Amount)			89,81			84,55			90,76

Any increase in the index is then deemed to be a decline in the liquidity of the undertaking.

Another ratio of which mention must be made is the *fixed charges coverage* ratio which expresses interest before interest and tax as a multiple of the sum of interest charges and such fixed charges as capital repayments on debt and lease payments. These can be obtained from the notes to the financial statements dealing with long term debt and with commitments. A further refinement of this ratio will be dealt with in chapter 16.

A ratio sometimes found is the *net current assets turnover*. This suffers from the same problems as the current assets turnover and also from those found in RONA. The ratio is calculated by comparing sales to net current assets (current assets−current liabilities). Since this is a composite figure improvements could be brought about by improvements in current asset management or by an increase in current liabilities. Flowing from this, though, is a very useful ratio: the *creditors payment period*. This period is calculated in a very similar fashion to the debtors collection period. Outstanding creditors are divided by the total of *goods and services* bought on credit during the year and then multiplied by 365 in order to obtain the average period taken to pay creditors. The total of goods and services bought on credit is not always easy to determine from the financial statements and it is often necessary to make assumptions about services bought. For practical purposes, all expenses are accepted as being bought on credit except salaries and wages, items which are normally prepaid such as rent and lease charges and of course non-cash items such as depreciation.

Calculations for the creditors payment period

	1985	1984	1983
Sales	4 650 000	4 550 000	3 665 000
Net operating income	102 000	184 000	183 000
Expenses for the year	4 548 000	4 366 000	3 482 000
Non-credit expenses	2 238 000	2 142 500	1 844 500
Salaries and wages	1 730 000	1 610 000	1 339 000
Rent	80 000	70 000	65 000
Lease charges	325 000	357 000	315 000
Depreciation	103 000	105 500	125 500
Credit financed purchases	2 310 000	2 223 500	1 637 500
Creditors	760 000	600 000	555 000
Creditors payment period	120	98	124

This period appears excessively long, but it raises one of the problems discussed below. Businesses of this type usually close down from about mid-December and re-open after the first week of January. Employees go on holiday leave and the factory undergoes its annual maintenance procedure. Most of their customers do the same. The result is that orders only start coming in during the second week of January and the factory only really gets back into full production in mid-January. Because of this dead period as little raw material as possible is purchased during late November and early December. Purchases during January and February are abnormally high because of this and creditors at the end of February are therefore also abnormally high, which gives a false impression of the length of time normally taken to pay them.

2. An alternative cascade based on the Du Pont formulation

There are also other ways of combining ratios when analysing an undertaking than the Du Pont cascade discussed above. Where the information is available to calculate contribution margins (see chapter 17) the combination described below is also effective. It measures the effect of pricing policy, marketing ability, asset utilisation and financial policy on return on equity.

The detailed income statement for EF is drawn up so as to reflect a direct margin (sales minus variable cost, which is the same as the gross profit in a trading concern). It also reflects a factory contribution, but this can be ignored for purposes of this analysis since it is determined after taking certain fixed costs (such as factory salaries) and indirect costs (such as maintenance) into account. The common size statement shows that the direct contribution margin is 28,82 % of sales in 1985, 29,23 % in 1984 and 33,15 % in 1983. This is regarded as an indication of *pricing policy*, and shows that EF has been cutting prices.

Once this figure has been calculated it is easy to determine the *breakeven point* of sales for EF. This is the amount of sales at which the company will make neither profit nor loss, and will simply be that amount of sales at which total indirect factory expenses and total administrative expenses equal 28,82 % of sales:

Indirect factory expenses	610 000
Administrative expenses	628 000
Total	1 238 000
Sales of which this is 28,82 %	4 295 628

Similar calculations will show the breakeven point in 1984 to be R3 920 629 and in 1983 R3 113 122. This figure is based on the assumption that all expenses will remain at current levels other than those which vary directly with the volume of production and which were included in the direct cost of sales. Obviously, as the contribution margin shrinks the breakeven point rises (the undertaking needs to sell more goods to break even).

The difference between the actual sales and the breakeven sales is known as the *margin of safety*. The margin of safety for 1985 was R354 372, for 1984 it was R629 371 and for 1983 it was R552 878. Expressed as a percentage of sales, the margin of safety has declined to 7,62 % of sales in 1985 from 13,93 % in 1984 and 15,08 % of sales in 1983. These percentages are regarded as an indicator of the *marketing ability* of the undertaking, since they show the amount by which sales could decline before wiping out the profits of the undertaking. The better the marketing, the larger the percentage should be. As far as EF is concerned, the figure for 1985 is extremely worrying.

Note at this point that net income is a function of the percentage contribution margin and the margin of safety sales. Ignoring the rounding off differences, the calculations to prove this are:

1985[1] 28,82 % × R354 372 = R102 000 *or* 28,82 % × 7,62 % = 2,19 %
1984   29,23 % × R629 371 = R184 000 *or* 29,23 % × 13,93 % = 4,04 %
1983   33,15 % × R552 878 = R183 000 *or* 33,15 % × 15,08 % = 4,99 %

The percentages calculated above are the net margin percentages calculated on p 253.

Asset utilisation is measured in the same way as before by the asset turnover ratio, and as before asset turnover multiplied by net margin will give return on assets. At this stage, then, this formulation is:

ROTA = Asset turnover × Contribution margin × Margin of safety.

There are two measures of *financial policy* which are brought into account: firstly, instead of the debt: assets ratio calculated previously a ratio of total assets to equity is calculated (preference shares are not regarded as part of the equity); and secondly, the ratio of net profit before tax but after interest to net profit before tax and interest. Preference dividends, if any, are treated in the same way as interest since they represent a fixed rate payment for a portion of the financing of the undertaking.

The assets to equity ratio multiplied by ROTA will give the return on equity before interest and tax. This is quite easy to prove:

Assets/Equity × PBIT/Assets (ROTA) = PBIT/Equity

In the case of EF the assets/equity ratio is as follows:

1985   2 081 000/696 000 = 2,99
1984   1 781 000/616 000 = 2,89
1983   1 590 000/505 000 = 3,15

The formulation to date then is:
Assets/equity × Asset turnover × Contribution margin × Margin of safety = PBIT/Equity

1985   2,99 × 2,23 × 28,82 % × 7,62 % = 14,66 %
1984   2,89 × 2,55 × 29,23 % × 13,93 % = 29,87 %
1983   3,15 × 2,31 × 33,15 % × 15,08 % = 36,24 %

Next, profit before tax to profit before interest and tax gives a measure of the gearing of the undertaking. For EF this ratio is:

1985   122 000/102 000 = 1,196
1984   156 000/184 000 = 0,848
1983   170 000/183 000 = 0,929

The figure for 1985 is an awkward one. In actual fact interest received should be taken out of the financial statements together with the investment which earned the interest. Since, according to the balance sheet, the investment did not exist at the end of the year but must have been an investment of surplus funds at some time during the year, the amount has been left in. These figures are a kind of reverse leverage index in that the greater the positive value of gearing over the period, the smaller will be this figure.

The effect of the cost of gearing is then obtained by multiplying the PBIT based ROE with this figure:

1985   14,66 % × 1,196 = 17,53 %
1984   29,87 % × 0,848 = 25,32 %
1983   36,24 % × 0,929 = 33,66 %

Finally, the reciprocal of the effective tax rate is calculated by dividing PAT by PBT:

1985   122 000/122 000 = 100,00 % (tax rate is 100,00 − 100,00 = 0)
1984   98 000/ 156 000 = 62,82 % (tax rate is 100,00 − 62,82 = 37,18 %)
1983   142 000/ 170 000 = 83,53 % (tax rate is 100,00 − 83,53 = 16,47 %)

If this reciprocal is multiplied by the PBT based ROE, the answer will be the ROE properly calculated on the basis of profit after tax:

1985   100,00 % × 17,53 % = 17,53 %
1984   62,82 % × 25,32 % = 15.91 %
1983   83,53 % × 33,66 % = 28.12 %

The whole layout of this method of analysis can be set out as follows:

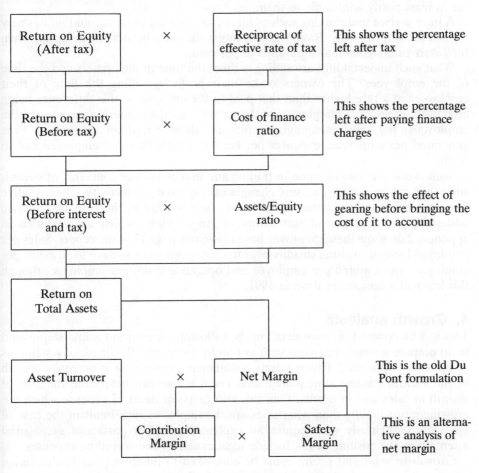

Figure 14.14

Any further analysis of the asset turnover would then proceed along the same lines as in the previous formulation of the expanded Du Pont formulation used in the analysis of EF.

3. The analysis of service undertakings

The ratios discussed thus far are wholly applicable to manufacturing and trading undertakings. However, they would not give all the information necessary for a satisfactory analysis of a service undertaking. There are not that many pure service undertakings other than professional practices, since businesses like banks (which are discussed below) are service organisations but they do have enormous investments in assets which are used to generate their income and the above ratios are at least partly applicable to them.

A pure service undertaking such as that of an attorney or an accountant has very little in the way of assets. Ratios such as return on assets become meaningless when they start running up into thousands of per cent.

What such undertakings are selling is time: the time of the owners and the time of the employees. The owners make their profit by selling the time of their employees at a rate higher than that paid to the employees, this difference being effectively their gross margin. Since the "assets" used to generate income are the employees, the most meaningful ratios are those based on employees: Fees generated per employee, expenses per employee, idle time per employee and so forth.

Such ratios are also of value in trading and manufacturing concerns, of course, since they can be used to measure changes in employee productivity. Their relative importance in such industries is, however, far less than in the case of a service undertaking. The financial statements of Anglo-Alpha which are included in appendix 2 do show these employee based ratios on page 17 of the report. Sales per employee have been rising steadily over the last seven years as have fixed assets per employee, value added per employee and operating profit per employee, though this last had a temporary drop in 1991.

4. Growth analysis

This will be covered in more detail in the following chapter but a first step would be to prepare a trend statement such as that included with the financial statements of EF in the appendix. This is simply a statement showing the percentage growth in the various income statement items. From it one can determine the rate of growth in sales and in profits. One can also pinpoint items of expense which are growing more rapidly than what sales are. Examples of such items in the case of EF, which obviously will require an explanation and/or particular managerial attention in the ensuing years, include legal expenses and travelling expenses.

Growth in sales and profits must be compared to inflation rates to determine whether the growth is real or only monetary. In the case of EF it is plain that there was no real growth since the inflation rates at the time under discussion were well above the nominal growth rates shown.

5. Factors specific to the analysis of listed companies

5.1 Annual financial reports of listed companies

The example of Engineering Firm (Pty) Ltd was used above to demonstrate how financial ratio analysis could be used to determine the trouble spots in a company.

Ratios could also be used to decide on whether or not to invest in a company and are part of the analysis of listed companies. The number of ratios which can be calculated for most listed companies is limited, however, because of the fact that the annual reports sent to shareholders do not contain enough detailed numerical information. The financial report of Anglo-Alpha Limited is exceptional in that it does include such items as the gross profit of the company, but Anglo-Alpha's financial reports have long been recognised as among the best produced in South Africa.

To compensate for the paucity of financial information there is a great deal of descriptive information contained in the various reports. Again, Anglo-Alpha gives much more than most but all companies must give a complete director's report as required by the Companies Act and additional information required by the regulations of the JSE. This information is usually contained in a separate report called a chairman's report or management report or some similar name. In addition, there are a number of statements of GAAP which are specifically applicable to listed companies. These require disclosure of such matters as sales and profits by segment of the business, capitalization of leased assets and accounting for the results of associated companies by the equity method. There is also the very important requirement that accounting policies be clearly stated.

The analysis of such a company will start with a review of the accounting policies, followed by a study of the director's report and the chairman's review. Where there are other reports, such as the social report of Anglo-Alpha, these must also be studied for relevant information. Only then will the ratio analysis be undertaken. This will usually follow the same lines as the analysis of Magrad Limited in chapter 13, with any changes being further analysed in terms of the Du Pont cascade in order to determine what effect they have had on overall performance.

5.2 Stock exchange ratios

The next step in the analysis is to examine information extrinsic to the financial reports. This would include reports in the financial press and an analysis of what investors generally feel about the share. This feeling is generally reflected in the share price on the Johannesburg Stock Exchange.

Several ratios are calculated on the basis of the trading price of a share and are published in the financial press. The three most commonly found are discussed here:

The *price/earnings ratio* (P/E) is determined by firstly taking the earnings for the year and dividing this by the number of shares in issue to get an Earnings Per Share (EPS) figure. This figure is not all that important on its own, but because it is used widely in share analysis people do want to see it. The EPS is then divided into the ruling price of the share. As an example, the EPS of Anglo-Alpha, as given in the notes to the financial statements, is 421,5 cents (based on historical costs) and the closing price of the share on the Johannesburg Stock Exchange at 31 December 1993 was 7 000 cents. The P/E ratio would have been 7 000/421,5 or 16,6. This is in the higher range of these ratios and indicates fairly high investor confidence in the company. By way of contrast, the p/e of a highly rated company like South African

Breweries at the same stage was 20,3, while that of Magrad, used as an example in the previous chapter, was only 3,93.

Rather than use the p/e, some people prefer its inverse which is known as the *earnings yield* (E Y). In the case of Anglo-Alpha this would be the EPS expressed as a percentage of the ruling share price, or 421,5/7 000 × 100 which comes to 6,0 %. In the case of this ratio, a low percentage expresses high investor confidence.

A third ratio of interest to investors is the *dividend yield* (D Y). This is determined by expressing the dividend per share as a percentage of the ruling stock exchange price of the share and tells an investor what cash return he would be getting if he bought shares in the company at the current price. In the case of Anglo-Alpha the notes give the dividend as 175 cents per share and the D Y is 175/ 7 000 × 100, or 2,5 %. This is a low return. Even if one bears in mind that no income tax is payable on dividends received, this would be equivalent to receiving taxable interest of about 4,8 % at a 48 % marginal personal tax rate. The fact that this is still low indicates that the market is sure that there will be growth in the future and that it is worthwhile accepting this low return now in order to obtain the expected future benefits.

A final ratio which could be calculated is the *dividend cover*. This is an indication of what proportion of its income the company is paying out to its shareholders and is calculated by dividing the E Y by the D Y. In the case of Anglo-Alpha this would be 6,0/2,5 or 2,4. This shows that the company is not paying out a very large amount since the dividends could be 2,4 times as big before exhausting all the income. This ratio could also be calculated directly from the financial statements. Simply take the net income for the year and divide by the ordinary dividend declared. This would give 126 786/52 634 = 2,4.

Anglo-Alpha, of course, calculates these ratios and publishes them in the financial statements. An interesting extra is the fact that this company, being one of the few which do actually make full adjustments for the effects of inflation, calculates and publishes these figures on both a historical cost and a current cost basis. A look at the statistics on page 17 of the financial statements shows that earnings per share drop from 421,5 cents to 254,9 cents when inflation is brought into account and that earnings yield then drops from 6,0 % to 3,6 %. Dividend cover drops from a conservative looking 2,4 down to 1,44.

Some people also use an inverted version of the dividend cover which is known as the *ploughback percentage*. It is calculated by subtracting the D Y from the E Y and expressing the result as a percentage of the E Y. In the case of Anglo-Alpha this would be (6,0 − 2,5)/6,0 × 100, or 58 %. This is the percentage of its income that Anglo-Alpha is ploughing back into the business. A high ploughback percentage is usually taken to mean that the company is holding back money in order to finance expansion or new ventures.

5.3 Problems associated with the analysis of banking and mining companies
Anyone setting out to analyse mining annual reports by using only the ratios quoted here is in for a shock. These companies differ from manufacturing and trading

companies in that they are working a depleting asset. The future of the company cannot only be evaluated on the basis of past performance but also on the amount of ore left in the ground and the economics of mining it. This information is provided in the form of technical reports which are required in terms of Johannesburg Stock Exchange regulations but in order to interpret these it is necessary to have some relevant technical knowledge. The analysis of mining reports, especially gold mining reports, has become a specialised field.

Banks (and insurance companies) have been granted special concessions as far as financial reporting is concerned, though not all of them take full advantage of these. Effectively, they are allowed to build up secret reserves in good years and to draw on these in bad years in order to smooth their reported profits. The longer term effect of this is minimal: all profits or losses are reported in the longer term. Only the timing of reporting them is changed from one year to another. This is justified by the special position the banks have in the community. They must be able to prove their stability, since any negative views could lead to a damaging or even fatal run on a bank, which would have widespread repercussions on the community as a whole. The trend in recent years, however, has been more and more towards fuller disclosure of the results of banking activities.

6. Problems with and limitations of financial statement analysis

The calculation of financial ratios is an easy arithmetical exercise. In practice the hard work comes before doing the sums. Financial ratios can only be meaningful if the figures used in performing the calculations are meaningful, and unfortunately the figures on financial statements are not always meaningful. The first problem is that the figures on the financial statements are all historical. While this is exactly what is needed for finding out where things have gone wrong in an undertaking, it is not always satisfactory for determining what will happen in the future. Past performance trends can be extrapolated, but such extrapolations have to be put into the perspective of changes in economic conditions, in the market in which the undertaking operates, in socio-political developments and various other factors which could influence it.

The biggest problem caused by the use of historical figures when doing an analysis of past performance is that of valuation. Fixed assets in particular are often reflected on financial statements at a figure which is based on historical cost. As a result, these assets are often under valued. This is particularly true of land and buildings. A very good example of the effects of inflation is shown in the Anglo-Alpha financial report. Profits for the year are reduced from R126,8 million to R76,7 million by a current cost adjustment, a reduction of 47 %. A large part of this decrease in the profit is due to the increased depreciation written off on the difference between the book value of assets at historical cost and the value at current cost (see note 8 to the financial statements).

There are also other specific problems related to depreciable assets. A firm which is depreciating its fixed assets shows a smaller asset base in every year in which it does not purchase new assets. Under such circumstances it will show a higher return on assets simply by maintaining its previous level of profit, even if inflation means that it is actually showing a smaller real profit! For example, say a firm has assets of R100 000 at the end of 1998. It depreciates these assets at 20 % per year and does not purchase any new assets during 1999, so that fixed assets are shown at a value of R80 000 at the end of 1999. If it shows a profit of R50 000 in both 1998 and 1999, the return on fixed assets will be 50 % in 1998 and will rise to 62,5 % in 1999, and the effect this would have on the ROTA will depend on the proportion of fixed to current assets. This would seem, at first glance, to indicate an improved performance. A moment's consideration should show that this is not necessarily so, particular if the monetary value of the equipment has remained constant or even increased due to changes in price levels.

Other problems occur in the case of leased assets. The requirement that leased assets be capitalised and reflected on the balance sheet applies only to listed companies. In other undertakings it is not always possible to determine the value of leased assets used in the course of production. This must have a distorting effect on the ratios calculated. If one compares two companies, one of which owns its assets and the other of which leases a substantial proportion of them, the first one will have a much larger asset base and would probably show a smaller ROTA. The argument has been offered that the costs of leasing will lead to smaller profits, which would compensate for the fact that the asset base is smaller. This argument does not hold water, since a company owning its assets has a larger depreciation expense than the other which would offset the lease charges to some extent.

There are other problems caused by the accounting policies of different undertakings. The rates used for writing off depreciation, stock valuation procedures and the way in which provision is made for expected expenses such as bad debts will all affect both profit figures and asset valuations.

A final major problem is that financial statements cover a financial year and present the financial position at the end of that year. This date is not necessarily representative of what the position is during the year, since nearly all businesses have at least a measure of seasonality. The calculation of the creditors payment period for Engineering Firm above showed the way in which this variation in business activity can affect the financial position. This factor must also be taken into account when comparing two companies. If they have different financial year ends their financial statements may not be directly comparable.

Before starting a ratio analysis it is therefore necessary to spend time examining the financial statements in detail to determine what policies have been applied and to make whatever adjustments may be necessary in order to arrive at figures which are meaningful enough to use. It is also necessary to examine factors other than financial, such as seasonality, and any other factors specifically affecting this type of business. A person having no knowledge of these factors could very easily misinterpret the results of his ratio calculations.

Key words

Time series analysis	Cross sectional analysis
Profit before interest and tax (PBIT)	Profit before tax (PBT)
Profit after tax (PAT)	Gearing
Financial leverage	Liquidity index
Price/earnings	Earnings yield
Dividend yield	Dividend cover
Ploughback percentage	Return on net assets (RONA)
Leverage index	Fixed charges coverage
Net current assets turnover	

Chapter 15

Further points in financial analysis

The previous chapters have dealt with the basics of financial statement analysis, both from the point of view of funds flow analysis and from the point of view of conventional ratio analysis. While these should be enough for a first time student to be able to gain a great deal of information from the statements there are obviously other factors and techniques which can assist in giving greater insight into the affairs of the undertaking. This chapter introduces new aspects, both quantitative and non-quantitative.

1. **Quality of earnings**
2. **More on trend and growth analysis**
3. **Failure prediction**
4. **Prospectuses and strategic financial analysis**
5. **Economic value added (EVA)**
6. **Financial risk analysis**

1. Quality of earnings

To date all discussion has been concerned purely with quantitative aspects of analysis although reference has been made to the fact that various other factors have to be borne in mind. Many of these factors can be grouped together under the heading of quality of earnings. Like most aspects of qualitative analysis, this is a rather fuzzy area, and the term means different things to different people. Broadly speaking, an undertaking has higher quality earnings when the earnings of a period are indicative of the earnings which can be expected in the future and which can quickly be realised, or turned into cash, compared to a firm which has variable earnings which are not indicative of future earnings or when it takes a long time for these earnings to be realised.

To be more specific, the following points can be mentioned:

Quality of Earnings

High	*Low*
1. *Conservative accounting practices*	*Liberal accounting practices*

Conservative accounting policies are those which take all possible liabilities into account before determining the profits for the period. This would include providing for deferred taxes, providing for increased replacement cost of fixed assets and writing off costs as they are incurred by using realistic stock valuation systems, such as LIFO, for cost determination.

2. *Profits that can quickly be converted to cash*	*Profits that are far from convertible to cash*

The old saw has it that profits are not profits until they are in the bank. If the cash flow of the company is falling behind its profit flow, the quality of its earnings is regarded as declining.

3. *Earnings that follow a steady trend*	*Volatile earnings*

A company whose profits fluctuate wildly from year to year is generally not regarded as a good bet because of the uncertainty of its profit patterns, which means that the quality is not very satisfactory.

4. *Recent earnings that are indicative of future earnings*	*Recent earnings that bear little relevance to the future*

This obviously ties in rather closely with the previous point. It is not exactly the same, for even if a company's earnings pattern is volatile its circumstances may be such that future profit performance is roughly determinable. Changing circumstances may also mean that a previously stable firm will no longer be so stable.

5. *Earnings that flow from the main business of the firm*	*Earnings that flow from extraordinary items*

If a firm is involved in numerous projects aside from its main business and it so happens that most of the profit is coming from these rather than from the main business the obvious judgement must be that the company is managing its resources wrongly and that the quality of its earnings must suffer because of this.

| 6. *Earnings from operations* | *Earnings from financial juggling (including tax concessions)* |

A company can improve its earnings by financial juggling. This has happened all too often in South Africa of recent years with some of the more lunatic of the so-called decentralisation incentives. Many people have taken advantage of various concessions regarding interest rates, relocation allowances and various subsidies and have thereby shown profits from an undertaking which is in actual fact so poorly managed or has prospects so poor that it is incapable of making a profit from its operations.

| 7. *Earnings from a sound balance sheet* | *Earnings from a balance sheet with possible hidden surprises* |

This may not always be easy to judge, but there are often warning signs in the notes to the statements. There may be contingent liabilities or contracts for capital expenditure which could materially affect the company in the future. A look at the assets structure may also indicate that there are assets which are in need of replacement due to ageing and, particularly in times of rising prices, the company may not be able to finance the cost of replacement.

| 8. *Earnings that are understandable* | *Earnings that can only be understood by a financial genius* |

The financial statements should be understandable and complete. Statements which conceal information, either by poor presentation or by hiding information in odd notes or statements which leave the analyst looking for more information, must always arouse suspicion. This may not always be justified since there are companies, like those in the Rembrandt group, which have been notoriously poor in providing information to their shareholders, but this has been accepted as a political necessity because of political hostility to South African companies operating overseas.

| 9. *Local earnings* | *Foreign earnings* |

This last item is not as clear cut as the previous ones. The main problem about foreign earnings is that they are not necessarily easily translated into tangible earnings for local shareholders because of, for example, various currency control regulations. Of course, foreign earnings may be of a very high quality depending on the country where they are earned. In recent years also, with the decline in the relative value of the South African Rand, certain overseas earnings have been very highly rated.

Factors which must also be taken into account when looking at quality of earnings are those which are outside of the company and which may affect its future, such as political factors. The opinions of the person doing the analysis will also affect the evaluation of the quality of the earnings, since this is a matter about which it is impossible to lay down more than general guidelines. A possible summary of the factors affecting the overall earnings of the undertaking and the changes in the overall earnings of the undertaking could be set out diagrammatically as follows:

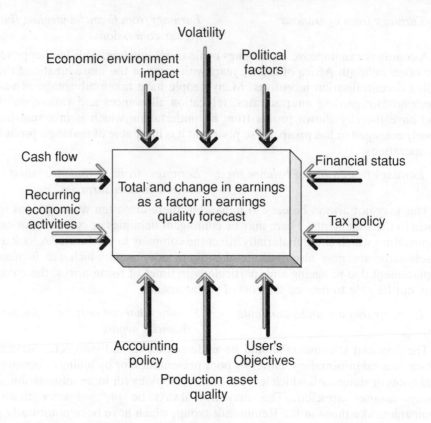

Figure 15.1

The volatility of the earnings of an undertaking is affected by many factors. Some sectors of the industry are volatile by nature, such as those dependent on agriculture. A poor crop means poor profits, and there is little management can do about this other than diversify into more stable areas of business. In some industries there are management factors which make the earnings pattern more or less volatile. A typical example would be a comparison between two firms producing similar products but using different production processes. One is more highly mechanised while the other makes more extensive use of manual labour. What are the factors which affect volatility? From a financial point of view the critical aspect is the one of operating leverage, which is illustrated below in fig 15.2.

Fixed costs are those which do not vary with the volume of production, such as the rent of the factory. Variable costs are those which do vary with volume of production such as raw materials consumed.

The more mechanised firm, with the higher operating leverage, is much more vulnerable to changes in the volume of production and sales because it cannot reduce its costs as easily as the firm with lower fixed cost structure. A small change in volume of sales can therefore have a dramatic effect on the profits of the organisation. Compare the effects on profits of a similar change in volume for the

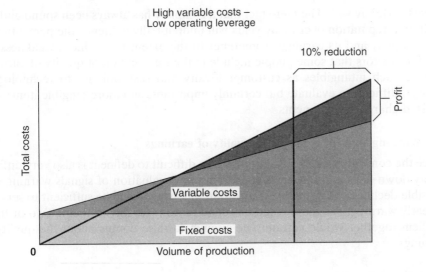

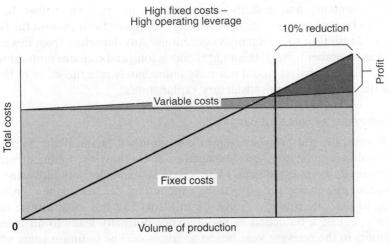

Figure 15.2

second company. Whereas the first has moved into a loss position, the second is merely showing smaller profits. An increase in volume will cause an equally dramatic rise in profits for the firm with the higher operating leverage, a far higher increase than that shown by the other firm. The earnings of the more highly leveraged firm are therefore far more volatile.

The political factors are of course partly a reality and partly a matter of personal evaluation. In the current South African situation they may play a major part in the evaluation of quality of earnings.

The financial status of the company should not really play a part in the evaluation of the quality of the company's earnings, but in something as subjective as this it almost certainly will. The mere fact that a company has always been sound and has built up a reputation over many years will undoubtedly influence the perception of the company and its earnings, sometimes to the extent that it hides weaknesses.

Other factors that some people include in their evaluation of quality of earnings include such intangibles as customer loyalty and susceptibility to technological change, difficult to evaluate but certainly important, and more tangible items such as fixed charge commitments.

1.1 Warning signs of a decline in quality of earnings

Since the concept of quality of earnings is so difficult to define it is also very difficult to lay down hard and fast rules concerning the evaluation of signals warning of a possible decline in that quality. Any of the following would be sufficient to serve as an early warning, but there could be sound reasons for any of them. Two or three of them together would certainly be enough to raise doubts about the quality of earnings.

1.1.1 *Audit report*

The audit report is normally a short statement that the auditor has examined the financial statements and underlying documents to the extent that he found necessary to be able to state that the financial statements fairly present the financial position and results of the company's operations. Any departure from this could be regarded as an amber light. If the audit report is long and contains unusual wording or is qualified, the analyst would normally immediately rate the value of the share down in the absence of any satisfactory explanations.

1.1.2 *Reductions in managed costs*

This will generally not be picked up in the published financial statements, since costs are unlikely to be itemised. Managed costs are those the timing of which can be determined by management. The classical examples are advertising and maintenance, and changes in advertising expenditure can usually be monitored by reference to external sources. A change in a cost like this must arouse concern, since the effect of a reduction in maintenance normally leads to an increase in stated profits in the relevant year but to a serious decline in future years when the effect of previous slack maintenance leads to extra maintenance costs and breakdown costs. Cuts in advertising reduce costs in the relevant year, but can lead to reduced sales in subsequent years and so on.

1.1.3 *Changes in accounting policy*

The figures appearing in the financial statements are prepared according to the accounting policies adopted by the undertaking. If these policies are changed there will obviously be changes in the nature of certain figures appearing on the statements and the question which will arise is why the change was made. There may be valid reasons, but the change could also have been made to give a better appearance to the operating results or the financial position of the undertaking.

1.1.4 *Excessive increases in accounts receivable, accounts payable, stock*

If there is a deterioration in the management quality of the undertaking there will also be a deterioration in the quality of the undertaking's earnings. It may take some time for the effects of the deterioration to become obvious in the financial ratios, but increases in these items of working capital are usually the first sign of a weakening of management.

1.1.5 *Increases in intangibles*

The intangibles which are normally the focus of this point are research and development costs and other development costs of various types. The accounting treatment of these has long been a matter of dispute, with some claiming that they should be written off as normal expenditure items and others claiming that the costs of development should be written off over the estimated benefit life of the product being developed. Most undertakings adopt the latter course, with lifetimes normally being estimated as fairly short. By lengthening the estimated lifetime, an undertaking could reduce the annual write off amount and so increase profits. The increased amount on the balance sheet would serve to alert the analyst to the possibility of this happening.

There could also be purchases of intangibles such as mineral rights which are very difficult to evaluate.

1.1.6 *Decline in gross or net income percentages*

The gross profit percentage would again not generally be available to the outside analyst, but both of these would have to be analysed in the light of prevailing economic circumstances. Cuts in gross profit margins may be in reaction to poor sales. A drop in net margin may be due to poor conditions which have forced a drop in production and, as can be seen in figure 13.2, this must lead to a decline in overall profits at a greater rate than the decline in sales. This must lead to a decline in net margin. Still, such a decline is indicative of problems in the undertaking and must cast doubts on the quality of earnings.

1.1.7 *Reduction of reserves*

This is so obvious that it is scarcely necessary to mention it. Obviously if a firm has been building up reserves and now starts running them down there will be questions asked, either concerning the running down or on the quality of management which led to unnecessary reserves being built up in the first place.

1.1.8 *Sharp increases in borrowings*

This has always been a red warning light, but it must again be viewed in the light of circumstances. Several South African undertakings have in recent years been offered outstanding opportunities for expansion due to the political pressure on overseas companies to withdraw from this country. In order to finance the purchase of perfectly healthy disinvesting companies they have been forced to borrow. The increase in debt may create some doubts, but on balance these companies have not been down rated by the market.

1.1.9 *Other sudden changes in operating methods, financing methods, deferred tax policies, balance sheet composition or management*

Again, none of these necessarily mean that the company is deteriorating, but they are still warning signs which the alert analyst will take into account in coming to conclusions about an undertaking's quality of earnings.

The above section should be enough to persuade doubters that analysis of financial statements is not the purely mathematical exercise which the chapter on ratio analysis may have led them to believe. The next section should show that this analysis is the field of specialists with a wide knowledge of the total business environment and an ability to apply this to the circumstances of the undertaking being analysed.

2. More on trend and growth analysis

The value of an undertaking or of its shares on the open market must ultimately depend on the value of its future earnings and its future dividend payment patterns, which will depend on the growth rates in its sales and margins. These will depend on the interaction of a number of factors such as the growth rate of the industry in which the undertaking is operating, the competitive position of the undertaking within that industry and the quality of management in formulating and carrying out a successful strategy.

Because of the importance of the growth rates they have become a focus of importance for many analysts. Investors study them to predict the growth in the value of their shares, banks and other suppliers of funding study them to predict future funding requirements, and companies study them to determine their performance in the light of their competitors' performance, to detect weaknesses in their competitors and to predict competitor behaviour.

Analysis of growth usually has three distinct phases. The first is the quantitative measurement of growth of the variables concerned. Reference to this process was made in chapter fifteen, but more sophisticated techniques are often used. The second phase is the analysis of the sources of growth, both within and without the undertaking, and the interaction of these various sources on each other. The third phase is using the information gleaned in the first two, together with other information such as economic conditions generally and in the particular industry and any announced strategies of the undertaking, to predict future growth patterns and growth rates and to examine the financial and operating consequences of such growth.

To understand the significance of the financial statements and ratios, historical, comparative and projected, it is essential that the analyst have an appreciation of modern business theory. In terms of this theory, an undertaking can maximise its net worth if it adopts certain determinable optimal policies regarding financing, pricing, cost structures and dividend policies. If the firm is following some sub-optimal policy, the analyst should be aware of this and be able to use this knowledge in his predictions of the future strategies likely to be adopted by the undertaking and their likely consequences. There are various models for the determination of optimum strategies but most of them are variations of the following simple one:

The market share of the undertaking and the growth rate of the industry will determine the optimum type of strategy to be adopted. A company with a high market share in a new industry with a high growth rate will normally adopt a policy which will enable it to consolidate its position as a leader in the industry before the growth rate of the industry slows down, as it must in due time. This costs a great deal of money, which absorbs the large cash flows which such a company can generate. As a result, such a company is usually strapped for cash. The intuitive belief is that such a company must generate a return on assets at least equal to the physical growth rate of the industry plus the rate of increase in the replacement cost of its asset base in order to generate sufficient cash flows to finance itself without recourse to external funds. Such companies usually employ a high degree of financial leverage, with the attendant exposure to a high degree of financial risk, often have recourse to rights issues and seldom pay more than nominal dividends.

The undertakings which have a low market share in a high growth industry are in a far weaker position than those with a high share. Particularly in a new industry one finds that market positions have not yet become entrenched and the smaller firms must fight to obtain a better share. Such firms are therefore usually enormously greedy for cash, and their future cash requirements position is even more strained than that of the high market share undertaking.

Undertakings which have a high market share in a mature, slowly growing industry are in a totally different position. They do not need to finance expansion programs, so are able to apply their cash flows to larger dividend payments and require very little external finance. They usually generate returns considerably larger than the industry growth rate plus inflation. Sometimes such undertakings do adopt strategies to further enlarge their market share at the expense of their other large competitors, but this is usually so expensive to achieve that mergers are far more likely.

An undertaking with a low market share in this type of industry is very poorly placed, since it must effectively spend all its funds trying to maintain its position because it will be impossible to improve its position in any way other than by taking market share from its bigger, wealthier competitors. There are exceptions, of course. Some companies with a small market share manage to exploit a niche within that market where they are able to act like market leaders because of geographical location, product differentiation or other successful strategies.

The above is a very rough guide. The actual structure of the industry concerned will affect this. There may be a distinct market leader in an industry, there may be two or three firms of equal size, growth rates may be uneven and so on. In each case an adjustment must be made to the basic four section model, which is graphically illustrated in figure 15.3. The desired flow of funds in various circumstances, and the one which will be found if the undertaking adopts an optimisation strategy, is indicated by the arrows. A firm trapped in a low growth, low market share position should either close down and repay the investment to the shareholders or invest in a high growth area, if it has sufficient cash. A firm in a low growth, high market share position has cash to invest and will be able to pump this into high growth areas as well as to pay dividends, and so forth.

The desired operations movement, which is not illustrated, is simpler. A firm in a low market share, high growth industry will attempt to move into a high market share position in the same industry. From the high growth, high market share position the only natural movement is into the high market share, low growth position as the market for the product matures.

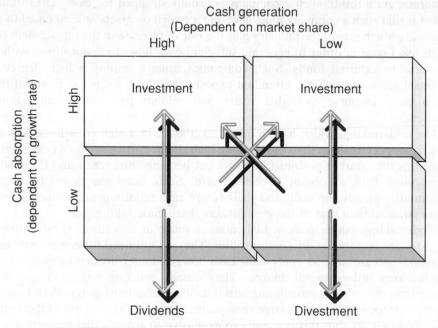

Figure 15.3

2.1 Financial strategies and sustainable growth rate

A moment's thought will serve to show that a company can grow by use of internal funds at the same rate as the rate of retention of profits within the company. Thus if a company earns 10% on its capital base after tax and pays no dividend, it can finance growth of 10% without recourse to external finance. If it earns 10% after tax but pays out half of its earnings as dividends, it will only be able to grow at 5%.

In order to increase its growth rate above the rate of return it earns, it will have to borrow money from outside. If it maintains a debt assets ratio of 1:2 and borrows money equal to the amount it earns, it can double the amount it can invest in growth and, in the first case mentioned above, be able to grow at 20%. These three cases can be illustrated by using simplified examples, with an assumption that annual sales equal three times assets:

Case 1: Ten per cent return on assets, no dividends, no borrowings

	Year 1	Year 2	Year 3
Total assets	4 000	4 400	4 840
Shareholders equity	4 000	4 400	4 840
Liabilities	—	—	—
Sales (say 3 × assets)	12 000	13 200	14 520
Net income (10% of assets)	400	440	484
Dividends	—	—	—
Sales growth rate	—	10%	10%
Profit growth rate	—	10%	10%

Growth, whether measured in terms of sales or earnings, is at a rate of 10%, which is the same as the after tax rate of return on total assets in a case where there is 100% retention of earnings and total reliance on internal funding.

Case 2: Ten per cent return on assets, 50% dividends, no borrowings

	Year 1	Year 2	Year 3
Total assets	4 000	4 200	4 410
Shareholders equity	4 000	4 200	4 410
Liabilities	—	—	—
Sales (say 3 × assets)	12 000	12 600	13 230
Net income (10% of assets)	400	420	441
Dividends	200	210	220
Sales growth rate	—	5%	5%
Profit growth rate	—	5%	5%

A 50% retention of earnings only allows a rate of growth of 50% of the after tax rate of return on assets where there is total reliance on internal funding.

Internally funded growth, which is growth without recourse to new share issues, can only take place at a rate not higher than that known as the sustainable growth rate, which is illustrated in the three cases above and is generally stated as:

g   = ROE × (1 − D/E)
where g= the sustainable growth rate,
ROE   = the after tax return on shareholder's interest at the start of the year,
D/E   = the dividend payout rate on shareholder's interest at the start of the year
        and (1 − D/E) = the profit retention rate.

Case 3: Ten per cent return on assets, 50% dividends, 50% borrowings

	Year 1	Year 2	Year 3
Total assets	4 000	4 400	4 840
Shareholders equity	2 000	2 200	2 420
Liabilities	2 000	2 200	2 420
Sales (say 3 × assets)	12 000	13 200	14 520
Net income (10% of assets)	400	440	441
Dividends	200	220	220
Sales growth rate	—	10%	10%
Profit growth rate	—-	10%	10%

Payment of dividends and a rate of growth equal to the rate of return on assets is only possible if outside funding is used.

These scenarios should be related to the rate of growth in the industry concerned. If the industry is growing at a faster rate than the company, then the company is losing market share. A company in the sort of position shown in case one above would then be heading for increasingly poor performance if it did not alter its financial strategy to permit a rate of growth at least equal to that of the industry concerned. This strategy will either involve borrowing money or continually issuing new share capital to finance growth. A one time issue of new share capital will only have the one time effect of increasing the capital available at the time of issue, and growth thereafter will continue at the same rate as before, albeit from a higher base than before. Since the continual issue of new shares will be virtually impossible to achieve in practice this effectively means that the company will make use of borrowing strategies with possible occasional issues of shares.

The various financial strategies which it can adopt do not mean that the company will grow at the rates indicated as possible. There are many reasons why a company can grow at a slower rate, such as industry growth rates and competitor activity, but it cannot grow at a faster rate than that permitted by its financial strategy.

Summarising everything said above, the possible growth rate of a company is determined by the following financial factors:

● The after tax rate of return on assets, which is determined by:
  The profit margin on sales before tax;
  The asset turnover ratio; and
  The tax rate.
● The rate of borrowings of the company.
● The rate of retention of profit, determined by the dividend payout ratio.

The simple sustainable growth rate model above ($g = ROE \times (1 - D/E)$) can be expanded to bring into account the extra factors mentioned. ROE, or after tax return on equity, can be expanded into its component parts:

$$\frac{\text{Profit before tax}}{\text{Sales}} \times \frac{\text{Sales}}{\text{Assets}} \times (1 - \text{Tax rate}) \times \frac{\text{Assets}}{\text{Shareholders' interest}} = \frac{\text{PAT}}{\text{S/h interest}}$$

This is essentially the Du Pont formula discussed earlier in a slightly different format. Using this, the expanded sustainable growth rate formula can be stated as

$$g = \frac{PBT}{S} \times \frac{S}{A} \times (1-T) \times \frac{A}{SI} \times (1-D/E)$$

The sustainable growth rate of a company can be changed by changing any of the components of the above equation, by improving the sales margin before tax, by improving asset turnover, by changing the tax rate, by changing the borrowing ratio or by changing the dividend payout rate.

This equation can now be applied to the firm's position in the four sector grid above. A firm in a high growth area will try to maximise all the factors in order to achieve the growth necessary to protect its position in the market. It will seek high profit margins, high asset turnover, high borrowings and low tax rates and dividend payout rates. A firm in a low growth area with little prospect of improving its market share will adopt a different policy, since its maximum growth rate is not determined by financial factors but by economic factors in the market.

The above analysis deals with the growth of the worth of the firm. A complete analysis will also deal with an analysis of the growth in earnings. The reasons for growth in earnings will generally be analysed in terms of the following factors in order to identify real growth.

● Accounting changes
   These are not true changes in income but are the result of changes in accounting policy. Changes in the rate at which depreciation is written off, for instance, will result in changes in reported earnings. The effect of such changes on the earnings of the undertaking should be shown in the notes to the financial statements and must be taken into account in the analysis of the income of the undertaking.

● Environment
   All factors in the environment which are beyond the control of the undertaking, except those specifically mentioned below, are included under this heading. Changes in exchange rates, changes in the business cycle, changes in the rates of inflation and technological changes which may benefit or disadvantage the particular undertaking. The analyst should try to quantify the effect of such changes on the reported earnings of the undertaking during each period.

● Infrequent, unusual or extraordinary items
   Such items obviously distort the earnings for a particular period, and their effect should be quantified in the financial statements and adjusted for by the analyst.

● Tax rates
   The actual tax rate of the undertaking is the subject of this heading. This rate may change because of a general change in tax rates or because of changes in the situation of a particular undertaking due to the exhaustion of allowances or assessed losses. The effect can be quantified by reference to pre tax income figures.

● Capital structure and interest structure
   Any changes in the capital structure of an undertaking will obviously change the financial gearing of the undertaking and will lead to changes in the income

available to ordinary shareholders. Changes in the interest rate structure, whether because of general changes in interest rates in the economy as a whole or because of changes in the nature of the undertaking's financial structure will also affect the earnings available for distribution. These changes can represent real growth, but an attempt must be made to quantify the effect of such changes.

● Operations

Growth resulting from the ongoing business of the operation can be regarded as real growth which is sustainable in the longer term, as distinct from the growth due to any of the above factors which are merely distortions of the real growth trend.

It must be borne in mind, however, that the growth reflected in the income statement of the undertaking is growth in terms of nominal monetary values. An inflation factor should be brought into account before stating whether the income of the undertaking has really grown over a period.

An analysis performed in terms of the above methodology should assist the analyst in determining the strategies being followed by the undertaking. This knowledge will then assist in determining whether the strategies are optimal in terms of the industry and the undertaking's position within that industry and the probable changes of the strategy leading to success for the undertaking. The analysis can only be performed by someone who has a thorough knowledge of the industry and of the factors affecting it over the short and longer term.

The four sector analysis assists in clarifying the concepts involved but is obviously not of very great practical help in the analysis. Very few undertakings actually fit into one of the categories, very few firms have dominant positions within an industry and the relevant position vis-à-vis competitors is not always available until some time after the analysis should be made. Many undertakings are also involved in several sectors of the economy, and it is then necessary to make use of the segmental reporting data required by AC 115 to prepare several different analysis of the segments of the undertaking before combining them to pronounce an overall judgement on the prospects of the undertaking as a whole.

3. Failure prediction

Many attempts have been made to use financial statements to predict the probability of failure of an undertaking. Failure can be defined in different ways, but most people automatically think of absolute failure as evidenced by bankruptcy. Several milder definitions have also been offered, ranging from reduction or non-payment of a dividend to failure to meet the terms of repayment of loans.

To date none of the predictors developed has been universally successful, but a few of those which have had some success are worth discussing. There are two basic groups of predictors which have been used, those which concentrate on only one factor, or univariate predictors, and those which use a combination of factors, or multivariate predictor models.

3.1 Univariate predictors

A great deal of research has been done into the performance of selected financial ratios of failed and non-failed firms to see whether there were any significant differences between these. One of the best known pieces of research is that performed by Beaver and published in 1966 as a supplement to *The Journal of Accounting Research*. The original work paired 79 failed companies with 79 similar non-failed companies and plotted their comparative ratios. Significant differences were found in nearly all the ratios calculated, but gross cash flow to total debt and net income to total assets were the most reliable predictors up to three years before failure, with the former becoming more reliable for periods of over three years and up to five years before failure.

The problem with this research was that it was purely empirical, and had no theoretical foundation to support Beaver's conclusions. While Beaver did attempt to explain the reasons for the fact that this ratio had been the best performer, subsequent replication of his work has led to findings which differ in various respects from the original. Factors which influence the actual percentage at which the undertaking's position becomes critical include the ratio between short and long term debt and the rates of inflation ruling at the time the analysis is done.

Nowadays very little attention is paid to the cutoff points determined by Beaver, but the basic principle is regarded as sound: if the undertaking's cash flow is declining as a percentage of total debt it will obviously experience increasing difficulty in meeting its obligations. The trend of this ratio is therefore regarded as being of paramount importance in assessing an undertaking's prospects of failure.

3.2 Multivariate predictors

Because of the difficulties in finding a single ratio which could adequately act as a predictor of financial distress several researchers investigated the possibility of combining a number of different ratios. The normal way of doing this was to give different weights to the various ratios and so come up with a single index figure which could be regarded as an indicator of failure or non-failure.

While many models have been developed, the best known is probably that of Edward Altmann which was first published in *The Journal of Finance* in September 1968. Altmann again performed an empirical analysis of a number of undertakings and developed the so-called "Z-function" which reads as follows:

$$Z = .012X_1 + .014X_2 + .033X_3 + .006X_4 + .010X_5$$

Where X_1 is working capital to total assets, X_2 is retained earnings to total assets, X_3 is earnings before interest and taxes to total assets, X_4 is market value of equity to book value of total debt and X_5 is sales to total assets. His results were very impressive in predicting bankruptcy one year before failure, but became less so as the time span prior to failure increased. Later research indicated that the Z factor applied to manufacturing concerns, and did not work very well when attempts were made to apply it to other types of undertaking.

The multipliers are so calculated as to indicate imminent bankruptcy when the sum is less than 1.81, but there is a fairly wide band of uncertainty since non-failure is only predicted when the value exceeds 2.99.

His selection of ratios, incidentally, appears to have been purely arbitrary. Different ratios could have been used and subjected to the same procedures of linear regression in order to obtain a predictor of failure. This appears to be what Altmann has subsequently done in developing his "Zeta factor", but this is a proprietary model and the details have not been published.

A similar model was developed by Dr J H de la Rey at the Bureau for Financial Analysis at the University of Pretoria. This model appears to have achieved a very high rate of success when used by one of the leading commercial banks in this country, but not very much information is available on these results.

3.3 Problems with failure predictors

All the models which have been developed have looked at the past. They have used data built up over a period of years in empirical determination of formulae, but there is very little theory to back up the results. For this reason it cannot be stated unequivocally that any one of these models will work under different conditions, and all of them must be used with great care in practice.

4. Prospectuses and strategic financial analysis

Section 145 of the Companies Act makes it illegal to make an offer to the public to subscribe for shares unless the offer is accompanied by a prospectus which complies with the requirements of the Act and which has been registered in the Companies Registration Office. The prospectus must state that it has been so registered. The following sections and Schedule 3 to the Act contain requirements regarding the matter to be specified in the prospectus. These sections of the Act are mainly concerned with extra documents which have to be lodged with the Registrar such as consent to act as directors by all the persons so named in the prospectus, consent to the publication of their opinions on the company or aspects of it by experts, copies of relevant contracts and a copy of the underwriting contract, if any.

The actual contents of the prospectus, which are summarised below, are largely prescribed by Schedule 3. Only the major points are listed here, and anyone wishing to know the detail must refer to the Act. The numbers in brackets at the end of each section here refer to the sections of Schedule 3 for those who want more detail.

1. The name of the company, the address of its registered office and transfer office and the date of incorporation. (1, 32)
2. The names, occupations and addresses of the directors or proposed directors, their terms of office and their remuneration or proposed remuneration in any capacity and the borrowing powers exercisable by the directors.(2, 34)
3. The names and addresses of the auditors, attorneys, bankers, stockbroker and trustees and underwriters, if any.(3, 4)
4. The name, address and professional qualifications, if any, of the secretary. (5, 35)
5. The general history of the company and any changes in the business of the company during the last five years, plus a statement of the profits or losses,

dividends and dividend cover over that period for the company and each of its subsidiaries. If the proceeds of the issue are to be used to purchase shares in another company so that it becomes a subsidiary, the same information must also be supplied in respect of that company and all its subsidiaries. There must also be a statement of the company's estimated commitment in respect of fixed assets and the date on which those assets will be brought into use. (6)

6. The purpose of the offer. (7,36)
7. Details of the share capital of the company, including the number of founders' and management or deferred shares and any special rights attaching to these. Details must also be given of preferential rights or options in respect of shares and of any shares issued or agreed to be issued otherwise than for cash. (8, 10, 11, 37, 39)
8. Details of material loans and particularly of loans other than in the normal course of business. (9)
9. Details of any fixed property and other fixed assets to be acquired partly or wholly out of the proceeds of the share issue. (12)
10. Preliminary and issue expenses, amounts paid to promoters and commission in respect of underwriting.(14, 15, 42)
11. Material contracts other than in the normal course of business and a reasonable time and place where such contracts may be examined. (16, 40)
12. Full details of the interest of any director or promoter in the promotion of the company and in any property to be acquired out of the proceeds of the share issue and of every property acquired by the company during the three years before the issue of the prospectus. (17, 41)
13. Particulars of the shares being issued, their issue price and the time and date of the opening and the closing of the offer, plus the minimum amount which the directors believe must be raised in terms of the issue. (18, 19, 20, 44)
14. A statement of whether the company has made an application to be listed on a stock exchange and, if so, which stock exchange. (23)
15. There must be a report by the auditor of the company which deals with the profits or losses, the dividends and the assets and liabilities of the company over the past five years. If the company has subsidiaries he has to deal with these matters in respect of the subsidiaries and of the group as well. If the proceeds of the issue are to be used to purchase shares in a company so that it becomes a subsidiary then the report must cover that company (or those companies) as well. Any adjustments made to the figures in this report must be noted, and the directors must also report any material changes which have taken place between the date of the last annual financial statements and the date of the prospectus. All references to five years must be shortened to the period of the company's existence where this is less than five years. (25 to 30, 47, 48).

Note that there is no requirement to present the annual financial reports for the last five years, but that each aspect can be dealt with separately: assets, liabilities, share capital and profits or losses and dividends. The analyst thus receives even less than what he would normally get in the annual financial statements, but he gets it for a longer period (five years compared to two) and he gets a lot more information about the company and its plans. This is enough to do some strategic financial analysis of the company with the objective of deciding on whether or not to invest. Such an analysis is related to much of what has been said in this chapter. It relates to quality of earnings and to failure prediction, though it is more positive than the latter since it attempts to do some success prediction as well.

Broadly speaking, there are four areas of analysis for which the prospectus can be used and which will be briefly discussed below.

4.1 Management
Probably the most important single factor in the success or otherwise of a company is the management of that company. The prospectus gives a great deal more information about the management of a company than what the annual financial statements have to and this information should be studied carefully. The management team should consist of people with a strong record in the particular industry plus the appropriate technical people. It is very seldom that technical people with only technical experience are good managers, but they are essential members of the team. It is also important that the managers be committed to the company rather than to their own enrichment in the company so take a look at the remuneration and proposed remuneration of the directors and managers. Also look to see whether they are putting their own money into the company. Are they shareholders? Did they purchase these shares at full market price or were they given them at lower prices or in exchange for certain assets? Look at all the contracts involving managers or directors. Have they been selling goods or services to the company, either directly or through other companies in which they have major investments? Do they have good reputations in the industry? In the business world generally? Have they been involved in any shady or doubtful dealings in the past? Only if a person is satisfied of the competence and commitment of the management of a company can he consider that company as an investment possibility.

4.2 Product and market
The other non-financial factor which must be examined before considering investing is the company's product and the market in which it operates. People with an intimate knowledge of the relevant market have an advantage in this type of investigation, but anyone can find out a great deal by going through the prospectus.

Before being listed on the main board of the Johannesburg Stock Exchange a company must have at least three years of trading behind it. All the information relating to the period of three to five years before the date of the prospectus must be included, so from the prospectus it should be possible to determine whether the company has a clear market focus or whether it does not really have a clear idea of what it is trying to market. It should also be possible to determine whether the company has a competitive advantage over its competition, whether in terms of technology or products or services which are recognised as superior by customers whether in terms of quality, price, service, image or some mixture of these. It can definitely be established whether the company has a good track record of growth in its market, and an examination of the material contracts section should help to determine whether the company has set up any alliances with other companies which could help it along the way, such as suppliers of specialised parts or large retail chains which could be customers.

It is usually a bit more difficult to find out about the product rather than the market unless the product is well known. It is all too easy for the outsider to be overly impressed with the claims made by promoters, but this is not too difficult a hurdle to overcome by referring the matter to someone who has the expertise.

4.3 Financial position

While the financial statements are not presented in their usual form, the basic information is there for analysis. The only important figure which the Act does not require is the turnover of the company, but most companies supply this anyway as part of the general overview of the company. A ratio analysis can be performed, a cash flow analysis can be performed and there is usually enough information to judge the quality of earnings.

4.4 Financial arrangements

While the first three factors mentioned above are fairly generally recognised as being of importance, Shilit and Shilit have identified this as another important factor. Looking at some South African issues since 1986 has confirmed that it is a very good predictor of success or otherwise. Two of the factors they mention which have specifically been applicable locally, the first being the use of the proceeds of the issue. Where the shares are being issued for funds to fuel growth the companies tend to be successful while where the shares are being issued to pay off old debt the companies have generally thereafter simply incurred new debt.

The second factor they mention is the equitability of the issue for new investors. Where the new investors are actually making a major contribution to the company's financing but are getting a very minor part of the power in the company it is usually a sign of the directors and promoters having more interest in enriching themselves, and it doesn't matter much whether this is through making a success of the company (which might be hard work) or simply at the expense of the other shareholders, which may be a lot easier.

5. Economic value added (EVA)

A topic which has enjoyed a great deal of publicity in recent years is that of economic value added and the idea of creating shareholder value. The economic value added idea has two aspects to it:

1. Certain expenses in the income statement are written back and treated as assets to be amortised over a period. Examples would be the expense of training personnel, which would presumably be of benefit to the undertaking in the future. Other items include research and development costs including market development costs. This information is not always available in published financial statements. Those of Anglo-Alpha, for instance, specifically mention

R4,6 million spent on formal training courses (Social report, page 11), but whether this is the total amount spent on training is not mentioned. There is also no obvious mention of any type of research and development costs, of which there must have been some.

2. The second aspect is to take into account the total cost of the capital used in the undertaking. This is the cost of all the finance which is invested in the assets of the undertaking and includes interest bearing debt, shareholders funds which must be recompensed in the form of dividends and non-interest bearing debt such as most current liabilities.

Economic value added is then defined as the excess of the adjusted income over the cost of the total capital.

Where the adjustments to the income statement cannot be made EVA is approximated by simply using the unadjusted income while knowing that the actual EVA must be higher than the figure so calculated.

6. Financial risk analysis

An aspect of interest to investors and to the owners is the matter of risk. While there are many aspects of risk, the two major ones are *business risk* and *financial risk* or financial security.

Business risk is beyond the scope of this book. It deals with the risks inherent in any business such as the risk of technical obsolescence, the risk of changing consumer tastes, the risks of political intervention and so forth. Financial risk is more limited in scope, being normally divided into just two separate components:

1. Security of capital, or the risk of going insolvent; and
2. Security of income, or the risk that the undertaking will not provide sufficient income.

Security of capital is normally measured from a long term perspective by looking at the various debt ratios (also referred to as *financial structure* ratios) such as total debt to total assets, (interest bearing) debt to equity, assets to equity and the Beaver ratio (discussed on page 289) and so forth. The better these ratios the bigger the cushion the undertaking has against adverse circumstances developing.

From a short term aspect security of capital is measured by looking at the various liquidity ratios, such as the current ratio and quick ratio, and the various working capital ratios such as stock turnover, debtors collection period and creditors payment period. Again, the better these ratios the less likelihood there is of a short term financial problem.

Security of income is measured in different ways depending on who is looking at the undertaking:

Shareholders would be interested in the dividend cover;

Lenders, such as the financial institutions, would be interested in the interest cover and the fixed charges cover;

Managers and owners or purchasers interested in running the undertaking would want to look at such matters as the breakeven sales and the margin of safety.

Key words

Quality of earnings
Growth analysis
Univariate failure predictors
Strategic financial analysis
Economic value added (EVA)

Trend analysis
Sustainable growth rate
Multivariate failure predictors
Financial arrangements

Chapter 16

Funds flow and cash flow analysis

By this stage of the book it should be clear that there is a great difference between profit and the amount of cash available. Profit or income has possibly been overemphasised in accounting practice over the years, partly because of its importance for purposes of determining tax liability. Businesses have often been in the position of showing good profits while their lifeblood, cash flow, has been so poor that they have been unable to pay the taxes on their profits! This chapter discusses the importance which accountants have been attaching to cash flows (and, for longer term decisions, funds flows) over the last thirty years or so.

1. **Accounting flows**

2. **The concept of funds**

3. **Preparation of the funds statement to show a net change in working capital**

4. **Preparation of the funds statement to show a net change in cash**

5. **Different applications of funds flow and cash flow**

1. Accounting flows

Up to this point the discussion of accounting statements has been in terms of the classical financial statements which have been prepared since the time of Paciolo. These are, firstly, the statement of financial position or balance sheet, which is a financial representation of the undertaking at a particular point in time. This is a static statement in that it measures a position at one point in time. It is often compared to a snapshot of the financial position of the undertaking.

Secondly, there is the income statement or trading and profit and loss statement, which is a list of income and expenses over a period of time. In other words, rather than showing a static position at a moment in time, this statement measures the flow of income into the business over that period and of the flow of expenses out of the business. Otherwise stated, this is the net operating flow over that period.

This is not the only flow with which accounting records are concerned. There are also the financial flows, which are the flow of cash and the flow of working capital into and out of the business. The financial flows are generally referred to as funds flows and are of equal importance to the business overall. Schematically, these various flows can be represented as follows:

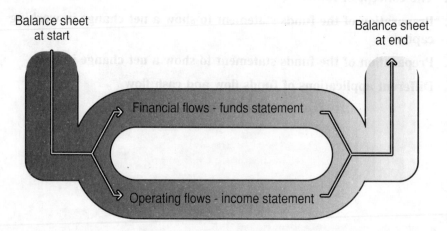

Balance sheet
at start

Balance sheet
at end

Financial flows - funds statement

Operating flows - income statement

Figure 16.1

The financial flows are all the flows of funds into and out of the undertaking and include the flows of cash resulting from operations as well as the flows generated by loans, by shareholders and by investment in capital assets.

The funds flow statement is a fairly recent addition to the accountant's repertoire. The American FASB only required the presentation of a funds statement in 1971, and the first requirement for a funds flow statement in South Africa was in the Companies Act of 1973. Since it is such a young statement not even the name has been settled. The South African Companies Act refers to it as a Statement of Sources and Applications of Funds and the Americans refer to it as a Statement of Changes in Financial Position, or SCFP for short. With even the name unsettled, it is hardly surprising that there is a great deal of argument still going on about the format which should be used. This argument will probably continue for a number of years to come since there are several arguments in favour of or against each proposal. The main argument concerns the particular concept of the term "funds" which must be used in the preparation of the statements. Statement AC 118, issued in July 1988, attempts to settle the matter in this country, but it is unlikely that the last has been heard of the matter here.

2. The concept of funds

The form of the funds statement and the ways in which it will eventually be used in the analysis of an undertaking will depend on the definition of funds which the undertaking uses. There are at least four different definitions of "funds" which are used by accountants in this country and overseas. In descending order of comprehensiveness, these are:

2.1 All financial resources

This is the widest-reaching and most commonly used definition of funds. All transactions involving any change in financial resources or their nature are reflected in a statement using this definition. This is the definition of funds which will be applied in this book and which is generally accepted as the one which is most informative. The bottom line of the statement will be a net increase or decrease in working capital or in cash.

2.2 Working capital

A statement using this definition is essentially the same as the one above, except that certain transactions which do not directly influence working capital may be excluded. A purchase of fixed assets financed directly by long term debt would, for example, not be reflected. The bottom line will be the same as in the first case.

2.3 Net monetary assets

This definition is again not very different from that in 2.2, except that it defines funds a little more narrowly as being only net quick assets, essentially cash and debtors less creditors. Here the bottom line will be the change in net monetary assets.

2.4 Cash and cash equivalents

This will obviously be the narrowest definition of all, with only those transactions directly affecting the cash balance being reflected on the face of the statement. Cash equivalents are items like money market instruments. While statement AC 118 on Cash Flow Information requires presentation on the all financial resources basis, the net figure at the end represents the change in cash and cash equivalents.

3. Preparation of the funds statement to show a net change in working capital

3.1 The purpose of the statement

A funds flow statement is prepared on this basis to show the net effect on working capital of the movement of all financial resources into and out of the undertaking over a period of time, usually one year. The accounting equation can be used to illustrate how these movements affect working capital, which is defined as being the difference between current assets and current liabilities. In its simplest form the equation reads:

Assets = Liabilities + Capital or	$A = L + C$
This can be expanded to read as follows: Current Assets + Long Term Assets = Current Liabilities + Long Term Liabilities + Capital or:	$CA + LTA = CL + LTL + C$
With a bit of transposition, this reads:	$CA - CL = LTL + C - LTA$
Since we have defined Working Capital as Current assets − Current liabilities, this can be changed to:	$WC = LTL + C - LTA$
Any change in working capital (ΔWC) will then be equal to the sum of the changes on the other side of the equation, or:	$\Delta WC = \Delta LTL + \Delta C - \Delta LTA$

Since all the components of the above equation appear on the balance sheet, preparation of a statement of changes in working capital over a period of time will involve an examination of the balance sheet to determine the changes which have taken place in the balance sheet over the relevant period of time. This means that the balance sheet should be broken down into its component parts and the various possibilities for change examined. Figure 16.2 on the next page sets this out.

The balance sheet shows the position of the various items at a point in time. In order to determine the changes that have taken place over a period of time it is necessary to compare a balance sheet at the beginning of that period with a balance sheet at the end of that period, and this is in essence how a funds statement is prepared. Unlike the income statement and balance sheet which are prepared directly from the financial records, this statement is prepared from the other statements with only occasional reference to the underlying records to expand the information which may only be shown in summary form in the balance sheet.

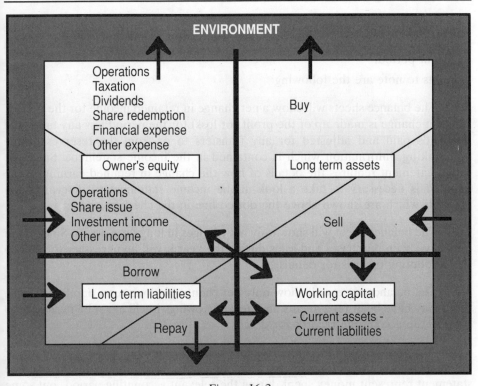

Figure 16.2

Working capital flows between the undertaking and its environment and within the undertaking

3.2 A simple method of preparation of the statement

Most funds flow statements are essentially very simple to prepare and can be drawn up directly from the particulars shown in fig 16.2. Simply set out the possible flows of funds enumerated there in the form of a checklist:

Inflows of funds		Outflows of funds	
Owner's equity			
Profits adjusted for non-		Losses adjusted for non-	
funds items	XXX	funds items	XXX
Investment income	XXX	Dividends	XXX
		Financing expense	XXX
		Taxation	XXX
Issue of shares	XXX	Redemption of shares	XXX
Long term assets			
Sell	XXX	Buy	XXX
Long term liabilities			
Borrow	XXX	Repay	XXX
Total inflow	XXX	Total outflow	XXX

The difference between the total inflow and the total outflow of funds over the period will determine whether the net working capital has increased or decreased over that period.

Points to note are the following:

3.2.1 The balance sheets will show a net change in retained income for the period. This net change is made up of the profit (or loss) for the period less any taxes and dividends paid and adjusted for any transfers to or from the reserves of the undertaking, information which is contained in the income statement. Since the funds statement requires the details of how the change in retained earnings came about it is necessary to take a look at the income statement to determine the amounts which are shown above the dotted line in the checklist above.

3.2.2 The balance sheet will show only net changes in long term assets. Since there may have been purchases and sales during the year it will be necessary to refer to the accounting records for details.

3.2.3 The balance sheet will show only net changes in long term liabilities. Since there may have been repayments and new borrowings it will again be necessary to refer to the accounting records for details.

3.2.4 A critical point in the preparation of a funds statement is the elimination of all items which do not represent flows of funds. Most items on the income statement represent money spent during the relevant accounting period, but some of the items are only book entries. Nobody spends money on depreciation, for instance, or on creating reserves. These entries which do not involve the actual spending of money during the period are referred to as "non-funds items".

Typical of such an item would be a reserve created on the revaluation of a fixed asset. While the balance sheet value of the asset would show a change, no money would have been spent on the asset and the extra "non-funds" value would have to be eliminated before preparing the funds statement. More typical, and absolutely critical in the preparation of a funds statement, is the elimination of depreciation. Depreciation is simply a book entry whereby an asset is written off over a period of time; the actual flow of funds takes place when the asset is purchased. This flow is reflected under the long term assets heading above and must not be duplicated in a future period by including depreciation.

Another non-funds flow item which is often found is a profit or loss on the sale of a fixed asset. The actual flow of funds here is the amount received for the asset. This amount can be split into two parts, the book value of the asset and the profit (or loss), since the so-called profit is based on the difference between book value and selling price. Looked at logically, the profit or loss can be regarded as an adjustment to depreciation: the asset was sold at a price higher than its book value because too much depreciation had been written off over the period of ownership to date, or at a price lower than its book value because not enough depreciation had been written off in the past. This gain or loss item is therefore treated in very much the same way as depreciation by being totally eliminated, and the total proceeds of the disposal entered as a source of funds. The amount of the proceeds will not be found in the balance sheet or income statement and is one of the items which will require a perusal of the original financial records.

Transfers to reserves and provisions, such as those for the increased replacement cost of fixed assets, are also non-funds items and must be eliminated in the preparation of the funds flow statement.

3.2.5 *An illustration of the preparation of the funds flow statement*

The funds flow statement of Engineering Firm (Pty) Ltd can be prepared using the checklist method shown above. The necessary information is contained in three documents: the balance at the start and at the end of the year and the income statement for the year. The balance sheets are obviously necessary for determination of differences by way of comparison, while the income statement is necessary for finding the details of the change in the retained earnings. The illustration below is of the worksheet used to prepare the funds flow statement included in the financial statements in appendix 1.

Inflows of funds		Outflows of funds	
Owners equity			
Profit adjusted for non-funds items[1]	289 500	Losses adjusted for non-funds items	nil
Investment income[2]	3 000	Dividends	nil
		Taxes[3]	58 000
		Financing expense[4]	31 000
Shares issued[5]	200	Shares redeemed	nil
Long term assets			
Sell	nil	Buy[6]	150 500
Long term liabilities			
Borrow[7]	12 800	Repay	nil
Total inflow	305 500	Total outflow	239 500
Net inflow			66 000
			305 500

Note that all the figures above the dotted line are obtained from the income statement and represent the change in retained earnings adjusted for the non-funds items:

289 500 + 3 000 − 31 000 − 58 000 = 203 500; 203 500 − 105 500 (depreciation) = 98 000; and 418 000 − 320 000 = 98 000 (change in retained earnings on the balance sheet from 1983 to 1984).

The workings for the above worksheet are as follows:

1	Net income before taxation for 1984	156 000
	Depreciation	105 500
	Interest paid	31 000
		292 500
	Interest received	3 000
		289 500

2, 3 and 4 are all taken from the income statement for 1984

5	Share capital per 1984 balance sheet	2 000
	Share capital per 1983 balance sheet	1 800
		200
6	Fixed assets per 1984 balance sheet	360 000
	Fixed assets per 1983 balance sheet	315 000
		45 000
	Add depreciation for 1984	105 500
		150 500

All depreciation prior to 1984 is included in both the 1984 and the 1983 figures, so that adding back the 1984 figures eliminates the effect of depreciation completely and leaves what is actually the change in the cost price of the fixed assets. Of course, this is the net change. If there were both purchases and sales of fixed assets in the same year it would not be possible to separate the two on the basis of the figures which appear on the face of the balance sheet. The directors' report might give sufficient information, but in this case it does not.

7	Directors' loans per 1984 balance sheet	196 000
	Directors' loans per 1983 balance sheet	183 200
		12 800

The second part of the funds statement is the easier to prepare. The *statement of changes in working capital* or *working capital variation statement* simply lists the changes in the various component items of working capital:

Working capital variation statement			
Increases in working capital		**Decreases in working capital**	
		Decrease in work in	
Increase in debtors	146 000	progress	15 000
Increase in cash and bank	15 000	Increase in creditors	45 000
		Increase in bank over-draft	15 000
		Increase in tax provision	20 000
Total increases	161 000	Total decreases	95 000
Net increase in working capital			66 000
			161 000

The net change here is obviously the same as the net change in the first part of the statement, and with these two parts of the statement together an analysis of the funds flow statement is possible.

The first part of the analysis is to answer the question "Why is there no cash if the firm is making a profit?"

3.2.6 *Analysis of the funds flow statement*

This statement shows just where the cash went. Of the profit of R289 500 no less than R150 500 went towards the purchase of fixed assets (there are no long term debts to help finance this purchase), interest consumed another R(31 000 − 3 000) = R28 000 and another R58 000 went on tax. The second part of the statement shows just what happened to the rest of the cash. Working capital increased by R66 000, but:

1. the increase in cash balances and the increase in the bank overdraft cancelled each other out;
2. debtors consumed R146 000, which was partly offset by increases in the amounts owed (ie money not yet spent) to creditors (R45 000) and the tax authorities (R20 000) and a decrease in the amount tied up in work in progress (R15 000), leaving a cash shortage in respect of these items of R66 000.

Not one cent of the increase in working capital was therefore available as cash. This means that anyone not looking beyond the net increase in working capital may misinterpret the undertaking's real liquidity position unless the debtors pay up very quickly.

The second part of the analysis is to examine the undertaking's financial policy and to decide on whether it is acceptable. In this case there is a large outflow in respect of fixed assets (a long term investment) which should theoretically be financed by a similar inflow in the form of long term finance, either share capital or long term loans in order to minimise financial risk. Since there is no such inflow the company is using a high risk financing policy, which is probably not appropriate at this stage of the firm's operations.

4. Preparation of the funds statement to show a net change in cash

4.1 The purpose of the statement

A funds flow statement is prepared on this basis to show the net effect on cash, or on cash and cash equivalents, of the movement of all financial resources into and out of the undertaking over a period of time, usually one year. The statement will obviously not differ very much from the one discussed above, and the arguments concerning its presentation can again be related to the balance sheet as in figure 16.3 on page 306.

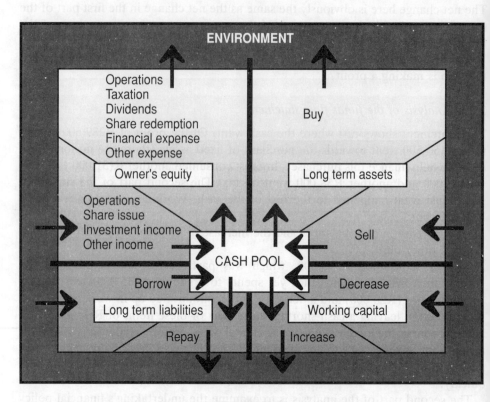

Figure 16.3

*Cash flows between the undertaking and its environment
and within the undertaking*

The only difference between this representation of the balance sheet base for flows of funds is that cash is separated from the other aspects of working capital and given a separate section for itself. Into this pool of cash will flow the results of a decreased investment in stock or debtors or an increased level of creditors, and from it will flow the results of increases in debtors or stock and decreases in creditors in addition to all the inflows and outflows mentioned in the previous section.

4.2 Statement AC118 and the preparation of the funds statement

This statement ruled it generally accepted accounting practice in South Africa to present a *cash flow statement* which is simply a funds statement in which the bottom line is the change in cash rather than the change in working capital. The Companies Act was subsequently amended to reflect this, though the statement did, with a little effort, meet the original requirements of that Act.

The statement requires separate presentation of:
* cash generated by operating activities, disclosing
* cash generated by operations
* investment income
* changes in the non-cash components of working capital
* cash effects of finance costs
* cash effects of taxation
* cash effects of investment activities
* cash effects of financing activities

A cash flow statement prepared for Engineering Firm (Pty) Ltd for the year ended 28 February 1984 in accordance with AC118 would look like this:

	Notes	
Cash retained from operating activities		
Cash generated by operations	1	289 500
Investment income		3 000
Cash used to increase working capital	2	− 86 000
Cash generated by operating activities		206 500
Finance costs		− 31 000
Taxation paid	3	− 38 000
Cash available from operating activities		137 500
Cash used in investing activities		
Investment to maintain operations		
Replacement of fixed assets	4	− 50 500
Investment to expand operations		
Additions to fixed assets	5	− 100 000
Cash generated		13 000
Cash effects of financing activities		
Increase in long term borrowings		12 800
Change in short term borrowings	6	0
Proceeds of share issue		200
Cash utilised		13 000

Notes: 1 Cash generated by operations

Operating income before tax	156 000
Depreciation	105 500
Interest paid	31 000
	292 500
Interest received	3 000
	R289 500

2	Cash used to increase working capital	
	Increase in debtors	146 000
	Decrease in work in progress	– 15 000
	Increase in creditors	– 45 000
		R86 000
3	Taxes	
	Tax provided	58 000
	Increase in tax provision	– 20 000
	Cash paid for taxation	**R38 000**

4 & 5 AC118 requires the separation of purchase of fixed assets into these two groups to show whether the firm is expanding by these purchases or merely maintaining its position by replacing fixed assets. Details would also have to be shown under both headings for each class of assets. The figures shown here are simply for purposes of example.

6	Change in short term borrowings	
	Increase in bank overdraft	15 000
	Increase in cash on hand	– 15 000
	Net change	**NIL**

Changes in cash are regarded as effectively being part of the change in short term borrowings since this cash is either available to redeem short term loans or has been generated from short term loans, either directly or indirectly.

4.2.1 *Analysis of the cash flow statement*

This statement shows exactly the same information as the funds flow statement above, but changes the concentration from working capital directly to cash. It is divided into three separate sections, each looking at a different aspect.

The first section deals with the operations of the undertaking and deducts from operating income those aspects of working capital which are directly related to operations as shown in note 2. The effect of this is to show how much cash is available from operations. This can differ dramatically from the working capital provided by operations if there are significant changes in the levels of stock, debtors or creditors. Compare this picture with the one provided above by the working capital based flow statement. It also shows the actual amount of tax paid as distinct from the amount provided by taking into account that element of working capital which refers to changes in the level of taxation due for payment.

The second section deals with investing activities, or what the company did with the funds it received, by detailing the assets in which the undertaking invested cash over the period, highlighting investment for maintenance of operations and investment for expansion.

The final part deals with the financing activities of the undertaking, showing the effects of borrowings and repayments and the effect of these on cash holdings. In this case the company borrowed nothing other than an amount of R12 800 from the directors, but used the funds generated by activities to purchase fixed assets. The overall effect is that the company was a net user of cash during the year to the extent of R13 000.

5. Different applications of funds flow and cash flow

A business cannot survive if it does not generate cash, which is the reason why there has been so much emphasis on cash flow during the past decade or so. However, cash does not provide the whole picture. To be successful the undertaking must also control the other aspects of working capital as reflected in the funds flow statement. In general terms, most people look at cash flow for short term evaluation and planning, but look to funds flow for the same purposes when it comes to the longer term. This is reflected in the following ratios which have been developed to assist in the analysis of the financial statements of an undertaking. Most of these ratios have fairly limited application.

5.1 Funds flow ratios

There is only one ratio in this category which is widely used. This is the *Beaver ratio*, named after its developer but also known as the *cash flow coverage ratio*. It makes use of what Beaver referred to as the *gross cash flow*, also referred to by others as *internal cash flow*, which is simply the operating profit of the undertaking before allowing for depreciation. It applies the very obvious concept that an undertaking with little debt and a high cash flow is in a financially sound position, but that as it moves towards having large debt and a low cash flow it becomes less financially sound. Beaver found that a company whose gross cash flow showed a declining trend would face almost certain financial failure if the gross cash flow continued declining to a point where it was less than 14 % of the total debt. His conclusions have since been attacked on various grounds, the most serious being that he did not take the term of the debt into account. If all the debt were long term the undertaking would obviously be in a better position than an undertaking with a similar total amount of debt most of which was short term.

Despite the criticisms the concept of this ratio is widely used, though the percentage which Beaver laid down is not regarded as being very meaningful. For Engineering Firm (Pty) Ltd the ratio would be as follows:

	1985	1984	1983
Operating income for the year	102 000	184 000	183 000
Depreciation	103 000	105 500	125 500
	205 000	289 500	308 500
Other funds flows—interest	20 000	− 28 000	− 13 000
	225 000	261 500	295 500
Total liabilities	1 385 000	1 165 000	1 085 000
Beaver ratio	16,25 %	22,45 %	27,24 %

The trend is sharply downward. While the 14 % mark is no longer regarded as very meaningful it is clear that EF is approaching this point and that a continued downward trend in this ratio must lead to serious problems for the company in the near future.

If directors' loans were to be treated as liabilities, of course, the picture would be much worse.

5.2 Short term cash and funds flow ratios

The Beaver ratio is essentially a measure of the long term survival prospects of an undertaking. Several other ratios have been developed for use in short term financial analysis. These mostly use the cash flow of the undertaking, but the funds flow or gross cash flow is sometimes used as an approximation of the actual cash flow. The most widely used of these include the ones discussed below.

5.2.1 *The defensive interval measure*

This is the cash flow equivalent of the quick ratio. It uses the quick assets and, instead of comparing them to the static picture of current liabilities, compares them to the daily cash outflow. The answer, instead of being a multiple of the current liabilities, is the number of days of operating expenses which the quick assets can cover.

The problem, of course, is that the analyst looking at the financial statements does not have any indication of the planned cash outflows of the undertaking. Since he has no budgeted figures available, he is forced to use the previous year's figures as a guideline. This is usually reasonably accurate, but changes in operating plans could mean that the next year's expenses could be very different, particularly in contracting firms where expenditures depend on the contracts in progress at any one time. The calculation of this ratio for Engineering Firm (Pty) Ltd would be as follows:

	1985	1984	1983
Sales for the year	4 650 000	4 550 000	3 665 000
Operating income	102 000	184 000	183 000
Operating expenses for the year	4 548 000	4 366 000	3 482 000
Non cash expense	103 000	105 500	125 500
Operating cash expenses	4 445 000	4 260 500	3 356 500
Daily operating expenses	12 178	11 673	9 196
Defensive (quick) assets	1 344 000	1 236 000	1 075 000
Defensive interval in days	110	106	117

The ratio tells one very little here, going down and then up again. This actually illustrates the weakness of this ratio, which lies in the fact that no account is taken of changes in current liabilities. Increases in quick assets can be funded by increases in current liabilities so as to increase this measure, which would give a distorted picture of the company's short term financial position.

Refinements have been suggested to this measure. They include proposals to take into account changes in the current liability position and an adjustment for those companies whose average debt differs markedly from the debt position at the year end. In the final analysis, it does provide an indicator of operating liquidity if there is no substantial change in the current liability position.

5.2.2 *Current liabilities to funds generated by operations*

Harold Bierman proposed several cash flow ratios on this theme for measurement of short term liquidity, but the figure he used throughout was the same gross cash flow figure used by Beaver. His proposals include:

Net current assets (Current assets − current liabilities) divided by funds generated by operations;
(Net current assets − stock) divided by funds generated by operations;
(Total liabilities − current assets) divided by funds generated by operations; and, for use when cash flow is negative,
Net current assets divided by funds lost in operations.

Each of these answers would then be multiplied by 365 to get the number of days involved. The first three would show how many days it would take to generate the funds currently involved, while the last would show the number of days for which operations could continue to drain funds from the undertaking before the company would be unable to meet its commitments.

5.2.3 *The liquidity flow index*

Kenneth Lemke proposed that the maximum funds outflow which an undertaking can bear be compared with the outflow actually required. This would again require knowledge which an outside analyst would not have of the undertaking's financial plans and is therefore actually only applicable within an undertaking. Practical maximum outflow is defined as the total of the opening cash balances plus total cash inflows for the period minus required closing balance of cash, while outflow required includes operating outflows and planned capital expenses.

An efficiently run undertaking should have an index of one. Less than one indicates financial weakness, more than one indicates poor cash management.

Key words

Funds flow
Working capital
Cash used for investment
Gross cash flow

Cash flow
Cash generated by operations
Cash effects of financial activities

Questions and exercises on Part Three

Test-yourself questions

1. The primary purpose of the cash flow statement is to report on the financial activities of the undertaking rather than on the operating activities.
   T   F
2. A set of the financial ratios derived from an annual financial report could replace the financial report itself.   T   F
3. A decrease in the accounts receivable collection period would indicate an improvement in credit control procedures.   T   F
4. There are universally acceptable standards for most financial ratios which allow the analyst to interpret them precisely.   T   F
5. Since financial statements are prepared on an annual basis the operating cycle of a business should not exceed one year.   T   F
6. The current ratio is calculated by dividing the current liabilities by the current assets.   T   F
7. If the accounts receivable collection period remains constant while sales are increasing, the amount of accounts receivable will decrease.   T   F
8. A decrease in the operating cycle of a business would indicate an improvement in the performance of lower level management.   T   F
9. Purchases for the year are equal to cost of sales plus the increase in stock over the period.   T   F
10. Gearing is a term used to describe the relationship between a company's long term debt and its current liabilities.   T   F

Assignment material

Question 3.1 Mu Company—Calculation of financial ratios

The following are the incomplete financial statements for Mu Company. You are required to fill in the missing figures by using the information following the financial statements.

Income statement for the year ended 28 February 1993

Sales	____
Cost of sales	____
Gross profit	____
Total expenses	____
Net profit before tax	____
Taxation	____
Increase in retained earnings	60 000

Balance sheet at 28 February 1993

Fixed assets
    Land and buildings   80 000
    Plant at cost
    Less accumulated depreciation
Net fixed assets
Current assets
    Cash
    Accounts receivable
    Stock

Shareholders equity
    Share capital   200 000
    Retained earnings

Long term liabilities
Current liabilities
                                                     200 000

Additional information:

1. The current ratio is 2:1
2. The ratio of current liabilities to long term liabilities is 2:1
3. Total debt to equity is 1:1
4. Plant is depreciated on a straight line basis at 10 % per annum and is currently four years old
5. Tax is paid at a rate of 40 % of net profit before tax
6. Total asset turnover is 2 times per year
7. Gross profit is 50 % of cost of sales
8. Stock turnover based on cost of sales is 3,2 times per year
9. Debtors collection period is 43,80 days.

Question 3.2 Gamma Corporation—calculation of financial ratios

On the night of 30 March 1999 most of the accounting records of the Gamma Corporation were destroyed by fire. Two days after that the sole effective shareholder was holding discussions with an investor about the possible takeover of the company. He needed as much information as he could get for this purpose but realised that it would not be possible to reconstruct the accounting records in such a short time. On the day after the fire the following were available:

1. The financial statements for the previous year shown as exhibit 2 below.
2. Certain fragmentary data and ratios that had been calculated from the financial statements for 1999. The statements themselves had been destroyed by the fire. These are included in exhibit 1 below.

3. The following data:
   3.1 The turnover for 1999 was R6 341 000;
   3.2 Current liabilities at end February 1999 were R1 256 000;
   3.3 No dividends were paid or declared during the 1999 financial year;
   3.4 No changes in share capital took place;
   3.5 No changes took place in long term investments;
   3.6 All short term investments were sold and the balance at end 1999 was nil;
   3.7 The cash balance was R42 000;
   3.8 New plant purchased during the year had cost R1 000 000; and
   3.9 The tax rate was 50%.

Exhibit 1

Available ratios	1999	1998
Acid test ratio (Quick ratio)	0,396:1	0,610:1
Current ratio	1,092:1	1,262:1
Stock turnover (Using cost of sales)	6,31 ×	7,15 ×
Gross profit margin	12,98 %	10,64 %
Net profit margin	0,52 %	(1,30 %)
Total asset turnover	1,55 ×	1,69 ×
Total debt/Equity ratio	1,25:1	0,94:1
Return on shareholders equity	?	(4,26 %)

Notes:
1. All ratio calculations have been rounded off. This may lead to small differences in calculations.
2. Year end figures have been used throughout in the calculation of ratios.

Exhibit 2

Balance sheet at 28 February 1998

Fixed assets		1910
Property, plant and equipment	3 014	
Less: Accumulated depreciation	1521	
	1 493	
Investments	417	
Current assets		1 548
Cash	16	
Short term investments	356	
Accounts receivable	377	
Stock on hand	729	
Prepaid expenses	70	
		3 458
Long term liabilities		449
Long term loans	449	
Current liabilities		1 227
Accounts payable and accruals	1 227	
Total liabilities		1 676
Shareholders equity		1 782
Ordinary share capital	208	
Retained earnings	1574	
		3 458

Income statement for the year ended 28 February 1998

Turnover		5 830
Cost of sales		5 210
Gross profit		620
Expenses		735
Depreciation	146	
Other expenses	589	
Net loss before taxation		115
Taxation adjustment		39
Net loss after taxation		76

Question 3.3 Elephant Company—Basic ratio analysis

A man with some money to invest safely on behalf of a maiden aunt has approached you to assist him in reaching a decision on whether to invest in Elephant Company Limited or Fieldmouse Company Limited. The two companies are in the same industry and have been steady performers over the years with little change taking place except that both have grown at a rate slightly higher than the inflation rate. Both companies are quoted on the Johannesburg Stock Exchange where the ruling price for Fieldmouse shares is currently about ten per cent higher than that for Elephant shares. You have at your disposal the following financial statements for the two companies:

	Elephant Limited	Fieldmouse Limited
Balance sheets		
Share capital	450 000	450 000
Retained earnings	280 000	380 000
	730 000	830 000
Long term loan	225 000	225 000
Current liabilities	180 000	225 000
	1 135 000	1 280 000
Fixed assets	745 000	780 000
Current assets	390 000	500 000
Stock	195 000	250 000
Accounts receivable	135 000	180 000
Cash	60 000	70 000
	1 135 000	1 280 000

	Elephant Limited	Fieldmouse Limited
Income statements		
Sales	1 800 000	2 100 000
Cost of sales	1 300 000	1 520 000
Gross profit	500 000	580 000
Operating expenses	425 000	500 000
Operating income	75 000	80 000
Interest	10 000	10 000
Net income before tax	65 000	70 000
Taxation	14 000	15 000
Net income after tax	51 000	55 000
Dividends	31 000	30 000
Increase in retained earnings	20 000	25 000

Required:

Prepare a report setting out your recommendations. Support these with any calculations you may feel necessary.

Question 3.4 Global Developments

(a) Complete the following cash flow statement by inserting the missing numbers in the spaces provided.

GLOBAL DEVELOPMENTS LIMITED
Cash flow statement for the year ended 28 February 1993
Cash retained from operating activities
  Cash generated by operations
  Investment income
  Cash used to increase working capital
Cash generated by operating activities
  Finance costs
  Taxation paid
Cash available from operating activities
  Dividends paid
Cash retained from operating activities
Cash used in investing activities
Purchase of fixed assets

Cash generated
Cash effects of financing activities
  Increase in long term borrowings
  Proceeds of rights issue
  Increase in cash and bank balances

Cash utilised

The balance sheets and income statements for 1993 and 1992 are given below:
GLOBAL DEVELOPMENTS LIMITED
Income statements for years ended last day of February

	1993	1992
Turnover	5 400 000	4 800 000
Cost of sales	4 320 000	3 840 000
Gross profit	1 080 000	960 000
Dividends received	20 000	10 000
Total income	1 100 000	970 000
Expenses	980 000	870 000
Depreciation	40 000	38 000
Interest paid	150 000	120 000
Salaries and wages	680 000	620 000
Other expenses	110 000	92 000
Net income before tax	120 000	100 000
Taxation	48 000	40 000
Net income after tax	72 000	60 000
Dividends declared	21 600	18 000
Increase in retained earnings	50 400	42 000

GLOBAL DEVELOPMENTS LIMITED
Balance sheets at end February

	1993	*1992*
Shareholders equity		
Share capita	200 000	100 000
Retained earnings	152 400	102 000
	352 400	202 000
Long term liabilities		
Mortgage loan	360 000	240 000
	712 400	442 000
Fixed assets	387 000	259 000
Land and buildings at cost	165 000	165 000
Plant and machinery	222 000	94 000
At cost	380 000	212 000
Accumulated depreciation	158 000	118 000
Investments at cost	30 000	30 000
Net current assets	295 400	153 000
Current assets	410 000	340 000
Stock	220 000	190 000
Accounts receivable	130 000	120 000
Cash and bank balances	60 000	30 000
Current liabilities	114 600	187 000
Creditors	54 600	137 000
Net provision for tax	38 400	32 000
Dividend payable	21 600	18 000
	712 400	442 000

(b) Referring only to the cash flow statement, comment briefly on the financial
position of the company at the end of February 1993.

Question 3.5 Tarragon Company—funds flow

Condensed balance sheets for Tarragon Company for the years ended last day of February, together with some additional information about the firm's activities, are given below.

Equities	1999	1998
Ordinary shares at par	55 000	45 000
Retained earnings	20 000	34 000
Shareholders equity	75 000	79 000
Accounts payable	20 000	16 000
	95 000	95 000
Assets		
Cash	7 000	13 000
Accounts receivable	20 000	17 000
Stock	23 000	25 000
Property, plant and equipment	70 000	60 000
Accumulated depreciation	− 25 000	− 20 000
	95 000	95 000

Additional information:

1. Used machinery was sold for R9 000 in cash. Original cost was R10 000 and accumulated depreciation was R3 000. The gain of R2 000 was treated as income.
2. New machinery was purchased for R20 000, of which R10 000 was paid in cash. The balance is included in accounts payable and is due for payment early in the new year.
3. There was a net loss of R4 000.
4. Cash dividends of R10 000 were paid.

Required:

1. Prepare a statement of changes in working capital for the year ended 28 February 1999.
2. Prepare a statement of source and applications of funds for the same year.
3. Comment briefly on the firm's financial position at 28 February 1999 in the light of the above statement. Do not do any other analysis or speculate on any other aspect of the firm.

Question 3.6 Shadow Company—funds flow

The following are the comparative balance sheets at end February for Shadow CC:

	1989	1988
Members' contributions	40 000	40 000
Undrawn profits	4 792	2 016
Member's loan	28 000	40 000
	72 792	82 016

Fixed assets		
Machinery and motor vehicles at cost	17 560	15 560
Accumulated depreciation	4 360	1 916
	13 200	13 644
Net current assets	59 592	68 372
Current assets	95 206	111 480
Stock	43 554	37 628
Accounts receivable	42 646	66 604
Loan to member	6 000	0
Short term deposit	2 000	6 000
Cash and bank	1 006	1 248
Current liabilities	35 614	43 108
Accounts payable	34 012	39 004
Taxation	1 602	4 104
	72 792	82 016

The following information is also available:
1. No fixed assets were sold or scrapped during the year.
2. Interest paid amounted to R2 346.
3. Provision for tax was R4 770.
4. R3 000 was distributed to members.

Required:
Prepare a cash flow statement for the year ended 28 February 1999.

Question 3.7 The Nightmare Factory Limited—

The balance sheets for the Nightmare Company Limited for the financial years ended 28 February 1998 and 1999 are given below, together with certain information extracted from the income statement for 1999:

THE NIGHTMARE FACTORY LIMITED

Balance sheets at	1999	1998
Share capital	300 000	250 000
Share premium	100 000	75 000
Retained earnings	174 150	137 900
	574 150	462 900
Long term liabilities	60 000	75 000
	634 150	537 900

Fixed assets	452 400	414 600
Land and buildings	254 400	184 600
Plant and machinery	198 000	230 000
Cost	290 000	290 000
Accumulated depreciation	92 000	60 000
Net current assets	181 750	123 300
Current assets	264 550	215 850
Stock	104 500	109 500
Debtors	94 950	63 850
Cash	65 100	42 500
Current liabilities	82 800	92 550
Creditors	67 800	82 550
Dividends	15 000	10 000
	634 150	537 900

The following relevant income statement information is also available:
1. Net income R96 250 (no tax was payable due to an assessed loss brought forward).
2. Depreciation for the year was R32 000.
3. Cash dividends of R60 000 were declared.

Required: Complete the following cash flow statement.

THE NIGHTMARE FACTORY LIMITED
Cash flow statement year ended 30 September 1999

	Note	
Cash from operations	1	
Cash used for working capital	2	
Net operating cash flow		
Financing cash flows		
Shares issued		75 000
Dividends paid	3	
Loan repaid		− 15 000
Net cash available for investment		
Investment cash flows		
Building		− 69 800
Net increase in cash		
Reflected by		
Increase in cash		22 600

Notes

1. Cash generated by activities	
Net income	96 250
Plus non cash expenses	_____
2. Cash used for working capital	
Stock	− 5 000
Accounts receivable	
Accounts payable	14 750
	40 850
3. Dividends paid	
Balance 1998	
Plus:	_____
Less:	_____
	_____

Question 3.8 Ajax and Lightning—Cash flow analysis

The following are the summarised financial statements for Ajax Company Limited and Lightning Company Limited:

AJAX COMPANY

Balance sheets at end February	*1999*	*1998*
Share capital	200	200
Retained earnings	220	180
	420	380
Long term liabilities	125	125
	545	505
Fixed assets at cost	280	250
Less: accumulated depreciation	125	100
	155	150
Net current assets	390	355
Current assets	615	470
Stock	455	350
Accounts receivable	120	100
Cash and bank balances	40	20
Current liabilities	225	115
Accounts payable	170	80
Dividends payable	30	15
Tax	25	20
	545	505

Income statement at end February 1999

Turnover	900
Operating income	150
Interest paid	20
Net income before tax	130
Tax	60
Net income after tax	70
Dividends	30
Net increase in retained earnings	40

Cash flow statement for the year ended 28 February 1999

Cash generated by operating activities	140
Finance costs	20
Dividends	15
Tax paid	55
Cash available from operating activities	50
Cash used in investment activities	
Additions to fixed assets	30
Cash generated	20
Cash effects of financing activities	
Decrease in long term borrowings	0
Change in cash and bank balances	20
	20

LIGHTNING COMPANY

Balance sheets at end February	*1999*	*1998*
Share capital	200	200
Retained earnings	140	120
	340	320
Long term liabilities	175	200
	515	520
Fixed assets at cost	280	260
Less: accumulated depreciation	130	105
	150	155
Net current assets	365	365
Current assets	485	500
Stock	340	350
Accounts receivable	120	120
Cash and bank balances	25	30
Current liabilities	120	135

	90	100
Accounts payable		
Dividends	20	15
Tax	10	20
	515	520

Income statement at end February 1999

Turnover	1 000
Operating income	110
Interest paid	30
Net income before tax	80
Tax	30
Net income after tax	50
Dividends	30
Net increase in retained earnings	20

Cash flow statement for the year ended 28 February 1999

Cash generated by operating activities	135
Finance costs	30
Dividends	25
Tax paid	40
Cash available from operating activities	40
Cash used in investment activities	
Additions to fixed assets	20
Cash generated	20
Cash effects of financing activities	
Increase in long term borrowings	25
Change in cash and bank balances	−5
	20

The two companies are about the same size in terms of sales, assets and personnel employed. They compete with each other and about another ten companies, all of which are smaller, in a highly competitive market. In 1999 Ajax Company Limited showed a larger income after tax than did Lightning Company Limited, but the cash generated by the two companies was exactly the same.

Required: Comment on the relative quality of the cash flows of the two companies. Show all the workings necessary to support your comments.

Question 3.9 Confident Company

Confident Company is run by its founder, a man who has that characteristic in abundance. An artisan who started his own business, he is a superb operator and plant manager but has little understanding of financial matters—or patience with them. He has just been handed the financial statements for the 1999 financial year and, while he has little knowledge of how to read such statements, has picked up from the income statement that net income after tax was R108 000, that cash dividends of R14 000 were paid and that depreciation written off amounted to R40 000. He was also aware that he had purchased fixed assets for R440 000 during the year, financing this partly by suspensive sale agreements. However, he finds himself very puzzled by the picture shown by the following balance sheets.

CONFIDENT COMPANY LIMITED
Balance sheets at 28 February

	1999	1998
Shareholders equity	414	320
Long term liabilities	300	0
	714	320
Fixed assets at book value	600	200
Net current assets	114	120
Current assets	324	180
Stock and work in progress	200	100
Accounts receivable	120	60
Cash and bank balance	4	20
Current liabilities	210	60
	714	320

Looking at the document, he complained to his accountant: "This company has been growing steadily for ten years. This last year was easily our best. We grew enormously and made our biggest profit ever. And what happens? Money has never been so tight! Just look at the current liabilities we have to settle with only four grand in the bank. It just doesn't make sense. It seems that the more you make, the poorer you get! These statements just can't be right."

Required:
Explain to the manager just why there is no money despite the fact that the company is making record profits. Prepare whatever statements you feel are necessary to make the position clear.

Question 3.10 Uno Fabrications

The following financial statements of Uno Fabrications have been laid before the managing director:

Balance sheets at 28 February

	1999	1998
Fixed assets	4 040	3 000
Stock and work in progress	1 400	1 000
Accounts receivable	800	560
Prepaid expenses	80	60
Cash and bank balances	200	500
	6 520	5 120
Share capital	2 000	2 000
Retained earnings	1 980	1 880
Long term loan	1 000	0
Accounts payable	1 480	1 200
Accrued expenses	60	40
	6 520	5 120

Income statement at 28 February 1999

Turnover		5 000
Cost of sales		2 800
		2 200
Depreciation	800	
Other expenses	1 100	1 900
Net income before tax		300
Taxes		120
Net income after tax		180
Dividends		80
Increase in retained earnings		100

From the notes and directors' report it is clear that the company purchased new machinery during the year, paying R840 000 in cash and signing a suspensive sale agreement for R1 000 000.

Required:

1. Prepare a cash flow statement to explain to the rather worried managing director why the company has so little cash even though the income statement reflects an income after tax of R180 000.
2. Write a brief report to Mr Uno explaining what this statement reveals about the cash position of the company and tell him why he has so little cash available.

Question 3.11 Chinese Puzzle Company

As the financial director of the Chinese Puzzle Company you have prepared the financial report which has been sent to shareholders. Included in the financial report is the cash flow statement shown below:

CHINESE PUZZLE COMPANY
Cash flow statement for the year ended 28 February 1999

Cash flows from operations Net income		180 000
Add: Depreciation		50 000
Deduct: Profit on sale of fixed assets		10 000
		220 000
Deduct: Cash used for working capital		12 000
Increase in stock	20 000	
Increase in prepaid expenses	1 000	
Decrease in accounts payable	9 000	
Decrease in accounts receivable	− 18 000	
Cash available from operating activities		208 000
Dividends paid		100 000
Cash retained from operating activities		108 000
Investment cash flows		
Purchase of fixed assets	130 000	
Sale of fixed assets	70 000	60 000
Cash generated		48 000
Cash effects of financing activities		
Increase in cash and bank balances		48 000

A shareholder has written to the company complaining about the cash flow statement and warning that he is going to ask the following specific questions at the annual general meeting of the company to be held one week from now:
1. How can depreciation be a cash flow?
2. The issue of shares to the seller of land purchased is not a cash transaction. Why is it included in a cash flow statement?
3. How can the profit on the sale of fixed assets be a deduction from net income in determining the cash flow from operating activities?
4. Why do you prepare this confusing statement anyway? I can easily compute the increase in cash from the comparative balance sheets for last year and this year.

Required: Draft the answers to these questions so that you can deal with them when they are raised at the meeting.

Question 3.12 Clyde Industrial Corporation Limited

Clyde Industrial Corporation Limited is a company which was first listed on the Johannesburg Stock Exchange during the boom year of 1987. The Report of the directors states that the nature of its business is the manufacture and distribution of secondary steel products to the mining, industrial and agricultural markets. The chairman's report states that the cutbacks in the mining industry have led to reduced margins in that industry with not much prospect of any substantial increase in business but that growth in the other sections is such that they should more than compensate for the loss in the mining sector. During the year under review the shares traded on the JSE at a substantial discount to the net assets value per share of 94,6 cents, the share price rising from a low of 25 cents to a high of 45 cents at the end of the year.

Below are the simplified balance sheet and income statement as sent to shareholders on 27 April 1993:

CLYDE INDUSTRIAL CORPORATION LIMITED (All figures in 000's)

Income statement to end February	1993	1992
Turnover	102 237	82 657
Operating income	5 528	4 494
Interest paid	1 124	1 015
Net income before taxation	4 404	3 479
Taxation	1 280	1 583
Net income after taxation	3 124	1 896
Extraordinary item	64	64
Net income attributable to shareholders	3 060	1 832
Dividend	572	572
Retained income for the year	2 488	1 260
Retained income at the beginning of the year	6 641	5 381
Retained income at the end of the year	9 129	6 641

Balance sheet at end February	1993	1992
CAPITAL EMPLOYED		
Share capital and premium	5 426	5 426
Non-distributable reserve	1 976	2 094
Distributable reserves	9 247	6 641
Shareholders equity	16 649	14 161
Long term liabilities	593	1 337
Deferred taxation	800	1 027
	18 042	16 525

EMPLOYMENT OF CAPITAL

Fixed assets	7 583	7 902
Loan levy	64	64
	7 647	7 966
Current assets Inventories	16 816	14 309
Accounts receivable	16 489	15 281
Cash	9	43
Current liabilities	33 314	29 633
Accounts payable and provisions	16 991	15 028
Shareholders for dividend	352	352
Short term loans	5 110	5 054
Taxation	466	640
	22 919	21 074
Net current assets	10 395	8 559
	18 042	16 525

The following relevant information is contained in the notes to the financial statements:

1. Operating income is arrived at after taking the following into account:

Depreciation	795	922
Profit on sale of fixed assets	205	61

2. Taxation
South African normal taxation

– Current	1 506	1 567
– Prior year adjustment	1	0
Deferred taxation	– 227	16
	1 280	1 583

3. Extraordinary item
Amortisation of goodwill arising from the purchase of companies.

4. Fixed assets

Land and buildings at valuation	2 850	2 850
Land and buildings at cost	539	533
Accumulated depreciation on industrial buildings	210	175
	3 179	3 208
Plant, equipment, vehicles and furniture at cost	10 097	10 468
Accumulated depreciation	6 027	6 172
	4 070	4 296
Goodwill at cost	641	641
Accumulated amortisation	307	243
	334	398
Net book value	7 583	7 902

Further information is that fixed assets with a cost of R958 were sold during the year for R848, and that of the new assets purchased R259 were for the expansion of operations.

Required: Prepare a cash flow statement for the year ended 28 February 1993.

CASES
3.1 Folly Fashions

(This case is based on "Delsowear', a case written by Trevor Albertyn for use at the Graduate School of Business Leadership, Unisa.)

Folly Fashions, a small manufacturer of women's and girls' clothing, was founded in 1955 by Koen Sosoon. Sosoon managed the firm himself for nearly twenty years before his other interest became so demanding of his time that he decided to appoint a professional manager. After what he believed was a thorough screening process he appointed Tom Taylor as the general manager of Folly Fashions with complete responsibility for all aspects of the operation of Folly Fashions. Taylor had been the production manager of one of Folly's competitors and Sosoon felt he had the requisite experience for his new post.

Taylor put his knowledge of production management to work immediately. Since roughly eighty per cent of Folly Fashions' sales took place in two short selling seasons (winter clothing around Easter time and summer clothing in early spring) the company had been following a seasonal production schedule. Smith viewed this as being indicative of poor planning and immediately changed the scheduling so that Folly Fashions produced evenly throughout the year. He realised that this would have cost implications since it would mean stockpiling, but reasoned that the increased productivity would more than compensate for this. He therefore had no qualms about arranging for a short term bank loan to finance this stockpiling, and making this a condition of transferring Folly's banking operations to First Enterprise Bank. This bank had long been angling for Folly's accounts, mainly because of the large cash balances which they built up after the selling seasons. The change in the nature of Folly's financing activities was nevertheless acceptable to them.

The arrangement with the bank at the end of 1979 was that Folly was entitled to use overdraft facilities up to a limit of R2 200 000 to finance the stock for a single season and that this overdraft would be settled in full before the start of the build up for the next selling season. The company had been taking full advantage of its arrangement with the bank and had, until recently, kept to the letter of its agreement. Until 1978 the company had managed to convert its stock into cash sufficiently rapidly to repay the loan in full before the end of February. This meant that the bank overdraft did not therefore appear on the financial statements at the year end which resulted in a far healthier looking balance sheet. Matters had deteriorated in the last two years, with Folly Fashions not being able to repay its loan in time so that it appeared on the balance sheets. The bank had allowed matters to drift without requiring any explanations or extra securities from Folly Fashions.

The company started producing new fashions for the 1979 Easter season in November 1978 and had used up R600 000 of its line of credit by 15 December for purchase of raw materials. By 1 February 1979 the company's overdraft had risen to R2 160 000 after completion of production for the winter season. Plans were being made for the spring fashion line, but Taylor knew that the company was in no position to meet the requirement of repaying the overdraft before production started.

The large unsold stock after the end of the previous season meant that Folly Fashions was only able to repay R200 000 of the overdraft by the end of February. It was also having problems in meeting its obligations in respects of accounts payable. Taylor believed that the problems were due to the fact that, for the first time ever, the design team had failed to correctly forecast the change in design, particularly in skirt lengths. This meant that sales were significantly below the levels for the previous season.

Taylor realised that some additional equity capital was necessary since it was obvious that sales in the next month or so would not generate sufficient cash to repay the overdraft. The Sosoon family, accepting that the problem was a short term one, agreed to invest a further R2 400 000 to settle the loan and to relieve some of the pressure from the most pressing of the accounts payable. This would enable Taylor to approach the bank with some confidence when negotiating the terms for the renewal of the overdraft.

It had become customary for Taylor to approach the bank early in May each year in connection with the renewal of the overdraft facility. This was normally a formality but Russell Morgan, the manager who had handled Folly's account ever since it had been transferred to First Enterprise Bank, had certain doubts in view of the way the company had been unable to meet its commitments over the last two years. In addition to the problems Folly was experiencing, the Reserve Bank had decided to use monetary policy to fight inflation and had increased lending rates. There were expectations of further increases in the prime overdraft rate which would automatically place further pressure on the earnings of all companies. Morgan was scrutinising all outstanding loans in the light of these circumstances and when Taylor approached him with a request of an increase in the overdraft limit to R3 000 000 he looked at the whole question very carefully. One of the keystones of his scrutiny was the financial statements of the company. These statements for the last three years are set out in the accompanying tables. In addition to the statutory financial statements in the first two tables, Morgan used the leverage supplied by being the lending banker to obtain the more detailed statements set out in the next two tables. He analysed all of these, comparing his results to the clothing industry averages shown in table 5, and came to certain conclusions. He noted that Folly Fashions' profits had declined while assets had increased. He also noted that the company had become a slow payer, a serious matter in an industry where most suppliers gave discounts for settlement within thirty days.

At their meeting Taylor admitted that they had misjudged the fashion trend and put the entire blame for the company's problems down to the sales decrease resulting from this. He also stated that certain steps had been taken to ensure that there was no recurrence of this problem. Morgan, while granting that the poor sales performance was a contributing factor, gave it as his opinion that the root of the company's problems lay in the fact that it had expanded its asset base too rapidly. He cited the recent purchase of equipment and the purchase of a building which had previously been rented as examples of actions which had placed an excessive drain on the company's cash resources. He also pointed out increases in certain expense categories and, in general, made it plain that the bank was not at all satisfied with the company's financial performance. While the injection of equity capital was regarded in a positive light the bank felt that it was necessary for the company to review its activities and to present a well thought out plan for the future before the question of an increased overdraft limit could be considered. Morgan even went so far as to state that he was reviewing the current limits and was not yet certain whether he could see his way clear to renewing the overdraft at its current levels.

Required:

1. Analyse the financial statements of the company using the Du Pont cascade. Determine which are the major problems of Folly Fashions and which are less important.
2. Prepare a cash flow statement for the period March 1977 to February 1979 and use this statement to analyse Folly Fashions' cash flow problems.
3. Use the above analyses, in conjunction with any other information which you have about the company, to determine the source of the company's problems and advise on how these should be sorted out.
4. Prepare pro forma financial statements at 1 March 1979 immediately after the injection of R2 400 000 equity capital. Use these statements as a base to prepare a budgeted income statement and balance sheet for presentation to the bank. Accept that 75 % of the stock on hand at end February 1979 is going to be sold as scrap for ten per cent of its value while the remainder will be sold at normal margins.

Table 1

FOLLY FASHIONS LIMITED
Income statements for years to end February

	1977	1978	1979
Turnover	19 500	20 260	20 400
Expenses	18 224	18 904	19 282
Depreciation	160	180	260
Interest	140	190	290
Non-disclosable expenses	17 924	18 534	18 732

	1977	1978	1979
Income before tax	1 276	1 356	1 118
Tax	536	556	458
Income after tax	740	800	660
Retained earnings brought forward	890	1 330	1 830
	1 630	2 130	2 490
Dividends paid	300	300	0
Retained earnings carried forward	1 330	1 830	2 490

Table 2

FOLLY FASHIONS LIMITED

Balance Sheets at end February

	1979	1978	1977
Shareholders' Equity	4 030	4 530	5 190
Share capital	2 000	2 000	2 000
Share premium	700	700	700
Retained earnings	1 330	1 830	2 490
Long term liabilities			
Mortgage loan	340	320	300
Current liabilities	1 560	3 026	6 292
Bank overdraft	0	780	1 960
Accounts payable	1 200	1 600	2 800
Non-trade accounts payable	0	200	900
Tax payable	40	80	40
Accrued expenses	320	366	592
	5 930	7 876	11 782
Fixed assets	1 590	1 996	2 942
Land and buildings	480	800	1 400
Plant and machinery	1 080	1 180	1 540
Other assets	30	16	2
Current assets	4 340	5 880	8 840
Stock and work in process	2 100	3 600	6 000
Accounts receivable	1 800	2 000	2 600
Cash on hand and in bank	440	280	240
	5 930	7 876	11 782

Table 3

FOLLY FASHIONS LIMITED

Manufacturing accounts for years to end February

	1977	*1978*	*1979*
Opening stock—raw materials	280	300	400
Opening stock—work in process	360	400	400
Purchases	8 400	9 400	9 800
Direct wages	5 040	5 480	5 880
Variable overheads	2 470	2 730	2 940
Fixed overheads	150	190	260
	16 700	18 500	19 680
Closing stock—raw materials	300	400	440
Closing stock—work in process	400	400	500
Cost of manufacture	16 000	17 700	18 740

Table 4

FOLLY FASHIONS LIMITED

Trading and profit and loss accounts to end February

	1977	*1978*	*1979*
Sales	19 500	20 260	20 400
Cost of sales	15 880	16 300	16 480
Opening stock	1 280	1 400	2 800
Cost of manufacture	16 000	17 700	18 740
Closing stock	1 400	2 800	5 060
Gross profit	3 620	3 960	3 920
Expenses	2 204	2 414	2 512
Administration	580	628	740
Depreciation	20	20	28
Marketing and sales	1 310	1 538	1 540
Other expenses	294	228	204
Operating income	1 416	1 546	1 408
Interest	140	190	290
Income before tax	1 276	1 356	1 118

Note: salaries included in the above expenses amounted to:

	750	790	840

Table 5
Selected ratios for the clothing industry

	1977	1978	1979
Current ratio	1,9:1	1,8:1	1,8:1
Acid test (Quick) ratio	1,0:1	1,0:1	0,9:1
Stock turnover *(a)*	10×	9×	9×
Debtors collection period *(b)*	30	29	30
Total asset turnover *(b)*	2,5×	2,6×	2,6×
Total debt to total assets	56%	60%	62%
Interest cover	8,3×	8,2×	8,2×
Return on equity *(c)*	20%	20%	21,3%
Return on total assets *(c)*	8,8%	8,0%	8,1%
Return on total assets *(d)*	15,3%	20,1%	19.1%
Net profit margin *(c)*	3,5%	3,1%	3,1%
Net profit margin *(d)*	6,1%	7,8%	7,3%
Tax rate	41%	42%	41%

(a) Sales to closing inventory
(b) Based on year end figures
(c) Based on after tax earnings
(d) Based on earnings before interest and tax.

3.2 Mantima Furniture Manufacturers

Mantima Furniture Manufacturers Limited [Mantima] supplies high quality furniture to department stores, furniture chains and independent furniture stores from its factory, which is located in an industrial area of Durban. The head office is in downtown Durban. On a morning in May 1987 Rina Venter, the assistant credit manager of Mantima, felt concerned about changes in the way two of her firm's clients, Zebra Home Furnishings (Pty) Ltd [Zebra] of Durban and Dube Furnishers CC [Dube] of Madadeni, were settling their accounts. She delegated upwards and laid the files of these two before her chief, Ralph Emerson.

Zebra sells from four shops, one in Durban itself and the others in nearby suburban areas. There is a measure of seasonality in their sales, with turnover being higher in December and lower during the winter months. Roughly 75% of Zebra's sales are hire-purchase sales, which are regarded as cash sales since they are immediately discounted, while the other 25% are instalment sales. These require a deposit of 25% and settlement over the next six months.

The history of the firm is as follows: a two man partnership was formed in 1947. When the sons of the original partners entered the business it was decided to form a company with each of the four holding an equal number of shares. This duly happened in 1963. When the older shareholders retired in July 1981, they transferred the shares to their sons. The business relationship with Mantima stretched back to 1949. They have purchased regularly from Mantima since that time and have always conducted their account satisfactorily.

Dube, on the other hand, is a relatively new customer who only started buying in 1983. There is just one store which is situated in a shopping complex in Madadeni, a black town just outside Newcastle. Several of the shops in the complex, including this one, belong to the owner of the complex and others are let out to various businesses. Since he also owns a soft goods store, a supermarket and a hardware store in the complex, Mantima has classified him as a department store. There have been no problems with this account until recently.

The credit terms for both of the firms have always been 30 days net. The terms provide for interest at 3 % above prime bank overdraft to be charged on arrear amounts, but to date this has not been necessary. Credit limits have been set at R40 000 for Zebra and R60 000 for Dube.

Mantima sells and advertises countrywide but tries to concentrate its efforts on strategically located shops within defined geographic areas. The recession which began about 1981 led to such changes in the furniture trade that product quality and customer service lost their primacy in marketing. Extended credit and financing of suppliers soon became so important that Mantima found itself in the undesirable position of having to support some customers financially in order to keep their products in the stores. Drastic increases in interest rates made this more and more expensive for Mantima to continue doing. In 1983 and 1984 interest rates rose to unheard of levels, the maximum prime overdraft rate reaching no less than 25 % during this time. It did drop back again, but at the end of February 1987 it was still at 15 %.

This requirement for credit on greater scale than before caused Emerson to insist on regular financial reports from his customers as a prerequisite for continued extension of credit. Most of the customers simply presented their annual financial reports, but whenever Emerson had any doubts he insisted on more regular reports, even requiring monthly reports from a few customers whose accounts he wanted to monitor on a constant basis.

When Venter received the financial statements of Zebra and Dube for the year ended 28 February 1987 towards the end of that month, she took a good look at the debtors accounts and decided to refer the account to Emerson. She provided him with the information contained in Exhibits 1 to 5 below.

To get the matter into perspective it is necessary to look at the state of the furniture trade over the last few years. Economic conditions remained extremely weak during 1985/6 and in such times shops such as Dube, which concentrate largely on the lower end of the market, are the first to feel the pinch. Continued weak trading conditions also eventually affect shops dealing in better quality goods. This is exactly what happened. It led to a decline in volume which in turn brought about a round of price cutting. This affected the margins of many retailers to such an extent that their financial positions became precarious.

Signs of an economic upturn appeared late in 1986, but these were so weak that people had little confidence that they should prepare to meet their boom. At any rate, there was no upturn in the orders placed on the furniture factories. The general feeling seemed to be that the upturn would take some time to affect the expenditure patterns of the man in the street, who was still crippled by a high rate of inflation which inhibited him from committing future income to hire purchase payments. Factory sales remained weak and could virtually only be maintained by generous extension of credit.

This led credit managers into the stressful position of having to grant credit in order to keep sales managers happy while being fully aware of the potential problems which could be created by the extension of credit to customers who were already financially extended.

You are required

1. to find out what these two customers are up to;
2. to support your answer in (1) with appropriate financial ratios together with any other calculations and comments; and
3. to state how Mantima should treat each of the customers.

Exhibit 1

Mantima Debtors analysis at 30 April 1987

	Total	April	March	February	January	Older
Zebra	44 512	4 106	14 098	3 655	22 653	0
Dube	79 068	36 448	17 308	4 102	19 575	1 635

Exhibit 2

ZEBRA HOME FURNISHINGS (PROPRIETARY) LIMITED
Balance sheets at 28 February (R 000)

Capital employed

	1987	1986	1985
Share capital—Ordinary shares	320	240	240
Preference shares	125	125	125
Retained earnings	− 25	5	125
	420	370	490
Mortgage loan[1]	1 560	1 500	1 520
Long term bank loan[2]	575	575	360
	2 555	2 445	2 370

Employment of capital

	1987	1986	1985
Buildings, plant and equipment	1 050	910	860
Accumulated depreciation	270	190	150
	780	720	710
Land	230	230	230
Long term investments	45	45	45
Total fixed assets	1 055	995	985
Net current assets	1 500	1 450	1 385

Current assets			
Stock	1 210	1 200	1 210
Debtors	1 070	1 000	900
Cash	30	40	60
	2 310	2 240	2 170
Current liabilities			
Creditors	620	580	575
Provision for tax	0	0	40
Current portion of long term debt	145	140	105
Accrued expenses	45	70	65
	810	790	785
	2 555	2 445	2 370

1. Secured by a mortgage over land and buildings.
2. Secured by a cession of debtors.

Exhibit 3

ZEBRA HOME FURNISHINGS (PROPRIETARY) LIMITED
Income statements for years ended 28 February (R 000)

	1987	1986	1985
Net sales	5 620	5 655	7 110
Cost of sales	3 400	3 415	4 305
Gross profit	2 220	2 240	2 805
Operating expenses	2 030	2 060	2 390
Operating income	190	180	415
Other income	50	55	255
	240	235	670
Interest	270	200	190
Profit (Loss) before tax	(30)	35	480
Tax	0	15	230
Profit (Loss) after tax	(30)	20	250
Dividends paid	0	140	140
Transferred to reserves	(30)	(120)	110

N.B.: *Stock at 28 February 1984 was R1 190 000*

Exhibit 4

DUBE FURNISHERS CC
Balance sheet at 28 February (R 000)

Capital Employed			
Members contributions	2 280	2 280	2 280
Undrawn profits	3 660	3 655	3 465
Members interest	5 940	5 935	5 745
Long term loan[1]	2 850	3 540	3 585
	8 790	9 475	9 330
Employment of capital			
Leasehold improvements	2 310	2 425	2 320
Other fixed assets	910	990	915
	3 220	3 415	3 235
Investments	220	225	230
Loans to members	90	45	70
Net current assets	5 260	5 790	5 795

Current assets			
Stock	3 285	3 580	3 630
Debtors	3 635	3 640	3 535
Cash and bank balances	315	495	375
Prepayments	105	95	90
	7 340	7 810	7 630
Current liabilities			
Creditors	1 775	1 625	1 545
Accrued expenses	305	395	290
	2 080	2 020	1 835
	8 790	9 475	9 330

Exhibit 5

DUBE FURNISHERS CC
Income statement for years ended 28 February

	1987	*1986*	*1985*
Net sales	17 835	18 930	19 465
Cost of sales	12 270	11 900	12 260
Gross profit	5 565	7 030	7 205
Operating expenses	5 730	5 365	5 420
Operating profit (loss)	(165)	1 665	1 785
Interest	635	635	445
	(800)	1 030	1 340
Abnormal items			
Provisions written back			
—stock obsolescence	690	0	0
—bad debts	120	0	0
Profit after extraordinary items	10	1 030	1 340
Tax	0	440	620
Profit after tax	10	590	720
Dividends	5	400	480
Increase in undrawn profits	5	190	240

1. The long term loan is secured by a notarial bond over debtors.
2. Figures for 1985, prior to the conversion to a close corporation, have been
   adjusted to ensure comparability with those of the later years.

Part four

Financial management

The previous sections have dealt with accounting as a record of historical events. This record shows what has happened within an undertaking, and was shown to be a valuable tool for analysis of the undertaking. Some aspects of this analysis have been predictive by nature, but the emphasis has been on reviewing past performance. Financial management, by contrast, is more concerned with the present and the future than with the past. History is important in that it provides guidelines for the future, but this section deals with the important matters of applying those guidelines in the management process.

Chapter 17

Budgeting and short term financial planning and control

Planning and control are two of the generally recognised functions of management. This chapter takes a look at the contribution which the budgeting process can make to these tasks.

1. **Budgeting and the functions of management**

2. **Profit planning and control outlined**

3. **The mechanics of budgeting**

4. **Using budgets for control**

1. Budgeting and the functions of management

A budget is a financial forecast covering a financial period of, usually, not more than one year. In its final format it is a detailed forecast of an undertaking's income statement for the ensuing year and a forecast of the balance sheet at the end of that year. This budget is a tool used by management to assist in the performance of the management task. While there are many descriptions of this task, the best broad one is probably that management is getting things done through people. In order to accomplish this the manager has to decide what he wants done, how he wants it done, who must do it, how the requirements must be communicated to the person who has to do it, how to motivate that person to do it and how to control that it has been done. Budgeting is a process whereby the manager

1. can set out what he wants done and broadly how he wants it done;
2. can communicate his requirements to the people concerned; and
3. can control that things have been done properly.

Business is a value creating process. The task of management is to plan and control that process to ensure the addition of maximum value in terms of the undertaking's objectives. These may be financial, such as maximisation of returns to shareholders, but most undertakings are likely to have a mixture of financial and social objectives. In order to achieve the addition of maximum value the manager has to take into the account a number of variables, both controllable and non-controllable. This can be illustrated as follows:

Population growth	Economic growth	Industry growth
Competitor activities		Product prices
	Politically inspired regulatory practices	

Inputs		Outputs
People		Products
Materials	The value creating process	Services
Services		Social effects
Capital		
	CONTROLLABLE VARIABLES	

NON-CONTROLLABLE VARIABLES

Figure 17.1

The list of variables mentioned here is not exhaustive, and there may be a number of different ones depending on the nature of the undertaking being managed.

Budgeting was defined above as being essentially short term, but if one were to use military terminology, the budget can be regarded as the tactics by which the strategy, or long term objectives, of the undertaking are to be attained. Page 5 of the annual report of Anglo-Alpha sets out a company mission, which is far too vague to be of any use for planning purposes. It then sets out a variety of business and social objectives which would form the basis for its strategies. One of their objectives is to at least maintain the real value of shareholders' investment, and a strategy would have to be developed to attain this. It might include a strategy for diversification, for moves into the retail sector of the cement industry, improvements in productivity or increasing market share or none of these. Whatever the strategy, however, it is going to be a long term one, laying down what should be achieved over the next five years or more. With a financial objective like this one, the strategic plan will have to develop goals which will enable the company to achieve its strategic objectives. The budgets drawn up within this strategic planning period will have to be designed with the objective of achieving these goals.

2. Profit planning and control outlined

The part played by the budget is primarily in the fields of planning and control. Planning is widely recognised as the most difficult of all management tasks and must be done in a structured manner with the objective of providing the manager with a feedforward framework which will assist him in the day to day decisions by laying down parameters within which these decisions can be made and the foundation of a feedback framework which will assist him in the control function. The control function is exercised through comparison of actual performance with planned performance. The results of this comparison must be communicated to the appropriate lower level managers or workers. Budgeting is *not* a dictatorial plan whereby workers are placed in a position of having to perform or suffer punishment for failing to meet budget. It is a co-operative process whereby all the parties involved should be able to make their inputs into the final plan so as to ensure personal commitment, which is an essential part of motivating the various parties. Once this feedback is sent to these people they must assist in analysing the variances from plan in order to determine the underlying causes, and they must be involved in formulating appropriate courses of action in order to remedy any deficiencies in performance. Regardless of the courses of action formulated, the responsible people must be aware of variances from budget so that the knowledge of this variance and its causes can be incorporated into future budget planning sessions.

The fact that these people are involved in the budgeting process presupposes that they have an area of managerial or performance responsibility. No one can plan meaningfully unless he has some control over the variables for which he is being asked to plan. These responsibilities must be clearly delineated and the accounting system must be so designed as to provide meaningful information about each area of responsibility. An organisation structure which permits meaningful separation of responsibilities and an accounting system which can produce reports on the separate activities are essential prerequisites for a successful budgeting system.

Other matters which are fundamental to any budget are that it must be timely and must be fully communicated so that all concerned in the management of any undertaking know what is expected of them. It must be drawn up with the full participation and approval of top management as well as of the lower levels and, above all, it must be realistic.

3. The mechanics of budgeting

The starting point of any budgeting exercise is to estimate the income which the operations of the undertaking will produce. It is also the most difficult part. Any estimate of sales of an undertaking's goods and services is subject to a number of uncontrollable or only partly controllable variables including general economic conditions, conditions specific to the industry and competitor activity. It is, however, possible to develop highly accurate sales forecasts.

This prediction of gross income is an aspect that is critical to the realisation of the undertaking's strategic plans so that it can only be developed in conjunction with the long term sales plan. This long term sales plan will be developed on a basis which includes such factors as predictions of economic growth, population growth and movement and age make up, past trends extrapolated into the future, plans for the development of new products or markets and expected competitor activities. Within the framework of such a long range sales plan the tactical sales plan for the shorter term must be developed.

The first step in this development must be a sales forecast. This forecast is a purely technical exercise of the "this is what will happen if we go on as we have been doing" type. Such a forecast must be developed for each product line before the sales budget is developed.

This forecast will be compared to the requirements of the strategic marketing plan. Management will then have to decide on a marketing plan which will involve decisions about the level of support the sales team is going to receive in terms of resource commitments. This will determine the amounts to be spent on advertising, on training the existing sales team or recruiting and training new sales team members. Decisions must be made about the release of new products and about pricing policies for the budget period. The limits of the undertaking's resources which can be applied must also be brought to bear on the sales plan before it is finalised, and the financial manager's department will have to look at the financial feasibility of the plan.

Any amendments to the original forecasts in the light of management's decisions concerning these factors must be discussed with the sales and marketing teams in order to get their full agreement and commitment to the plan, for without this commitment the plan is unlikely to be met.

In practice the plan is usually developed in fine detail, but with all assumptions clearly noted. As the year progresses, actual figures are compared with these budgeted figures and the plan modified, if this is necessary, once any variances have been analysed.

The whole budgeting process can best be shown by way of an example. Engineering Firm's financial statements to 28 February 1985 are available and can be used as the basis for the budget for 1986. (In actual fact, the budget should have been prepared long before the end of the financial year and based on the data available at the time of preparation.)

The start of the process is the development of a sales plan. This is based on projections of past results tempered with management intervention in the light of knowledge of the environment and the industry. This forecast cannot be made purely on the basis of the income statement as it stands since the company has two distinct product lines which, as the background to the company makes clear, are behaving differently and are expected to behave more differently in the future. The trend statement shows that the overall growth rate in sales has slowed dramatically lately, with the 24 % growth from 1983 to 1984 down to a mere 2 % in 1984/1985, but sales of the new products have been rising. Within the firm, for management purposes only, more detailed information for the past year is available:

ENGINEERING FIRM (PROPRIETARY) LIMITED
Budget working paper for 1986

	1985	Old—72 %	New—28 %
Sales	4 650 000	3 348 000	1 302 000
Direct cost of sales	3 310 000	2 252 700	1 057 300
Opening stock/work in process	185 000	124 200	60 800
Design fees	55 000	42 000	13 000
Direct wages	1 475 000	958 750	516 250
Power and water	50 000	35 000	15 000
Purchases	1 490 000	983 400	506 600
Subcontracted work	250 000	240 000	10 000
	3 505 000	2 383 350	1 121 650
Deduct: Closing stock/work in process	195 000	130 650	64 350
Direct contribution	1 340 000	1 095 300	244 700
Percentage contribution	28,82	32,72	18,79
Percentage of total contribution	100	82	18

Figure 17.2

This statement confirms that the new products now constitute 28 % of the sales, but also gives a very good idea of how low the margins on these products actually are. What it does not show is that the growth rate in sales for these products has been very good, however, with sales for 1985 being up 20 % on those of 1984. The difference in the direct contribution which each product makes to overall profits is very clear from this statement. The direct contribution only takes into account the sales price and the variable costs directly traceable to a product line. If there were to be no changes in the costs of inputs or selling prices, then this percentage could be applied directly to the predicted sales for the ensuing year in order to obtain the contribution of each product.

However, there are bound to be changes. The expectations of the directors are that volume sales growth will continue at a rate of 20 % for the new products, while sales for the old ones will be down by about 5 % for 1986. Colin Dover is also confident that prices for the new products will increase by 20 % during the year as the products have become more established in the market, while prices for the old products will rise by about 10 %, which is the expected rate of inflation for the next year.

On this basis, total sales for the 1986 financial year will be:

ENGINEERING FIRM
Sales forecasts for 1986

	Old products % change		New products % change	
Sales for 1985		3 348 000		1 302 000
Volume change	− 5 %	3 180 600	+ 20 %	1 562 400
Price change	+ 10	3 498 660	+ 20 %	1 874 880

Figure 17.2

The managers must now decide whether there are any factors which would lead to their not being able to meet these targets. If not, these are used as the basis for the whole sales plan and resources will have to be committed to the marketing section. Since in this case marketing is virtually all by direct contact this will mean having to accept an increase in the amount spent on travelling to customers and on entertainment.

Once the sales plan has been finalised the rest of the budget begins to fall into place. The production plan is next in line and is totally dependent on the sales plan. Once one knows how much of each product one believes one is going to sell then one can plan the production of those items, with the addition of ensuring that there is enough produced to meet stock requirements. These last are also derived from the sales plan, since there must be enough stock on hand at the end of the period to meet expected demand in the next period. The budget will have to be broken down into great detail, looking at staffing requirements which will have to be based on the hours of labour required for meeting production requirements, expected changes in the prices of the various inputs and changes in the relative growth of the various product lines.

The production budget for Engineering Firm will be based on producing what the sales budget says will be sold, since there is no real need to increase stocks at the year end. The forecast can first be prepared mechanistically, but it must be modified in the light of management knowledge of possible changes. Say that, since the plant is not yet working at its full productive capacity, no increase in the work force is expected but that a ten per cent increase in wages has been agreed. Input prices of raw materials and electricity are expected to increase by 10 %, while the ratio of design fees and subcontracted work to sales is expected to remain constant. The direct variable costs can then be easily calculated and this figure can be used for determining a new direct contribution and a contribution margin for each of the product lines. In addition, certain fixed costs can be directly allocated to the different lines such as depreciation or lease charges on machines bought specifically for one of the lines and the salary of the workshop supervisor for each of the lines:

ENGINEERING FIRM (PROPRIETARY) LIMITED
Budget working paper for 1986

	Total	*Old*	*New*
Sales	5 373 540	3 498 660	1 874 880
Direct cost of sales	3 800 478	2 504 633	1 295 845
Opening stock/work in process	195 000	130 650	64 350
Design fees	62 615	43 894	18 721
Direct wages	1 622 500	1 054 625	567 875
Power and water	64 529	38 393	26 136
Purchases	1 785 608	1 116 896	668 712
Subcontracted work	265 225	250 824	14 401
	3 995 478	2 635 283	1 360 195
Deduct: Closing stock/work in process	195 000	130 650	64 350
Direct contribution	1 573 062	994 027	579 035
Percentage direct contribution	*29,27*	*28,41*	*30,88*
Indirect factory expenses	505 000	235 000	270 000
Depreciation	95 000	35 000	60 000
Lease charges on plant	230 000	105 000	125 000
Salaries—factory	180 000	95 000	85 000
Product contribution	1 068 062	759 027	309 035
Percentage contribution	*19,88*	*21,69*	*16,48*

Figure 17.4

As could be expected, the new products show a significant improvement in direct margin as a result of price increase in excess of the cost increases, but the old products show a decline in margin due to the fact that prices can only be increased with circumspection due to the declining market. After the direct fixed costs have been brought into account the new products actually show a better margin than the old ones. This statement will form the master production budget in monetary terms, but will still have to be translated into physical terms by the people concerned. This will then result in a statement of labour inputs expressed in hours, material inputs in kilograms and any other items expressed in terms of whatever units may be most appropriate.

There is a factor of variability in the sales plan because it is virtually impossible that actual sales will exactly match budgeted sales. Since production will vary according to sales volumes, there must be a similar factor in the production plan, This is taken into account by preparing a flexible production budget. A flexible budget is based on the different cost behaviour patterns of the various factors involved in the production process.

1. Some of the cost factors are (directly) variable, which means that they increase proportionately to production volume. A typical example would be raw material, since a fixed quantity of raw material would be used for each unit of production.
2. Some of the factors are fixed, at least in the short term. A typical example would be the rent of the factory building, which will remain constant regardless of how much is produced—or whether anything is produced at all.
3. Some factors have what is known as a step pattern. They are fixed over certain ranges of production, but then increase sharply before reaching a new level at which they remain fixed for another range of production levels. Examples would be those costs which are incurred per shift like a shift foreman's salary. As long as only one shift is operated there will only be one salary to pay, but as soon as production requires two shifts the salary doubles as another foreman is required.
4. Many factors have some sort of semi-variable pattern. Wages will increase as production increases, but not in direct proportion. A certain level will be paid even at low levels, but as production increases more workers will be taken on or overtime wages will increase.
5. Other factors have a mixed pattern. Telephone costs, as a simple example, have a fixed base element in the rental of the telephone plus a variable element in the charges for calls which will almost certainly not vary in direct proportion to production

The determination of the behaviour pattern for each cost over various ranges of production involves a detailed study of the cost records. It is normally found that the total costs per unit increase in a straight line fashion over limited ranges of production, and this fact is used in preparing production budgets to determine the expected costs over various ranges of production. A flexible budget is necessary for control purposes since the actual volume of production will almost certainly vary from that planned. When this does happen it does not make sense to measure performance in respect of costs or efficiency against the volumes in the master budget. After all, one should not be rewarded for using less material than planned if this is due to the fact that less was produced, nor should one be punished for using more if this was due to higher production.

The flexible budget is not intended to give a most pessimistic forecast and most optimistic forecast type of analysis, but it is an attempt to show the range of volumes which can be realistically expected and to make allowances for fluctuations from the master budget over that range. For Engineering Firm the directors believe that the actual sales will be within +10% and −10% of the master budget figure.

ENGINEERING FIRM (PROPRIETARY) LIMITED
Flexible budget for 1986

	Projected	+ 5 %	+ 10 %	− 5 %	− 10 %
Sales old products	3 498 660	3 673 593	3 848 526	3 323 727	3 148 794
Direct contribution	994 027	1 043 705	1 093 405	944 304	894 604
(28,41 %)					
Indirect factory expenses	235 000	235 000	235 000	235 000	235 000
Product contribution	759 027	808 705	858 405	709 304	659 604
Sales new products	1 874 880	1 968 624	2 062 368	1 781 136	1 687 392
Direct contribution	579 035	607 970	636 921	550 068	521 117
(30,88 %)					
Indirect factory expenses	270 000	270 000	270 000	270 000	270 000
Product contribution	309 035	337 970	366 921	280 068	251 117

Figure 17.5

This flexible budget should serve to show the difference between the direct contribution margin and the product contribution margin. Once the direct contribution margin has been determined it should be applicable to any volume of sales within a demarcated range, in this case up to 10 % greater or less than forecast. This range is known as the *relevant range* for these costs. At some stage, of course, the direct contribution margins will change as for instance when volume increases to such an extent that it becomes necessary to pay labour at a higher rate for overtime work than the rate normally charged.

The direct product contribution, on the other hand, is a combination of the direct contribution margin based on costs that vary with production and certain fixed costs which remain unaltered in total over the relevant range, but which are directly related to a particular product or product line. They will also vary at some stage as for instance when an increase in production requires the leasing of an extra machine.

There are a great many costs which cannot be associated directly with either of the products, such as rent. The general test for deciding on whether a cost can be attributed directly to a product is simply to ask whether that cost would cease to be incurred if production of that product were to cease.

These other costs must now be brought into account in the pro forma income statement which is part of the master budget for the undertaking. Each individual expense item must be scrutinised to decide on what is likely to be spent on that head in the ensuing year. Some of these are easy to determine. Rent, for instance, will be in accordance with the escalation clause in the lease contract; lease charge commitments will be known, salaries can be estimated by taking into account expected increases and so forth. Others will be very much an estimate, such as the amount to be spent on cleaning material and the audit fee, but even these estimates can be very realistic.

ENGINEERING FIRM (PROPRIETARY) LIMITED
Master budget for 1986—Income statement

	1986	*1985*
Sales	5 373 540	4 650 000
Direct cost of sales	3 800 477	3 320 000
Opening stock/work in process	195 000	195 000
Design fees	62 615	55 000
Direct wages	1 622 500	1 475 000
Power and water	64 529	50 000
Purchases	1 785 608	1 490 000
Subcontracted work	265 225	250 000
	3 995 477	3 515 000
Deduct: Closing stock/work in process	195 000	195 000
Direct contribution	1 573 063	1 330 000
Indirect factory expenses	635 000	610 000
Depreciation	95 000	100 000
Lease charges on plant	230 000	235 000
Maintenance and repairs	40 000	30 000
Rent	90 000	80 000
Salaries—factory	180 000	165 000
Factory contribution	938 063	720 000
Administrative expenses	636 500	628 000
Audit fees	15 000	14 000
Bank charges	10 000	10 000
Cleaning and refreshments	8 000	6 000
Depreciation	3 000	3 000
Directors' salaries	180 000	180 000
Entertainment	18 000	13 000
Insurance	45 000	40 000
Lease charges on motor vehicles	70 000	80 000
Lease charges on office equipment	10 000	10 000
Legal expenses	500	4 000
Motor expenses	100 000	100 000
Railage and airfreight	5 000	5 000
Salaries	99 000	90 000
Stationery and printing	12 000	13 000
Subscriptions	4 000	4 000
Sundry expenses	20 000	21 000
Telephone and telex	12 000	10 000
Travelling expenses	25 000	25 000
Operating income for the year	301 563	92 000

Figure 17.6

The picture looks almost too wonderful, but at least the company has tried to develop a reasonable budget for the next year and can now seriously start looking at the possibilities of improving performance even further by either increasing income or reducing expenses. The best bet would of course be to go for higher sales, since the flexible budget shows to what extent the overall performance would be improved by an increase in the direct contribution.

The final part of the budgeting process would now seem to be the production of a forecast balance sheet, but this cannot be prepared directly from the income statement. There are at least three other budgets which have to be prepared before reaching the stage of the budgeted balance sheet. These are the cash flow budget, the investment budget and the finance budget.

The investment budget would deal with company plans for the purchase of new fixed assets, with full details of the costs and the timing of the purchase of these. The finance budget would deal with any new finance to be obtained during the year and the repayment of any currently outstanding debt. This could be in the form of money paid in by the shareholders (share capital or loans), borrowings from the financial institutions to cover the cost of new assets purchased, repayment of such debt or money to be raised by the sale of fixed assets. In the case of Engineering Firm there were no such plans for raising money or repaying the only long term debt, that of the directors' loans.

There are two forms of the cash flow budget. The one is simply a forecast of the cash flow statement for the following year, while the other one is a detailed one presented on a monthly or even weekly basis and giving precise estimates of when cash will actually be received or disbursed. This latter one is the one which is necessary for the preparation of the budgeted balance sheet. It is also essential for the control of the cash flow of the company. Since cash is so volatile one cannot wait until the end of the year for control purposes, but must have a budget so that the cash flow can be controlled on a regular basis throughout the year.

Engineering Firm's detailed cash flow budget can be drawn up on the basis of the following assumptions, which are developed from past history and the directors' knowledge of market conditions:
1. All sales will be on credit. 60% of these will be settled in the second month following invoicing and 40% in the following month.
2. All purchase of materials are on credit and will be settled at the end of the second month after date of statement.
3. 90% of all other expenses will be paid for on a cash basis, with the other 10% being paid in the month following statement.
4. Interest will be paid on overdraft at the rate of 21% per annum, while interest will be received on credit balance on the current account at a rate of 6% per annum.
5. Funds surplus to requirements at any time will be placed on 32 call at 15% per annum.
6. Sales will take place evenly throughout the year, but sales for December will only be 40% of the average monthly sales and sales for January will be 60% of the average.

The cash budget shows that the company is going to experience severe liquidity problems during the first part of the year, with interest payments over this period consuming a large part of the operating profit. This interest has been built into the monthly operating budget, which has to be prepared together with the cash budget, for the monthly cash flows cannot be determined until the monthly operating budget has been prepared, but the interest flows can only be determined from the cash budget. (See Figures 17.7 and 17.8 on pages 357 and 358 respectively.)

The opening balance is the net of the closing balance of the bank overdraft of R635 000 and the cash on hand of R14 000. It does not matter very much for budgeting purpose where the money is lying, as long as it is brought into account. It must make a small difference to the interest paid, but when on overdraft most people would try to keep as little cash on hand and as much in the bank as possible.

This cash flow budget illustrates the problems of expansion. As the company is called upon to finance ever more production, the cash resources become very stretched and it is only towards the end of the year that cash levels come back towards the balance at the beginning of the year. If production does not expand further during the next year, the bank overdraft should gradually become smaller.

This statement provides the necessary information for the preparation of the budgeted balance sheet. It gives the closing bank balance and also allows, conjunction with the income statement, a determination of the closing debtors and creditors balances. Debtors are calculated by taking the opening balance, adding sales for the year and deducting the amounts received from debtors, and creditors by taking the opening balance, adding purchases of goods and services and deducting the amounts paid to creditors. With these calculations done the only remaining matter is to look at the tax position. The 1985 balance sheet shows an amount of R10 000 paid to the tax authorities in excess of the tax liability. Tax at a rate of 50 % on the profit for the year would amount to R41 960. No particulars are given of the company's tax calculations, but with a nil tax payment the peculiarities of the provisional tax system would allow the company to make no provisional payments during the year to end February and only to pay the necessary tax amount six months after the end of the tax year. There would therefore be no tax flow implications, but the amount must be provided for in the balance sheet.

ENGINEERING FIRM (PROPRIETARY) LIMITED

Monthly operating budget for 1986

	March	April	May	June	July	August	September	October	November	December	January	February	Total
Sales	488 504	488 504	488 504	488 504	488 504	488 504	488 504	488 504	488 504	195 401	293 102	488 504	5 373 540
Direct cost of sales	330 234	330 234	330 234	330 234	330 234	330 234	330 234	330 234	281 535	267 975	278 863	330 234	3 800 477
Purchases	162 328	162 328	162 328	162 328	162 328	162 328	162 328	162 328	113 630	324 66	178 561	162 328	1 785 608
Other	167 906	167 906	167 906	167 906	167 906	167 906	167 906	167 906	167 906	235 510	100 302	167 906	2 014 869
Direct contribution	158 270	158 270	158 270	158 270	158 270	158 270	158 270	158 270	206 968	− 72 574	14 240	158 270	1 573 063
Indirect factory expenses	52 917	52 917	52917	52 917	52 917	52 917	52 917	52 917	52 917	60 417	45 417	52 917	635 000
Depreciation	7 917	7 917	7 917	7 917	7 917	7 917	7 917	7 917	7 917	7 917	7 917	7 917	95 000
Other	45 000	45 000	45 000	45 000	45 000	45 000	45 000	45 000	45 000	52 500	37 500	45 000	540 000
Factory contribution	105 353	105 353	105 353	105 353	105 353	105 353	105 353	105 353	154 052	− 132 991	− 31 177	105 353	938 063
Administration expenses	53 042	53 042	53 042	53 042	53 042	53 042	53 042	53 042	53 042	53 042	53 042	53 042	636 500
Depreciation	250	250	250	250	250	250	250	250	250	250	250	250	3000
Other	52 792	52 792	52 792	52 792	52 792	52 792	52 792	52 792	52 792	52 792	52 792	52 792	633 500
Operating income	52 312	52 312	52 312	52 312	52 312	52 312	52 312	52 312	101 010	− 186 032	− 84 219	52 312	301 563
Net interest	− 15 570	− 23 395	− 21 624	− 20 847	− 20 054	− 19 246	− 18 421	− 17 580	− 16 722	− 17 199	− 14 157	− 12 828	− 217 643
Net income	36 741	28 916	30 688	31 465	32 257	33 066	33 891	34 732	84 288	− 203 231	− 98 376	39 483	83 920
Cumulative net income	36 741	65 658	96 345	127 810	160 067	193 133	227 024	261 755	346 044	142 813	44 436	83 920	

Figure 17.7

ENGINEERING FIRM (PROPRIETARY) LIMITED

Cash budget for 1986

	March	April	May	June	July	August	September	October	November	December	January	February	Total
Opening balance	−621 000	−794 075	−1 193 168	−1 102 817	−1 063 186	−1 022 762	−981 529	−939 472	−896 574	−852 818	−877 132	−722 029	−621 000
Receipts from debtors	320 000	350 000	540 000	488 504	488 504	488 504	488 504	488 504	488 504	488 504	488 504	371 263	5 489 292
Cash available	−301 000	−444 075	−653 168	−614 314	−574 682	−534 258	−493 026	−450 969	−408 070	−364 314	−388 628	−350 766	4 868 292
Cash payments	477 505	725 697	428 025	428 025	428 025	428 025	428 025	428 025	428 025	495 619	319 244	290 653	5 304 896
Payments for materials	260 000	460 000	162 328	162 328	162 328	162 328	162 328	162 328	162 328	162 328	113 630	32 466	2 164 719
Other payments	169 505	212 906	212 906	212 906	212 906	212 906	212 906	212 906	212 906	280 499	152 823	205 395	2 511 468
Administration	48 000	52 792	52 792	52 792	52 792	52 792	52 792	52 792	52 792	52 792	52 792	52 792	628 708
Bank balance	−778 505	−1 169 773	−1 081 194	−1 042 339	−1 002 708	−962 284	−921 051	−878 994	−836 096	−859 933	−707 872	−641 419	−436 604
Interest paid	−15 570	−23 395	−21 624	−20 847	−20 054	−19 246	−18 421	−17 580	−16 722	−17 199	−14 157	−12 828	−217 643
Closing balance	−794 075	−1 193 168	−1 102 817	−1 063 186	−1 022 762	−981 529	−939 472	−896 574	−852 818	−877 132	−722 029	−654 247	−654 247

Figure 17.8

With these items taken into account the budgeted balance sheet can be drawn up:

ENGINEERING FIRM (PROPRIETARY) LIMITED
Budgeted balance sheet at February 1986

	1986	1985
Capital employed		
Share capital	2 000	2 000
Retained earnings	581 960	540 000
	583 960	542 000
Loans	154 000	154 000
	737 960	696 000
Represented by		
Fixed assets	474 000	572 000
Net current assets	263 960	124 000
Current assets		
Stock and work in progress	195 000	195 000
Debtors and deposits	1 184 248	1 300 000
Cash and bank balances	0	14 000
	1 379 248	1 509 000
Current liabilities		
Creditors and accruals	429 081	760 000
Bank overdraft	654 247	635 000
Provision for tax	31 960	− 10 000
	1 115 288	1 385 000
	737 960	696 000

Figure 17.9

Finally, one can prepare a budgeted cash flow statement to give the overall picture of what will happen to the undertaking's cash flows during the year that lies ahead. This statement emphasises the fact that as large part of the cash flow problem experienced by the company is the sharp reduction in the amounts owing to creditors, but that this is partly offset by a reduction in debtors.

ENGINEERING FIRM (PROPRIETARY) LIMITED
Budgeted cash flow statement for 1986

	Note	1986	1985
Cash retained from operating activities			
Cash generated by operations	1	399 563	205 000
Investment income		0	24 500
Cash used to increase working capital	2	215 167	− 60 000
Cash generated by operating activities		184 396	289 500
Finance costs		217 643	4 500
Taxation paid		0	40 000
Cash available from operating activities		− 33 247	245 000
Cash used in investment activities			
Investment to maintain operations			
Replacement of fixed assets		0	65 000
Investment to expend operations			
Additions to fixed assets		0	250 000
Cash generated		− 33 247	− 70 000
Cash effects of financing activities			
Increase in long term borrowings		0	− 42 000
Change in short term borrowings		33 247	112 000
Cash utilised		33 247	70 000
Notes:			
Cash generated by operations			
Operating income before tax		301 563	102 000
Adjustment for non-cash expenses			
Depreciation		98 000	103 000
		399 563	205 000
Cash used to increase working capital			
Change in stock/W I P		0	10 000
Change in debtors		115 752	90 000
Change in creditors		330 919	− 160 000
		215 167	− 60 000

Figure 17.10

This completes the process of preparing the budget, but that is only the planning part of the process. The second part, that of using the budget for control, still needs to be taken into account.

4. Using budgets for control

As stated at the beginning, two of the processes of management are planning and control. The part which budgeting plays in planning has been briefly sketched above, but a plan is meaningless unless it is put into action and this progress is monitored. The budget provides a mechanism for the process of monitoring since the actual results can be constantly compared with budget expectations as the year progresses. Deviations from budget should be quickly noticed and analysed and appropriate action taken. This action will depend entirely on the reasons for the variance which must be identified by analysis.

If the analysis shows that the variance has resulted from an uncontrollable external factor the next step would be to decide whether this factor is of such a nature as to make the assumptions on which the budget is based untenable. if so, the budget must be redrawn in the light of the new knowledge of the environment. If not, action plans must be formulated to modify the way in which the plan is being carried out so as to nullify the effect of this factor.

If the analysis shows that the variance has resulted from deviations in the execution of controllable variables, then the reasons for this deviation must be determined. Sloppy execution must be tightened up, but failure to execute because of unreasonably high budgetary expectations must lead to a revision of the budget.

In order to be able to use the budget for control purposes it is essential that the budget be prepared as meaningfully as possible. Any poor budget planning must mean that the budget is not only a poor plan but also a poor control mechanism.

5. The behavioural effects of budgets

The function of managers is to be able to work through people to accomplish tasks. All communication between managers and those under their command must play a role in the performance of this function, and budgets are an important of the process of communication both downwards from management and upwards from those under them. If this process is not handled intelligently the effect of the budgeting process on the whole operation can be negative in the extreme.

It is firstly of the utmost importance that the objectives of budget setting be clear not only in the minds of the managers but also of all those involved. If people feel that the budget will be used as a big stick to punish them when they under perform they will try to set their budget targets as low as possible to make sure that they can be achieved. They will also attempt to work to these unrealistically low budgets since if they perform too well in relation to budget their next budgets may not be accepted as realistic. The budget can thus lead to a lowering of productivity in all respects except that of producing reasons for the low levels of activity budgeted.

Another example of a negative effect can occur when people believe that their expense budgets will be cut next time round if they do not spend all the money available to them this time. No money saving practices are therefore sought and, if there should be budgeted money left unspent at the end of the budget period there is a desperate last minute to waste this money on something just to ensure that the budget is not cut.

On the other hand, if the objectives are clearly set out so that everyone knows that the budget is primarily a planning tool; that the control function will be carried out by analysing variances from budget in order to improve planning and not for the purposes of apportioning blame; if all concerned are drawn in to the process in such a way that their commitment to the budget is obtained; and if the reward system is tied to factors other than meeting of budget targets, then budgets can be one of the greatest motivational tools which management has at its disposal.

Key words

Sales forecast	Sales budget
Production budget	Flexible budget
Direct costs	Direct product costs

Chapter 18

Working capital management

One of the prime uses of financial analysis for middle order managers is in the area of working capital management, which is also known as cash flow management. This last name is actually misleading since, while the result of effective working capital management is improved cash flow, much more is involved than the simple management of cash.

1. Introduction

2. The operating cycle and the cash cycle

3. Fluctuations in working capital requirements

4. Managing the elements of working capital

1. Introduction

A business survives by having cash to meet its obligations. Overall, this cash can be provided by a variety of sources: shareholders or owners, creditor and lenders of various kinds, the operations of the undertaking and the conversion of other assets into cash as set out in figure 16.2 during the discussion of funds flows

No business can survive simply by turning its fixed assets into cash. Fixed assets are necessary to the survival of the undertaking and can only be converted into cash once. Current assets, however, are turned into cash in the normal course of business operations. Figure 16.3 shows the total flows of cash, including the flows occasioned by increases or decreases in working capital. It stands to reason the more quickly and more efficiently these assets are converted into cash, the more cash they provide for business operations. This can probably be best illustrated by a discussion of the operating cycle and the cash cycle of the undertaking.

2. The operating cycle and the cash cycle

The *operating cycle* of a trading or manufacturing undertaking is the length of time it takes to turn its stock into cash. It can be illustrated graphically for a manufacturing concern as follows:

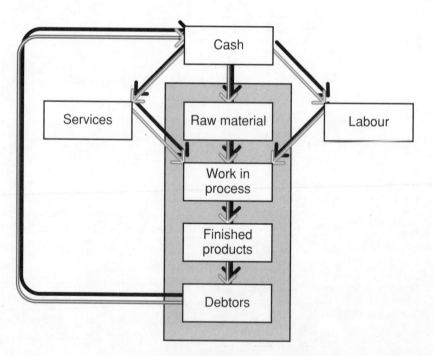

Figure 18.1

The operating cycle of the undertaking

Cash is used to purchase raw materials and services and to pay for labour. The combination of these inputs leads to work in process and ultimately to finished products. The sale of finished products means that these inputs are now contained in the amounts owed by debtors, who at some stage pay for the goods and so complete the cycle by putting cash back into the business.

The length of this cycle is calculated by the combination of two financial ratios, the stockholding period and the cash collection period, which is a variation of the debtors collection period.

As a matter of fact, if all sales are on credit it is identical to the debtors collection period which was discussed in chapter thirteen. The debtors collection period was defined as the outstanding debtors at the end of the year divided by the credit sales for the year multiplied by the days (or weeks or months) in the year, and was intended to give an idea of how efficiently the collection of cash from credit sales was being done.

The *cash collection period* has a different objective. It determines how long, on average, it takes to collect cash in respect of *all* sales, whether cash or credit. It is calculated by dividing debtors by total sales for the year and multiplying by the number of days in the year. A simple example should be enough to show the difference between the two. Say that a firm had credit sales of R1 200 000 and cash sales of R800 000 in a particular financial year and that its outstanding debtors at the end of that year totalled R200 000. The debtors collection period would be 200 000/ 1 200 000 × 365 = 61 days. This could then be compared to the laid down credit policy of the firm to decide on the efficiency of the debt collection function. If the policy was one of settlement within sixty days, for instance, the performance of the debt collection department would not be particularly satisfactory.

The cash collection period would be 200 000/2 000 000 × 365 = 37 days. This means that the undertaking was financing all sales for an average of 37 days. This figure could be improved in one of two ways, either:
1. by improving the debtors collection period; or
2. by increasing the ratio of cash sales to credit sales.

The stockholding period was discussed in chapter thirteen. It is determined by dividing total stock on hand by cost of sales and multiplying by 365 in order to determine how long it takes, on average, to sell stock.

These two ratios, both of which are expressed in days, together provide the length of the operating cycle of the undertaking in days. For Engineering Firm (Pty) Ltd, which was used as the example in that chapter, the debtors collection period was seen to be equal to the cash collection period at 106 days in 1983. The stockholding period was determined at 30 days in that same year. The operating cycle for each of the three years was as follows:

All numbers represent days	1985	1984	1983
Cash collection period	102	97	106
Stockholding period	22	21	30
Operating cycle	124	118	136

Figure 18.2

The importance of the period of this cycle is that is shows how much finance the undertaking needs in order to maintain its *operations* as distinct from finance needed for its capital expenditure. In 1983 EF needed enough finance to maintain its operations for no less than 136 days. To determine how much this actually is in terms of cash one simply needs to determine average daily expenses and multiply by the number of days. The simplest way to determine this is by taking sales, deducting the net income before tax, adding back non cash expenses and dividing by 365:

Average daily expenses	1985	1984	1983
Sales	4 650 000	4 550 000	3 665 000
Profit before tax	122 000	156 000	170 000
Total expenses	4 528 000	4 394 000	3 495 000
Deduct depreciation (non cash)	103 000	105 500	125 500
Total cash expenses	4 425 000	4 288 500	3 369 500
Daily expenses	12 123	11 749	9 232
Operating cycle	124	118	136
Finance required	1 503 252	1 386 382	1 255 552

Figure 18.3

The table shows clearly that, while the period requiring finance has fluctuated, the amount of finance required to maintain operations has been rising steadily.

The question now arises of how to finance the operating cycle. Part of it will be financed by the use of long term funds, but a significant part of the operating cycle is normally financed by trade credit as shown in figure 18.4

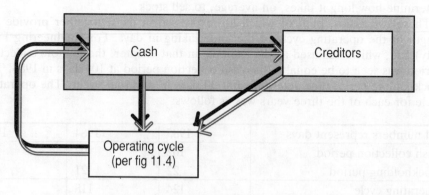

Figure 18.4
The cash cycle of the undertaking

Again a variation of an earlier ratio is used to determine just how much of this cycle is financed by the creditors. The creditors payment period discussed earlier was used to determine how long creditors waited before being paid. The *creditors finance period* shows how much of the operating cycle is financed by trade credit, and takes into account total expenses less depreciation, which does not involve the outlay of cash. The difference between the operating cycle and this creditors finance period is the *cash cycle* of the undertaking. This is the period that has to be financed out of longer term investments, either shareholders' funds or long term borrowings. The longer this cycle, the more long term money has to be pumped into the company.

For Engineering Firm the total cash expenses have already been calculated above. These must now be related to the creditors of the company:

	1985	1984	1983
Operating cycle in days	124	118	136
Total cash expenses	4 425 000	4 288 500	3 369 500
Creditors outstanding	760 000	600 000	555 000
Creditors finance period	63	51	60
Cash cycle of EF in days	61	67	76

Figure 18.5

This is interesting. It shows that the creditors finance period fell as the operating cycle fell. Money was flowing in (136 − 118) 18 days earlier, so creditors were paid quicker, but not to the same extent as the inflows and the cash cycle fell by 9 days. In 1985 the operating cycle rose by 6 days, but creditors payments were slowed down by 12 days, reducing the cash cycle by a further 6 days. As shown above, by 1985 the daily expenses averaged out at R12 123, which means that this drop of altogether fifteen days in the cash cycle meant that the company was saving itself an investment in operations of (15 × 12 123) R181 845.

This is what working capital management is all about. It shows why this aspect of management is also referred to as *cash management*, though this term is misleading in that working capital management is both wider than short term cash management and narrower than long term cash management.

3. Fluctuations in working capital requirements

3.1 Seasonal fluctuations

The above discussion of the operating and cash cycles centred around the figures which appeared on the balance sheets at the end of the financial year. There are very few businesses which have no seasonal changes in their working capital requirements, which means that the working capital needed at some times of the year is greater than at others. There are also cyclical fluctuations which move in accordance with economic cycles and which have the same effect but over longer periods of time.

A business which has extreme seasonal fluctuations is the toy business. Most of the sales, roughly 60 %, take place in the period September to November, with sales for each other three month period being about 15 % of the total.

It would not make sense from a production point of view to match production to sales. This would require a very large production facility which would be idle for about nine months of the year, with a labour force which would have to be increased just before the start of the peak season, trained to manage the machinery and then made redundant just before Christmas. This would be a terribly inefficient way of manufacturing, and no manufacturer tries it. Instead, they budget their production carefully and produce at an even rate throughout the year. This allows them to work with a smaller production facility and to maintain a constant labour force, but it has serious implications for working capital requirements.

For the sake of simplicity, take the case of a toy manufacturer who produces R12 million of toys each year at a constant rate of R1 million per month. He sells goods to a cost of R600 000 per month except for the months September to November, when his sales per month soar to the level of goods costing R2 400 000. He sells goods at a gross markup of 25 %, and at the end of February he has stock on hand of R180 000 and debtors of R1,5 million. Debtors settle at sixty days after date of invoice. His pattern of finance required for working capital would be as follows:

Month	Production	Deliveries	Stock	Sales	Debtors	Working capital
			All figures in R000 000			
March	1	0,6	2,4	0,75	1,5	3,9
April	1	0,6	2,8	0,75	1,5	4,3
May	1	0,6	3,2	0,75	1,5	4,7
June	1	0,6	3,6	0,75	1,5	5,1
July	1	0,6	4,0	0,75	1,5	5,5
August	1	0,6	4,4	0,75	1,5	5,9
September	1	2,4	3,0	3,6	4,35	7,35
October	1	2,4	1,6	3,6	7,2	8,8
November	1	2,4	0,2	3,6	7,2	7,4
December	1	0,0	1,2	0,75	4,35	5,55
January	1	0,6	1,6	0,75	1,5	3,1
February	1	0,6	20	7,5	1,5	3,5

Figure 18.6

His stock will increase steadily by R400 000 per month, rising to R4,4 million by the end of August. As the selling season starts, stock holdings will fall until he is virtually out of stock by the end of November, which ends the selling season. The level of finance required for stock steadily rises until the selling season starts, and then falls right down. But this is only part of the finance needed, and the finance pattern for debtors differs from that of stock. With two months sales unpaid at any one time, his debtors will remain constant at R1,5 million until September, when they will climb to R4,35 million and then rise to R7,2 million for the next two months before sinking back to previous levels. The final column shows the combined finance requirement, which rises from R3,9 million at March to R8,8 million at the end of October, before falling and hitting its low point at January of R3,1 million.

3.2 The effects of growth in sales

Growth in sales can cause working capital problems out of proportion to the growth experienced. To illustrate, say a company produces desks at a cost of R300 per unit and sells them at R400 per unit. All sales are on credit, with terms of thirty days net. In the first month they produce and sell 300 units at a cost of R90 000. In the second month demand soars and they produce and sell 500 units. At a cost of R300 per unit, this comes to R150 000. Collections from sales in the first month, however, only provide R120 000 so that the company is immediately strapped for cash. The problem is not that they are pricing badly and that their cash is drying up because profits are too low, it is simply that the growth in sales demands extra cash because of the timing differences between incurring the costs of production and the receipt of cash thirty days later. This is the greatest single problem facing the growing company. It is often forced to curtail growth to match the funding available, and this curtailment can mean the loss of customers which leads to a permanent stunting of the company. This can be tied back to the sustainable growth rate discussed in chapter 15. The rate at which a company can grow is determined by its profitability and the financial resources which are needed to support its growth. In general, the higher the rate of growth, the greater the need for funding to support it.

3.3 The effects of inflation

The effects of inflation on working capital requirements for a business like that mentioned above would be very similar to the effects of a growth in sales, but not quite as healthy. The monetary values would increase rather than the real values, and the greater the timing differences between incurring the costs and receiving payment in depreciating currency, the greater the funding requirements will be. This leads to an interesting point: what if the timing differences are positive? Say that you are running a supermarket and selling only for cash, but that you buy your goods on credit and have thirty days from date of statement to pay for the goods. It obviously is to your benefit to buy immediately after the statement date each month, since this gives nearly two months credit instead of the nominal thirty days, but what of the further effects? Say that you have an average of forty five days from date of purchase until date of payment for the goods, but that you have a very good system of stock control and sell your goods, on average, in fifteen days. This means that you receive money from your customers thirty days before you have to pay the suppliers in respect of the goods. If inflation is running at 120 % per annum, the following table shows the position that would apply. The supermarket would get the benefit of inflation from his suppliers and customers, and the greater the rate of inflation and the greater the timing difference between receipt and payment the better the business would fare. If this table were to be extended over the course of a full year, the supermarket would be in the position of owing R42 600 and having R316 386 cash in the bank! Using a more realistic rate of inflation would still give the same effect, but the difference would not be drastic enough to illustrate the point very well.

	Cash +/−	Balance	Purchases	Owing
Starting cash balance	0			
Purchases month 1			10 000	10 000
Sales month 1	+ 12 000	12 000		
Purchases month 2			11 000	21 000
Sales month 2	+ 13 200	25 200		
Payment	− 10 000	15 200	10 000	11 000
Purchases month 3			14 520	25 520
Sales month 3	+ 15 840	31 040		
Payment	− 11 000	20 040	11 000	14 520

4. Managing the elements of working capital

While the supermarket owner in the previous example needs little in the way of knowledge of management of working capital, there are very few undertakings which are in the fortunate position of having a negative cash cycle. The principle is clear, however. The shorter the cash cycle, the less finance the undertaking needs to provide in order to maintain its operations. The elements that need to be controlled are stock, debtors and creditors. The last one is not easy for most undertakings to control, since the creditors are more likely to be doing the controlling, but all three aspects will be covered briefly.

4.1 Controlling debtors

There are two main factors determining the length of the debtors collection period: economic conditions and the credit policy of the firm. Neither of these two is under the control of the undertaking to more than a limited extent except in the case of a monopoly. Economic conditions are beyond the control of the firm but can be taken into account in granting credit to minimise the effects of poor economic conditions, which invariably lead to lengthening of the time firms take to pay.

The undertaking's credit policy will have to be more or less in line with those of its competitors. If it is more stringent, the firm will lose orders to its competitors. If it is more lenient, not only will the firm get more sales and so provoke retaliatory action from competitors but it will also get all the poor credit risks which the other firms turned down and so will almost certainly have a higher incidence of bad debts. While this must be borne in mind, the variables which can be taken into account when determining a credit policy are the length of the credit period granted, the quality of the debtors, special policies regarding cash or quick settlement discounts and the collection enforcement programme followed. These together will determine the average collection period and the incidence of bad debts.

4.1.1 *The quality of debtors*

The process starts with the quality of the debtors to whom credit is granted. This is largely a matter of the perceptions of the persons setting the quality standards. The tighter the credit standards, the fewer customers the firm will have, while the looser the standards the poorer the collection is likely to be in terms of collection period and the incidence of bad debts. There are also other costs to be borne in mind: the more credit one grants, the larger the accounting department to deal with the paperwork and the more finance is required to support the increased monetary volume of credit granted.

The ultimate decision, in logical terms, should be to relax the standards until the extra cost of the increased credit granted exceeds the benefit of the extra sales generated by the extra credit, and there is no absolute way of determining when this point is reached.

The evaluation of credit is a fairly standardised procedure in most undertakings, with certain minimum requirements in terms of income and/or net worth of the customer and his credit record elsewhere, which is usually determined by confirming the references which are a standard requirement and checking with the credit information services.

4.1.2 *The credit terms*

Once again the firm is faced with a trade off situation. The easier the credit terms the higher the credit sales are likely to be, but the higher the incidence of delinquency in terms of slow payment and non-payment are likely to be and the conclusion is likely to depend purely on the perception of the management of the undertaking concerned. A business like Edgars, for instance, grants extended credit to virtually anyone who applies for it provided the person has a source of income like steady employment. Edgars is apparently willing to accept a very high level of delinquency in order to generate extra sales, but has, of course, to maintain a fairly high profit margin to finance the high level of debtors and the potentially high level of delinquency.

Another aspect which must be taken into account is that of seasonal variations in credit terms. Some firms try to stimulate sales by offering looser credit terms in their off seasons, and again the extent of this must depend on the extent to which management believes sales will be stimulated compared to the cost of stimulating those sales.

4.1.3 *Discount policies*

There are two categories of discount: Those tied to quick settlement of outstanding amounts such as cash discount or settlement discount, and discount tied to specific customers, known as trade discount, or specific volumes of sales, generally known as quantity discount.

Trade discounts are negotiated with customers or with groups of customers, e g garage owners, and have nothing to do with credit management. Quantity discounts are also part of a general marketing strategy and have little to do with this subject. The first category mentioned above, though, is directly tied to the credit policies of the undertaking. Granting settlement discounts can be an extremely expensive way of ensuring quick payment. Granting 2,5 % for settlement at thirty days instead of sixty days means paying 2,5 % per month, which comes to 34,49 % per annum if compounded monthly. Such a cost can only be justified if the margins are big enough to ensure that there is a profit on the sales which are settled in time to gain the benefit of the settlement discount, and that the inflow of cash at an earlier date assists the firms financing requirements in respect of working capital.

4.1.4 *Collection policy*

This only becomes of importance in dealing with delinquent accounts. If a firm has laid down a credit policy and has a customer not abiding by it, it has to have a policy whereby the policy is enforced. Failure to enforce a policy simply means giving the green light to those who would flout it. The firm must decide on the combination of letters, telephone calls and legal action it will take in order to enforce its policy, plus of course the stage at which it will refuse to supply goods to a particular customer. Generally speaking, the higher the expenditure on these items the lower the rate of delinquency becomes, up to a certain point beyond which further expenditure has virtually no direct effect. The undertaking may decide to continue with procedures, regardless of cost, *pour encourager les autres*, or to put it differently, to let it be known that it will not allow itself to be bilked by non-payers.

4.2 Stock control

Stock control is a vast topic, covering control of raw materials, work in process and finished goods and therefore involving production scheduling and planning. There must be enough raw materials to keep the process running without delays caused by stockouts, but there must not be too much raw material beyond what is immediately needed. The more efficiently production is scheduled, the less stock can be held. This is the reason for various stock systems like the so-called J(ust) I(n) T(ime) system, which demands that suppliers deliver the raw materials just before they are required for production, but such systems are really only applicable to continuous production lines.

There are other sides to the story. Higher raw material stock allows the undertaking flexibility in its production if it does not produce just one standard line, but higher stock has a cost in the form of the finance needed to carry it. Again, a firm should increase the raw materials stock until the cost of carrying that extra stock equals the extra income generated by the flexibility it engenders.

Higher stocks of finished goods give flexibility in marketing, since the undertaking can fill orders without having to produce the goods first, but the same considerations apply as in the case of raw materials. Work in process, of course, is determined by the length of the production process. There is no advantage to be gained from having extra work in process, so that this process should be shortened by whatever means are technically possible and otherwise desirable—shortening the process may lead to changes in the quality of the product, for instance.

There are a few techniques which are specifically applied to the management of stock. The first is the economic order quantity, used for determining the optimal order quantity of a particular item taking into account its ordering cost, its forecast usage rate and its carrying cost.

Ordering cost, normally indicated by the letter O, consists of the clerical costs of placing an order and checking the order when it arrives. This cost is assumed to be constant, regardless of the size of the order. if one is looking at self produced finished goods, this cost would take into account the costs of scheduling the production run.

The carrying costs per unit, which include the costs of storage, handling, insurance and the cost of the funds used to finance the stock, are designated by the letter C. The total carrying costs for a line of stock would be the average quantity on hand multiplied by C, the carrying costs per unit, or CQ/2.

If the usage of an item is at a constant level over time and there is no safety stock (see below), the order quantity is indicated by the letter Q and average stock of the item is expressed as Q/2. For simplicity it is assumed that stock is used at a constant tempo, so that the stockholding pattern can be approximated by straight lines:

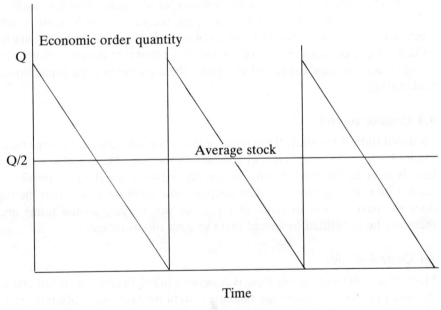

Figure 18.8

The total number of orders placed during a period is the total usage of that item per period, S, divided by Q, so that the total cost of orders during that period is SO/Q.

The total cost for stock, designated by T, in a situation like this would be the carrying costs plus the ordering costs, both of which have been defined above, so

Stock in units

$$T = (CQ/2) + (SO/Q)$$

There will be an obvious trade off here between large orders and small ones, with the large orders having lower ordering costs (fewer orders) but higher carrying costs (more stock) than smaller ones. The optimal order quantity (Q^*) can now be obtained by setting $T = 0$ in the above equation and simplifying to

$$0 = (C/2) - (SO/Q^2), \text{ which leads to } CQ^2 - 2SO = 0$$
$$Q^2 = 2SO/C$$
$$Q^* = \sqrt{2SO/C}$$

This formula can then be used to determine the optimal order size for any item to be purchased or produced. In practice, the application becomes more complex because of the fact that usage is not always constant and that there are lead times between the placing of the order and its execution.

This factor leads to another consideration, that of safety stock levels. Because there are disruptions in delivery from suppliers, stock is normally not allowed to reach zero level. There is always a buffer stock which is maintained to cover the time between placing the order and receiving it. This is based on the lead time and on the reliability of the supplier in meeting order delivery dates, so that the EOQ is normally determined as being the amount which must be ordered when the safety stock level is reached. This level is obviously known as the reorder level.

Beyond the application of these techniques, there is little to be done about stock control from a financial manager's point of view. It will simply be necessary for him to keep an eye on stock levels overall and to see to it that these levels do not reach a stage where the funds required to support them are beyond the capabilities of the undertaking.

4.3 Creditor control

As stated right at the start, there is not really very much that can be done here. You cannot keep on claiming that your cheque is in the post. The actual work to be done here is right at the start, when one should negotiate for the best possible credit terms with every supplier and then keep to those terms to ensure that the supplier does not have reason to claim that you are not keeping to the terms and that therefore he is entitled to amend them to your disadvantage.

4.4 Control of cash

Much of the research on this topic is American in origin and has no real application in a country like this where the banking system operates on a different basis. The fact of the matter is that cash management simply means getting the money to the bank as quickly as possible, especially if you are on overdraft in order to minimise interest costs, and to invest any temporarily surplus funds at the best rates possible.

Getting the money to the bank quickly can involve various aspects of electronic banking and making use of the services which the banks and other institutions offer, but these change rapidly and are not worth discussing in a textbook.

Key words

Working capital
Operating cycle
Cash cycle
Economic order quantity (EOQ)

Chapter 19

Long term financial planning

1. **Financial management and strategic planning**
2. **Creating shareholder wealth**
3. **Cost of capital**
4. **Elements of capital budgeting**

1. Financial management and strategic planning

One fact must be made clear right at the start of this chapter: strategic planning, which is the self important name of long term planning, is not the domain of the accountant or financial manager—alone. It is rather an exercise performed by a team consisting of all facets of management. Marketing, production and finance are the three main branches of managerial activity in any organisation, and all of them must combine with each other and with the more specialised sections of any particular undertaking to develop the long term plan for the undertaking. The broad general directions are normally established by those working directly with the market environment, the marketers and specialists like those doing environmental scanning and that broad, ill-defined management function, developing a vision. This vision plus all the other aspects of management must be teamed to realise the objectives of the undertaking, the main one of which must be the maximisation of shareholder wealth. Without this objective being realised, the undertaking will not have the financial power to accomplish any other objectives such as providing employment for those who choose to work for it.

The part of the accountant or financial manager is often perceived as the negative one of saying that certain dreams cannot be realised because of the financial constraints, but, more realistically, the part of the accountant in the development and implementation of long range plans is to provide the following information and services:

1. Evaluating alternatives and assessing financial feasibilities
2. Providing information about the financial foundation on which the long range plans can be built, plus analyses of past performance, cash flow, product mix and product profitability and capital expenditure.
3. Assembling and co-ordinating the plans of the various departments into one company-wide master plan, and breaking this down into detailed schedules of anticipated costs, profit and financial condition.
4. Using the information in point 4 to prepare detailed operating budgets.
5. Assisting in the review of these plans as they are put into operation by analysing variances in financial terms.
6. Importantly, but not covered in this book, instituting operating controls so that the planned objectives may be more easily achieved.

2. Creating shareholder wealth

The ultimate objective of any long range plan is to assist in the development of shareholder wealth. The ultimate measurement of shareholder wealth increase is not only the dividends paid to shareholders to increase their disposable wealth, but also the increase in the value of the shares of the company, so that their realisable wealth also increases. While the operationalisation of any plan to achieve this may be very complex, the concept is simple: the company has to generate returns greater than the cost of the capital used to generate those returns. A company may be profitable, but if the profits are not sufficient to cover the total cost of all capital employed, the shareholder will ultimately become poorer.

3. Cost of capital

Every undertaking is financed by a variety of different sources of funds, the major ones being share capital (or its equivalent in non-company forms of organisation), long term, interest bearing debt, short term interest bearing debt and short term interest free credit. For purposes of financial management these funds are referred to as "capital", a rather different meaning of the word from that which has been used throughout this book. Each of these sources of capital, then, has a cost, implicit or explicit, and the total cost of capital of an undertaking depends on the extent to which it is financed by each of these and what the costs of each are. The methodology for determining an undertaking's cost of capital is to determine the cost of each component and then to calculate a weighted average cost of capital.

3.1 The cost of interest bearing debt

For interest bearing debt there is an explicit cost which is easy to calculate by taking into account the two relevant factors: the interest rate and the tax rate, since the cost will be the net cost after allowing for the fact that interest is deductible for tax purposes. The formulation is generally taken as $k_i = k(1 - t)$ where k_i is the after tax cost, k is the nominal cost and t is the nominal tax rate. Complications arise where the debt consists of debentures which, in addition to their nominal yield, also have a premium payable on redemption or have been issued at a discount to their face value, but these variations can easily be catered for by modifying the formula.

A further problem is created by the use of overdraft financing, not in calculating the cost per Rand of debt but in calculating the average amount of debt used by the undertaking in view of the fact that this is fluctuating daily. This can be solved easily enough within the undertaking when one has full access to the financial records, but is impossible to solve simply by using the information appearing on the financial statements.

3.2 The cost of preference shares

Preference shares also have an explicit cost, determined in accordance with the rate for which the shares have preference (the coupon rate). Since dividends are not deductible for tax purposes, no adjustment has to be made for tax.

There are also possible complications in this case arising from the fact that certain preference shares can be redeemable or convertible. If they are issued and to be redeemed at par, there is no problem, but an adjustment to the cost of raising finance by this method would have to be made if the shares were to be redeemed at a premium or if they were issued at a value other than face value. If the shares were to be convertible into ordinary shares the value would have to be adjusted in accordance with the formula laid down for conversion. This could vary from an effective par conversion (the par value of the preference shares to be applied to purchasing ordinary shares at market value on date of conversion) through to a formula which would effectively be the same as redemption at a premium.

3.3 The cost of equity share capital

There are various approaches to the valuation of ordinary shares and the determination of the value of the share must obviously influence the determined cost of using this source of finance. In a market context, the cost of equity capital can be defined as the minimum rate of return which a company must earn for its ordinary shareholders in order to ensure that the market price of its shares will not change. A discussion of the Capital Asset Pricing Model (CAPM) is beyond the scope of this book, but this model implies that the required rate of return on ordinary shares is $R_j = i + (R_m - i) \beta_j$ *where i* is the risk free rate, R_m is the expected return on the market portfolio (all the shares quoted on a particular market), and β_j is the measure of responsiveness of the excess return for a particular share to the excess return for the market portfolio, or in other words a measure of whether the particular share's return (or price) varies more or less than the return (or price) of the market as a whole. A share perceived by the market to be risky will fall further than quality shares when the market falls, but will rise rather more when the market rises and such a share would have a Beta measure larger than one by the ratio of its greater movement to the movement of the market as a whole.

The exercise becomes rather technical, since it requires inputs concerning the movements over a whole market, expected market rates of return and risk free rates of return, all of which are constantly changing. Since the model not only assumes perfect market conditions but also cost free transfer of shares, adjustments have to be made to it to take real world conditions into account. It is the model which is preferred, however, particularly on the more sophisticated markets where such information is available.

In less sophisticated economies, however, the more primitive but still difficult to calculate discounted value of future expected dividends is the approach generally used to determine a price per share. The difficulty here lies in estimating the future dividend flow, particularly in the light of growth conditions and inflation. If one can develop a reasonable estimate of these, it is easy to solve for the discount rate that would equate them to the present price of the share, which rate would then be the cost of using equity capital for this company.

If this technique is applied accurately, and a similar exercise using CAPM is done accurately, the two approaches should yield the same answer. However, since both involve making certain assumptions about the future and even about present conditions, it must be accepted that both are going to give no better than an approximation of the cost of using equity capital.

3.4 The cost of using creditor finance

The use of creditor finance for anything other than operating costs is not normally a recommended practice. The cost of creditor finance can be virtually zero, though this will depend on credit terms and the extent to which use of creditor finance for longer term operations prevents taking advantage of settlement discounts. The disadvantage of creditor finance is its short term and the risk factor that the company making use of it will not be able to meet its obligations towards creditors if any untoward event should occur. Many firms have been forced into liquidation because of the inability to meet these short term obligations, while they could possibly have met the less onerous obligations in respect of longer term, fixed period obligations.

3.5 The determination of the weighted average cost of capital

This is a simple mathematical calculation once the above more difficult parts have been performed. It is simply a matter of determining the proportion of the finance provided by each type of finance and finding a weighted average of these. Say that a company is financed 40 % by ordinary shareholders funds, 20 % by preference shares and 40 % by debt. The calculations above have been performed and it has been found that the cost of ordinary shareholders funds is 15 %, that of preference shares 10 % and that of debt 8 %. The next step is simply to put these together as follows:

	Proportion	Cost	Weighted cost
Ordinary shareholders	40 %	15 %	6,0 %
Preference shareholders	20 %	10 %	2,0 %
Debt	40 %	8 %	3,2 %
			11,2 %

Figure 19.1

This shows that the historical cost of capital for this particular company is 11,2 %, and this is the hurdle rate, or minimum rate of return required, that should be used to evaluate new projects *provided* that new capital for a new project is raised in the same proportion as the existing capital structure. If new capital is raised in a different proportion then the weighted average cost of capital will change, and the new figure is the one that should be used. Over time, though, companies tend to raise new capital in the same proportions as before, even though the capital for any specific project may be different.

This last fact begs the question that is often posed: if a new project is being evaluated, should the rate of return required be the weighted average cost of capital of the undertaking or should it be the marginal cost of the new capital being raised? The answer is that in large companies with many projects these two tend to be equal, but in a smaller company entering into one off projects the answer is both. The company must obtain a higher rate of return on the project than it is paying for the finance used for that project, but it must also be higher than the weighted average cost of capital of the undertaking if the average rate of return on company projects is not to decrease. This minimum rate which a project must achieve is known as the hurdle rate.

4. Elements of capital budgeting

Joel Dean[4] laid down the component parts of capital budgeting over forty years ago as follows:

1. A creative search for investment opportunities.

---

[4] Dean, Joel *Controls for capital expenditure* Financial Management Series no 105, American Management Association, New York, 1953

2. Long range plans and projections for the company's future development.
3. A short range budget of supply of funds and demanded capital.
4. A correct yardstick of economic worth *(for the company as a whole)*.
5. Realistic estimation of the economic worth of individual projects.
6. Standards for screening investment proposals that are geared to the company's economic circumstances.
7. Expenditure controls of outlays for facilities by comparison of authorizations and expenditures.
8. Candid and economically realistic post completion audits of project earnings.
9. Investment analysis of facilities that are candidates for disposal.
10. Forms and procedures to ensure the smooth working of the system.

The previous section dealing with cost of capital tried to show how a correct yardstick of economic worth could be derived, and this section will deal with the realistic estimation of the economic worth of individual projects. The other points listed are either beyond the scope of a book on accounting and financial management or have been dealt with in other chapters.

4.1 Cost benefit analysis

In order to determine whether or not a project is worth undertaking the costs of that project must be measured against the benefits. In order to create wealth for the shareholders, the financial benefits must outweigh the financial costs of the project. One has now to argue about whether to measure the benefits in terms of extra profits generated or in terms of extra cash flow generated. While both have advantages and, as mentioned before, must be equal to each other over the long term, the fact of the matter is that the project is going to be financed by *cash outflows, not profit outflows*, and the only logical way to evaluate a project requiring cash outflows is to measure the resultant cash inflows. This does, however, have the potential to create some dysfunctional behaviour, as will be discussed below.

There are four possible cash flow benefits which must be considered when undertaking a project:

1. Cost reductions from replacing a costly process with a more efficient, cheaper one.
2. Cash flows (and profits) from increased sales.
3. Cash received when replaced equipment is sold.
4. Cash received when the equipment for the project is sold at the end of its useful life.

Against these must be measured three types of cash outflow:

1. The initial cost of the project.
2. The operating costs of the project.
3. The cost of capital improvements or upgrades to be made over the life of the project.

From an accounting point of view one of the operating costs of the project would be the depreciation on the capital equipment. Obviously, when evaluating cash flows this must be excluded here, but the effect of depreciation on cash flows via the reduction in taxable profit and therefore in tax payable must be borne in mind. Depreciation cannot just be ignored altogether.

4.2 Non-discounting methods of evaluating capital projects

The methods discussed here, while widely encountered in practice, have little to recommend them from a theoretical point of view. In many cases they lead to the taking of dysfunctional decisions which ultimately lead to destruction rather than creation of shareholder wealth.

4.2.1 The first, and the most widely used, is the *payback period*. This simply looks at the incremental cash flow (or sometimes incremental profit) which will result from the acceptance of the project and divides the cost of the project by this to see how long it will take the project to pay for itself. Cut off points are usually set by deciding to accept only projects which will pay for themselves within, say, three years. This then requires a notional return of 33,3 % per annum on the cost of the project for that period. The problem with this approach is that it takes no note of the timing of the cash flows. A project with a high cash inflow in the first two years of its life but with declining cash flows thereafter would stand a much better chance of acceptance than a project with low initial cash inflows which increase as the project develops, even though this latter may be a far better project for the firm to undertake. Effectively, this method measures only recoupment of investment outflows and does not measure the profitability of the investment.

Example 1: Cash flow payback

A project will cost R30 000 and will result in an increased cash inflow of R10 000 per year. The machines will last about eight years, at the end of which time scrap value will be nil, but they will be depreciated over five years for tax purposes. Tax rate is 50 %.

$$\text{Actual increase in cash flow} = \text{increase in cash flow} - \text{increased tax}$$
$$= \text{R10 000} - 50\% \text{ of } (\text{R10 000} - \text{R6 000})$$
$$= \text{R10 000} - \text{R2 000} = \text{R8 000}$$

$$\text{Payback is } \frac{\text{R30 000}}{\text{R8 000}} = 3 \text{ years } 273 \text{ days}$$

Example 2: Accounting payback

For the same example as above, the accounting profit per year will be R10 000 (the cash saving) less R6 000 (the annual depreciation) plus R3 000 (the tax saving due to depreciation) = R7 000.

Accounting payback period is R30 000/R7 000 = 4 years 106 days

Acceptance or rejection of these projects using this method would depend on the cut off period laid down, ignoring everything happening after that date.

4.2.2 A second method used is the *accounting rate of return* which uses the conventional accounting model for determining a pre tax rate of return. The formula is:

$$\text{Accounting rate of return} = \frac{\text{Increase in future annual net income} \times 100}{\text{Initial increase in required investment}}$$

Example:

Assume the same facts as in the previous example. The annual increase in accounting profit would be the increased cash flow minus the cost of the machine spread over its estimated useful life (not the depreciation which would be used for tax purposes). This would come to R10 000 − R3 375 = R6 625. The accounting rate of return would then be R6 625/R30 000 = 22,1 %.

This method does make an attempt to measure profitability, but again it does not take into account the timing of the cash flows. In most projects cash flows will not be constant, at least not in the first few years of operation, but this method simply smooths the forecast profits over the period in order to get an average rate of return. The only way in which the timing of cash flows can be brought into account is by using a method which discounts the value of future cash flows.

4.3 Discounted cash flow methods

4.3.1 *Discounting explained*

Many people seem to have problems with the idea of discounting future cash flows. This is odd, since no one seems to have any trouble with the idea of receiving interest on money invested, which is just the other side of the discounting coin. For instance, it is obvious that if you invest R100 today at a rate of 10 % per annum, this will grow to R100 + (R100 × 10/ 100) = R110 over the next year. It should be just as obvious that if you want R110 in one year's time and can invest at a rate of 10 % per annum, you would have to invest R110 − (R110 × 10/ 110) = R100 now. This second calculation discounts the value of the future cash amount of R110 to its net present value (NPV) of R100, and is no more complex than the calculation of interest.

Included as appendix 6 are some present value tables, but any financial calculator will have a net present value function built into it and is a lot easier to use than the tables. If you do intend to use the tables, however, note that there are two of them:
1. The first gives the present value of R1 after a number of years at various percentage rates. For instance, if you wish to know how much you have to invest today at a rate of 12 % to have R100 after ten years, you simply go down the 12 % column until you reach the ten year row which gives you your answer of 0,32197 per Rand, which means that you must invest R32,197 to get R100 after ten years.
2. The second tells you how much you must invest now to ensure an income of R1 per year for a number of years at various rates of return. For instance, if you want an income of R100 per year for the next twenty years and can invest at 14 %, you go down the 14 % column until you reach the 20 year row, which gives you 6,62313 per Rand. You would therefore have to invest R662,313 now at 14 % to ensure an income of R100 per year for 20 years, the first R100 being payable one year from now. If you don't believe this, work it out for yourself.

To summarise, then, discounting is simply working back from what an investment is going to be worth at a certain rate of interest after a number of years to what that investment is worth now without all the interest. The net present value of a series of fixed payments over a period in the future is simply the calculation of the sum of the present values of a series of investments maturing at regular intervals over that period.

Methods of evaluation of projects which use discounted cash flows require estimates of the amount and timing of future cash flows. These can then be discounted back to present values to determine the attractiveness or otherwise of the projects. The method therefore presumes that future cash flows can be estimated with certainty. Since this is not applicable to the real world, the application of some method of sensitivity analysis is necessary. This can vary from a simple model examining the effect of changes in one variable at a time through to highly complex computer models which measure the effect of simultaneous changes in any number of variables. These variables include direct changes in any of the factors mentioned in the cost benefit analysis section above, but also include such matters as technological changes which may make the project irrelevant or comparatively expensive to operate, and so impact indirectly on those variables, plus of course general economic or socio-political changes.

4.3.2 *Internal rate of return*

The internal rate of return (IRR) is the rate of discount at which future cash flows must be discounted in order to have their net present value equal the value of the outflows on the investment. Say a project costing R50 000 will provide an improved cash flow of R10 000 per year for ten years. The IRR can be calculated as follows:

Outflow = R50 000
Cash inflow = R10 000 per year for 10 years.
From the tables, R1 per year for 10 years at 14 % will give R5,21611 and at 16 % will give R4,83322, so that R10 000 per year will give R52 161,1 and R48 332,2 at those rates. The actual rate lies between these two percentages and can be calculated by interpolation:
R50 000 = R10 000 × F (F is the factor to be found in the tables)
F = 50 000/10 000 = 5,00000
Difference between the factors for 14 % and 16 %
    = 5,21611 − 4,83322 = 0,38289
Difference between the factor for 14 % and the actual factor
    = 5,21611 − 5,00000 = 0,21611
The actual rate is therefore
    14 % + (0,21611/0,38289 × 2 %) = 15,12901 %

This rate would then be used to decide whether or not to accept the project. If the costs of capital from the project were less than this percentage, the decision would be to carry on with the project.

The use of the Internal Rate of Return method is popular in practice, presumably because it gives a percentage which can be directly applied to the decision. It also gives an easy way of ranking projects when there are insufficient funds to actually accept all those which give returns in excess of the hurdle rate.

In reality, the method has a major shortcoming. For a simple project which simply requires a one time outlay this does not arise, but as soon as the project becomes more complex and requires more than one outlay then the equations used for solving the IRR can have more than one answer. A project which lasts several years but requires major outlays for maintenance or upgrading after a few years may have more than one period of cash outflow and IRR is generally not a suitable method for evaluating such projects.

4.3.3 *Net present value*

The preferable method, from theoretical and practical points of view, is to use DCF methods to determine the Net Present Value (NPV) of a project. This is done by determining the present value of all predicted cash flows for the project by discounting at the hurdle rate. If the Net Present Value of all cash flows is positive, then the project is acceptable. As a straightforward example, take the case of a machine to be purchased for R100 000. The machine is expected to increase Cash inflows by R20 000 per year for ten years, requiring a major overhaul after the end of the fifth year and having no scrap value after ten years. The applicable hurdle rate is 10 % per annum. A schedule such as the following would be prepared to reflect all the cash flows relating to the project over the period:

Project cash flows	Year	Out	In	Present value
Purchase price of machine	0	100 000	0	− 100 000
	1		20 000	18 182
	2		20 000	16 529
	3		20 000	15 026
	4		20 000	13 660
	5		20 000	12 418
Major overhaul	6	30 000	20 000	− 5 645
	7		20 000	10 263
	8		20 000	9 330
	9		20 000	8 482
	10		20 000	7 711
Net present value of the project at a discount rate of 10 %				5 956

Figure 19.2

In this case the present value is positive which means that the return on the project is greater than the hurdle rate, making the project acceptable.

This method is more soundly based theoretically than the IRR method, but does not give a direct ranking of competing projects. One cannot simply accept the project with the largest NPV, but should look at the project which gives the largest NPV in relation to the original outlay. A project requiring an outlay of R100 000 and having a NPV of R10 000 is not a better one than a project requiring an outlay of R40 000 but having a NPV of R6 000, since the larger NPV of the first one is only 10 % of the outlay required while that of the second is 15 % of the outlay required.

Factors to be considered when using a DCF approach include the following:
1. The initial outflows and inflows.
   The initial outflow for a project will always be the initial cost of the project, but one must not forget initial inflows which can arise from the disposal of the equipment which is being replaced by the new equipment being evaluated. If one does a DCF analysis comparing the existing situation and the proposed situation if the new project is accepted this can be one of the critical factors in arriving at a decision.

2. Future inflows from disposal of the assets at the end of the project.
   The above example did not bring this into account, but the fact is that the machine will still have a residual value at the end of its economic life, even if this is purely as scrap. This value should be brought into account as a future cash inflow.
3. Investments in stocks and debtors
   The cost of a project is not simply the cost of the machinery or the building. There is often an associated cost of extra required stocks of materials to be used or extra debtors to be financed if the project leads to an increase in turnover.
4. Increases in overhead costs
   Just as a project may require an increased investment in stocks or debtors, so it may require an increase in overhead costs. This increase may be very difficult to isolate unless it arises from a specific project related expenditure.
5. Income taxes
   The cash outflow of a project is decreased over the years if there are tax write offs resulting from the project. One of the obvious write offs is depreciation, which is ignored for purposes of calculating cash flows but does decrease the profits and therefore the amounts of tax paid. The timing of the tax payments has to be accounted for, however, since the tax saving may occur a year or more after the depreciation is written off in the financial records depending on whether the company has an assessed loss for tax purposes or not.
6. Rationing of funds
   Any undertaking can generate any number of projects, but only a few can be accepted because of the limitation on the funds available to finance such projects. In some cases projects may also be mutually exclusive: there may be two different projects each of which is aimed at the same task. Acceptance of the one would then automatically mean the rejection of the other.

4.3.4 *A problem with NPV*

NPV analysis evaluates projects to determine whether they have positive net present values over the whole of their economic lives. A problem arises when there is a need to decide between two projects, both of which have positive NPV's, when the economic lives of the two projects differ. Project A may have a NPV or R10 000 over five years, but Project B a NPV of R15 000 over ten years. There is no wholly satisfactory way of deciding between these two projects. One either evaluates them over the life of the shorter project, which ignores possible major inflows for the longer project after this, or one evaluates over the life of the longer project making assumptions about the disposal value of the shorter lived project and the re-investment of any funds released by the termination of the project, including possibly the replacement of the project.

4.3.5 *Negative effects of DCF on employee behaviour*

Many employees are sceptical about the value of DCF calculations because of the way in which their performance is evaluated. Most evaluations of employee and managerial performance are made on the basis of accounting figures, and accounting figures are generally not merciful to cash flow figures. If an employee has a project accepted on the basis of cash flow projections but is then evaluated on the basis of accounting figures which decrease the cash flow impact by the amount of depreciation, the evaluation is almost invariably negative, at least in the early stages of a project.

To overcome this it is necessary to evaluate those who have capital expenditure authority on a basis which compares the actual results with the projected results using the DCF analysis.

4.4 Conclusion

This chapter is a very brief survey of the methodology and terminology of capital planning. Anyone reading it should be aware that it is not a how-to manual, but that the topic is a highly complex one requiring detailed knowledge before putting it into practice.

Key words

Discounted cash flow	Internal rate of return
Net present value	Payback period
Shareholder wealth	Cost of capital

Questions and exercises on Part Four

Test-yourself questions

True or false

1. "Disposal value of assets being replaced are relevant to the replacement decision."   T   F
2. "The higher the hurdle rate, the more an undertaking would be willing to pay for cost-saving equipment."   T   F
3. "The higher the hurdle rate, the less need there is to worry about errors in predicting residual values."   T   F
4. "Net present values can never be negative."   T   F
5. Variable costs fluctuate directly in proportion to sales.   T   F
6. Relaxing credit terms usually results in an increase in debtors   T   F
7. Which of the following is a carrying cost of stock?
   (a) Insurance of stock
   (b) Storage cost
   (c) Losses through wear and tear (shop-soiled goods)
   (d) All of the above
8. A decrease in a share's beta value, other things being unchanged, will result in an increase in the market price of the share   T   F
9. Aubergine Limited is looking at the purchase of a new machine. The analysis done to date indicates that the following cash inflows will be realised:

Year	Amount (R000)
1	8 000
2	16 000
3	25 000
4	45 000
5	35 000

   If the cost price of the machine is R55 000, what is the cash flow payback period?
10. Broccoli Limited uses a Net Present Value approach to the evaluation to the assessment of capital expenditure using a hurdle rate of 15 %. Say whether a project costing R2 500 000 would be accepted if it had the following cash inflows:

Year	Net cash inflow (R000)
1	800
2	850
3	830
4	1 200
5	700

PROBLEMS

Question 4.1

You have been appointed manager of a branch of a national chain of clothing stores with effect from the end of February 1999. The company believes in participative management and one of the first tasks assigned you is to prepare a master budget for your store for March, April and May, the first three months of the new financial year. As you know, your background is in marketing and merchandising and you have no experience of this type of work. Since all accounting work is done at head office you will not have any local assistance in preparing the budget, but the current branch manager, who has been promoted to a larger branch, will be there to assist you and you are invited to call on head office staff at any time. From currently existing records and the information supplied by the current manager you come up with the following information:

Branch balance sheet at end February 1999

Head office account	764 000
Accounts payable	680 000
	1 444 000
Fixed assets	300 000
Stock on hand	600 000
Accounts receivable	522 000
Cash at bank	22 000
	1 444 000

Actual and forecast sales:
January—R400 000; February—R500 000; March—1 000 000; April—R600 000; May—R600 000; June—R400 000.

Cash sales make up ten per cent of total sales, and there are no bad debts on the ninety per cent credit sales. Eighty per cent of credit sales are collected in the month following the sale and the balance in the following month. No discounts are granted and the gross profit on all sales is forty per cent of selling price.

The policy is to hold only enough stock at the end of the month to meet the expected sales for the following month, and purchases are paid for in the month following purchase. Other monthly cash disbursements are as follows:

Fixed monthly expenses	R80 000
Variable expenses	24 % of sales

During March a payment of R80 000 must be made for fixtures purchased during February. The only other expenses is depreciation which is charged at R4 000 per month.

Head office lays down certain financial guidelines. The branch is not entitled to borrow from the bank and must maintain a minimum cash and bank balance of R20 000 to ensure this. Any money required must be borrowed from head office at the beginning of a month and must be repaid at the end of a month, with both borrowings and repayment being in multiples of one thousand Rand. The branch will be charged interest at 8 % per annum on such loans and interest must be repaid along with the principal.

Required:

1 Prepare a budgeted income statement for your first three months as manager as well as a cash budget for the period and a balance sheet at the end of the period. Remember that taxes will be paid by head office so that you need not bother about them.
2 Explain why a need for a loan from head office could arise and show how the branch could repay such a loan out of operating sources.

Question 4.2

Because of government funding cutbacks to universities the business school of the university of the Nation (UNINABS) is under pressure to cut costs. One of the large expense items is that of preparing study material and handouts and the management of UNINABS is considering the purchase of a special high volume photocopying machine. The cost of this machine will be R380 000, but it is expected to generate net savings of R100 000 per year for the six years that it is expected to last. The salvage value at the end of this time is expected to be R50 000.

Because of the nature of the machine a stock of special supplies and spares must be kept on hand, the value of this being R40 000. While this amount will be constant for the whole period, it will be recovered in full at the end of the six years.

Required:

1 Compute the payback period.
2 Compute the accounting rate of return on the initial investment.
3 Compute the net present value (NPV) if the hurdle rate of return is 14 %.
4 Compute the internal rate of return (IRR) to the nearest percentage.

Question 4.3

The Marvellous Merchandise Mart has been operating for some years, but has recently moved to new, more accessible premises because of the increased interest being shown in their merchandise. Despite the growth in sales which has taken place the company often finds itself short of cash. Since this has led to delaying payments to certain suppliers the business has lost some goodwill, and this has led to a decision to borrow a lump sum of money from the bank to pay all the suppliers happy, rather than to request fluctuating overdraft facilities. With the Christmas season approaching, the owner has asked you to prepare a cash budget for the period from December to February so that he can determine the amount that he should borrow.

The actual and budgeted information with which they have supplied you is given below. On the basis of this information,

1   Prepare a cash budget for December, January and February
2   Prepare a second cash budget showing what the effect would be if sales terms were altered from cash to thirty days net and all customers accepted these terms, while all other factors remained the same.

All sales are on a cash basis. Goods purchased for resale are paid for in the month following purchase. The only expenses for which you have to make provision are the rent of R4 000 per month and the owner's salary of R9 600 per month, but he also has provisional taxes of R24 000 to pay at the end of February. He has also decided that he wants to maintain a month end cash balance of R 12 000, although the balance at end of November is only R800. The purchases during November amounted to R280 000, and the budgeted purchases and sales are as follows:

	Sales	Purchases
December	320 000	80 000
January	80 000	80 000
February	120 000	80 000

Question 4.4

The Fabulous Factory produces two products, Wotisits and Nonsums. There are two sales managers, one for the PWV and northern area and one for the rest of the country, who have prepare the following information for use in the preparation of the budgets for the following year:

	Wotisits		Nonsums	
	Northern	Rest	Northern	Rest
March	4 000	6 000	6 000	8 000
April	4 400	6 800	6 600	9 000
May	4 600	6 800	7 000	9 200
2nd quarter	13 200	18 000	16 000	20 000
3rd quarter	14 000	19 800	17 000	20 600
4th quarter	10 000	14 000	12 000	16 000

Budgeted sales prices are R0,05 higher per unit in the rest of the country than in the Northern area, where it is intended to sell Wotisits at R1,65 and Nonsums at R2,15. Returns and allowances country-wide are expected to be one per cent (1 %) of the gross sales of Wotisits and one and one half per cent (1,5 %) of the gross sales of Nonsums.
Monthly fixed distribution expenses are expected to be R1 000 for Wotisits and R1 500 for Nonsums for each of the districts and variable distribution expenses are budgeted at four per cent (4 %) of gross sales, while monthly promotion expenses are budgeted at R2 000 per area for Wotisits and R2 200 for Nonsums.

Required:

1   Name the three basic components of the sales plan.
2   Prepare the sales plan using the above inputs.

3 Prepare budget schedules for the sales plan for each of the components in such a way as to reflect relevant classifications such as products and responsibility.

Question 4.5

(a) Nero Cosmetics Limited is expecting very strong growth during 1999. This will obviously lead to cash flow problems and you are required to prepare documents for submission to the company's bankers as part of the company's request for overdraft facilities. While a month-by-month cash flow forecast will be required once management has had time to think over the implications of this fast growth, you are at this stage only required to prepare a budgeted income statement for the year to 28 February 1999 and a forecast balance sheet at that date based on the 1998 financial statements given below and the assumptions which follow.

NERO COSMETICS LIMITED

Income statement for the year ended 28 February 1998

Sales		2 625 000
Cost of goods sold		1 933 050
Gross profit		691 950
Operating expenses	525 000	0
Depreciation	35 700	560 700
Operating profit		131 250
Taxes		52 500
Net profit		78 750

NERO COSMETICS LIMITED

Balance sheet at 28 February 1998

Share capital		700 000
Retained earnings		210 000
		910 000
Long term debt		875 000
		1 785 000
Fixed assets		805 000
Net current assets		980 000
Current assets		
Inventory	655 000	
Accounts receivable	325 000	
Cash and bank balances	525 000	
		1 505 000
Current liabilities		525 000
Accounts payable	165 000	
Bank overdraft	360 000	
		1 785 000

The following assumptions have to be built into your model:
1   Sales will grow by 60 % (sixty per cent)
2   Cost of goods sold will be 75 % (seventy-five per cent of sales).
3   There will be no changes in share capital, long term liabilities or fixed assets.
4   The depreciation charge will be R56 000.
5   Average receivables collection period will be sixty days.
6   All payables will be settled within thirty days.
7   Inventory will be turned over three times per year.
8   The tax rate is 40 % (forty per cent).
9   Operating expenses will grow by 10 % (ten per cent).
10 No dividends will be declared or paid during the year.

(b) Management believes that it can improve matters by turning inventory over four times per year and settling all payables at forty-five days. Prepare a new balance sheet to reflect the effect of these changes.

Question 4.6

Zigzag Zipper Company has been approached to purchase a new, higher volume machine for the production of zippers. This machine, which has a cost price of R200 000, can produce 192 000 zippers against the 130 000 units which the current machine can produce. The new machine would also have a contribution of R0,25 per unit against the R0,20 of the old machine. The existing machine, which can currently be sold for R40 000, has a remaining useful life of eight years, which is the same as the expected life of the new machine. However, the old machine is expected to have a zero salvage value while the new machine should have a salvage value of R40 000 at the end of its economic life. The only other costs relevant to the decision of whether to buy the new machine are the overhaul costs: the old machine will require a major overhaul in two years time at a cost of R20 000, while the new machine will only require a major overhaul after four years at a cost of R16 000. The firm's hurdle rate is ten per cent.

Required:

Use the net present value method to determine whether the new machine should be purchased to replace the old one.

CASES

Case 4.1 Comprehensive Company—comprehensive case on cash flows and cash budgets

D J Kenn had invented a new telescopic night sight which he felt would revolutionise the hunting industry and was suitable for all sorts of sport shooting as well. He had been granted a patent with a life of fourteen years and wanted to market the product. Unfortunately, as is so often the case, he had no money to manufacture and market the product. Acting on the advice of knowledgeable friends he decided to float a company with a share capital of R100 000. He would sell the patent to the company as his contribution, keeping half the shares for himself, and would sell the rest of the shares to raise money for development of the product.

He laid his proposal before a number of people, all of whom expressed interest, but only one of whom, a well known venture capitalist, actually showed enough interest to carry the matter further. He was willing to put up the necessary money but only on certain conditions. Firstly, D J would have to keep the majority of the shares ("I'd rather it was your money. That way you will work harder to make a success of the company."). Secondly he wanted to have some financial projections. The statements he specifically required were:

1. A projected balance sheet on the day that the company was ready to start production;
2. A projected income statement for the first year of operations based on the studies already done by D J;
3. A cash budget for the first year of operations;
4. A cash flow statement for the first year of operations; and
5. A working capital based funds statement for the first year of operations.

D J consulted with the people who had helped him build his prototypes and came up with the following information which he presented to his accountant with a request that he prepare the required documents:

1. The venture capitalist would pay in R40 000 for forty per cent of the share capital. The remaining sixty per cent would be used to purchase the patent from D J.
2. The estimated costs of registration and organisation of the company, including salary during the pre-production period, would be R7 000.
3. The cost of buying and modifying the necessary machinery, which would have a useful life of ten years, would be R20 000.
4. It would be necessary to purchase about R2 000 worth of raw materials before starting production. Sixty per cent of this would be used in pre-production trial runs.
5. Budgeted sales for the first year were R320 000, R20 000 per month for the first four months and R30 000 per month thereafter. Terms of sale would be 30 days net.
6. Budgeted purchases of raw materials and supplies would be R108 000. These would be purchased in equal monthly amounts and would be paid for within thirty days of purchase.
7. It would probably be necessary to borrow from the bank during the year, although any such loan would be repaid before the end of the year. The cost of such funds would be two per cent per month.
8. Expected manufacturing costs would be about R144 000 including wages. There would also be about R24 000 administrative costs for the year. These costs would be incurred evenly throughout the year.
9. Office equipment would cost about R4 000.
10. Since all manufacture would be to firm order only there would be no stock of finished goods on hand at the end of the year.

11. D J decided to get intangible assets off the balance sheet as quickly as possible. The costs of the development of the product, including the cost of registering the patent, would therefore be written off over the first two years in equal instalments.
12. All assets would be depreciated at 10 % p a on the straight line basis.
13. Tax would be payable at the ruling company rate of forty per cent.
14. Dividends would be paid at thirty per cent of net income after tax.

Required:

1. Prepare the balance sheet at the start of operations on 1 March 1998.
2. Prepare the projected income statement for the first year of operations.
3. Prepare the cash budget for the first year of operations, listing your assumptions.
4. Prepare the cash flow statement for the first year of operations; and
5. Prepare a working capital based funds statement for the first year of operations.
6. Contrast the statements prepared in 3, 4 and 5 above. Which of the three do you think would be most useful to a shareholder, a banker and the management of the company respectively?

Appendix 1

Financial statements of a small private company

The financial statements on the next few pages are those of a small engineering company which has done quite well for itself but has declined somewhat of late. The name has been changed to protect the guilty but shy people involved; the figures have all been multiplied by a constant factor and comparative figures for 1983 have been added. Otherwise the statements are just as they first appeared. No attempt has been made to doctor them for purposes of demonstration or to improve their presentation.

They are not to be regarded as perfect models of financial statements. Rather, they are typical of the statements one would receive in practice if one were to be approached for a loan or if one were thinking of investing in a company.

ENGINEERING FIRM (PROPRIETARY) LIMITED

Financial Statements at 28 February 1985

The following reports and financial statements, together with the annexed notes and schedules (hereafter referred to jointly as the financial statements) for the year ended on the above date are presented in accordance with the requirements of the Companies Act, 1973:

The financial statements on pages 2 and 7 hereafter have been approved by the board and are signed on its behalf by:

A Baker
30 June 1985

C Dover

Green, Ink & Co

Chartered Accountants (SA)
Public Accountants and Auditors

Telephone (012) 98-7654
PO Box 1234
0001 Pretoria

Auditors' report

REPORT OF THE AUDITORS TO THE MEMBERS OF ENGINEERING FIRM (PROPRIETARY) LIMITED

We have examined the annual financial statements set out on pages 2 to 7 hereafter which, in our opinion and subject to the fact that all operations are under the direct control of the directors, fairly present the financial position of the company at 28 February 1985 and the results of its operations for the year ended on that date.

With the written consent of all the shareholders we have performed certain accounting and secretarial duties during the course of the year under review.

30 June 1985

ENGINEERING FIRM (PROPRIETARY) LIMITED

Report of the directors for the year ended 28 February 1985

Business and operations
The principal activity of the company is medium engineering work under contract or to order. The factory is situated in rented premises in Pretoria.

Review of the company's affairs and results of operations for the year
The strong upward trend in the company's fortunes which started in the previous financial year continued during the year under review. All other relevant matters under this heading are fully covered in the attached financial statements.

Dividends and reserves
No dividends were paid or proposed, nor were any amounts transferred to or from reserves.

Fixed assets
Details of changes in fixed assets are given in the attached financial statements.

Directors and secretary
Messrs A Baker and C Dover continued to act as directors throughout the year under review. Mr E Forester of the same address as the company continued to act as secretary.

Events subsequent to the end of the financial year
No material events, knowledge of which would be necessary for an evaluation of these financial statements, have occurred between the date of these financial statements and the date of this report.

A Baker
30 June 1985

C Dover

ENGINEERING FIRM (PROPRIETARY) LIMITED

Balance sheet at 28 February 1985

	Note	1985	1984	1983
Capital employed				
Share capital	2	2 000	2 000	1 800
Retained earnings		540 000	418 000	320 000
		542 000	420 000	321 800
Loans	3	154 000	196 000	183 200
		696 000	616 000	505 000
Represented by				
Fixed assets		572 000	360 000	315 000
Net current assets		124 000	256 000	190 000
Current assets				
Stock and work in process		195 000	185 000	200 000
Debtors and deposits		1 300 000	1 210 000	1 064 000
Cash and bank balances		14 000	26 000	11 000
		1 509 000	1 421 000	1 275 000
Current liabilities				
Creditors and accruals		760 000	600 000	555 000
Bank overdraft		635 000	535 000	520 000
Provision for tax		−10 000	30 000	10 000
		1 385 000	1 165 000	1 085 000
		696 000	616 000	505 000

C Dover   A Baker

The above balance sheet and attached statements and notes are subject to our report of even date.

Green, Ink & Co
29 July 1985

ENGINEERING FIRM (PROPRIETARY) LIMITED

Income statement for the year ended 28 February 1985

	1985	*1984*	*1983*
Turnover	4 650 000	4 550 000	3 665 000
Interest received	24 500	3 000	0
Expenses	4 552 500	4 397 000	3 495 000
Audit fees	14 000	12 000	11 000
Depreciation	103 000	105 500	125 500
Directors' remuneration for			
managerial services	180 000	108 000	99 000
Interest paid	4 500	31 000	13 000
Lease charges	325 000	357 000	315 000
Other expenses	3 926 000	3 783 500	2 931 500
Net income before taxation	122 000	156 000	170 000
South African Companies Tax 1985	0	58 000	28 000
Net income after taxation	122 000	98 000	142 000
Retained earnings brought forward	418 000	320 000	178 000
	540 000	418 000	320 000

ENGINEERING FIRM (PROPRIETARY) LIMITED

Statement of sources and applications of funds for the year ended 28 February 1985

	1985	1984	1983
Funds were obtained from:			
Net operating income before charging depreciation	205 000	289 500	308 500
Interest received	24 500	3 000	0
Shares issued	0	200	0
Loans from directors	0	12 800	0
Reduction in working capital	132 000		
	361 500	305 500	308 500
These funds were applied to:			
Purchase fixed assets for	315 000	150 000	122 500
Pay interest of	4 500	31 000	13 000
Increase working capital by	0	66 000	85 000
Repay loans from directors	42 000	0	60 000
Taxation	0	58 000	28 000
	361 500	305 500	308 500
Statement of changes in working capital			
Increases in working capital			
Cash and bank balances	0	15 000	9 000
Stock and work in progress	10 000	0	48 000
Debtors and deposits	90 000	146 000	40 000
Provision for tax	40 000	0	0
	140 000	161 000	97 000
Decreases in working capital			
Cash and bank balances	12 000	0	0
Stock and work in progress	0	15 000	0
Creditors and accruals	160 000	45 000	7 000
Bank overdraft	100 000	15 000	0
Provision for tax	0	20 000	5 000
	272 000	95 000	12 000
Net increase in working capital	− 132 000	66 000	85 000

ENGINEERING FIRM (PROPRIETARY) LIMITED

Cash flow statements for the year ended 28 February 1985

	1985	*1984*
Cash retained from operating activities		
Cash generated by operations	205 000	289 500
Investment income	24 500	3 000
Cash used to increase working capital	− 60 000	86 000
Cash generated by operating activities	289 500	206 500
Finance costs	4 500	31 000
Taxation paid	40 000	38 000
Cash available from operating activities	245 000	137 500
Cash used in investment activities		
Investment to maintain operations		
Replacement of fixed assets	65 000	100 500
Investment to expend operations		
Additions to fixed assets	250 000	50 000
Cash generated	− 70 000	− 13 000
Cash effects of financing activities		
Increase in long term borrowings	− 42 000	12 800
Change in short term borrowings	11 200	0
Proceeds of share issue	0	200
Cash utilised	− 30 800	13 000
Notes:		
Cash generated by operations		
Operating income before tax	102 000	184 000
Adjustment for non-cash expenses		
Depreciation	103 000	105 500
	205 000	289 500
Cash used to increase working capital		
Change in stock/W I P	10 000	− 15 000
Change in debtors	90 000	146 000
Change in creditors	− 160 000	− 45 000
	− 60 000	86 000

ENGINEERING FIRM (PROPRIETARY) LIMITED

Notes to the financial statements at 28 February 1985

1. ACCOUNTING POLICIES

   The financial statements are prepared in accordance with generally accepted practices with the following policies being specifically adopted:

   1.1 Fixed assets are depreciated at appropriate rates on the reducing balance basis.

   1.2 Lease charges are shown as expenses in the year in which they are incurred. At the conclusion of the lease the assets, if they are retained, are brought into account at a reasonable market value, this value (less any settlement amount paid to the lessor) being reflected as income.

   1.3 Stock is valued at the lower of cost, based on the FIFO method, or market value. Work in process is based on full cost of work performed to the end of the financial year less appropriate provisions for losses where in the opinion of the directors these may be necessary.

2. SHARE CAPITAL

	1985	1984
Authorised		
4 000 Ordinary shares of R1 each	R4 000	R4 000
Issued		
2 000 Ordinary shares of R1 each	R2 000	R2 000

3. LOAN

   The loans from the directors are unsecured, free of interest and repayable on demand

4. FIXED ASSETS

	Cost	Depreciation	Net	1984
Plant, machinery and workshop equipment	R850 000	R315 000	R535 000	R335 000
Loose tools	15 000	—	15 000	10 000
Office equipment	20 889	4 000	16 000	8 000
Office furniture	10 000	4 000	6 000	7 000
	R895 000	R323 000	R572 000	R360 000

5. TAXATION

   Taxation has been provided on the basis of an assessed loss brought forward being fully utilised. The amount of the assessed loss is still the subject of dispute with the authorities.

6. LEASE CHARGES

   The company has commitments in respect of lease contracts amounting to R300 000 over the next four years, R100 000 of is due within the next financial year.

ENGINEERING FIRM (PROPRIETARY) LIMITED

Common size income statements

% OF SALES

	1985	1984	1983	
Sales	100,00	100,00	100,00	
Direct cost of sales	71,18	70,77	66,85	
Opening stock/work in process	3,98	4,40	4,91	
Design fees	1,18	1,10	1,09	
Direct wages	31,72	30,77	31,38	
Power and water	1,08	1,10	1,09	
Purchases	32,04	36,15	32,47	
Subcontracted work	5,38	1,32	1,36	
	75,38	74,84	72,31	
Deduct: Closing stock/work in process	4,19	4,07	5,46	
Direct contribution	28,82	29,23	33,15	*COMMON*
Indirect factory expenses	13,12	14,13	15,55	
Depreciation	2,15	2,31	3,41	
Lease charges on plant	5,05	6,22	6,41	
Maintenance and repairs	0,65	0,88	0,68	
Rent	1,72	1,54	1,77	
Salaries—factory	3,55	3,19	3,27	
Factory contribution	15,70	15,10	17,60	
Administrative expenses	13,51	11,05	12,61	
Audit fees	0,30	0,26	0,30	
Bank charges	0,22	0,20	0,23	
Cleaning and refreshments	0,13	0,18	0,16	
Depreciation	0,06	0,01	0,01	
Directors' salaries	3,87	2,37	2,70	
Entertainment	0,28	0,40	0,27	
Insurance	0,86	0,77	0,68	
Lease charges on motor vehicles	1,72	1,32	1,77	
Lease charges on office equipment	0,22	0,31	0,41	
Legal expenses	0,09	0,01	0,03	
Motor expenses	2,15	2,20	2,37	
Railage and airfreight	0,11	0,22	0,38	
Salaries	1,94	1,43	1,88	
Stationery and printing	0,28	0,31	0,30	
Subscriptions	0,09	0,09	0,05	
Sundry expenses	0,45	0,51	0,53	
Telephone and telex	0,22	0,46	0,48	
Travelling expenses	0,54	0,02	0,03	
Operating income for the year	2,19	4,04	4,99	*Common*
Non-operating expense	− 0,43	0,62	0,35	
Interest paid	0,10	0,68	0,35	
Interest received	0,53	0,07	0,00	
Net income before tax	2,62	3,43	4,64	*Common*

ENGINEERING FIRM (PROPRIETARY) LIMITED

Trend statements
(Percentage change year on year)

	85/84	84/83
Sales	2,20	24,15
Direct cost of sales	2,80	31,43
Opening stock/work in process	− 7,50	11,11
Design fees	10,00	25,00
Direct wages	5,36	21,74
Power and water	0,00	25,00
Purchases	− 9,42	38,24
Subcontracted work	316,67	20,00
	2,94	28,49
Deduct: Closing stock/work in process	5,41	− 7,50
Direct contribution	0,75	9,47
Indirect factory expenses	− 5,13	12,81
Depreciation	− 4,76	− 16,00
Lease charges on plant	− 16,96	20,43
Maintenance and repairs	− 25,00	60,00
Rent	14,29	7,69
Salaries—factory	13,79	20,83
Factory contribution	6,26	6,51
Administrative expenses	24,85	8,87
Audit fees	16,67	9,09
Bank charges	11,11	5,88
Cleaning and refreshments	− 25,00	33,33
Depreciation	500,00	0,00
Directors' salaries	66,67	9,09
Entertainment	− 27,78	80,00
Insurance	14,29	40,00
Lease charges on motor vehicles	33,33	− 7,69
Lease charges on office equipment	− 28,57	− 6,67
Legal expenses	700,00	− 50,00
Motor expenses	0,00	14,94
Railage and airfreight	− 50,00	− 28,57
Salaries	38,46	− 5,80
Stationery and printing	− 7,14	27,27
Subscriptions	0,00	100,00
Sundry expenses	− 8,70	17,95
Telephone and telex	− 52,38	20,00
Travelling expenses	2 400,00	0,00
Operating income for the year	− 44,57	0,55
Non-operating expense	− 171,43	115,38
Interest paid	− 85,48	138,46
Interest received	716,67	N/A
Net income before tax	− 21,79	− 8,24

ENGINEERING FIRM (PROPRIETARY) LIMITED

Selected ratios

	1985	*1984*	*1983*
Solvency			
Assets/liabilities (1)	2 081 000	1 781 000	1 590 000
	1 539 000	1 361 000	1 268 200
	1,35	1,31	1,25
Assets/liabilities (2)	2 081 000	1 781 000	1 590 000
	1 385 000	1 165 000	1 085 000
	1,50	1,53	1,47
Short term liquidity			
Current ratio	1 509 000	1 421 000	1 275 000
	1 385 000	1 165 000	1 085 000
	1,09	1,22	1,18
Acid test (Quick) ratio	1 314 000	1 236 000	1 075 000
	1 385 000	1 165 000	1 085 000
	0,95	1,06	0,99
Long term liquidity (leverage, gearing)			
Debt/assets (1)	1 539 000	1 361 000	1 268 200
	2 081 000	1 781 000	1 590 000
	0,74	0,76	0,80
Debt/assets (2)	1 385 000	1 165 000	1 085 000
	2 081 000	1 781 000	1 590 000
	0,67	0,65	0,68
Debt/equity (1)	1 539 000	1 361 000	1 268 200
	542 000	420 000	321 800
	2,84	3,24	3,94
Debt/equity (2)	1 385 000	1 165 000	1 085 000
	696 000	616 000	505 000
	1,99	1,89	2,15
Interest bearing debt/equity (1)	635 000	535 000	520 000
	542 000	420 000	321 800
	1,17	1,27	1,62
Interest bearing debt/equity (2)	635 000	535 000	520 000
	696 000	616 000	505 000
	0,91	0,87	1,03
Interest cover	102 000	184 000	183 000
	4 500	31 000	13 000
	22,67	5,94	14,08
Activity ratios			
Total asset turnover	4 650 000	4 550 000	3 665 000
	2 081 000	1 781 000	1 590 000
	2,23	2,55	2,31
Net asset turnover	4 650 000	4 550 000	3 665 000
	696 000	616 000	505 000
	6,68	7,39	7,26
Fixed asset turnover	4 650 000	4 550 000	3 665 000
	572 000	360 000	315 000
	8,13	12,64	11,63

	1985	1984	1983
Current asset turnover	4 650 000	4 550 000	3 665 000
	1 509 000	1 421 000	1 275 000
	3,08	3,20	2,87
Stock and WIP turnover	4 650 000	4 550 000	3 665 000
(Based on sales in this case)	195 000	185 000	200 000
	23,85	24,59	18,33
Debtors collection period in days	4 650 000	4 550 000	3 665 000
	1 300 000	1 210 000	1 064 000
	102,04	97,07	105,96
Creditors payment period in days	2 230 000	2 165 000	1 627 500
	760 000	600 000	555 000
	124,39	101,13	124,47
Profitability ratios			
Return on equity (1)	122 000	98 000	142 000
	542 000	420 000	321 800
	22,52	23,33	44,13
Return on equity (2)	122 000	98 000	142 000
	696 000	616 000	505 000
	17,53	15,91	28,12
Return on total assets	102 000	184 000	183 000
	2 081 000	1 781 000	1 590 000
	4,90	10,33	11,51
Return on net assets	102 000	184 000	183 000
	696 000	616 000	505 500
	14,66	29,87	36,24
Return on sales (Net margin)	102 000	184 000	183 000
	4 650 000	4 550 000	3 665 000
	2,19	4,04	4,99

(1) Directors' loans treated as debt
(2) Directors' loans treated as equity

Appendix 2

Financial statements of a company quoted on the Johannesburg Stock Exchange

The annual report of Anglo-Alpha Limited occupies the next pages. I should like to express my appreciation to Anglo-Alpha Limited for permission to reproduce these statements and to comment on them.

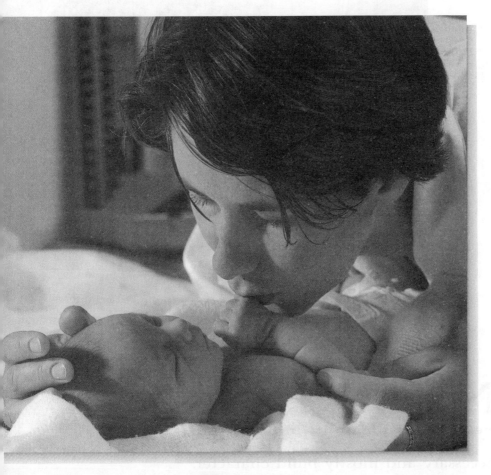

Each new day brings new beginnings, new challenges and new experiences. How we cope with these will depend on how we have been taught by those who have gone before. The success of the future will be influenced by the quality of the example we leave.

1

Not all of life's experiences are welcome or pleasant, but they are necessary and mostly build character. They are part of the subconscious learning process which has no power of discernment. We can, however, choose how we accept them and use them in shaping the future.

Market capitalisation

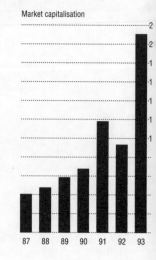

Sales increased by 15,9 per cent due mainly to the inclusion of Pioneer Ready Mixed Concrete's sales with effect from 1 August 1993, moderate price increases and improved product mix in the Stone and Ready Mixed Concrete and Industrial divisions.

Operating profit increased by 36,7 per cent to R199 million on slightly lower sales volumes due mainly to the benefits of productivity improvement plans introduced in 1992. This resulted in an increased margin of 22,7 per cent (1992: 19,3 per cent).

Attributable profit for the year increased by 47,3 per cent due largely to the improved operating margin and relatively low increase in the current cost adjustment. This improvement is, however, off a low base and the profit is only slightly above that achieved in 1989.

Cash available from operations increased by 42,4 per cent to a record R205 million due mainly to the improvement in profitability and lower working capital requirements.

Dividends for the year totalled 175 cents, 15,1 per cent up from 1992, resulting in a cover on a current cost basis of 1,5 times.

Net capital expenditure and investments increased by 34,9 per cent to R112 million and related mainly to replacement of plant and equipment and investments in Parem Enterprises (Pty) Limited, the holding company of Pioneer Ready Mixed Concrete and The Cement Organisation (Swaziland) (Pty) Limited, the holding company of Inter-Africa Supplies (Swaziland) Limited.

Return on net assets improved to 14,6 per cent but is still well below the Company's cost of capital of 18,0 per cent.

Prospects 1994: Sales volumes on average are expected to increase marginally in 1994. Net earnings are forecast to increase by slightly more than inflation in 1994.

| | 31 December | | % |
	1993	1992	change
...les (Rm)	877	757	+ 15,9
...erating profit (Rm)	199	146	+ 36,7
...ofit attributable to ordinary ...areholders (Rm)			
...current cost basis	77	52	+ 47,3
...historical cost basis	127	100	+ 27,2
...ash available from operations (Rm)	205	144	+ 42,4
...vidends per share (cents)	175	152	+ 15,1
...apital expenditure and investments (Rm)	112	83	+ 34,9
...turn on net assets	14,6 %	12,5 %	
...ebt to equity percentage	14,6 %	19,2 %	
...arket capitalisation (Rm)	2 105	932	+125,8

3

A child's development and growth are directly affected by the quality and variety of influences received. Developing the positive influences is to recognise and build on the strengths of others and to form sound, meaningful inter-relationships for the future.

Main Mission

To manufacture and market concrete
and concrete ingredients and other
products allied to the Group's technical
and marketing expertise.

Objectives

Business

- To satisfy customer requirements through superior service and to ensure the prompt, reliable delivery of high quality products.
- To achieve and sustain a growth in sales and earnings to provide shareholders with a competitive return on their investment.
- To at least maintain the real value of shareholders' investment.
- To maintain sound financial strength to support the Group's growth objectives.
- To uphold fair and ethical business practices in achieving the Group's goals.
- To exercise professionalism and leadership in the Group's fields of expertise.

Social

- To develop one of the Group's most important resources – people – and, through positive leadership and participative management, create opportunities and provide an environment in which they can be innovative and stimulated to greater productivity and self-improvement.
- To acknowledge and satisfy the realistic needs and aspirations of employees through enlightened and progressive personnel practices.
- To fulfil the Group's commitment to environmental conservation.
- To participate actively in the development of communities affected by Group operations.
- To contribute to and be constructive in the development of South Africa's social and economic future.

Peter Byland

South Africa is a land of opportunity and I have considerable confidence that we will make the right decisions which will lead to economic prosperity and the development of all South Africans.

Dear stakeholders

Your Company faced yet another difficult trading year to 31 December 1993 due to the continued recessionary conditions in the South African economy aggravated by the political uncertainty and deplorable violence in the country. However, I am able to report that, despite poor trading conditions, the Group's productivity improvement plans, introduced during 1992, were most successful. Accordingly, the Group is able to report improved results for the year.

With inflation adjusted attributable profit after tax at R77 million (1992: R52 million), earnings per share increased by 47,3 per cent from 173 cents to 255 cents.

It is important to note, however, that although the percentage increases are pleasing, they are off a very low base as the Group reflected declining earnings between 1989 and 1992. Sales volumes for the year remained below 1989 levels.

Nevertheless, the Group has still some way to go to achieve its target returns. The return on net assets was 14,6 per cent compared with a target of 18,0 per cent while the return on equity target is 22,0 per cent against 15,4 per cent achieved.

During the year we purchased the remaining 50 per cent interest in Parem Enterprises (Pty) Limited, the holding company of Pioneer Ready Mixed Concrete, because the

company is not only a major user of our products but also is likely to yield significant returns in a growing economy. In addition, we acquired a controlling interest in Inter-Africa Supplies (Swaziland) Limited, a cement blending and trading company, as part of a programme of obtaining sales outlets in key market areas. After restructuring our indirect investment in the concrete paving industry, previously held through a 50 per cent interest in Roozeboom Brick Works (Pty) Limited, we now hold 40 per cent of Grinaker Precast (Pty) Limited. Having re-considered our involvement in coal we concluded that the investment was no longer appropriate for Anglo-Alpha. We have accordingly disposed of our interest in East Rand Coal Holdings (Pty) Limited and also entered into an agreement for the conditional sale of our interest in Anglovaal Coal Holdings (Pty) Limited.

As a result of a 42,4 per cent increase in cash available from operations, to R205 million, we were able to fund the cost of these investments internally as well as repay borrowings.

In the light of the improved results, the Board of Directors has declared a total dividend for the year of 175 cents per share resulting in a dividend cover of 1,5 times on a current cost basis (1992: 1,1 times). Although this cover is below the Group's target of 2,0 times, the Board is satisfied that in the absence of planned major capital expenditure over the next five years as

well as the present favourable level of cash flow, the lower cover is justified.

In aggregate, the success of management's hands-on approach in positioning the Group to remain competitive, the positive signs of an economic upturn and an acceptable outcome to the forthcoming elections leave me optimistic about the future of the Group and South Africa.

There is still uncertainty about future economic and fiscal policy in South Africa, particularly as it will impact on the revenue requirements of the new government. Its focus will have to be on economic growth, thereby creating additional employment and being able to provide additional housing. This is required in order to meet the expectations of the majority of South Africans. In this regard my fervent wish is for responsible communication and action, not rhetoric, from all political parties now and during the election and for consultation with business and labour before the implementation of far-reaching legislation which could harm investment and thus the very objectives the new government will be trying to achieve.

Certain suggestions on the future ownership and exploitation of the mineral wealth of South Africa have recently received much publicity. These are naturally of concern to us being, as we are, dependant on mining. These proposals if implemented, aside from the negative impact that they have already had on investor confidence, could have a serious impact on the viability of the building material supply industry, particularly that of the stone and sand aggregate industry weakened as it has been from years of diminishing demand and increased competition from alternative products.

South Africa is a land of opportunity and I have considerable confidence that we will make the right decisions which will lead to economic prosperity and the development of all South Africans.

The cement cartel

South Africa is fortunately self-sufficient in terms of cement supply, having a healthy industry with adequate spare capacity to meet the immediate future needs of the new South Africa at lowest delivered costs which arise through supplying from the closest factory. It is therefore ironic that whilst other African countries are offering incentives in the form of tax holidays, tariff protection and soft loans, to establish or rehabilitate cement manufacturing plants, and have considerably higher prices, critics of the local industry call for the termination of the present selling arrangements of the South African cement producers.

Unlike many other countries which can rely on neighbours for cement in times of shortage, South Africa is remote from those countries with the capacity to supply. Consequently, imported cement, particularly in the case of inland markets such as the PWV, would be extremely expensive and consume large amounts of foreign exchange, which of course is the reason why countries dependant on imports are so anxious to become self-sufficient themselves in this regard.

The selling arrangements of the South African cement producers were implemented, with the approval of the authorities, over 20 years ago and were designed to improve efficiency and to ensure that no customers would be prejudiced by virtue of their location during periods of possible product shortage. Prior to this, customers in remote areas experienced shortages during periods of high demand as the returns earned by the producers on such deliveries were less attractive than sales to customers closer to the cement factories. These arrangements have been amended from time to time to take into account concerns expressed by the Industry's

customers and by Government.

The selling arrangements also go a long way toward reducing the risk of what is traditionally, because of its capital intensity, a high risk business. The reduced risk in turn permits lower returns, lower selling prices and gives financiers (banks and shareholders) the confidence to make investments in the Industry. It also affords the Industry the confidence to undertake timeous capacity expansion rather than being reactive to product shortages.

The pricing system applied by the producers offers stability and consistency, is both logical and transparent and, with the exception of volume discounts, makes no distinction between customers, thus ensuring everyone can compete on equal terms. If the pricing system were to fall away, for whatever reason, overseas experience is that the larger, more powerful customers would succeed in negotiating even larger discounts at the expense of smaller operators.

The Competition Board, after a detailed investigation, including a visit to North and South America, Europe and the Far East, concluded that the South African Cement Industry's selling arrangements were in the interests of customers and producers alike and granted the Industry an exemption from the prohibitions of the Competitions Act. There has been no change in subsequent events or circumstances that would seem to justify a review of this exemption and its withdrawal would not only jeopardise the Industry, but also place customers, particularly those inland, at the mercy of expensive imported cement.

Cement will be a vital material in a future South Africa and the general and free availability of a quality product at reasonable prices is essential.

Prospects

The present uncertain economic and political climate in South Africa makes it difficult to forecast the Group's performance in 1994. However, as mentioned earlier, I am confident about the future prospects for the country.

From all appearances South Africa is experiencing a bottoming-out of its economic recession and the broad consensus amongst economists is that

growth in the gross domestic product for 1994 will be approximately 2 per cent. Inflation, measured by the change in the consumer price index, should be between 8 and 9 per cent for the year while the prime overdraft rate is expected to be down by a further 1 or 2 per cent from the present 15,25 per cent. Accordingly, we are forecasting a modest increase in sales volumes which, together with continued successful cost containment, should lead to a rate of increase in profitability slightly in excess of the inflation rate. The Group's cash flow is expected to decline by 3 per cent due mainly to the payment of increased tax.

Directorate

On 4 August 1993 Mr Don Mkhwanazi was appointed a non-executive director of the Company to fill a vacancy on the Board. His business and marketing expertise qualify him to contribute to the Board's deliberations. I welcome him and look forward to his contribution to the affairs of the Group.

Appreciation

I am grateful to my fellow directors for their support and valuable guidance during the year as well as to the management of the Anglo-Alpha Group for their loyalty and commitment to its future. Management's hands-on approach has enabled Anglo-Alpha to reflect satisfactory results in difficult circumstances.

My thanks also go to the associate service organisations: Cement Distributors SA; The Portland Cement Institute and the South African Cement Producers Association for their assistance and contribution to our business activities.

Finally, I thank our customers for their support and Anglo-Alpha Group employees for their loyalty and consistent contribution in a most challenging year.

Yours sincerely

P Byland
9 February 1994

Johan Pretorius

I am pleased to report that the Group's results reflect a significant improvement ... It must, however, be borne in mind that the improvement is off a low base ...

Performance review

As a result of the continued recessionary conditions in the South African economy during 1993, demand for the Group's products in general declined compared with 1992.

Despite this, I am pleased to report that the Group's results reflect a significant improvement due mainly to the productivity improvement plans introduced during 1992. It must, however, be borne in mind that the improvement in our results is off a low base as the Group has reflected declining earnings during the period 1989-1992 as a result of the poor trading conditions in South Africa. This year's earnings are only in line with those achieved in 1989. In addition, the target returns on net assets and equity are still not being achieved.

Operating profit improved by 36,7 per cent to R199 million due mainly to the cost efficiencies referred to and the operating margin accordingly increased from 19,3 per cent to 22,7 per cent.

As a result of the decline in interest rates, the Group's borrowing costs were 19,6 per cent lower at R24 million (1992: R30 million).

The taxation charge increased by 96,2 per cent to R64 million (1992: R32 million) due to the higher profitability and the effective tax rate increasing from 24,5 per cent to 33,4 per cent.

Despite the increase in the taxation charge, profit attributable to ordinary shareholders increased by 47,3 per cent to R77 million (1992: R52 million). On a historical cost basis, profit after tax increased by 27,2 per cent to R127 million (1992: R100 million).

Capital expenditure and investments

Net capital expenditure and investments for the year totalled R112 million compared with R83 million in 1992. The major portion of this expenditure related to the replacement of plant and equipment and investments.

During the year Parem Enterprises (Pty) Limited which trades under the name of Pioneer Ready Mixed Concrete became a wholly-owned subsidiary of the Company and now forms part of our renamed Stone and Ready Mixed Concrete Division. This investment complements our existing construction aggregate business. Previously we held 50 per cent of Parem. In addition, the Group acquired a controlling interest in The Cement Organisation (Swaziland) (Pty) Limited, the holding company of Inter-Africa Supplies (Swaziland) Limited, a cement blending and trading company in Swaziland. We restructured our indirect investment in the concrete paving industry, previously held through a 50 per cent interest in Roozeboom Brick Works (Pty) Limited, and now hold a 50 per cent interest in Grinaker Precast (Pty) Limited. We also disposed of our interest in East Rand Coal Holdings (Pty) Limited and also entered into an agreement for the conditional sale of our interest in Anglovaal Coal Holdings (Pty) Limited.

Capital expenditure and investments for the period 1994 to 1998 are estimated to total R555 million (present-day cost) including pre-production finance costs.

Of this amount R94 million is for expansion, R400 million is for the replacement of plant and equipment and R61 million for quality-of-worklife improvements.

The expansion expenditure includes expanding the wet mill and flotation plant at Umzimkulu Carbonates, palletising and shrink-wrapping facilities, a cement blending plant and other investment opportunities.

Financial strength
The Group remained in a financially sound position with cash available from operations increasing by 42,4 per cent to R205 million (1992: R144 million). This was due mainly to the improved profitability and working capital management and enabled the Group to reduce borrowings and fund the cost of its investments internally.

Cash flow as a percentage of total interest bearing and non-interest bearing debt amounted to 55,3 per cent (1992: 42,2 per cent). The cash flow per share at 683 cents (1992: 479 cents) is 2,7 times earnings per share.

Interest bearing borrowings, net of cash resources, at year-end amounted to R126 million (1992: R151 million) resulting in the debt to equity percentage decreasing to 14,6 per cent (1992: 19,2 per cent). This is below the Group's target of 33 to 67 per cent and it can borrow an additional R448 million before reaching the upper level of its target range.

In view of the higher level of earnings and the decrease in borrowing costs, the interest cover increased from 5,2 times in 1992 to 8,5 times.

The 1994 business plan indicates that after providing for dividends and capital expenditure, the Group should have a net cash inflow which will contribute to the further reduction in borrowings.

Appreciation
I thank all employees in the Anglo-Alpha Group for their loyalty, dedication and contribution to the success we have achieved in 1993. I know it's not been an easy year especially with the social stresses caused by continued violence, political uncertainty and retrenchments.

Thank you too, to my colleagues on the Board and to the Group Executive Committee for their loyalty and commitment to making Anglo-Alpha the success it is today.

J G Pretorius

9 February 1994

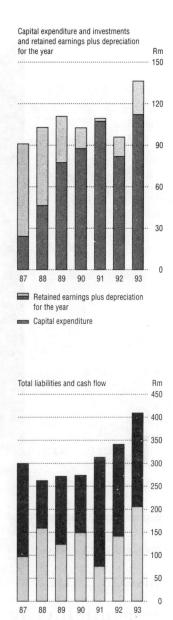

Capital expenditure and investments and retained earnings plus depreciation for the year | Rm

87 88 89 90 91 92 93

▨ Retained earnings plus depreciation for the year
▬ Capital expenditure

Total liabilities and cash flow | Rm

87 88 89 90 91 92 93

▬ Total liabilities
▭ Cash flow

Thandere are
certain basic
e l e m e n t s
necessary to
sustain life.
Responsibility for these elements

belongs to everyone and requires

proper planning and practical strategies

to ensure a continuing future for all.

10

forum and to give guidance on particular issues.

The Group does not tolerate any discriminatory practices and recently introduced a policy and procedure concerning the management of harassment in the workplace. Our non-discriminatory practices were publicly recognised by the Federation of Business and Professional Women at their annual Gold Medal Award function. Anglo-Alpha won the Award in 1990 and was a finalist in 1992 and 1993.

The Company's approach to improvements in conditions of employment for the coming year has been a conservative one, notwithstanding the encouraging financial results at year-end. In recent years the Company has granted overall increases at least in line with inflationary trends; this has been in pursuance of Anglo-Alpha's remuneration philosophy and also in order to achieve and maintain a consistent wage curve and compensation integrity within the Company. The effect has been to maintain salary and wage increases which have been closely comparable to, but marginally favourable as against the CPI during the period 1989 to 1993.

Anglo-Alpha recognises that many of its employees face difficult circumstances resulting from the political instability and prevailing economic recessionary conditions in South Africa. In this regard the Group's managers are encouraged to keep an "open door" policy and to assist employees by providing support counselling by suitably trained and qualified people.

It is expected that the forthcoming pre and post election periods will be ones of further political uncertainty and violence. If this scenario materialises, the Group will continue to do its utmost to ensure the safety of each employee at the workplace.

Industrial relations

The Group experienced another year of industrial peace during 1993. This was due mainly to the positive relationships established with representative trade unions and employees through open and honest communication and the emphasis placed on the training of our representatives, supervisors and managers in industrial relations. This has created an environment of trust and a willingness to negotiate.

To date the Group has signed twenty-three recognition agreements with nine different representative trade unions.

Another contributing factor to Anglo-Alpha's sound industrial relations is the production of an annual employee report in five languages. This document is aimed at keeping employees informed about the Group's activities which, we believe, they have a right to know. In fact, we feel so strongly about the value of communicating with employees that Anglo-Alpha sponsors an employee report competition presented by The South African Institute of Chartered Accountants.

Training

The Anglo-Alpha Group believes that for employees to play their full role in achieving corporate and personal objectives, it is essential that a comprehensive and effective training system exists at all levels. Despite the difficult economic situation in South Africa, the Group has maintained its focus on training.

Of importance is on-the-job training provided for all employees to ensure the development of skills suitable to our industry.

Of particular relevance is a training programme designed to train trainers to prepare employees for voting in the forthcoming elections. This programme is complete and has been implemented at some of our operations. It is envisaged that the trainers will also go into the various communities around the Group's operations to educate them on the voting process. Forty-five trainers, including shop stewards, participated in this programme. This was achieved at minimum cost and has been effective and well received.

In 1993 the Group registered 4 512 formal course attendances at a total cost of R4,6 million. Particularly noteworthy was the progress made in cross-cultural training as well as the implementation of the Group's five year overseas training programme.

Three of the apprentices trained at the Group's technical training centre did exceptionally well in their respective fields in the South African Skills

Employees

Employee well-being is of prime importance at Anglo-Alpha. Being a caring organisation of integrity summarises the contents of the Group's Social Policy which is a document, first published in 1976, outlining the expected approach and attitude towards all employees.

The Social Policy has been developed in consultation with employees and is gularly reviewed and updated to sure that it remains current in dressing the needs of employees in e broader South African vironment. To ensure the success of e Policy, the Group's Human sources Department, together with erational management, conducted gular Social Policy implementation ive audits during the year. These dits were intended not only to sure compliance with the Policy but so to provide an experience-sharing competition and one of them was chosen to represent South Africa in the International Skills Olympics held in Taiwan.

New directions in training for the future include mentoring and coaching skills for supervisors and managers and a move to formalise self-directed work teams.

Affirmative training

The Group remains firmly committed to the implementation of affirmative training. During 1993 a task force reviewed our affirmative training policy which was first introduced in 1978. The policy builds on the principles embodied in the Group's Social Policy and the already established non-discriminatory practices of the Group.

Manpower planning in the Group continued to focus on strengthening Anglo-Alpha's technical competence and multi-skilling.

Benefits and facilities

The Anglo-Alpha Group provides health care, retirement, disability and death benefits for all employees.

As a result of rising medical attention and medicine costs, the Group established a task force to evaluate alternative schemes to provide the best possible health care at the lowest possible cost. The task force has made its findings known to management who will in turn evaluate and authorise any changes beneficial to the Group.

One significant change already implemented is that it is no longer compulsory for an employee to be a member of the medical aid scheme.

The Group has also introduced retirement planning flexibility and has offered employees the choice of remaining members of the Pension Fund or of joining a newly formed employees' provident fund.

Employees are encouraged to purchase their own homes and to this end the Group provides financial assistance in the form of cash loans for improvements and guarantees to financial institutions in order to make larger sums available to employees to acquire homes. This policy has been actively pursued for 15 years, having been finalised and implemented since 1979.

Care for employees on retirement continued under the Pensioner Assistance Programme which is designed to teach past employees to supplement their income through self-help programmes.

Safety

Anglo-Alpha believes that it is the right of every employee to work in a safe and healthy environment and the Group is committed to achieving the highest safety standards.

Eight operations achieved 5 star NOSA ratings, five have 4 star ratings and four operations have been awarded NOSCARs, NOSA's supreme award. Our Roodepoort cement plant has achieved its 18th NOSCAR.

General public

The Group's environmental conservation and property rehabilitation efforts continued during the year.

Further to the establishment of a Group Environmental Consultant portfolio during 1992, an environmental policy will be introduced during 1994. This policy is consistent with the internationally accepted "principles of sustainable development".

An integral part of the policy is the Anglo-Alpha "code of practice" which defines the Group's standards, applicable legislation and work practices conducive to the improvement of Anglo-Alpha's environmental performance. The "code" will form part of the Group's standard operating procedures and will be subject to annual internal audit.

During the year the Group financially supported a wide variety of community projects, social, cultural and environmental organisations as part of its Corporate Social Investment programme. We regard this programme as being very important in contributing to the restructuring of the communities in which we operate.

12

Human nature drives us towards independence which is an admirable goal for all. To achieve it requires trust, courage and a belief in the people entrusted with our future.

Value Added Statement

for the year ended 31 December 1993

The Statement reflects the value that the Group's activities add to the cost of the raw materials and services used to manufacture its products.

The statement below, compiled on a current cost basis, details how the value added is applied to meet certain obligations, reward those responsible for its creation and the portion that is reinvested in the business for the continued operation and expansion of the Group.

	Note	1993 Rm	%	1992 Rm	%	1991 Rm	%	1990 Rm	%	1989 Rm	%
Sale of goods and services		877		757		728		697		625	
Less: Cost of materials and services		412		374		367		339		287	
Value added from trading operations		465		383		361		358		338	
Add: Income from investments		15		16		13		10		14	
Total value added	1	480		399		374		368		352	
Distributed as follows:											
Employees Salaries, wages, pensions and other benefits	2	204	42,5	187	46,7	177	47,3	150	40,9	130	36,9
Providers of finance Borrowing costs	3	24	5,0	30	7,6	21	5,7	14	3,8	18	5,1
Government Taxation	4	67	13,9	34	8,5	26	6,9	62	16,8	58	16,6
Providers of capital		53	11,0	46	11,5	46	12,2	39	10,6	34	9,7
Minority shareholders		–	–	–	–	–	–	(1)	(0,1)	(1)	(0,1)
Dividends to ordinary shareholders		53	11,0	46	11,5	46	12,2	40	10,7	35	9,8
Replacement of assets Depreciation	5	108	22,6	96	24,1	92	24,6	82	22,3	76	21,5
Expansion and growth Retained earnings for year	6	24	5,0	6	1,6	12	3,3	21	5,6	36	10,2
		480	100,0	399	100,0	374	100,0	368	100,0	352	100,0

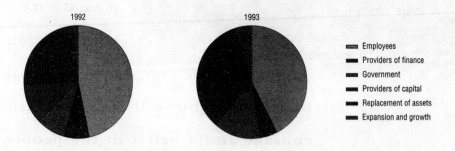

1992   1993

- Employees
- Providers of finance
- Government
- Providers of capital
- Replacement of assets
- Expansion and growth

14

Total value added increased by 20,0 per cent due mainly to the 15,9 per cent increase in the sale of goods and services which was partly offset by a 10,4 per cent increase in the cost of materials and services following the inclusion of the operations of Pioneer Ready Mixed Concrete from August 1993.

The portion of value added distributed to employees increased by 9,2 per cent to R204 million (1992: R187 million) which is in line with the inflation rate for 1993.

Resignations and dismissals amounted to 122 for the year which, together with 122 retrenchments, resulted in a staff turnover of 7,6 per cent. Excluding retrenchments, staff turnover was only 3,7 per cent.

Staff complement of the Group at 31 December comprised:

	1993	1992
* Sales and marketing	735	311
* Production and technical	3 066	3 016
* Administration	127	132
	3 928	3 459

Borrowing costs include the dividend of R63 000 (1992: R168 000) paid to the holder of the cumulative redeemable preference shares.

Taxation paid includes:	1993 Rm	1992 Rm
Amounts included in taxation distribution:	67	34
SA normal tax and deferred tax	64	32
Regional Service Council levies	2	2
Rates and taxes paid to local authorities	2	1
	68	35
Less: Government grants	(1)	(1)

Other exchanges with the Government include value-added tax levied on purchases, customs duties, import surcharges and excise tax.

The total amount reflected above excludes the following amounts collected by the Group on behalf of Government:

Value-added tax charged on supplies	128	81
PAYE and SITE deducted from employees' remuneration	30	27
Non-resident shareholders' tax deducted from dividends paid	–	1
	158	109

Depreciation comprises:

Historical cost depreciation	60	52
Current cost depreciation	87	81
	147	133
Financial gearing adjustment	(39)	(37)
	108	96

Retained earnings for the year excludes extraordinary items and share of earnings retained by associates so as not to distort the value added to raw materials.

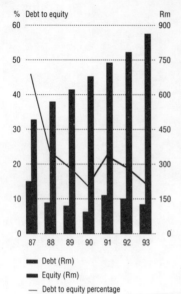

% Debt to equity   Rm
60 ·· 900

50 ·· 750

40 ·· 600

30 ·· 450

20 ·· 300

10 ·· 150

 0   0
   87   88   89   90   91   92   93

- ■ Debt (Rm)
- ■ Equity (Rm)
- — Debt to equity percentage

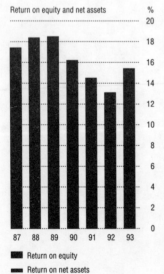

Return on equity and net assets   %
·· 20

·· 18

·· 16

·· 14

·· 12

·· 10

··· 8

··· 6

··· 4

··· 2

                                                             0
   87   88   89   90   91   92   93

- ■ Return on equity
- ■ Return on net assets

	ANNUAL COMPOUND GROWTH 1987-1993 %	1993 Rm	1992 Rm	1991 Rm	1990 Rm	1989 Rm	1988 Rm	198 Rr
RESULTS								
Sales	13,1	877,2	757,0	728,2	697,3	624,7	530,6	418,
Operating profit	12,0	199,3	145,9	135,6	167,8	169,2	149,5	100,
Income from investments		15,2	16,3	13,1	9,5	13,9	8,8	3,
Profit before borrowing costs, taxation and current cost adjustment	12,7	214,5	162,2	148,7	177,3	183,1	158,3	104,
Borrowing costs		24,2	30,0	21,0	13,6	17,5	19,0	23,
Profit before taxation and current cost adjustment	15,2	190,3	132,2	127,7	163,7	165,6	139,3	81,
Taxation		63,5	32,4	24,4	58,6	55,0	41,1	0,
Preference dividends		0,1	0,2	0,3	0,4	0,5	0,6	0,
Outside shareholders' interest		–	–	–	(0,5)	(0,3)	–	0,
Profit before current cost adjustment attributable to ordinary shareholders	7,9	126,7	99,6	103,0	105,2	110,4	97,6	80,
Current cost adjustment		50,1	47,6	45,0	45,0	39,9	32,4	26,
Profit attributable to ordinary shareholders	6,2	76,6	52,0	58,0	60,2	70,5	65,2	53,
Share of equity earnings retained by associates		1,9	0,3	5,3	5,2	7,2	9,0	0,
Extraordinary items		2,0	(6,9)	–	(5,0)	(1,2)	(2,5)	
Profit for year	6,9	80,5	45,4	63,3	60,4	76,5	71,7	54,
FINANCIAL POSITION								
Employment of capital								
Property, plant and equipment		1 419,4	1 359,7	1 443,1	1 390,4	1 241,4	1 146,2	1 094,
Investments		218,0	177,8	152,2	120,0	115,0	90,9	95,
Current assets		415,0	347,1	303,6	267,0	248,9	201,9	169,
Total assets	7,1	2 052,4	1 884,6	1 898,9	1 777,4	1 605,3	1 439,0	1 359,
Non-interest bearing debt		228,1	141,5	127,9	172,5	151,0	124,9	74,
	6,0	1 824,3	1 743,1	1 771,0	1 604,9	1 454,3	1 314,1	1 285,
Capital employed								
Stated capital		442,3	413,2	366,8	304,3	251,2	226,5	226,
Non-distributable reserves		271,1	250,0	248,8	266,3	277,6	262,2	41,
Retained earnings		143,8	121,6	122,2	109,9	93,4	80,7	223,
Ordinary shareholders' equity – historical value	9,7	857,2	784,8	737,8	680,5	622,2	569,4	491,
Capital revaluation reserve		773,9	753,3	842,5	816,7	707,5	605,8	566,
Ordinary shareholders' equity – current value	7,5	1 631,1	1 538,1	1 580,3	1 497,2	1 329,7	1 175,2	1 058,
Outside shareholders' interest		4,8	0,1	0,1	0,7	1,3	0,1	0,
Tax deferments		7,8	5,1	5,2	5,8	2,7	1,5	1,
Interest bearing long-term borrowings		125,0	161,5	139,8	86,0	78,0	87,1	158,
Capital employed	6,4	1 768,7	1 704,8	1 725,4	1 589,7	1 411,7	1 263,9	1 217,
Current portion of long-term borrowings		55,6	38,3	45,6	15,2	42,6	50,2	67,
Total capital employed	6,0	1 824,3	1 743,1	1 771,0	1 604,9	1 454,3	1 314,1	1 285,
CASH FLOW INFORMATION								
Cash available from operations	13,3	205,4	144,2	75,8	149,1	123,3	158,9	96,
Ordinary dividends		(46,9)	(45,7)	(40,6)	(35,5)	(31,6)	(22,3)	(19,
Cash retained from operations		158,5	98,5	35,2	113,6	91,7	136,6	77,
Net capital and investment expenditure		(112,2)	(83,1)	(107,5)	(87,7)	(77,6)	(46,5)	(24,
Net inflow/(outflow) for the year		46,3	15,4	(72,3)	25,9	14,1	90,1	53,

	ANNUAL COMPOUND GROWTH 1987-1993 %	1993	1992	1991	1990	1989	1988	1987
...atistics								
...rnings, dividends and ordinary shares								
...rnings per share								
...current cost basis	6,2	254,9c	173,0c	192,9c	200,1c	234,3c	216,8c	177,5c
...historical cost basis	7,9	421,5c	331,3c	342,6c	349,8c	367,2c	324,6c	266,9c
...vidends per share	16,5	175,0c	152,0c	152,0c	132,0c	115,0c	95,0c	70,0c
...vidend covered by earnings								
...current cost basis		1,5	1,1	1,3	1,5	2,0	2,3	2,5
...historical cost basis		2,4	2,2	2,3	2,7	3,2	3,4	3,8
...et worth per share								
...current cost basis	7,5	5 423c	5 114c	5 254c	4 978c	4 421c	3 907c	3 518c
...historical cost basis	9,7	2 850c	2 609c	2 453c	2 262c	2 069c	1 893c	1 633c
...umber of shares in issue (000)		30 077	30 077	30 077	30 077	30 077	30 077	30 077
ash flow								
...ash flow margin		23,4%	19,0%	10,4%	21,4%	19,7%	29,9%	23,2%
...ash flow per share	13,3	682,8c	479,4c	252,1c	495,7c	410,0c	528,2c	322,1c
...vidend covered by cash flow		3,9	3,2	1,7	3,8	3,6	5,6	4,6
...rrowing costs covered by cash flow		9,1	5,6	4,3	10,7	7,8	9,0	5,0
...rrowings covered by cash flow		1,1	0,7	0,4	1,5	1,0	1,2	0,4
...ash efficiency ratio		1,0	1,0	0,6	0,9	0,7	1,1	1,0
...ash flow return on net assets		20,1%	15,0%	8,8%	19,4%	17,0%	22,3%	13,5%
ofitability, liquidity and leverage								
...erating profit as a percentage								
...sales		22,7%	19,3%	18,6%	24,1%	27,1%	28,2%	24,1%
...ective tax rate		33,4%	24,5%	19,1%	35,8%	33,2%	29,5%	0,2%
...turn on net assets		14,6%	12,5%	13,4%	14,7%	16,5%	15,1%	13,0%
...turn on equity		15,4%	13,1%	14,5%	16,2%	18,5%	18,4%	17,4%
...ebt to equity percentage		14,6%	19,2%	22,5%	13,8%	19,2%	23,6%	45,7%
...urrent ratio		1,4	1,8	1,6	1,3	1,2	1,0	1,1
...rrowing costs covered by earnings		8,5	5,2	6,6	11,6	10,1	8,0	4,3
ock exchange performance								
...arket value per share								
...at year end	31,6	7 000c	3 100c	3 925c	2 250c	1 950c	1 575c	1 350c
...highest		7 000c	4 350c	4 300c	2 600c	2 450c	1 575c	1 850c
...owest		3 100c	2 400c	2 250c	1 950c	1 575c	1 250c	1 200c
...erage price of shares traded		3 926c	3 167c	3 805c	2 427c	2 218c	1 378c	1 542c
...lue of shares traded (R000)		48 491	29 581	22 295	20 851	18 101	11 174	18 966
...umber of share transactions recorded		720	387	368	466	639	449	606
...are volumes traded (000)		1 235	934	586	859	816	811	1 230
...are volumes traded as a percentage								
...total issued shares		4,1%	3,1%	1,9%	2,9%	2,7%	2,7%	4,1%
...are price index								
...ase: January 1987 = 100)		583,3	258,3	327,1	187,5	162,5	131,3	112,5
...E actuaries index – industrial								
...ase: January 1987 = 100)		391,6	306,6	293,0	212,1	196,0	136,5	101,6
...E actuaries index – building and ...nstruction								
...ase: January 1987 = 100)		414,6	211,7	246,5	168,5	154,3	138,1	100,6
...rnings yield								
...urrent cost basis		3,6%	5,6%	4,9%	8,9%	12,0%	13,8%	13,1%
...historical cost basis		6,0%	10,7%	8,7%	15,5%	18,8%	20,6%	19,8%
...vidend yield		2,5%	4,9%	3,9%	5,9%	5,9%	6,0%	5,2%
mployees								
...umber of employees		3 928	3 459	3 991	4 236	4 365	4 105	3 992
...les per employee		R223 312	R218 842	R182 467	R164 607	R143 107	R129 251	R104 705
...erating profit per employee		R 50 750	R 42 169	R 33 989	R 39 606	R 38 762	R 36 426	R 25 273
...xed assets per employee		R196 863	R202 192	R171 321	R151 427	R136 703	R138 158	R141 337
...lue added per employee		R122 087	R115 496	R 93 788	R 86 800	R 80 684	R 72 618	R 56 708
oductivity index		1,23	1,18	1,17	1,23	1,30	1,31	1,23

NOTES

1. All ratios and statistics exclude the asset revaluation reserve except the ratios which are shown on a current cost basis.

2. The redeemable preference share capital is included as interest bearing debt.

3. Earnings exclude the Group's share of earnings retained by associates and extraordinary items.

DEFINITIONS

1. *Earnings per share* – profit attributable to ordinary shareholders divided by the number of shares in issue during the year.

2. *Dividend cover* – earnings/cash flow per share divided by dividends per share.

3. *Net worth per share* – ordinary shareholders' equity divided by number of shares in issue.

4. *Cash flow* – cash available from operations.

5. *Cash flow per share* – cash flow divided by the number of shares in issue during the year.

6. *Borrowing costs covered by cash flow* – cash flow before borrowing costs, including preference dividends, divided by borrowing costs paid including borrowing costs capitalised, preference dividends and lease finance charges.

7. *Borrowings covered by cash flow* – cash flow divided by interest bearing long-term borrowings.

8. *Cash efficiency ratio* – cash flow divided by operating profit.

9. *Cash flow margin* – cash flow expressed as a percentage of sales.

10. *Cash flow return on net assets* – cash flow expressed as a percentage of average net assets.

11. *Return on net assets* – profit after taxation before borrowing costs adjusted for taxation expressed as a percentage of average net assets.

12. *Return on equity* – profit attributable to ordinary shareholders expressed as a percentage of average ordinary shareholders' equity.

13. *Debt to equity percentage* – interest bearing borrowings net of cash resources expressed as a percentage of ordinary shareholders' equity and outside shareholders' interest.

14. *Current ratio* – current assets divided by current liabilities.

15. *Borrowing costs covered by earnings* – profit before borrowing costs, tax and current cost adjustment divided by borrowing costs paid including borrowing costs capitalised, preference dividends and lease finance charges.

16. *Earnings yield* – earnings per share as a percentage of market value per share at year-end.

17. *Dividend yield* – dividends per share as a percentage of market value per share at year-end.

18. *Productivity index* – sales divided by total current cost excluding borrowing costs and taxation.

The setting of financial objectives and the establishment of sound financial policies are the standards against which the Group can measure the quality of its performance in striving to maximise shareholders' wealth.

These objectives and policies are reviewed on a regular basis and, if required, amended to reflect changing circumstances.

The Group's target returns are based on market-related returns required by investors and lenders of capital. In comparing the Group's performance against its targets, th target returns on net assets and equity are calculated on a historical cost basis.

The Group's actual performance against the financial targets is outlined below.

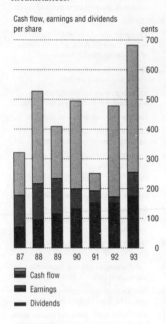

Cash flow, earnings and dividends per share — cents

- 700
- 600
- 500
- 400
- 300
- 200
- 100
- 0

87 88 89 90 91 92 93

■ Cash flow
■ Earnings
▬ Dividends

	Target	Actual 1993	1992	Averag 1987-199
Return on net assets	18%	14,6%	12,5%	14,2
Return on equity	22%	15,4%	13,1%	16,2
Debt to equity percentage	33-67%	14,6%	19,2%	22,6
Dividend cover	2,0	1,5	1,1	1

Return on net assets

The target return on net assets is to at least equal the Group's overall cost of capital which serves as a basis for investment evaluation. Cost of capital is the Group's weighted average cost of debt and equity.

Cost of equity is estimated by reference to the capital asset pricing model and other recognised methods.

The return achieved for 1993 reflects an increase over 1992 due mainly to the increased profitability achieved as a result of the productivity improvement plans introduced, the reduction of unutilised assets and effective working capital management. The return, however, remains below the target due to the under-utilisation of capacity.

The low average return is the result of the poor performance of the South African economy during the past seven years as evidenced by the 2,1 per cent real annual compound decline in Gross Domestic Fixed Investment over the same period.

Return on equity

It is the Group's policy to use financial leverage to earn a return on equity in excess of the return on net assets. The return for 1993 improved due to a 27,2 per cent increase in historical cost profit for the year.

The return achieved for 1993 remains below the target of 22 per cent due mainly to the low return on net assets and low level of debt.

Debt to equity percentage

The Group's target debt to equity is to be within the stated range depending on capital expenditure requirements, economic circumstances and the cost of debt.

The debt to equity percentage for the current year remained below the target in the absence of any major expansion expenditure.

The Group's business plan indicates that the debt to equity percentage is expected to decline further.

Dividend cover

The objective is to achieve an optimum long-term balance between dividends and retentions. The policy is to achieve an average dividend growth higher than the inflation rate. Dividends are to be covered 2,0 times on average by current cost earnings.

Although the cover for 1993 of 1,5 is below the target, management is of the opinion that the present high level of cash flow and relatively lower estimated capital expenditure in the next five years permits the lower cover.

The compound growth in dividends for the past seven years was 16,5 per cent compared to an average inflation rate for the same period of 13,7 per cent.

December 1993

Size of holding		Number of shareholders	% of total	Number of shares	% of total
1	–	500	2 838	80,6	540 528	1,8
501	–	1 000	263	7,5	212 988	0,7
1 001	–	5 000	323	9,2	774 222	2,6
5 001	–	10 000	33	0,9	261 545	0,9
10 001	–	50 000	32	0,9	733 707	2,4
50 001	–	100 000	10	0,3	782 177	2,6
+ 100 000			21	0,6	26 771 681	89,0
			3 520	100,0	30 076 848	100,0

	Number of shareholders	Number of shares	% of total
nsion funds, insurance companies, banks and her institutions	50	4 481 075	14,9
her corporate bodies	121	5 619 230	18,7
dividuals	3 347	1 739 156	5,8
areholders with an interest of 5% or more in the ued capital:			
ltur Investments Limited	1	16 475 596	54,8
A Mutual Group	1	1 761 791	5,8
	3 520	30 076 848	100,0

cluded above are the following beneficial shareholdings of Directors and Group Executives.

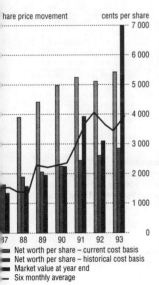

share price movement   cents per share

- ▬ Net worth per share – current cost basis
- ▬ Net worth per share – historical cost basis
- ▬ Market value at year end
- ▬ Six monthly average

	Beneficial		Held in terms of the Employees' Share Participation Scheme	
	1993	1992	1993	1992
B E Hersov	1 000	1 000		
D R Baker	1 000	1 000		
R Bock	15 000		22 500	33 750
M B Burgess	2 000	2 000		
M Germena	5 750			7 500
M M Doyle			22 500	18 750
P Ferreira	8 500		18 750	23 500
Clive S Menell	400	400		
J G Pretorius			59 500	62 500
Francis J Ridsdale	7 000	7 000		
A E Schrafl	73 000	73 000		
R F C Searle			25 500	23 000
R L Straszacker	400	400		
T G Wagner			25 000	20 500

Mr M B Burgess has disposed of his 2 000 shares subsequent to 31 December 1993.

The Company has not been notified of any other changes in these interests during the period 1 January 1994 to the date of this Report.

The Directors have pleasure in presenting their report for the year ended 31 December 1993.

Nature of business
There has been no change in the nature of business since the previous report.

General review of operations
Despite poor trading conditions and lower sales volumes, operating profit increased by 36,7 per cent to R199,3 million (1992: R145,9 million) due mainly to the cost efficiencies introduced during 1992.

The performance of the Group in the six months ended 30 June 1993 and 31 December 1993 respectively, compared with the same periods last year, is reflected in the following salient features:

	Total 1993 Rm	31.12.93 Rm	30.06.93 Rm	Total 1992 Rm	31.12.92 Rm	30.06.92 Rm
Sales	877,2	472,5	404,7	757,0	382,2	374,8
Profit attributable to ordinary shareholders:						
– current cost basis	76,7	52,1	24,6	52,0	33,1	18,9
– historical cost basis	126,8	74,8	52,0	99,6	56,5	43,1

Employees' Share Participation Scheme
The following movement of shares took place during the year:

Shares held by employees at 31 December 1992	868 70
Shares allocated during the year	76 25
Shares transferred to participants being fully paid for	(160 15
Shares held by employees at 31 December 1993	784 80
Shares available per shareholder approval	3 007 68
Available for future allocations	2 222 88

Share Scheme shares were acquired on the open market b the Trustees using loan funds provided by the Company terms of the Scheme Trust Deed.

Divisional contributions to Group sales, operating profit, cash flow and net operating assets are detailed below:

	Sales				Operating profit				Cash flow				Net operating assets**			
	1993		1992		1993		1992		1993		1992		1993		1992	
	Rm	%	Rm	%	Rm	%	Rm	%	Rm	%	Rm	%	Rm	%	Rm	%
Cement	448,2	48,0	415,2	51,5	142,4	69,6	110,8	74,6	112,2	54,6	87,3	60,5	803,2	51,8	831,5	5
Stone and ready mixed concrete	183,4	19,6	123,4	15,3	9,2	4,5	(6,7)	(4,5)	22,9	11,1	5,6	3,9	281,0	18,1	223,2	1
Industrial	285,8	30,6	251,2	31,1	54,2	26,5	44,8	30,1	40,0	19,5	42,6	29,5	471,2	30,4	449,3	2
Other	16,4	1,8	16,9	2,1	(1,2)	(0,6)	(0,3)	(0,2)	*30,3	14,8	* 8,7	6,1	(4,1)	(0,3)	12,2	
	933,8	100,0	806,7	100,0	204,6	100,0	148,6	100,0	205,4	100,0	144,2	100,0	1 551,3	100,0	1 516,2	10
Internal transactions	(56,6)		(49,7)		(5,3)		(2,7)		–		–		–		–	
Total	877,2		757,0		199,3		145,9		205,4		144,2		1 551,3		1 516,2	

* Includes investment income.
** Excludes investments.

Share capital
During 1993 the Company redeemed the remaining 132 redeemable preference shares of R1 each at a premium of R9 999 per share.

The number of authorised preference shares and authorised and issued ordinary shares remained unchanged.

In terms of a special resolution dated 7 May 1993, an amount of R28 990 000 was transferred from non-distributable reserves to the Stated Capital account.

The Company will request shareholders on 4 May 1994 to approve a further transfer not exceeding R30,0 million to Stated Capital. The effect of this transfer will be to increase Stated Capital from R442,2 million to R472,2 million.

Holding company
The Group's holding company is Altur Investments Limited which is held by Anglovaal Limited and Swiss-based Holderbank Financière Glaris Limited. Altur Investments holds 54,8 per cent of the issued shares of the Company.

Unsecured loan stock
In accordance with the Trust Deed, the Company redeemed the remaining 10 cent unit of the R20 million 9,5 per cent unsecured 1984/1993 loan stock on 31 December 1993.

Dividends
Details regarding dividends declared and payable on the ordinary shares in respect of 1993 are as follows:

No.	Declaration date	Last date to register	Amount per share	Payment date
86	4 August 1993	20 August 1993	50,0c	10 September 1993
87	9 February 1994	25 February 1994	125,0c	18 March 1994
	Total dividends for the year ended 31 December 1993		175,0c (1992: 152,0c)	

Dividends in respect of the cumulative redeemable preference shares totalled R63 000 for 1993 (1992: R168 000).

ubsidiaries and investments

uring the year the Group acquired the remaining
 per cent of Parem Enterprises (Pty) Limited from
etoria Portland Cement Company Limited. We
structured our indirect investment in the concrete
ving industry, previously held through a 50 per cent
terest in Roozeboom Brick Works (Pty) Limited, and now
ld 40 per cent in Grinaker Precast (Pty) Limited. In
dition a 66,7 per cent interest was acquired in The
ement Organisation (Swaziland) (Pty) Limited, the
lding company of Inter-Africa Supplies (Swaziland)
mited. The Group disposed of its interest in East Rand
al Holdings (Pty) Limited and also entered into an
reement for the conditional sale of its interest in
glovaal Coal Holdings (Pty) Limited.

rofits and losses of subsidiaries

ofit after tax earned by subsidiaries and attributable to
e shareholders of Anglo-Alpha Limited totalled R16,2
illion (1992: R10,8 million) while losses totalled R23 000
992: nil).

etirement benefit information

 employees of the Group are, on engagement, required
 become members of the Anglo-Alpha Pension Fund,
ich is managed outside the Group.

wever, to meet the changing needs of employees, the
oup has established a provident fund and with effect
m 31 March 1994 employees have the choice of
longing to either the Pension Fund or Provident Fund,
pending on their personal requirements.

e Pension Fund is registered in terms of the Pension
nd Act, 1956 and is a defined benefit plan. The formula
ed to determine pensions is based on the employee's
al year's remuneration and aggregate period of
embership.

ntributions are at the rate of 17,25 per cent of
nsionable emoluments of which employees pay
 per cent. Employee and employer contributions
ounted to R9,4 million and R13,9 million respectively
r the year.

e Fund's investment income, with the exception of
come from fixed property, is brought to account at the
te of accrual. Investments, with the exception of direct
d indirect investments in property, are revalued
nually and stated at market value in the Fund's balance
eet. Direct and indirect investments in property are not
preciated. Properties are valued on a periodic basis (not
ceeding three years) on an open market value basis.

e second valuation of the Anglo-Alpha Pension Fund
s performed during 1993 and indicated that the Fund
s in a sound financial position as at 31 December 1992.
e actuaries use the most common form of accrued
nefit valuation, being the projected unit credit method.
is method sees each year of service as giving rise to an
ditional unit of pension entitlement and values each
it separately to build up a total retirement benefit
ligation.

e Fund held 263 000 Anglo-Alpha Limited ordinary
ares at 31 December 1993. The market value of the

Fund's quoted shares at 31 December 1993 was
R374,7 million, an appreciation of R224,5 million over
book value.

Surplus funds in the Pension Fund as determined by the
actuarial valuation done as at 1 July 1990 were used to
introduce a range of benefit improvements. These
improvements make the Anglo-Alpha Pension Fund's
benefits competitive in the market and provide members
with most of the benefits normally associated with a
provident fund. Pensions are adjusted annually for the
impact of inflation, subject to the performance of the
Fund.

Insurance and risk management

The Group's insurance and risk management philosophy is
aimed at protecting its assets, earnings and legal liabilities
against unacceptable financial loss at minimum cost
commensurate with satisfactory cover.

Even though the insurance market has begun to harden,
the Group's good claims experience has resulted in its
insurance premiums not increasing.

All fixed assets are insured at current replacement value.
Possible catastrophe-type risks are identified and insured,
while risks of a non-catastrophic nature are self-insured.

Self-insurance programmes are in place where the cost-
benefit relationship exceeds the risk and the incidence of
loss is infrequent or of a minor nature. These programmes
supplement insurance cover and are designed to assist
divisions with their deductibles in the event of claims. The
programmes are reviewed on an annual basis to ensure
adequate cover and stop-loss protection.

The Group's risk management programme is reviewed on
an ongoing basis and remains an integral part of ensuring
that catastrophe risks threatening the Group are
investigated and either eliminated, reduced or transferred
to the insurers. Risk surveys are, where necessary, carried
out at the major plants every two years.

No major losses were experienced during the year under
review and claims of a general nature were adequately
covered in terms of the Group's insurance policies.

Directorate and Secretary

The names of the Directors and Secretary in office at the
date of this report are set out on page 52.

Mr D D B Mkhwanazi was appointed a Director of
Anglo-Alpha Limited with effect from 4 August 1993.

In terms of the Company's Articles of Association, Messrs
M B Burgess, D D B Mkhwanazi, F J Ridsdale, A E Schrafl
and R L Straszacker will retire at the forthcoming Annual
General Meeting but, being eligible, offer themselves for re-
election.

Review of Operations – Cement Division

Salient features	1993 Rm	1992 Rm	% Change	1991 Rm	1990 Rm	1989 Rm
Sales – non-Group	448,2	415,2	+ 7,9	397,8	371,8	320,3
Operating profit	142,4	110,8	+28,6	105,6	119,3	103,9
Cash flow	112,2	87,3	+28,5	31,6	93,3	67,9
Capital expenditure and investments	25,5	31,2	–18,1	51,2	29,0	19,4
Net operating assets						
– current value	803,2	831,5	– 3,4	951,2	889,0	849,5
– historical value	487,6	493,7	– 1,2	487,9	392,2	398,1
Operating profit to operating assets	29,0%	22,6%		24,0%	30,2%	25,9%
Productivity index	1,30	1,22		1,22	1,31	1,32
Number of employees	1 278	1 193		1 491	1 406	1 413

Results

The Construction Industry remained in a depressed state during 1993 as a result of the continued economic recession in South Africa. Accordingly, the Division's cement sales volumes for 1993 were 1,7 per cent below the previous year.

Operating profit increased by 28,6 per cent from R110,8 million in 1992 to R142,4 million due mainly to the containment of production costs. This was achieved primarily by rationalisation throughout the Division and the benefits of the Dudfield refurbishment programme conducted over the past three years.

The Division's cash flow increased by 28,5 per cent to R112,2 million (1992: R87,3 million) due mainly to the increased profitability.

Capital expenditure and investments

Capital expenditure and investments for the year amounted to R25,5 million (1992: R31,2 million) which included the commissioning of a palletiser and bag warehousing facility at Dudfield at a cost of R10,9 million.

During the year the Division strengthened its distribution base by establishing distribution facilities in key markets and by expanding its transport capability. This included the acquisition of a 66,7 per cent shareholding in The Cement Organisation (Swaziland) (Pty) Limited, the holding company of Inter-Africa Supplies (Swaziland) Limited, a cement trading company in Swaziland.

The Division's projected capital expenditure for the next five years is estimated at R326 million (present-day cost) including pre-production finance costs of which 57 per cent is earmarked for replacement of plant and equipment.

Environmental actions

At its plant at Witbank, the Division densifies silica fume, a by-product of the ferrosilicon manufacturing process, which in its undensified form is extremely difficult to handle and dusty. By densifying the product and using it as a cement and concrete additive, the silica fume preserves natural resources (lime and clay) and limits gas emissions generated in the cement clinker manufacturing process.

Together with the rest of the Cement Industry, the Division continued to use other cement additives which not only put waste products such as fly ash and blast furnace slag to good use but lead to a reduction in the quantity of coal burned and gas emissions generated.

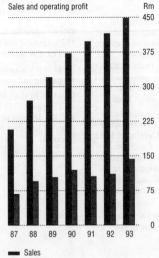

Sales and operating profit — Rm

■ Sales
■ Operating profit

Prospects

Although a number of large projects will come on stream during 1994, including the Columbus Stainless Steel plant and the Alusaf project at Richards Bay, the demand for cement during the first half of 1994 is expected to remain sluggish as a result of political uncertainty affecting both domestic and foreign investor confidence. Economic growth is expected to manifest itself only during the second half of the year, gaining momentum in the last quarter. A small increase in sales volumes is therefore expected.

Incorporating

Concrete Additives (Pty) Limited	100%
Macdonald & Volck (Pty) Limited	100%
Inter-Africa Supplies (Swaziland) Limited	67%

Location of operations

Factories

Dudfield	Western Transvaal
Ulco	Northern Cape
Roodepoort	West Rand
Witbank	East Rand

Distribution terminals

Brakpan	East Rand
Alrode	East Rand
Manzini	Swaziland

Area offices

Bloemfontein	Orange Free State
East London	Eastern Cape

Main products

Ordinary portland cement, rapid hardening portland cement, ordinary portland cement 15, portland fly ash cement and masonry cement. Portland cement is a major ingredient in concrete production, plaster and mortar and is used in cementation processes in mines and soil stabilisation. Condensed silica fume is used as a pozzolan in specialised concrete applications.

Annual production capacity

3,6 million tons (clinker).

Divisional Director: Ron Searle CA (SA), Age 52, joined 1964.

Senior Management:
Rowan Dent CA (SA), Age 47, joined 1972. (Director – Marketing).

Robbie Jones Pr Eng, BSc(Elec Eng), MBL, Age 47, joined 1972. (General Manager – Dudfield).

Hennie Potgieter Dip Eng, Age 50, joined 1970. (General Manager – Roodepoort).

gene Richards BSc(Elec Eng), HBA,
e 46, joined 1974. (General Manager –
:o).

aham Volck CA (SA), Age 51, joined
58 (Managing Director – Macdonald
Volck).

*anges subsequent to 31 December
93:*

Marco Germena was appointed
Director: Cement Division with effect
from 1 January 1994.

Ron Searle was appointed Director:
Management Services with effect
from 1 January 1994.

Robbie Jones was appointed General
Manager – Ulco and Eugene Richards
was appointed General Manager –
Dudfield with effect from 10 January
1994.

It is the small and seemingly insignificant aspects of life that often require the greatest attention. Having a macro focus is a useful gift but to be effective in the longer term requires building upon attention to detail.

Review of Operations –
Stone and Ready Mixed Concrete Division

Salient features	1993 Rm	1992 Rm	% Change	1991 Rm	1990 Rm	1989 Rm
Sales – non-Group	183,4	123,4	+ 48,6	126,4	135,1	123,9
Operating profit/(loss)	9,2	(6,7)	POS	(2,9)	14,3	27,2
Cash flow	22,9	5,6	+308,9	1,0	14,6	15,5
Capital expenditure and investments	7,8	14,5	– 46,2	14,4	31,7	34,4
Net operating assets						
– current value	281,0	223,2	+ 25,9	228,2	232,9	171,4
– historical value	211,7	162,0	+ 30,7	167,0	157,6	131,6
Operating profit to operating assets	4,9 %	(4,1)%		(1,8)%	9,9 %	23,7%
Productivity index	1,04	0,94		0,97	1,08	1,21
Number of employees	1 408	954		1 130	1 242	1 352

Note: The results of Parem Enterprises (Pty) Limited, the holding company of Pioneer Ready Mixed Concrete (Pty) Limited, are included with effect from 1 August 1993.

Results
Sales of sand and stone increased marginally over 1992 due mainly to strong demand in certain areas, notably Natal, partially offset by very depressed sales in the Transvaal.

Sales revenue increased by 48,6 per cent to R183,4 million (1992: R123,4 million) due mainly to the inclusion of Parem Enterprises' results for the first time and a favourable sales mix of aggregates.

Operating costs decreased in 1993 due to the productivity improvement plans introduced in 1992 including retrenchments and plant closures. The Division accordingly returned to profitability, improving operating profit by R15,9 million compared with 1992.

The Division's cash flow improved substantially to R22,9 million (1992: R5,6 million) due to the improved profitability and reduced working capital levels.

Capital expenditure and investments
Capital expenditure and investments decreased by 46,2 per cent to R7,8 million (1992: R14,5 million) and related mainly to plant and equipment replacement. Following the restructuring of the investment in Roozeboom Brick Works (Pty) Limited, the Division acquired a 40 per cent interest in Grinaker Precast (Pty) Limited, a manufacturer of paving products in the Transvaal and Natal.

The projected capital expenditure over the next five years is estimated at

R111 million (present-day cost) including pre-production finance costs and relates mainly to plant and equipment replacement as well as the establishment of ready-mixed concrete operations in the Durban and Cape Town markets in order to utilise the Division's spare capacity and to create a viable distribution channel for aggregates.

Environmental actions
The Division participated fully in the Aggregate and Sand Producers Association of South Africa (ASPASA) "About Face" environmental management programme designed to encourage greater environmental awareness, and was awarded three of the four "Five Fish Eagle" Awards made in 1993.

As a member of ASPASA the Division subscribes to the view that wise environmental stewardship of our natural resources is essential to ensure quality of life for the society of today as well as the generations of tomorrow. ASPASA encourages its members to strive for excellence in its environmental management. This involves not only meeting all legal requirements but, where possible, doing more than the law requires.

Prospects
Due to major contracts in the Division's market areas coming to an end without new contracts of equal size being available to replace them and the generally pessimistic view held by customers of the market

situation immediately preceding an following the forthcoming election an increase in sales volumes is not expected in 1994. However, with th inclusion of Pioneer Ready Mixed Concrete and the entry into the ready-mixed concrete markets in Durban and Cape Town, sales of ready-mixed concrete are expected increase significantly.

Incorporating
Hippo Quarries Granite (Pty) Limited	100%
Pioneer Ready Mixed Concrete (Pty) Limited	100%

Location of operations
Operations	Depots
44 in Transvaal	1 in West Rand
8 in Natal	1 in East Rand
3 in Cape	2 in Cape
3 in Orange Free State	

Transport	Area offices
Transvaal	2 in Johannesbu
Natal	1 in Durban
Cape	1 in Cape Town

Main products
Crushed stone used in the producti of concrete, road and railway line construction and ready-mixed concrete. Sand and agricultural limestone. Stone for gold extraction

Ready-mixed concrete for the construction industry.

Annual production capacity
Stone and sand 10,2 million tons.

Ready-mixed concrete 1,2 million cubic metres.

Divisional Director: Mike Doyle BCom, Age 48, joined 1971.

Senior Management:
Dries Erlank H Dip(Mining), MBA, Age 40, joined 1980. (General Manager – Hippo Cape).

Alan Jones FCA, CA (SA), MBA, Age 47, joined 1982. (General Manager Commercial).

Karl Meissner-Roloff BSc(Civ Eng) (Hons), Age 41, joined 1979. (Gene Manager – Hippo Natal).

Dallis Pattle ACIS, Age 54, joined 1969. (General Manager – Hippo Transvaal).

Eugene Pienaar BSc(Civ Eng), Age 5 joined 1988. (General Manager – Pioneer Ready Mixed Concrete).

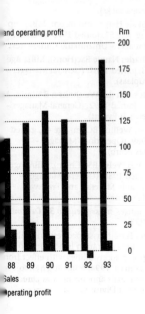

and operating profit

Rm
200
175
150
125
100
75
50
25
0

88 89 90 91 92 93

Sales
Operating profit

Preparing for the uncertainties of tomorrow requires some experience and a great deal of courage. The quality of the future will depend on good corporate citizenship and active social responsibility programmes.

Review of Operations – Industrial Division

Salient features	1993 Rm	1992 Rm	% Change	1991 Rm	1990 Rm	1989 Rm
Sales – Group	42,9	37,1	+ 15,6	35,8	29,2	24,3
– non-Group	242,9	214,1	+ 13,5	200,0	188,0	176,2
	285,8	251,2	+ 13,8	235,8	217,2	200,5
Operating profit	54,2	44,8	+ 21,0	38,5	36,2	40,6
Cash flow	40,0	42,6	– 6,1	26,3	32,8	24,8
Capital expenditure and investments	23,9	21,0	+ 13,8	22,9	29,0	13,2
Net operating assets						
– current value	471,2	449,3	+ 4,9	421,3	348,2	327,8
– historical value	208,8	194,3	+ 7,5	189,4	171,9	169,3
Operating profit to operating assets	26,9 %	23,4 %		21,3%	21,2%	25,0%
Productivity index	1,19	1,17		1,15	1,15	1,20
Number of employees	1 099	1 156		1 208	1 420	1 434

Results

Sales volumes for all of the Division's products declined further during the year as a result of markets served remaining in a depressed state. However, an improved product mix at Umzimkulu Carbonates following the introduction of wet milled products and moderate selling price increases throughout the Division resulted in the sale of goods and services increasing by 13,8 per cent to R285,8 million (1992: R251,2 million).

Operating profit increased by 21,0 per cent from R44,8 million to R54,2 million due mainly to the benefits of productivity improvement plans introduced during 1992 and improved plant performance.

The Division's cash flow decreased by 6,1 per cent to R40,0 million (1992: R42,6 million) due to higher tax payments following the improved profitability in 1992.

Capital expenditure and investments

The Division spent R23,9 million on capital expenditure during 1993, a 13,8 per cent increase over 1992, which includes R10,5 million in respect of the second phase of the wet mill project at Umzimkulu Carbonates.

Projected capital expenditure for the next five years is estimated at R113 million (present-day cost), including pre-production finance costs, divided equally between expansion and diversification capital and replacement of plant and equipment.

Environmental actions

In terms of the environmental rehabilitation plan submitted to the Department of Mineral and Energy Affairs, the lowest quarry bench has been established at Ouplaas to allow reject rock to be backfilled. The backfill process commenced during 1993. The advancing backfill will then be landscaped and vegetated with self-sustaining indigenous vegetation.

Cappa Sacks addressed the potential negative impact on the environment through the usage of lead-free inks and bio-degradable (starch-based) adhesives.

Prospects

The markets being served by the Division are expected to reflect marginal growth in 1994 and sales volumes are therefore forecast to increase at the same rate.

Incorporating

Plastocarb (Pty) Limited   100%

Location of operations

Lime
Ouplaas   Northern Cape

Industrial Minerals
Ceramic Minerals   Benoni
Lewis & Everitt   Cape Town, Durban, Johannesburg & Port Elizabeth
Transvaal Magnetite   Phalaborwa
Umzimkulu   near Port
  Carbonates   Shepstone
Plastocarb   Harrismith

Packaging
Cappa Sacks   Isithebe, Kwazulu

Main products

Lime
Burnt lime in the form of unslaked and hydrated lime used in gold and uranium mining, metallurgical, carbide, paper, chemical and sugar industries. Limestone for metallurgical, agricultural and ceramic industries.

Industrial Minerals
Calcite, dolomite, silica, feldspar, magnetite, pyrophillite used in the paint, plastics, paper, chemical, agricultural, glass, ceramic, construction and coal mining industries, and calcium carbonate masterbatch for the plastics industry.

Packaging
Multi-wall paper sacks used mainly for cement, chemicals, industrial mineral, lime and limestone products and refractory materials.

Annual production capacity

Lime	0,7 million tons
Industrial Minerals	0,7 million tons
Packaging	62 million units

Divisional Directors:
Lime: Marco Germena CA (SA), Age 4█ joined 1970.

Industrial Minerals and Packaging: Pi█ Ferreira BSc(Hons), ACIS, MBA, Age 4█ joined 1971.

Senior Management:
Joshua Bhengu Dip IPM, MBA, Age 3█ joined 1976. (General Manager – Cappa Sacks).

Frikkie Hansmann BCom, MBL, Dip Eng, Age 51, joined 1975. (General Manager – Umzimkulu Carbonates).

Charles Naude BSc(Hons), MBL, Age 38, joined 1981. (General Manager – Ouplaas).

Alex van der Westhuizen BAdmin, Age 47, joined 1992. (General Manager – Lewis & Everitt).

Carl Welling BCom, Age 48, joined 1989. (Operations Manager – Plastocarb).

James Welsh BSc(Chem), MBA, Age 3█ joined 1988. (General Manager – Ceramic Minerals and Transvaal Magnetite).

Changes subsequent to 31 December 1993:

Piet Ferreira assumed responsibility for the lime operation in addition to his other responsibilities with effect from 1 January 1994, following Marco Germena's appointment as Director: Cement Division.

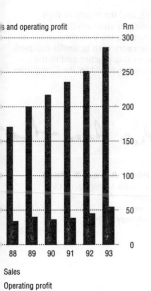

Trust is a fundamental element in building interpersonal relationships and to be an effective leader requires acknowledging the strengths of others and often relinquishing control and allowing them to lead.

27

Report of Management

The annual financial statements and other financial information contained in this Annual Report were prepared under the direction of management which is responsible for the integrity and objectivity thereof. The financial statements have been prepared in conformity with generally accepted accounting practice applied on a consistent basis throughout the year.

To meet its responsibility with respect to financial information, management maintains a system of internal accounting controls designed to provide reasonable assurance that transactions are performed in accordance with management's authority and that assets are adequately protected against loss. The system includes an appropriate delegation of authority and segregation of responsibilities and is supported by written policies and procedures, which are regularly reviewed and, if necessary, modified in response to changes in business conditions, and by the selection and training of qualified personnel who are required to maintain a high standard of ethical conduct.

The Group's internal auditors independently assess the effectiveness of the internal control structure and recommend possible improvements where necessary.

KPMG Aiken & Peat, who were appointed auditors at the inception of the Company, are engaged to express an independent opinion on the financial statements. Their audit is conducted in accordance with generally accepted auditing standards and includes a review of internal controls and a test of transactions to the extent necessary to allow them to report on the fairness of the operating results and financial position of the Group.

The annual financial statements which appear on pages 20 to 27 and 30 to 52 were approved by the Board of Directors on 9 February 1994 and have been signed on its behalf by:

P Byland
CHAIRMAN

J G Pretorius
GROUP MANAGING DIRECTOR

Report of the Independent Auditors

To the members of Anglo-Alpha Limited.

We have audited the annual financial statements and group annual financial statements set out on pages 20 to 27 and 30 to 52 which have been prepared on the bases of accounting set out on pages 30 and 31.

Our responsibility is to report on these financial statements.

We conducted our audit in accordance with generally accepted auditing standards. These standards require that we plan and perform the audit to obtain reasonable assurance that, in all material respects, fair presentation is achieved in the financial statements. The audit included an evaluation of the appropriateness of the accounting policies, an examination, on a test basis, of evidence that supports the amounts included in the financial statements, an assessment of the reasonableness of significant estimates and a consideration of the appropriateness of the overall financial statement presentation. We consider that our auditing procedures were appropriate to enable us to express our opinion presented below.

In our opinion these financial statements fairly present the financial position of the Company and of the Group at 31 December 1993, and the results of their operations and cash flow information for the year then ended in conformity with generally accepted accounting practice and in the manner required by the Companies Act.

KPMG Aiken & Peat
Chartered Accountants (SA)
Auditors
Johannesburg
9 February 1994

Index to the Financial Statements

Current Cost Subject Index

29

The principal accounting policies of the Group, set out below, conform in all material respects with statements of Generally Accepted Accounting Practice and standards issued by the Board of the International Accounting Standards Committee. The policies are consistent with those followed in the previous year.

The annual financial statements incorporate current value accounting procedures which include the revaluation of property, plant and equipment, investments and inventories. Current value accounting procedures reflect the Group's capital requirements for the maintenance of its existing productive capacity and the cost of conducting business during prolonged periods of rising costs. Current value accounting procedures are especially relevant due to the capital intensive nature of the Group's business.

1. Basis of consolidation

The consolidated financial statements include the financial position and operating results of the Company and all its subsidiaries. The results of subsidiaries are included from the dates of acquisition until the dates of disposal.

On acquisition of a subsidiary, asset values are adjusted to the values placed on them for the purpose of the acquisition and any goodwill is written-off over a period not exceeding five years. Accumulated depreciation on plant, property and equipment acquired is not reversed on consolidation. Unrealised profits arising from transactions within the Group are eliminated.

2. Property, plant and equipment

Property, plant and equipment are stated at depreciated current replacement cost except where otherwise indicated. The assets are revalued every five years and during the intervening years asset values are updated by applying an inflation index to determine current values. The revaluation is performed by the Group's engineers and is based on the estimated current replacement cost of the existing production capacity.

The remaining useful lives of the assets are reassessed simultaneously with their revaluation. The net surplus arising on revaluation is transferred to the capital revaluation reserve.

The total annual depreciation charge is based on the current replacement cost of property, plant and equipment at rates which have been determined in relation to the useful lives of the assets, using the straight line method.

Investment properties are reflected at their open market value and are not depreciated. Valuations are undertaken annually by management and by external valuers at least every five years.

Land, mineral rights, quarry properties and certain other assets which are not used directly in the process of manufacture, or which will not be replaced, are not revalued.

Land on which specialised buildings are situated is shown at cost. Provision is made to recognise permanent declines in value. Specialised buildings and the remaining assets are depreciated over their estimated useful lives, using the straight line method.

Borrowing costs incurred on funds raised specifically to finance the construction of property, plant and equipment and which are incurred prior to the assets being commissioned, are capitalised.

3. Leases

Where the substance of a lease is a financing arrangement and all risks and rewards associated with ownership are transferred to the Group, the cash value of the leased assets are capitalised and stated in the balance sheet at depreciated current replacement cost with the corresponding liability to the lessor.

Depreciation is provided over the estimated useful lives of leased depreciable assets on a straight line method. Lease payments are allocated between a reduction of the liability to the lessor and a lease finance cost which is charged against income, based on the effective rate of interest.

4. Investments

Investments are stated at current values. In arriving at current values the market value, carrying value, earnings yield method, dividend yield method or net realisable value are used as appropriate. Current values are determined on an annual basis by management.

Investments are valued individually and provision is made to recognise permanent diminutions in the value of investments.

Investments in which the Group exercises significant influence and which it intends holding on a long-term basis, are classified as associates and are stated at their carrying values. Significant influence is defined as the ability to participate in the financial and operating policy decisions of the investee and applies to instances where the Group holds an equity interest of between 20 per cent and 50 per cent. The Group's post-acquisition share of retained earnings of associates is incorporated in the consolidated income statement from their effective dates of acquisition and is transferred to non-distributable reserves. Dividends received from or declared by associates are included in income from investments.

The excess of the current value of investments over the carrying values or cost is reflected separately in the capital revaluation reserve.

Income from investments in which the Group holds an equity interest of less than 20 per cent is brought to account only to the extent of dividends received or declared.

5. Inventories

Inventories, with the exception of machinery spares, are valued at the lower of current replacement cost and net realisable value. Machinery spares are valued at depreciated current replacement cost. Cost is determined on either the first-in first-out or the average cost method. The cost of work in progress and finished goods includes an appropriate allocation of production overhead expenditure. Due account is taken of obsolete, redundant or slow-moving items in valuing machinery spares and stores.

6. Non-distributable reserves

These reserves comprise:

6.1 Capital revaluation reserve

The balance on this reserve comprises:

6.1.1 The net surplus on the revaluation of property, plant and equipment, investments and inventories. Annual increases in revaluations less capital expenditure of a replacement nature are credited directly to this reserve. Decreases are shown in the income statement as extraordinary charges only to the extent that they exceed surpluses previously transferred to this reserve.

6.1.2 The Group's share of post-acquisition reserves retained by associates.

6.2 Capital replacement reserve

This reserve represents the current cost adjustments in respect of cost of sales and additional depreciation on property, plant and equipment and machinery spares less the financial gearing adjustment.

6.3 Deferred taxation

This reserve represents the deferred tax balance at 1 January 1988 which is no longer required in terms of the partial basis of accounting for deferred taxation.

7. Tax deferments

Tax deferments comprise:

7.1 Deferred taxation

Deferred taxation is provided on the liability method using the partial basis. Accordingly, deferred taxation is provided only where it is probable that taxation will become payable in the foreseeable future (currently defined as five years) as a result of the reversal of timing differences exceeding future originating differences.

7.2 Taxation on LIFO reserve

The LIFO reserve is taxable over a 10 year period with effect from 1991. Provision has been made in full for the taxation to be paid.

8. Foreign currencies

Foreign currency borrowings are translated to South African Rand at rates of exchange ruling at the balance sheet date or, where borrowings are covered by foreign exchange contracts, at the rates applicable. Costs of forward cover incurred on foreign borrowings are included in borrowing costs.

Foreign currency adjustments are included in operating profit where they relate to normal trading transactions. Where borrowings denominated in foreign currency are raised specifically to finance the construction of capital assets, foreign currency adjustments arising prior to the commissioning of the assets are capitalised.

9. Sales

Sales comprise all sales of goods and services to customers after deducting value-added tax, trade discounts, returns and delivery charges and include sale of quota and commissions received. Internal transactions are excluded on consolidation.

10. Retirement benefits

Retirement benefit contributions paid by the Group to fund obligations for the payment of retirement benefits are charged against income in the year of payment.

11. Current cost adjustment

11.1 The adjustment reflects the effect on the income statement of applying current cost accounting policies and comprises the following adjustments:

11.1.1 Additional depreciation

This represents the difference between depreciation based on the current replacement cost of property, plant and equipment and machinery spares and on the historical cost of those assets.

11.1.2 Cost of sales

This represents the difference between the current cost and the historical cost of inventories consumed. The current cost of inventories consumed is arrived at using the averaging method.

11.1.3 Financial gearing

This represents that portion of the additional depreciation and cost of sales adjustments which will be financed from borrowings. The proportion is based on the Group's long-term average debt percentage.

11.2 Outside shareholders' interest

The current cost adjustment is net of outside shareholders' interest where applicable.

12. Extraordinary items

Extraordinary items are material items of income and expenditure resulting from occurrences, the underlying nature of which is not typical of the ordinary trading or operating activities of the Group. Extraordinary items include results arising from discontinued operations which are defined as significant identifiable business units which management has formally decided to sell or close.

13. Earnings per share

Earnings per share is based on the profit attributable to ordinary shareholders divided by the weighted average number of shares in issue during the year. Earnings exclude the Group's share of earnings retained by associates and extraordinary items.

14. Presentation

All amounts in the financial statements, reports and supporting schedules are stated to the nearest R000 except where otherwise indicated. Comparative figures are regrouped or restated where necessary.

Cash Flow Statements

for the year ended 31 December 1993

Anglo-Alpha Limited	Note	Group 1993 R000	Group 1992 R000	Company 1993 R000	Company 1992 R000
Cash generated by operations	1	244 070	177 149	230 497	168 744
Income from subsidiaries				3 600	4 556
Income from investments		15 190	16 372	10 843	13 721
Borrowing costs		(24 155)	(30 040)	(26 693)	(33 388)
Preference dividends		(63)	(168)	(63)	(168)
Taxation	2	(29 678)	(19 130)	(28 174)	(16 113)
Cash available from operations		205 364	144 183	190 010	137 352
Ordinary dividends	3	(46 920)	(45 717)	(46 920)	(45 717)
Cash retained from operations		158 444	98 466	143 090	91 635
Investment in existing operations		(36 124)	(60 519)	(43 698)	(66 043)
Replacement capital expenditure	4	(45 559)	(68 997)	(44 348)	(68 361)
Proceeds from the disposal of property, plant and equipment	5	7 293	8 478	3 098	5 609
Proceeds from the disposal of investments		2 142	–	2 142	–
Net advancement of loans to subsidiaries				(4 590)	(3 291)
Investment in future operations		(76 042)	(22 601)	(61 624)	(10 604)
Expansion capital expenditure	6	(15 641)	(9 326)	(14 005)	(7 635)
Acquisition of investments		(3 843)	(1 026)	(2 150)	(1 026)
Acquisition of subsidiaries	7	(36 616)	–	(36 616)	–
Long-term receivables advanced		(23 945)	(7 664)	(22 353)	(7 664)
Long-term receivables repaid		13 500	5 721	13 500	5 721
Investment in fixed deposit		(9 497)	(10 306)	–	–
Net inflow for the year		46 278	15 346	37 768	14 988
Cash effect of financing activities					
Repayment of long-term borrowings		(32 993)	(56 755)	(32 059)	(56 421)
Repayment of preference shares		(1 320)	(1 240)	(1 320)	(1 240)
Decrease in bank overdraft		(7 686)	(160)	–	(135)
Increase in cash resources		(4 279)	(29 791)	(4 389)	(29 792)
Long-term borrowings raised		–	72 600	–	72 600
Cash utilised		(46 278)	(15 346)	(37 768)	(14 988)
Cash flow per share	8	683 c	479 c		

32

Anglo-Alpha Limited	Group		Company	
	1993 R000	1992 R000	1993 R000	1992 R000
1. Calculation of cash generated by operations				
Operating profit	199 347	145 863	184 316	137 172
Depreciation and other non-cash items	53 179	45 844	53 758	47 961
Retained to finance working capital	(8 456)	(14 558)	(7 577)	(16 389)
Increase in inventories	(4 374)	(4 322)	(3 570)	(5 200)
Increase in receivables	(19 445)	(12 100)	(24 033)	(8 984)
Increase/(Decrease) in payables	15 363	1 864	20 026	(2 205)
	244 070	177 149	230 497	168 744
2. Reconciliation of taxation paid				
Charge per income statement	63 533	32 375	57 977	28 759
Attributable to extraordinary item	–	(1 666)	–	(637)
Movement in taxation payable	(31 230)	(11 712)	(30 565)	(12 090)
Movement in deferred taxation	(2 625)	133	762	81
	29 678	19 130	28 174	16 113
3. Reconciliation of ordinary dividends paid				
Amount owing at beginning of the year	31 882	31 882	31 882	31 882
Current charge per the income statement	52 634	45 717	52 634	45 717
Amount owing at end of the year	(37 596)	(31 882)	(37 596)	(31 882)
	46 920	45 717	46 920	45 717
4. Replacement capital expenditure				
Land	1 526	1 260	1 526	1 260
Buildings	4 476	7 065	4 383	7 065
Plant and equipment	39 557	60 672	38 439	60 036
	45 559	68 997	44 348	68 361
5. Proceeds from disposal of property, plant and equipment				
Book value of assets disposed of	3 425	5 011	1 563	4 124
Profit on disposal	3 868	3 467	1 535	1 485
	7 293	8 478	3 098	5 609
6. Expansion capital expenditure				
Land	116	581	116	46
Buildings	478	–	478	–
Plant and equipment	15 047	8 745	13 411	7 589
	15 641	9 326	14 005	7 635

7. Acquisition of subsidiaries
The cost of acquiring the remaining interest in Parem Enterprises
(Pty) Limited and shares in The Cement Organisation (Swaziland)
(Pty) Limited is represented by the following:

Cash payment			36 616	–
Property,plant and equipment	75 926	–		
Goodwill	3 846	–		
Long-term receivables	1 343	–		
Inventories	7 371	–		
Trade and other receivables	30 536	–		
Taxation prepaid	43	–		
Cash resources	1 642	–		
Long-term borrowings	(15 126)	–		
Deferred taxation	(15)	–		
Trade and other payables	(34 341)	–		
Bank overdraft	(7 686)	–		
Net assets acquired	63 539	–		
Outside shareholders' interest	(4 744)	–		
Transferred from investments	(2 179)	–		
Receivable advanced prior to acquisition	(20 000)	–		
	36 616	–	36 616	–
8. Reconciliation of cash flow per share (cents)				
Earnings per share – current cost basis	255	173		
Current cost adjustment	167	158		
Earnings per share – historical cost basis	422	331		
Add: Depreciation and other non-cash items	177	152		
Deferred and unpaid taxation	112	44		
Less: Increase in working capital	28	48		
	683	479		

33

for the year ended 31 December 1993

Anglo-Alpha Limited and subsidiary companies	Note	1993 R000	1992 R000
Sales	1	877 168	756 973
Cost of sales		543 311	495 184
Gross profit		333 857	261 789
Historical cost depreciation	2	60 429	51 964
Selling and administration expenses		74 081	63 962
Operating profit	3	199 347	145 863
Income from investments	5	15 190	16 372
Borrowing costs	6	24 155	30 040
Profit before taxation and current cost adjustment		190 382	132 195
Taxation	7	63 533	32 375
Preference dividends		63	168
Profit before current cost adjustment attributable to ordinary shareholders		126 786	99 652
Current cost adjustment	8	50 115	47 617
Profit attributable to ordinary shareholders		76 671	52 035
Share of earnings retained by associates		1 943	269
Profit before extraordinary items		78 614	52 304
Extraordinary items	9	1 969	(6 938)
Profit for year		80 583	45 366
Retained earnings at beginning of year		121 580	122 200
		202 163	167 566
Ordinary dividends	10	52 634	45 717
		149 529	121 849
Transfer to non-distributable reserves – share of earnings retained by associates	12	(5 710)	(269)
Retained earnings at end of year		143 819	121 580
Earnings per share			
– current cost basis		255c	173c
– historical cost basis		422c	331c
Dividends per share		175c	152c
Weighted average number of shares in issue (000)		30 077	30 077

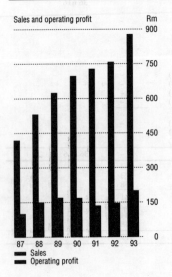

Sales and operating profit (Rm)

■ Sales
■ Operating profit

34

31 December 1993

Anglo-Alpha Limited and subsidiary companies	Note	1993 R000	1993 R000	1992 R000	1992 R000
Capital employed					
Stated capital	11		442 246		413 256
Non-distributable reserves	12		271 108		249 983
Retained earnings			143 819		121 580
Ordinary shareholders' equity					
– historical value			857 173		784 819
Capital revaluation reserve	12		773 948		753 298
Ordinary shareholders' equity					
– current value			1 631 121		1 538 117
Outside shareholders' interest in subsidiaries			4 790		46
Tax deferments	13		7 773		5 133
Preference share capital and premium			–		1 320
Long-term borrowings	14		125 046		160 202
			1 768 730		1 704 818
Employment of capital					
Property, plant and equipment	18		1 419 397		1 359 721
Investments	20		217 985		177 774
Current assets					
Inventories	21	150 743		138 726	
Trade and other receivables		209 207		159 226	
Cash resources		55 038		49 117	
		414 988		347 069	
Current liabilities					
Current portion of long-term borrowings	14	55 570		38 281	
Taxation payable		40 917		9 730	
Trade and other payables		149 557		99 853	
Ordinary dividend payable		37 596		31 882	
		283 640		179 746	
Net current assets			131 348		167 323
			1 768 730		1 704 818
Net worth per share					
– current cost basis			5 423c		5 114c
– historical cost basis			2 850c		2 609c

35

for the year ended 31 December 1993

Anglo-Alpha Limited	Note	1993 R000	1992 R000
Sales	1	796 642	733 498
Cost of sales		496 805	486 725
Gross profit		299 837	246 773
Historical cost depreciation	2	54 170	49 403
Selling and administration expenses		61 351	60 198
Operating profit	3	184 316	137 172
Income from subsidiaries	4	3 600	4 556
Income from investments	5	10 843	13 721
Borrowing costs	6	26 693	33 388
Profit before taxation and current cost adjustment		172 066	122 061
Taxation	7	57 977	28 759
Preference dividends		63	168
Profit before current cost adjustment attributable to ordinary shareholders		114 026	93 134
Current cost adjustment	8	49 991	47 486
Profit attributable to ordinary shareholders before extraordinary items		64 035	45 648
Extraordinary items	9	2 048	(2 315)
Profit for year		66 083	43 333
Retained earnings at beginning of year		96 217	98 601
		162 300	141 934
Ordinary dividends	10	52 634	45 717
Retained earnings at end of year		109 666	96 217

31 December 1993

Anglo-Alpha Limited	Note	1993 R000	1993 R000	1992 R000	1992 R000
Capital employed					
Stated capital	11		442 246		413 256
Non-distributable reserves	12		228 025		207 024
Retained earnings			109 666		96 217
Ordinary shareholders' equity					
– historical value			779 937		716 497
Capital revaluation reserve	12		831 883		803 973
Ordinary shareholders' equity					
– current value			1 611 820		1 520 470
Tax deferments	13		3 013		3 775
Preference share capital and premium			–		1 320
Long-term borrowings	14		115 298		160 153
			1 730 131		1 685 718
Employment of capital					
Property, plant and equipment	18		1 315 254		1 318 589
Interest in subsidiaries	19		120 957		57 991
Investments	20		174 707		152 906
Current assets					
Inventories	21	138 509		134 849	
Trade and other receivables		161 131		137 098	
Cash resources		53 494		49 105	
		353 134		321 052	
Current liabilities					
Current portion of long-term borrowings	14	50 968		38 172	
Taxation payable		42 173		11 608	
Trade and other payables		103 184		83 158	
Ordinary dividend payable		37 596		31 882	
		233 921		164 820	
Net current assets			119 213		156 232
			1 730 131		1 685 718

Anglo-Alpha Limited	Group		Company	
	1993	1992	1993	1992
	R000	R000	R000	R000
1. Sales (refer accounting policy 9)				
Sales of goods and services	**877 168**	756 973	**796 642**	733 498
Sales exclude:				
Internal transactions	**65 694**	49 667	**44 983**	38 678
Value-added tax	**128 159**	81 119	**114 223**	78 782
Management fees	**1 263**	826	**1 263**	826
Rental received on leasing of properties	**808**	189	**808**	189
Dividends and interest received are shown as income from investments (refer note 5)				
2. Depreciation				
Historical cost depreciation				
Owned assets				
Land, quarry properties and mineral rights	**548**	459	**473**	459
Buildings	**5 212**	4 609	**5 048**	4 534
Plant and equipment	**50 110**	42 446	**44 099**	39 960
	55 870	47 514	**49 620**	44 953
Leased assets				
Plant and equipment	**3 935**	3 715	**3 935**	3 715
	59 805	51 229	**53 555**	48 668
Machinery spares	**624**	735	**615**	735
	60 429	51 964	**54 170**	49 403
Current cost depreciation	**87 394**	80 744	**87 230**	80 604
	147 823	132 708	**141 400**	130 007
3. Operating profit				
is stated after:				
Administration, management and technical fees	**6 149**	5 635	**6 144**	5 635
Auditors' remuneration				
Audit fees	**1 029**	894	**883**	812
Expenses	**35**	36	**25**	29
Other services	**–**	83	**–**	80
	1 064	1 013	**908**	921
Directors' emoluments				
For services as directors	**139**	143	**139**	143
For managerial services	**1 937**	1 891	**1 937**	1 891
	2 076	2 034	**2 076**	2 034
Profit on disposal of:				
Property	**2 260**	1 792	**796**	96
Plant and equipment	**1 608**	1 675	**739**	1 389
	3 868	3 467	**1 535**	1 485
Operating lease expenses				
Plant and equipment	**1 337**	802	**499**	574
4. Income from subsidiaries				
Dividends			**3 600**	4 396
Fees			**–**	160
			3 600	4 556

Anglo-Alpha Limited	Group		Company	
	1993 **R000**	1992 R000	**1993** **R000**	1992 R000
5. Income from investments				
Dividends				
Associates				
Listed	**4 254**	4 356	**4 254**	4 356
Unlisted	**4 777**	7 019	**4 777**	6 940
	9 031	11 375	**9 031**	11 296
Other investments				
Listed	**–**	35	**–**	–
Unlisted	**934**	427	**934**	427
	9 965	11 837	**9 965**	11 723
Interest	**5 225**	4 535	**878**	1 998
	15 190	16 372	**10 843**	13 721
6. Borrowing costs				
Interest paid (including forward cover costs)	**12 444**	16 565	**14 982**	19 913
Lease finance charges	**18 910**	16 272	**18 910**	16 272
	31 354	32 837	**33 892**	36 185
Less: Amount capitalised (refer accounting policy 2)	**914**	769	**914**	769
Interest received on cash resources	**6 285**	2 028	**6 285**	2 028
	24 155	30 040	**26 693**	33 388
7. Taxation				
South African normal taxation				
Current	**56 097**	35 550	**54 428**	32 907
Secondary	**6 086**	–	**5 546**	–
Deferred	**2 585**	896	**(762)**	(81)
	64 768	36 446	**59 212**	32 826
Prior year taxation				
Current	**(1 275)**	(4 071)	**(1 235)**	(4 067)
Deferred	**40**	–	**–**	–
Aggregate tax charge	**63 533**	32 375	**57 977**	28 759
Reconciliation of rate of taxation				
	%	%	**%**	%
Normal taxation rate	**40,0**	48,0	**40,0**	48,0
Decrease in rate of taxation due to:				
Unprovided timing differences	**(4,4)**	(13,6)	**(5,4)**	(14,6)
Dividend income	**(2,1)**	(4,3)	**(3,1)**	(6,3)
Capital profits	**(0,4)**	(1,0)	**(0,3)**	(0,3)
Other special allowances	**(0,1)**	(0,2)	**(0,1)**	(0,1)
Tax losses utilised	**(2,2)**	(1,5)	**–**	–
Prior year over-provision	**(0,6)**	(3,1)	**(0,7)**	(3,3)
Rate adjustment	**(0,4)**	–	**(0,3)**	–
	(10,2)	(23,7)	**(9,9)**	(24,6)
Increase in rate of taxation due to:				
Secondary tax on companies	**3,2**	–	**3,2**	–
Disallowed expenditure	**0,4**	0,2	**0,4**	0,2
	3,6	0,2	**3,6**	0,2
Effective rate on historical cost income	**33,4**	24,5	**33,7**	23,6
Estimated tax losses available for set-off against future taxable income attributable to ordinary shareholders (R000)	**11 133**	1 033		

Anglo-Alpha Limited	Group		Company	
	1993 R000	1992 R000	1993 R000	1992 R000
8. Current cost adjustment (refer accounting policy 11)				
Current cost depreciation:				
on property, plant and equipment	86 513	79 893	86 349	79 753
on machinery spares	881	851	881	851
Cost of sales adjustment	3 725	5 835	3 664	5 736
	91 119	86 579	90 894	86 340
Less: Financial gearing adjustment (refer note 12)	41 004	38 962	40 903	38 854
	50 115	47 617	49 991	47 486
9. Extraordinary items (refer accounting policy 12)				
Share of extraordinary items of associate companies:				
Deferred tax rate changes	2 923	–	–	–
Surplus on disposal of property	844	–	–	–
	3 767	–	–	–
Profit on disposal of investment	2 048	–	2 048	–
Goodwill arising on the acquisition of subsidiaries	(3 846)	–	–	–
Loss on discontinuance of two quarry operations	–	(7 762)	–	(2 952)
Permanent diminution in value of investment	–	(842)	–	–
	1 969	(8 604)	2 048	(2 952)
Attributable taxation				
Current	–	637	–	637
Deferred	–	1 029	–	–
	1 969	(6 938)	2 048	(2 315)
10. Ordinary dividends				
No. 86 50,0 cents per share paid				
10 September 1993 (1992: 46c)	15 038	13 835	15 038	13 835
No. 87 125,0 cents per share payable				
18 March 1994 (1992: 106c)	37 596	31 882	37 596	31 882
175,0 cents per share (1992: 152c)	52 634	45 717	52 634	45 717
11. Share capital				
Authorised				
36 000 000 (1992: 36 000 000) ordinary shares of no par value				
Issued				
Stated capital				
30 076 848 (1992: 30 076 848) ordinary shares of no par value	413 256	366 776	413 256	366 776
Transfer from non-distributable reserves (refer note 12)	28 990	46 480	28 990	46 480
	442 246	413 256	442 246	413 256

Unissued shares totalling 5 923 152 are under the control of
the Directors until the forthcoming Annual General Meeting.

Anglo-Alpha Limited

	Group 1993 R000	Group 1992 R000	Company 1993 R000	Company 1992 R000
12. Non-distributable reserves (refer accounting policy 6)				
Balance at beginning of year	1 003 281	1 091 325	1 010 997	1 104 973
Transfer to stated capital	(28 990)	(46 480)	(28 990)	(46 480)
	974 291	1 044 845	982 007	1 058 493
Surplus/(Deficit) on revaluation of property, plant and equipment	72 293	(19 126)	79 779	(24 598)
Surplus on revaluation of associates and other investments	27 352	10 455	33 486	9 945
Transfer from income statement – share of earnings retained by associates	5 710	269		
Net assets acquired in associates in excess of purchase consideration	623	–		
Surplus/(Deficit) on revaluation of inventories	1 185	(886)	994	(576)
Cost of sales adjustment	3 725	5 835	3 664	5 736
Current cost depreciation on machinery spares	881	851	881	851
Transfer to income statement – financial gearing adjustment	(41 004)	(38 962)	(40 903)	(38 854)
Balance at end of year	1 045 056	1 003 281	1 059 908	1 010 997
Represented by:				
Capital revaluation reserve				
Extent by which interest of shareholders has been increased as a result of revaluing assets:				
Property, plant and equipment	646 120	660 340	706 276	712 846
Investments	60 240	32 888	102 577	69 091
Inventories	24 463	23 278	23 030	22 036
	730 823	716 506	831 883	803 973
Share of post-acquisition reserves retained by associates	43 125	36 792		
	773 948	753 298	831 883	803 973
Capital replacement reserve				
The movement on this reserve is made up primarily of the current cost adjustment per the income statement net of the transfer to stated capital	82 622	61 497	50 997	29 996
Deferred taxation				
Balance at 1 January 1988 no longer required as a result of the change to the partial basis of deferred taxation	188 486	188 486	177 028	177 028
	271 108	249 983	228 025	207 024
	1 045 056	1 003 281	1 059 908	1 010 997
13. Tax deferments (refer accounting policy 7)				
Deferred taxation				
Balance at beginning of year	2 083	2 135	725	725
Balance of newly acquired subsidiary	15	–	–	–
Transfer from/(to) income statement	3 266	977	(121)	–
Attributable to extraordinary items	–	(1 029)	–	–
Balance at end of year	5 364	2 083	604	725
Taxation on LIFO reserve				
Balance at beginning of year	3 050	3 131	3 050	3 131
Transfer to income statement	(641)	(81)	(641)	(81)
Balance at end of year	2 409	3 050	2 409	3 050
	7 773	5 133	3 013	3 775

	1993 Provision made R000	1993 Contingent liability R000	1993 Potential liability R000	1992 Provision made R000	1992 Contingent liability R000	1992 Potential liability R000
Analysis of deferred taxation:						
Group						
Accelerated property, plant and equipment allowances	691	179 882	180 573	804	215 761	216 565
Working capital allowances	7 210	22 071	29 281	4 329	28 336	32 665
Capitalised lease allowances	–	44 731	44 731	–	39 180	39 180
Tax losses	(128)	(356)	(484)	–	(730)	(730)
	7 773	246 328	254 101	5 133	282 547	287 680
Company						
Accelerated property, plant and equipment allowances	592	177 437	178 029	710	214 454	215 164
Working capital allowances	2 421	22 957	25 378	3 065	26 759	29 824
Capitalised lease allowances	–	44 731	44 731	–	39 180	39 180
	3 013	245 125	248 138	3 775	280 393	284 168

The contingent liability for deferred taxation at 31 December 1993 has been reduced for the decrease in the rate of taxation from 48% to 40%.

41

Anglo-Alpha Limited	Group		Company	
	1993 R000	1992 R000	1993 R000	1992 R000
14. Long-term borrowings				
Fixed rate borrowings				
Loans	34 049	36 158	34 000	36 000
Financial lease and suspensive sale obligations				
Local	31 848	41 928	31 848	41 928
Foreign	483	–	–	–
	66 380	78 086	65 848	77 928
Variable rate borrowings				
Loans	75	96	75	96
Financial lease and suspensive sale obligations	114 161	120 301	100 343	120 301
	180 616	198 483	166 266	198 325
Amount repayable within one year	55 570	38 281	50 968	38 172
	125 046	160 202	115 298	160 153
Long-term borrowings are repayable as follows:				
1993	–	38 281	–	38 172
1994	55 570	50 988	50 968	50 939
1995	90 744	80 587	86 214	80 587
1996	25 056	19 627	20 082	19 627
1997	3 084	3 000	3 002	3 000
1998	3 084	3 000	3 000	3 000
1999 and later	3 078	3 000	3 000	3 000
	180 616	198 483	166 266	198 325

(Details of long-term borrowings are given on page 50.)

	Group		Company	
15. Commitments				
Capital expenditure including escalation and pre-production interest				
Authorised but not contracted for	14 658	21 951	9 614	21 951
Contracted for	11 880	19 654	10 837	19 654
Amounts payable within one year	26 538	41 605	20 451	41 605

Funds to meet these commitments will be provided from cash flow and existing loan facilities.

	Group			
16. Borrowing capacity				
Borrowing capacity in terms of the most restrictive covenants imposed by loan agreements and Articles of Association	1 081 183	989 090		
Total borrowings excluding financial leases	97 718	81 287		
Unutilised borrowing capacity	983 465	907 803		
Unutilised borrowing facilities	181 548	141 361		

	Group		Company	
17. Contingent liabilities				
Guarantees in terms of housing assistance schemes for employees	2 690	2 772	2 690	2 772
Less: Fixed deposits advanced as security (refer note 20)	80	92	80	92
	2 610	2 680	2 610	2 680
Other guarantees	1 000	–	1 000	–
	3 610	2 680	3 610	2 680

The Group's policy is to provide for dividend distributions from current profit. Any liability for secondary tax on companies has not been provided on undistributed earnings as the possibility of future dividend distributions from retained earnings is remote.

Anglo-Alpha Limited	Group		Company	
	1993 R000	1992 R000	1993 R000	1992 R000

18. Property, plant and equipment (refer accounting policy 2)

Assets at estimated current replacement cost

	Group 1993	Group 1992	Company 1993	Company 1992
Buildings – valuation	263 405	241 431	263 405	241 431
Accumulated depreciation	162 402	140 873	162 402	140 873
	101 003	100 558	101 003	100 558
Plant and equipment – valuation	3 059 746	2 705 447	2 959 931	2 698 025
Accumulated depreciation	1 911 508	1 604 263	1 862 682	1 601 976
	1 148 238	1 101 184	1 097 249	1 096 049
Investment properties – valuation	68 238	68 107	44 915	44 332
Assets at historical cost				
Land, quarry properties and mineral rights – cost	25 529	22 743	21 075	18 689
Accumulated depreciation	5 122	4 539	4 536	4 247
	20 407	18 204	16 539	14 442
Buildings – cost	30 975	14 816	13 294	12 568
Accumulated depreciation	9 534	7 224	5 068	5 013
	21 441	7 592	8 226	7 555
Plant and equipment – cost	101 284	81 514	67 957	65 120
Accumulated depreciation	70 201	51 648	49 142	43 570
	31 083	29 866	18 815	21 550
Capital work in progress – cost	28 987	34 210	28 507	34 103
Total cost or estimated current replacement cost	3 578 164	3 168 268	3 399 084	3 114 268
Total accumulated depreciation	2 158 767	1 808 547	2 083 830	1 795 679
	1 419 397	1 359 721	1 315 254	1 318 589
The historical cost of assets valued at estimated current replacement cost is	1 107 142	955 919	922 909	872 826
Accumulated depreciation	435 783	346 410	386 018	344 733
	671 359	609 509	536 891	528 093
Surplus arising from revaluation of assets (refer note 12)	646 120	660 340	706 276	712 846
	1 317 479	1 269 849	1 243 167	1 240 939
Net book value of assets at cost	101 918	89 872	72 087	77 650
	1 419 397	1 359 721	1 315 254	1 318 589

(i) Included under investment properties are assets leased with a historical cost and book value of

	7 581	7 581	7 581	7 581

(ii) Included under plant and equipment are assets leased or acquired under suspensive sale agreements with a historical cost of

	Group 1993	Group 1992	Company 1993	Company 1992
	92 356	91 800	91 506	91 506
Accumulated historical cost depreciation	35 484	31 515	35 156	31 221
	56 872	60 285	56 350	60 285

(iii) Certain assets with a book value of

	945	3 219	859	.795

have been mortgaged or pledged as security for loans as set out on page 50.

(iv) Investment properties were valued during November and December 1993 by internal management. The basis of valuation used was the open market value in continuation of existing use.

The historical cost of investment properties is:

	Group 1993	Group 1992	Company 1993	Company 1992
Land	13 806	11 654	4 221	4 279
Buildings	13 862	11 323	11 323	11 323
	27 668	22 977	15 544	15 602

(v) Asset revaluations in respect of all divisions have been carried out during the past three years. Where applicable and in accordance with accounting policy 2 an inflation index of 9,0 per cent (1992: 12,0 per cent) was applied to the assets of the Group to determine current values.

(vi) A register of land and buildings is available for inspection at the registered office of the Company.

Details of the movement in the net book value of fixed assets is given on page 45.

43

Anglo-Alpha Limited	Group		Company	
	1993 R000	1992 R000	1993 R000	1992 R000
19. Interest in subsidiaries				
Unlisted shares at cost less amounts written-off			42 535	24 162
Amounts owing by subsidiaries			88 275	41 212
			130 810	65 374
Less: Amounts owing to subsidiaries			9 853	7 383
			120 957	57 991
Details of subsidiary companies are given on pages 46 and 47.				
20. Investments (refer accounting policy 4)				
Investments in associates				
Shares at cost	45 656	44 101	43 052	43 190
Share of post-acquisition reserves				
Non-distributable	746	746		
Retained earnings	42 379	36 046		
	88 781	80 893		
Loans to associates	12 779	16 587	12 779	16 587
Total investment in associates:				
At carrying value	101 560	97 480		
At cost			55 831	59 777
Surplus arising on revaluation of associates	51 128	27 380	93 516	63 583
	152 688	124 860	149 347	123 360
Other share investments – valuation	9 188	5 584	9 097	5 544
Fixed deposit	36 883	23 300		
Deposit advanced	29 879	20 382		
Interest accrued	7 004	2 918		
The Group has entered into a fixed deposit agreement for the purpose of establishing a sinking fund in order to settle its suspensive sale obligation in favour of the Standard Bank of South Africa Limited. The deposit earns interest at 13,99 per cent (1992: 15,89 per cent) and is presently unencumbered.				
Long-term receivables – cost				
Employees' Share Participation Scheme Trust	15 139	15 569	15 139	15 569
Staff assisted housing scheme	80	92	80	92
Other	4 007	8 369	1 044	8 341
	217 985	177 774	174 707	152 906
Historical cost of investments				
Listed shares	9 411	9 411	9 371	9 371
Unlisted shares	36 321	34 766	33 717	33 855
Fixed deposit	36 883	23 300	–	–
Long-term receivables	32 005	40 617	29 042	40 589
	114 620	108 094	72 130	83 815
Shares of post-acquisition reserves of associates	43 125	36 792		
Surplus arising from revaluation of associates and other investments (refer note 12)	60 240	32 888	102 577	69 091
	217 985	177 774	174 707	152 906
The valuation of investments is:				
Listed shares at market value –				
Associate	75 971	51 660	75 971	51 660
Other	91	40	–	–
	76 062	51 700	75 971	51 660
Unlisted shares at current value (Directors' valuation)	73 035	62 157	69 694	60 657
	149 097	113 857	145 665	112 317
(Details of investment in associates and other share investments are given on pages 48 and 49.)				
21. Inventories (refer accounting policy 5)				
Inventories, which are stated at current values, comprise:				
Raw materials	10 374	6 584	7 260	6 107
Waste rock dumps	17 145	14 634	17 145	14 634
Work in progress	8 958	10 223	8 958	10 223
Finished goods	37 321	33 075	32 669	29 920
Machinery spares and stores	76 945	74 210	72 477	73 965
	150 743	138 726	138 509	134 849
Historical cost of inventories	126 280	115 448	115 479	112 813
Surplus arising from revaluation of inventories (refer note 12)	24 463	23 278	23 030	22 036
	150 743	138 726	138 509	134 849

Anglo-Alpha Limited	Group		Company	
	1993 R000	1992 R000	1993 R000	1992 R000
Net book value at beginning of year	1 359 721	1 443 100	1 318 589	1 401 545
Add:				
Replacement capital expenditure	45 559	68 997	44 348	68 361
Expansion capital expenditure	15 641	9 326	14 005	7 635
Surplus/(Deficit) on revaluation of property, plant and equipment (note (i))	72 293	(19 126)	79 779	(24 598)
Assets of newly acquired subsidiaries	75 926	–		
Less:				
Depreciation (note (ii))	146 318	137 565	139 904	130 230
Proceeds on disposal of property, plant and equipment	7 293	8 478	3 098	5 609
Profit on disposal of property, plant and equipment	(3 868)	(3 467)	(1 535)	(1 485)
Net book value at end of year (per note 18)	1 419 397	1 359 721	1 315 254	1 318 589

Notes

(i) *Surplus/(Deficit) on revaluation of fixed assets includes:*

Surplus on revaluation of assets	108 517	64 972	116 003	59 500
Book value of disposals not affecting capacity	627	1 860	627	1 860
Cost of additions not affecting capacity	(36 851)	(85 958)	(36 851)	(85 958)
	72 293	(19 126)	79 779	(24 598)

(ii) *Depreciation includes:*

Historical cost				
Normal	59 805	51 229	53 555	48 668
Extraordinary	–	6 443	–	1 809
Current cost	86 513	79 893	86 349	79 753
	146 318	137 565	139 904	130 230

31 December 1993

Subsidiary companies

| | Issued share capital | | Interest in capital | | | | Interest of Company | | | |
| | | | Direct | | Indirect | | Shares | | Indebtedness | |
	1993 R	1992 R	1993 %	1992 %	1993 %	1992 %	1993 R000	1992 R000	1993 R000	1992 R000
Cement Division										
Anglo-Alpha (Bophuthatswana) (Pty) Limited	1 000	1 000	100	100	–	–	1	1	20	20
Concrete Additives (Pty) Limited	400 000	400 000	100	100	–	–	–	–	(1 742)	(944)
Inter-Africa Supplies (Swaziland) Limited	5	–	–	–	67	–	–	–	–	–
Macdonald & Volck (Pty) Limited	20 000	20 000	100	100	–	–	2 785	2 785	1 379	4 328
National Portland Cement Company Limited	1 240 000	1 240 000	100	100	–	–	1 240	1 240	(615)	(282)
Mortacem (Pty) Limited *(formerly Specialised Concrete Products (Pty) Limited)*	10 000	10 000	100	100	–	–	85	85	(95)	(95)
Swaziland Cement Products (Pty) Limited	300	–	–	–	67	–	–	–	–	–
The Cement Organisation (Swaziland) (Pty) Limited	300	–	67	–	–	–	13 333	–	–	–
Stone and Ready Mixed Concrete Division										
Anglo-Alpha Stone Limited	2 925 079	2 925 079	100	100	–	–	12 871	12 871	8 468	13 080
Benoni Crushers (Pty) Limited	30 000	30 000	–	–	100	100	–	–	–	–
Brakpan Crushers (Pty) Limited	84 000	84 000	–	–	100	100	–	–	–	–
Constone Limited	4 800 000	4 800 000	–	–	100	100	–	–	–	–
Crankshaw Quarries (Pty) Limited	1 200	1 200	–	–	100	100	–	–	–	–
Crown Crushers (Pty) Limited	998	998	–	–	100	100	–	–	–	–
Hipcon Crusher Holdings (Pty) Limited	100 000	100 000	–	–	100	100	–	–	–	–
Hippo Quarries (Pty) Limited	1 000	1 000	–	–	100	100	–	–	–	–
Hippo Quarries (Lesotho) (Pty) Limited	1 000	1 000	–	–	100	100	–	–	–	–
Hippo Quarries (Natal) (Pty) Limited	600	600	–	–	100	100	–	–	–	–
Hippo Quarries (Transvaal) (Pty) Limited	2	2	–	–	100	100	–	–	–	–
Hippo Quarries Granite (Pty) Limited	100	100	–	–	100	100	–	–	–	–
Ital Holdings (Pty) Limited	56 000	–	–	–	100	–	–	–	–	–
Italservice (Pty) Limited	15 000	–	–	–	100	–	–	–	–	–
Klipstone Transport (Pty) Limited	1 000	1 000	–	–	100	100	–	–	–	–
Libanon Transport (Pty) Limited	2	2	–	–	100	100	–	–	–	–
Luipaardsvlei Crushers (Pty) Limited	200	200	–	–	100	100	–	–	–	–
Middelburg Klipbrekery (Edms) Beperk	96	96	–	–	100	100	–	–	–	–
Ngagane Quarrying Company (Pty) Limited	18	18	–	–	100	100	–	–	–	–
Olifantsfontein Quarries (Pty) Limited	600 000	600 000	–	–	100	100	–	–	–	–
Parem Enterprises (Pty) Limited	4 000 000	–	100	–	–	–	5 462	–	46 078	–
Philippi Properties (Pty) Limited	600	600	–	–	50	50	–	–	–	–
Pioneer Crushers (Pty) Limited	54 510	54 510	–	–	100	100	–	–	–	–
Pioneer Ready Mixed Concrete (Pty) Limited	200 000	–	–	–	100	–	–	–	–	–
Pioneer Ready Mixed Concrete (Bophuthatswana) (Pty) Limited	100	–	–	–	100	–	–	–	–	–
Pioneer Ready Mixed Concrete Services (Pty) Limited	250 000	–	–	–	100	–	–	–	–	–
Power Crushers Transvaal (Pty) Limited	4 000	4 000	–	–	100	100	–	–	–	–
Prima Mixed Concrete (Pty) Limited	100	–	–	–	100	–	–	–	–	–
Randfontein Crushed Stone Distributors (Pty) Limited	13 100	13 100	–	–	100	100	–	–	–	–
Reef Quarries (Pty) Limited	8 590	8 590	–	–	100	100	–	–	–	–
Rheebok Quarries (Pty) Limited	100	100	–	–	100	100	–	–	–	–
Roozeboom Brick Works (Pty) Limited	200 000	–	–	–	100	–	–	–	–	–
Springs Crushers (Pty) Limited	34 002	34 002	–	–	100	100	–	–	–	–
Steyns Sand (Pty) Limited	2	2	–	–	100	100	–	–	–	–
Transit – Mixed Concrete South Africa (Pty) Limited	1 822 796	–	–	–	100	–	–	–	–	–
Unified Stone Crushers (Pty) Limited	150 000	150 000	–	–	100	100	–	–	–	–
Venterspost Crushers (Pty) Limited	58 000	58 000	–	–	100	100	–	–	–	–
Verulam Quarries (Pty) Limited – ordinary	20 000	20 000	–	–	100	100	–	–	–	–
– preference	480 000	480 000	–	–	100	100	–	–	–	–
West Crushers (Pty) Limited	148 368	148 368	–	–	100	100	–	–	–	–
Windmill Quarries (Pty) Limited	100 000	100 000	–	–	100	100	–	–	–	–
Industrial Division										
Anglo-Alpha Industrial Minerals Limited	1 428 750	1 428 750	100	100	–	–	3 214	3 214	(3 236)	(3 233)
Ceramic Minerals (Pty) Limited	100 000	100 000	–	–	100	100	–	–	–	–
E R Properties (Pty) Limited	750 000	750 000	100	100	–	–	665	665	(772)	(772)
Industrial Sealants (Pty) Limited	400 000	400 000	100	100	–	–	168	168	(168)	(168)
Lewis & Everitt (Pty) Limited	6 000	6 000	–	–	100	100	–	–	5	5
Messina Dolomite (Pty) Limited	2	2	–	–	100	100	–	–	–	–
New Kusasa Mining (Pty) Limited	36 500	36 500	–	–	55	55	–	–	–	–
Oribi Lime Works (Pty) Limited	150	150	–	–	100	100	–	–	–	–
Plastocarb (Pty) Limited	3 000	3 000	100	100	–	–	2 329	2 329	(2 759)	(799)
Transvaal Graphite & Mineral Company (Pty) Limited	200	200	100	100	–	–	–	–	–	–
Transvaal Magnetite (Pty) Limited	300	300	–	–	100	100	–	–	–	–
Union Lime Company Limited	3 900 000	3 900 000	100	100	–	–	–	–	–	–

Subsidiary companies

	Issued share capital		Interest in capital				Interest of Company			
			Direct		Indirect		Shares		Indebtedness	
	1993	1992	1993	1992	1993	1992	1993	1992	1993	1992
	R	R	%	%	%	%	R000	R000	R000	R000
Property and mineral rights										
Bleskop Stone Crushers (Pty) Limited	16 000	16 000	–	–	100	100	–	–	–	–
Bon Accord Quarries (Pty) Limited	150 000	150 000	–	–	100	100	–	–	–	–
Cannon Quarries (Pty) Limited	11 604	11 604	–	–	100	100	–	–	–	–
Canonby Quarries (Pty) Limited	20 000	20 000	–	–	53	53	–	–	–	–
Cappa Sacks (Pty) Limited (Deregistered)	–	422 000	–	100	–	–	–	422	–	(422)
Cleveland Crushers (1934) (Pty) Limited	24 000	24 000	–	–	100	100	–	–	–	–
Constone (Reef) (Pty) Limited	300	300	–	–	100	100	–	–	–	–
Effingham Quarries (Pty) Limited	12 000	12 000	–	–	100	100	–	–	–	–
Eland Quarries (Pty) Limited	100	100	–	–	100	100	–	–	–	–
Falcon Investments Limited	10 000	10 000	–	–	100	100	–	–	–	–
Highland Enterprises (Pty) Limited	2	2	–	–	100	100	–	–	–	–
Hillcrest Quarries (Pty) Limited	66 000	66 000	–	–	100	100	–	–	–	–
Hillside Mobile Crushers (Pty) Limited	1 000	1 000	–	–	100	100	–	–	–	–
Hilton Quarries Holdings (Pty) Limited	140 000	140 000	–	–	100	100	–	–	–	–
Hippo Crusher Holdings (Pty) Limited	600 000	600 000	–	–	100	100	–	–	–	–
Kliprug Quarries (Pty) Limited	2	2	–	–	100	100	–	–	–	–
Korhaan Investments Limited	10 000	10 000	–	–	100	100	–	–	864	864
Leach & Brown Holdings (Pty) Limited	20 000	20 000	–	–	100	100	–	–	–	–
Metal Recovery Buying Company (Pty) Limited	1	1	100	100	–	–	14	14	–	–
Natal Crushers (Pty) Limited	14	14	–	–	100	100	–	–	–	–
New Capital Granite Quarries (Pty) Limited	15 000	15 000	–	–	100	100	–	–	–	–
Peninsula Quarries (Pty) Limited	851 400	851 400	–	–	100	100	–	–	–	–
Philippi Industrial Townships (Pty) Limited	2 000	2 000	100	100	–	–	2	2	393	383
Poort Crushers (Pty) Limited – ordinary	200	200	–	–	100	100	–	–	–	–
– preference	200	200	–	–	100	100	–	–	–	–
Pretoria Amalgamated Quarries (Pty) Limited	870 000	870 000	–	–	100	100	–	–	–	–
R Snow Enterprises (Pty) Limited	100	100	100	100	–	–	150	150	14	14
The Northern Cape Milling Company Limited	2 000	2 000	–	–	100	100	–	–	–	–
Trans-Atlas Limited	80 000	80 000	–	–	100	100	–	–	–	–
WMG Estates (Pty) Limited	100	100	–	–	100	100	–	–	–	–
Zeekoewater Crushers (Pty) Limited	3 000	3 000	–	–	100	100	–	–	–	–
Group management, financial and technical service companies										
Angalp-Air (Pty) Limited	100 000	100 000	100	100	–	–	211	211	(461)	(663)
Anglo-Alpha Finance (Pty) Limited	100	100	100	100	–	–	–	–	31 054	22 518
Anglo-Alpha Technical Services Limited	5 000	5 000	100	100	–	–	5	5	(5)	(5)
Per note 19							42 535	24 162	78 422	33 829

47

Investments

Name of company	Issued share capital		Percentage held		Carrying/Current value	
	1993	1992	1993	1992	1993	1992
	R	R	%	%	R000	R000
Associate companies						
Listed						
Chemicals and oil						
Omnia Holdings Limited*	73 707 000	73 707 000	26	26	36 742	32 805
Unlisted						
Coal						594	2 981
Anglovaal Coal Holdings (Pty) Limited**	55 001	55 001	50	50	573	544
Corondale Prospecting and Mining Company (Pty) Limited**	200	200	50	50	21	25
East Rand Coal Holdings (Pty) Limited	–	2 000	–	50	–	2 412
Building and construction						47 194	40 934
Ash Resources (Pty) Limited***	200	200	25	25	1 147	478
Cement Distributors (South Africa) (Pty) Limited	1 500	1 500	33	33	–	–
Grinaker Precast (Pty) Limited***	400 000	–	40	–	2 650	–
Namibia Portland Cement Limited	400 000	400 000	50	50	–	–
Natal Portland Cement Company (Pty) Limited***	60 000 000	60 000 000	33	33	35 372	29 098
Parem Enterprises (Pty) Limited	–	4 000 000	–	50	–	2 996
Roozeboom Brick Works (Pty) Limited	–	200 000	–	50	–	853
Southern Cement Distributors (Pty) Limited	1 000	1 000	20	20	1 043	1 013
Slagment (Pty) Limited***	11 600 001	11 600 001	33	33	6 982	6 496
Other						4 251	4 173
ABCP Finance Company (Pty) Limited	1 146	1 146	33	33	–	–
Spilo (Pty) Limited****	1 000 000	1 000 000	26	26	4 251	4 173
Per note 20 – carrying value					88 781	80 893
Other investments						
(Equity interest of less than 20 per cent)						
Listed						
Gold						
The South African Land & Exploration Company Limited	3 213 945	3 213 945	2	2	91	40
Unlisted						
Other						9 097	5 544
Ciments de Bourbon SA (FRF)	9 200 000	9 200 000	7	7	9 097	5 544
Small Business Development Corporation "A" shares	273 093 448	260 912 136	–	–	–	–
Per note 20 – at valuation					9 188	5 584

Twelve month period taken into account to:

   * *31 December 1993*
  ** *30 June 1993*
 *** *30 November 1993*
**** *28 February 1993*

Anglo-Alpha Limited	Group	
	1993	1992
	R000	R000
The Group's proportionate share of retained earnings is as follows:		
Sales	340 077	334 113
Operating profit	33 081	30 111
Borrowing costs	9 898	13 194
Profit before taxation	23 183	16 917
Taxation	12 209	5 273
Profit after taxation	10 974	11 644
Brought to account by the Group as dividend income	9 031	11 375
Profit before extraordinary items	1 943	269
Extraordinary items	3 767	–
Profit for year	5 710	269
Net assets acquired during year	2 178	1 013
Carrying value at beginning of year	80 893	79 611
Carrying value at end of year	88 781	80 893
The Group's proportionate share of assets and liabilities is as follows:		
Property, plant and equipment	109 522	135 330
Investments	8 758	14 556
Current assets	105 624	108 972
	223 904	258 858
Less: Borrowings – interest bearing debt		
long-term	9 365	39 223
current	23 610	44 067
– non-interest bearing debt	102 148	94 675
Equity	88 781	80 893
Loans	12 779	16 587
Total investment (per note 20)	101 560	97 480

(i) The net assets and results of the above companies in which the Group holds an equity interest are reflected at historical cost and deferred tax is accounted for on the liability method using the comprehensive basis.

(ii) No adjustments have been made for any unrealised profits arising from transactions between the Group and the associate companies.

(iii) The above figures are determined from the latest audited financial statements but where these are older than six months the latest financial information available is used.

(iv) Had the Group's share of net attributable retained earnings for the year been included in Group earnings, earnings per share, on a historical cost basis, would have increased by 1,5 per cent or 6 cents per share (1992: increased by 0,3 per cent or 1 cent per share).

(v) The financial position of the associates has not been affected by any significant events occurring between the dates of the associates' financial statements and the Group's annual report.

31 December 1993

	Terms of repayment	Final repayment date	Closing rate of interest 1993 %	1992 %	Group 1993 R000	1992 R000	Company 1993 R000	1992 R000
Fixed rate borrowings								
Loans								
(i) Standard Merchant Bank Limited Unsecured loan	R7 000 000 on 27 June 1994 and R12 000 000 on 27 December 1994	1994	15,67	15,67	**19 000**	19 000	**19 000**	19 000
(ii) Unsecured debentures 1995/99	R3 000 000 p.a. commencing 30 June 1995	1999	10,95	10,95	**15 000**	15 000	**15 000**	15 000
(iii) Industrial Development Corporation of South Africa Limited. Mortgage secured over mining rights and equipment with book value of R86 000 (1992: R86 000)	R7 000 monthly including interest	1994	14,00	14,00	**49**	133	**–**	–
(iv) Repaid during the year					**–**	2 025	**–**	2 000
					34 049	36 158	**34 000**	36 000
Financial lease and suspensive sale obligations (refer note 18)								
(v) First National Bank of Southern Africa Limited. Capitalised lease of plant	R13 812 267 p.a.	1996	13,54	13,36	**31 848**	39 928	**31 848**	39 928
(vi) Stanbic Bank Swaziland Limited (Swaziland Emalangeni)	R12 366 monthly	1999	16,00	–	**483**	–	**–**	–
(vii) Repaid during the year					**–**	2 000	**–**	2 000
					32 331	41 928	**31 848**	41 928
Variable rate borrowings								
Loans								
(viii) Allied Bank Limited. Mortgages secured over immovable property with a book value of R859 000 (1992: R795 000)	R2 443 monthly including interest	1996	11,82	11,73	**75**	96	**75**	96
					75	96	**75**	96
Financial lease and suspensive sale obligations (refer note 18)								
(ix) Nedcor Bank Limited Capitalised lease of plant	R25 860 058 p.a.	1995	14,39	16,68	**41 859**	58 194	**41 859**	58 194
(x) Standard Bank of South Africa Limited	R46 165 610 on 5 January 1995	1995	12,46	15,75	**46 166**	40 353	**46 166**	40 353
(xi) First National Bank of Southern Africa Limited	R2 555 624 half-yearly including interest	1996	7,77	–	**13 818**	–	**–**	–
(xii) Anglo-Alpha Pension Fund Capitalised lease of property	R6 134 735 p.a.	1996	21,00	14,00	**12 318**	14 987	**12 318**	14 987
(xiii) Repaid during the year					**–**	6 767	**–**	6 767
					114 161	120 301	**100 343**	120 301
					180 616	198 483	**166 266**	198 325
Amounts repayable within one year					**55 570**	38 281	**50 968**	38 172
Per note 14					**125 046**	160 202	**115 298**	160 153

Notice is hereby given that the fifty-ninth Annual General Meeting of the shareholders of Anglo-Alpha Limited will be held at Anglovaal House, 56 Main Street, Johannesburg, on Wednesday 4 May 1994, at 12:00 for the following purposes –

1. To receive and consider the annual financial statements for the year ended 31 December 1993.

2. To re-elect the following Directors who retire in terms of the Articles of Association: Messrs M B Burgess, D D B Mkhwanazi, Francis J Ridsdale, A E Schrafl and R L Straszacker.

3. To extend the authority granted to the Directors to issue the unissued shares of the Company at their discretion, subject to the usual rules and regulations of The Johannesburg Stock Exchange, until the next Annual General Meeting of members.

4. To consider and, if deemed fit, to pass with or without modification the following resolutions:

As an ordinary resolution

"That Annexure "A" to the Anglo-Alpha Employees' Share Participation Scheme Trust Deed be amended as follows:

– Paragraph 5

Limit
The aggregate number of Scheme Shares shall at no time exceed the limit that is approved by the Company in General Meeting from time to time. The limit, approved at a General Meeting of the Company held on 12 November 1987, is 10 per cent of the number of issued shares of the Company. This, subject to any movement in the issued share capital of the Company, represents a present limit of 3 007 685 shares.

– Paragraph 6

Offer of Scheme Shares
The Trustees shall, whenever so directed by the Board, offer Employees the Right to Ordinary Shares at the Current Market Price in quantities determined from time to time by the Board, subject to a maximum total entitlement of 210 000 shares per participant."

As a special resolution

"That the Company transfer an amount not exceeding R30 million from the non-distributable reserve to Stated Capital."

Reason for transfer
The reserves are in respect of shareholders' funds retained in the Company and invested in assets and should therefore be treated as permanent capital.

Effect of transfer
The Stated Capital of the Company will increase from R442,2 million to R472,2 million.

The transfer books and register of members of the Company will be closed from 30 April 1994 to 7 May 1994, both days inclusive.

Any member entitled to attend and vote at the meeting is entitled to appoint a proxy or proxies to attend, speak and vote in his stead. The proxy so appointed need not be a member. Proxy forms should be forwarded to reach the Company's Transfer Secretaries not less than 48 hours before the time of holding the meeting.

By order of the Board

P D Buchner
Group Secretary

Sandton
25 February 1994

Board of Directors

NON-EXECUTIVE DIRECTORS

Chairman
P Byland (55)
Appointed to Board in 1970.
A member of the Executive Committee of
Holderbank Financière Glaris Limited
and director of companies.

Deputy Chairman
B E Hersov (67)
Appointed to Board in 1967.
Chairman and Managing Director of
Anglovaal Limited, Chairman of First
National Bank Holdings Limited and
director of companies.

D R Baker (72)
Appointed to Board in 1973.
Former Group Managing Director of
Anglo-Alpha Limited and director of
companies.

W M Grindrod (58)
Appointed to Board in 1985.
Chairman of Grindrod Unicorn Group
Limited and director of companies.

Clive S Menell (62)
Appointed to Board in 1970.
Deputy Chairman of Anglovaal Limited
and director of companies.

D D B Mkhwanazi (40)
Appointed to Board in 1993.
Marketing consultant and director of
companies.

Francis J Ridsdale (81)
Appointed to Board in 1978.
Former senior partner of Deneys Reitz
and director of companies.

J C Robbertze (57)
Appointed to Board in 1984.
Managing Director of Anglovaal
Industries Limited and director of
companies.

T M Schmidheiny* (48)
Appointed to Board in 1976.
Chairman of Holderbank Financière
Glaris Limited and director of companies.

A E Schrafl* (61)
Appointed to Board in 1967.
Deputy Chairman of Holderbank
Financière Glaris Limited and director of
companies.

R L Straszacker (83)
Appointed to Board in 1980.
Former Chairman of Eskom and director
of companies.

EXECUTIVE DIRECTORS

J G Pretorius (58)
Group Managing Director
Appointed to Board in 1983.

R F C Searle (52)
Deputy Group Managing Director
Appointed to Board in 1985.

M B Burgess (53)
Director: Human Resources
Appointed to Board in 1990.

ALTERNATE DIRECTOR

U Bieri* (51)
Appointed to Board in 1989.
A member of the Executive Committee of
Holderbank Financière Glaris Limited.

* Swiss

Group Executive Committee

Johan G Pretorius (58) BSc MBL
*Chairman (35)**
Joined the Group in October 1958 and
held various positions in the Cement,
Stone, Lime and Industrial Minerals
Divisions before being appointed Group
Managing Director in September 1985.

Randolph Bock (52) BSc HBA
*Director: Technical Services (31)**
Joined the Group as a Works
Chemist in 1962. He was seconded to
Holderbank as a Technical Consultant in
1971. In 1982 he was appointed General
Manager of the Ulco cement operation.
He was appointed Director: Technical
Services in March 1990.

Mike B Burgess (53) BA Dip Pers Man
Hon FIPM
*Director: Human Resources (27)**
Joined the Group as Assistant to
Personnel Manager in 1967. In 1981 he
was promoted to Director: Human
Resources. In addition, he served as
Director: Industrial Minerals Division
from 1985 until 1989 and he was
subsequently appointed an Executive
Director in February 1990.

Mike M Doyle (48) BCom
*Director: Stone and Ready Mixed
Concrete Division (22)**
Joined the Group in 1971 as assistant
to the company secretary. He was
appointed General Manager: Hippo
Quarries Transvaal in 1979 and General
Manager: Hippo Quarries in 1982. In
1984 he was appointed General Manager:
Natal Portland Cement, a position he
held until he was appointed Director:
Stone Division in January 1990.

Piet Ferreira (48) BSc(Hons) ACIS MBA
*Director: Industrial Minerals Division
and Director: Cappa Sacks (22)**
Joined the Group in 1971 as assistant
to the company secretary. He was
appointed Company Secretary of Union
Lime in 1976, Financial Manager of
Union Lime and Industrial Minerals in
1978 and Joint General Manager of the
same division in 1980. He was appointed
Director: Industrial Minerals Division in
March 1990 and Director: Cappa Sacks in
November 1991.

Marco Germena (46) CA(SA)
*Director: Lime Division and Director:
Management Services (23)**
Joined the Group as Management
Accountant in 1970. In 1985 he was
appointed Director: Finance and
Administration. He was appointed
Director: Management Services in 1988
and Director: Industrial Minerals Division
in 1989. In May 1990 he was appointed
Director: Lime Division.

Ron F C Searle (52) CA(SA)
*Director: Cement Division (29)**
Appointed Deputy Group Managing
Director in 1985 after 21 years of service.
He joined the Group in 1964
as an assistant in the secretarial and
accounting department. He was
appointed Director: Finance and
Administration in 1981 and Director:
Cement Division in 1985.

Trevor G Wagner (46) CA(SA) MBL
*Director: Finance and Administration
(16)**
Joined the Group in 1977 as Assistant
Group Secretary. He was appointed
Group Secretary in 1979 and Director:
Finance and Administration in January
1988.

* Years of service

Changes subsequent to 31 December 1993:

1. Ron Searle, in addition to being Deputy
   Group Managing Director, was appointed
   Director: Management Services with effect
   from 1 January 1994.

2. Marco Germena was appointed Director:
   Cement Division with effect from 1 January
   1994.

3. Piet Ferreira was appointed Director:
   Industrial Division with effect from
   1 January 1994, incorporating the Lime
   Division into his existing responsibilities.

Administration

Group Secretary
P D Buchner ACIS H Dip Co Law H Dip
Tax Law (Wits)

Registered Office and Postal Address
Anglo-Alpha Limited
Reg No 05/05750/06
94 Rivonia Road, Sandton 2199
PO Box 781868, Sandton 2146
Telephone (011) 780-1000
Fax (011) 783-8950
Telegraphic address – Angalp
International Telex – 4-22075 SA

Transfer Secretaries
Anglovaal Limited
56 Main Street, Johannesburg 2001
PO Box 62379, Marshalltown 2107
Telephone (011) 634-9111

Bankers
First National Bank Limited

Attorneys
Deneys Reitz

Auditors
KPMG Aiken & Peat

Appendix 3

Glossary

This short glossary is intended to assist in understanding the terms used by the accountant. Where they could be found Afrikaans equivalents have also been included, but sometimes there is no direct Afrikaans translation. Descriptive terms in Afrikaans have not been included.

Note: Items in italics within a definition have a definition of their own in this glossary.

Above the line: A term coined to describe that part of the income statement which deals with income and expenses up to the point of determination of *net income*. Extraordinary items and appropriations of income are "below the line".

Account: Originally, the page in the ledger reserved for recording transactions of a particular type. The menacing is still basically the same, but has been extended to include page equivalents in mechanised and electronic data processing systems. (Rekening)

Accounting: The whole conventional art, science and practice of maintaining financial records, preparing reports on the basis of these records and interpreting these reports. To be pedantic, it must be added that the maintaining of records, known as *bookkeeping*, is often excluded from this definition. (Rekeningkunde)

Accounting conventions: Those practices which have become so universally accepted by accountants that they form the basis of accounting theory.

Accounting entity: Any organisation having a separable financial being for which separate financial records can be maintained. This organisation need not be a separate legal being: different branches of the same business may have separable, though connected, financial records. (Rekeningkundige entiteit)

Accounting period or reporting period: The period covered by a financial report. For purposes of income tax and the Companies Act this period is one year, but for internal periods this may be any suitable period. A manager may want monthly reports of income and expenses, for instance, while large construction contracts may cover two or more years. (Rekeningkundige tydperk, verantwoordingstydperk)

Accounting practices: The formalised practices recognised by the organised accounting profession and by which the members of the profession are bound to regulate their financial reporting. In a set of financial statements, the note on accounting practices will refer to those practices which are applied in the financial statements or explain why certain practices have not been applied. (Rekeningkundige praktyke)

Accounts payable or creditors: The amounts owing by the undertaking to outsiders. There will normally be a split between short term and long term creditors, and there will often be a split between *trade creditors* and other creditors. (Rekeninge betaalbaar of krediteure)

Accounts receivable or debtors: The amounts owing to the undertaking by outsiders. There will normally be a split between short term and long term debtors, with long term debtors often being further split between instalment sale debtors and other long term debtors. (Rekeninge ontvangbaar of debiteure)

Amortisation: A concept similar to *depreciation*, which involves the writing off of an asset over a period of time. The two terms are used interchangeably by some American writers but amortisation generally applies to the writing off of *intangible assets*. (Amortisasie)

Appropriation account or retained earnings statement: The final part of an income statement in an accounting entity where more than one party is entitled to share in the *profits*, this statement shows how the profits are divided among the various entitled parties including, where applicable, the tax authorities. (Verdelingsrekening, winsverdelingsrekening)

Arms-length transaction: A transaction which takes place at market values as though the parties were totally unconnected, even though there may be a substantial connection between them.

Articles of association: The document which regulates the relationship between a company, its shareholders and outside parties. It is maintained on register by the Registrar of Companies and anyone dealing with a company is deemed to have constructive knowledge of the contents of the Articles because they are available for inspection. (Statute van 'n Maatskappy)

Asset: Any item, tangible or intangible, which belongs to the organisation concerned. (Bate)

Associated company: A company in which a company has a long term direct interest less than an absolute controlling interest, but which either exceeds twenty per cent of the equity of the investee company or is large enough to allow the company to exercise significant influence over the activities of the investee company. This interest should be accounted for by the equity method. (Geassosieerde maatskappy)

Audit: A word which has become used far more widely than just in the accounting world, it derives from the latin "audire", meaning to hear. From an accounting point of view the word indicates an examination of the financial and other records of an undertaking to determine the reliability of any reports prepared on the basis of those records.

It is necessary to distinguish between internal and external audits. The former are part of the normal management process, and can vary from elementary checks of cash on hand to extensive reviews of systems employed by an undertaking. The extent of the responsibilities of the internal auditor is prescribed by the management of the undertaking.

The external auditor is required to report on the financial statements of the undertaking and to state whether they fairly present the state of affairs and the financial results for the period under review. While his duties can be extended by management, the minimum duties are often prescribed by laws such as the Companies Act. (Oudit, ouditering)

Audit report: The report prepared by the auditor certifying his satisfaction with the financial statements in accordance with his brief, or stating which aspects have not satisfied him. (Ouditverslag)

Auditor: The functionary who performs the audit. In terms of the Companies Act only persons registered with the Public Accountants and Auditors Board may act as auditors for companies. Other audits may have less stringent requirements. (Ouditeur)

Authorised share capital: The amount and classification of share capital which a company is authorised to issue in terms of its *Memorandum of Association*. This amount can be changed by means of a *special resolution*. (Gemagtigde aandelekapitaal)

Balance sheet or statement of financial position: A list of all assets and liabilities of an organisation, with monetary values, on a specified date and of the difference between the monetary values of the two which is known as *capital* or owners equity. (Balansstaat)

Bear: One who deals in securities in expectation of a fall in prices.

Bear market: A period during which the prices of securities quoted on the stock exchange are falling.

Below the line: A term coined to cover that part of the income statement after the determination of normal operating profits. It includes extraordinary items and appropriations of profits.

Bookkeeping: Maintaining financial records. This is part of *accounting*, but is nowadays often distinguished from it. (Boekhou)

Book value or net book value: The value of assets as shown in the financial statements. This will usually be cost or valuation less depreciation written off and may bear little relationship to actual market values of the assets. (Boekwaarde, netto boekwaarde)

Budget: A detailed estimate of future revenue and expenses used as a planning and control tool. (Begroting)

Bull: One who deals in securities in expectation of a rise in prices.

Bull market: A period during which the prices of securities quoted on the stock exchange are rising.

Business trust: see *Trading trust*

Capital: Also known as "net worth", "owner's equity", "shareholders' equity", "net assets", "owner's contribution" or "owner's interest", this represents the difference between the monetary values of the assets and liabilities. (Kapitaal, eienaarsbelang, aandeelhouersbelang)

Capital income or expense: *Income or expense* which does not affect the operating profit of an undertaking such as the profit or loss on the sale of a fixed asset. (Kapitaalwins, kapitaalverlies)

Capital gains tax: A form of taxation on capital profits not currently in effect in South Africa, but fairly common throughout the world. The base on which this tax is levied differs considerably from country to country. (Kapitaalwinsbelasting)

Capital transfer duty: A tax levied on transactions whereby any item of capital value, whether land or cash or anything in between, is transferred from one party to another. (Kapitaaloordragreg)

Cash flow statement: Either a funds flow statement prepared using cash as the definition of funds or a simple summary of the cash transactions of an organisation over a period. (Kontantvloeistaat)

Chairman's statement or report: A document required to be attached to the published financial statements of companies listed on the Johannesburg Stock Exchange, dealing with broad issues concerning the company and including a forecast for the following year. (Voorsittersverslag)

Chartered Accountant (SA): A member of the South African Institute of Chartered Accountants who has met all the requirements detailed in chapter three. (Geoktrooieerde Rekenmeester (SA))

Close corporation: A small business corporation having juristic personality. It is limited to a maximum of ten members and is registered in terms of the Close Corporation Act of 1984. (Beslote Korporasie)

Company: A corporation with juristic personality registered under the Companies Act of 1973 or any of its predecessor Acts. (Maatskappy)

Consolidated financial statements: The combined financial statements of a group of companies, giving the financial results and position of the group rather than just of one company. (Gekonsolideerde finansiële state)

Contingent liability: A liability which does not yet exist but which will come into existence if a certain event occurs. This could include such cases as a guarantee issued for payment of a debt by someone else which will only become a liability if that person fails to meet his obligations. (Gebeurlikheidslas)

Co-operative: A special class of juristic person registered under the Co-operatives Act of 1981. (Koöperasie)

Cost of control of subsidiary or goodwill arising upon consolidation: The excess of the amount paid for the shares of a subsidiary over the book value of the assets pertaining to those shares.

Cost of sales, cost of goods sold: An item in the *trading account* which is normally determined by adding opening *stock* to purchases and allied costs and deducting closing stock. (Koste van verkope)

Credit: 1. The right-hand side of ledger account or journal entry. Amount with net credit balances represent sources of cash, either permanent inflows such as income or temporary inflows such as loans or purchases of goods or services not yet paid for. (Krediet, kredit) 2. The right to pay for goods or services some time after receiving them. (Krediet)

Creditors: see *Accounts payable*

Cum div: The price at which a share is traded after the announcement of a dividend is paid but before the right to the dividend is finally vested in the owner of the shares. In other words, the price paid for the share includes an amount in respect of the dividend which will be recovered as soon as this is paid.

Current assets: Cash and assets which should, in the normal course of operations, be turned into cash within one year. (Bedryfsbates, vlottende bates)

Current liabilities: Liabilities which have to be settled within one year. (Bedryfslaste, vlottende laste)

Debentures: Loan certificates issued by a company or other organisation. They normally entitle the holder to a fixed or determinable rate of interest and repayment on or after a specified date on defined terms. They may also be convertible to shares in the company. (Skuldbriewe)

Debit: The left-hand side of a ledger account or journal entry. Accounts with net debit balances represent applications of cash, either on assets or expenses. (Debiet, debit)

Debtors: see Accounts receivable.

Deferred tax: Income tax which, because of allowances incorporated into the tax laws, will only become payable in an accounting year subsequent to the one in which the taxable income is earned. (Uitgestelde belasting)

Depreciation: The expensing of assets over an appropriate period of time by writing an amount off operating profits to a provision for depreciation. (Waardevermindering, voorsiening vei waardevermindering)

Director: A person elected by the shareholders of a company to manage the company on behalf of the shareholders. (Direkteur)

Direct taxes: Taxes levied directly on the income of the taxpayer. (Direkte belasting)

Discussion paper: A document issued by the Accounting Practices Board for discussion prior to refinement and possible eventual incorporation into an accounting or auditing standard. Discussion papers carry numbers in the series DP. (Besprekingsdokument, BD)

Dividend: That proportion of the profits of a company paid out to the shareholders rather than being retained within the company. (Dividend)

Donations tax: A tax levied on donations made. Effectively it represents *Estate duty* paid in advance since it was designed to overcome the evasion of estate duty by way of giving away the taxable estate to one's future heirs. (Geskenkbelasting)

Equity, equities: 1. The total investment in an undertaking, whether by the owner(s) or by creditors. (Belange)
2. The investment in the undertaking by the owner(s), more property referred to as Owners' equity. (Eienaarsbelang)

Estate duty: a tax levied on the value of the estate of a deceased person (Boedelbelasting)

Ex div: The price paid for a share as soon as the rights to a dividend not yet paid still accrue to the seller.

Expenditure: Any moneys laid out, whether in cash immediately or by making use of credit and so paying out cash at a later date including purchases of capital items.

Expense: Any transaction which decreases the *profit* of the undertaking. (Uitgawe)

Exposure draft: A preliminary draft of a proposed accounting standard which is sent out for comment, after which it may be adopted or revised and again sent out as an exposure draft. These drafts carry numbers in the range ED. (Geopenbaarde konsep, GK)

Finance, financial management: This is the most complex aspect of the whole accounting process and involves decisions concerning investments in the broadest sense, sourcing of funds and capital structures for organisations. (Finansiële bestuur)

Financial statements: The reports presented after an accounting period dealing with financial flows during that period and the financial position at the end of that period. (Finansiële state, finansiële jaarstate)

Fixed assets: *Assets* used in the production of income but not a source of cash within the normal operating pattern of the undertaking. (Vaste bates)

Funds statement, statement of sources and applications of funds: A statement dealing with the sources and applications of funds, as variously defined, by an organisation during the course of an accounting period. (Fondsestaat, bronne en aanwendings van fondse staat)

Gearing of financial gearing: 1. The effect which the use of borrowed funds has on the return of *owners' equity*. (Hefboomeffek)
2. The ratio between borrowings and *owners' equity*. (Hefboom, finansiële hefboom)

Generally accepted accounting practice: A formalised practice, recognised by the organised accounting profession, which lays down how a specific type of transaction is to be dealt with in the financial statements. Generally abbreviated to GAAP. (Algemeen aanvaarde rekeningkundige praktyk)

General sales tax: A tax introduced in South Africa on certain types of transactions at a flat rate. Generally abbreviated as GST (Algemene Verkoopsbelasting, AVB)

Goodwill: An amount paid for a business in excess of the tangible value of its assets, usually because the business as a going concern is worth more than the separate value of the assets. (Klandisiewaarde)

Gross profit: The difference between the selling price of goods sold and the cost of goods sold. (Bruto wins)

Holding company: A company which has control of *subsidiary companies*, either by virtue of holding a majority of shares in those companies, having a majority of the voting power or being able to control the composition of the boards of directors of those companies.

Income: 1. Money or value received by an organisation for its own account. (Inkomste)

2. The net income or *profit* of an undertaking. (Netto inkomste, wins)

Income statement: 1. The name specified by the Companies Act for the financial report dealing with the operating activities of a *company* leading to the determination of a *profit* or *loss* and the appropriation of any profit. This report need only contain certain minimum information as required by the fourth schedule to the Companies Act.

2. Due to the influence of the Companies Act this name is now commonly applied to the complete operating reports of most undertakings. Such reports are commonly split into several parts as may be applicable, including *manufacturing account, trading account, profit and loss account* and *appropriation account*. (Inkomstestaat)

Income tax: A tax levied directly on income earned by a taxpayer. (Inkomstebelasting)

Indirect taxes: Taxes levied not directly on the taxpayers income but on some indirect basis such as a transaction tax or value added tax. (Indirekte belasting)

Inflation accounting: A still not finalised series of techniques for taking into account the effects of inflation on the financial reports of an undertaking. (Verantwoording vir inflasie)

Intangible assets: Assets such as goodwill or unexpired patents or copyrights which have no physical value in themselves but which may nevertheless produce income. In any evaluation of financial statements they should be treated with great circumspection since their value subsists purely in the use to which they may be put. In different circumstances they may be worthless. (Ontasbare bates)

Inter vivos trust: A *trust* created during the life time of the founder for the benefit of certain beneficiaries at some future date or even in the present.

Inventory: 1. A list of items such as *fixed assets* or trading *stocks* held on a particular date. (Inventaris)

2. Used in America to mean the physical trading *stock* on hand. (Voorraad)

Issued share capital: The share capital actually issued by the company and for which it has received payment. This may be the full *authorised share capital* or some lesser amount. (Uitgereikte aandelekapitaal)

Juristic personality or legal persona: Existence granted to a corporate body in terms of a law so that it can exist separately from its members, possess its own assets and incur its own liabilities. (Regspersoonlikheid)

Legal persona: see juristic personality

Leverage or operating leverage: The effect on a firm's operating profit of operating at a capacity utilisation in excess of its break even level of operations. (Bedryfshefboom)

Listed company: A company whose shares are quoted on a recognised stock exchange. (Genoteerde maatskappy)

Long term liabilities: In balance sheet classification, liabilities which do not have to be settled within the next financial year. (Langtermynlaste)

Loss: An excess of expenditure over income in an operating period or in respect of a particular transaction. (Verlies)

Manufacturing account: The first section of an *income statement* for a manufacturing concern in which the cost of production for a period is determined. (Vervaardigingsrekening)

Mark-up: The percentage, or less commonly the absolute amount, added to the cost price of an item in order to determine the selling price. (Toeslag, toeslagpersentasie)

Market capitalisation: The total market value of the shares of a company quoted on a stock exchange, obtained by multiplying the current market price by the number of shares in issue. (Mark kapitalisasie)

Memorandum of Association: The document of registration of a company under the Companies Act. It contains details of the name of the company, the objects for which it was formed, the *authorised share capital* and the names of the first signatories.

Minimum tax on companies (MTC): A tax introduced in the 1988 budget in order to bridge the gap in government finances. Theoretically it was not a new tax but merely a forced payment of tax in advance of the liability for tax being incurred.

Net income: see *Profit*

Net monetary liabilities: In inflation accounting, the amount by which monetary liabilities, cash and amounts owing to the company determinable in cash, exceed monetary assets, amounts owing by the company determinable in cash.

Nominal value: see *Par value*

No par value shares: Shares issued with no par value attached to them. This was an innovation in South Africa when introduced by the Companies Act of 1973 but was already long established in other countries at that time. It was simply a realistic acceptance of the fact that the par value has little meaning after the shares have been issued. (Geen pari-waarde aandele)

Owners' equity: see *Capital*

Partnership: An undertaking organised by two or more people for the purpose of making a profit which they will share amongst themselves. (Vennootskap)

Par value: The legal value attached to shares in a company at the time of registration of the company and the minimum value at which the shares may normally be issued by the company. (Pari-waarde)

Profit: An excess of income over expenditure over a period or in respect of a particular transaction. (Wins)

Profit and loss account: That section of an *income statement* in which the operating expenses are set out for deduction from the gross income or *gross profit* and sundry income added in order to determine the *net profit* for the period. (Wins- en verliesrekening)

Prospectus: An invitation to the public to subscribe for shares in a public company. It is a very comprehensive document and must comply with the requirements of Schedule 3 to the Companies Act. (Prospektus)

Provision: An amount set aside from profits to meet a specific obligation or loss of a company which cannot be precisely determined at the date of the financial statements. Provisions for depreciation are strictly speaking incorrectly named. (Voorsiening)

Quoted company: see *Listed company*

Retained earnings: That part of the profits of a company not paid out as dividends or transferred to a reserve but generally available for use in the company's operations. (Onuitgekeerde winste, opgehoopde winste)

Reserve: An amount set aside to meet future requirements for which there is no method of estimating the amount. There are two types of reserve:

1. Distributable reserves are created out of profits, the most common being retained earnings. They are available at any time for the payment of dividends to shareholders. (Uitkeerbare reserwes)

2. Non-distributable reserves are not available for payment of dividends. They are not created normally by appropriations of profit. Included are the legally non-distributable reserves such as share premium account and the voluntarily non-distributable reserves

such as reserves for the increased replacement cost of fixed assets. (Nie-uitkeerbare reserwes)

Retained earnings statement: see *Appropriation account.*

Revenue income or expense: Transactions which have the effect of increasing or reducing the operating income of an undertaking.

Section 21 company: A company registered in terms of Section 21 of the Companies Act which makes provision for the registration of organisations which do not have the making of a profit as an object. If a company of this type was registered under the preceding Companies Act it will still be known as an Incorporated Association not for Gain.

Sole proprietorship: A business owned by one person. (Eenmansaak)

Special resolution: Certain transactions can only be performed by a company if the requirements of a special resolution are met, these requirements being that twenty-one days written notice of the resolution to be proposed and a three quarter majority of shareholders present approving the resolution. Holders of at least one quarter of the shares of the company must be present in person or by proxy. Full details are given in section 199 of the Companies Act. (Spesiale besluit)

Stag: One who applies for a new issue of shares in the expectation that the opening price of the shares will be higher than the issue price so that he can immediately sell at a stagging profit.

Statement of financial position: see *Balance sheet*

Stock: 1. The trading goods which a business has on hand for resale. (Voorraad)

2. A number of shares in a company put together in a bundle in terms of section 100 of the Companies Act. Once shares have been converted to stock the stock bundle can be bought or sold in any fraction of the bundle and not necessarily in a proportion representative of the shares which originally went into the bundle.

Stock exchange: A market place where securities of various types are traded through agents know as *stockbrokers*. (Beurs, aandelebeurs, *aandelemakelaars*)

Subsidiary company: A company which is controlled by another company, either by that other company having a majority of the shares or a majority of the voting power or being able in some way to control the composition of the board of directors. (Filiaal-maatskappy)

Tangible assets: *Assets* of an organisation the physical existence of which can be verified. (Tasbare bates)

Testamentary trust: A trust created in terms of the will of a deceased person.

Trade creditors: Persons or organisations to which money is owed in respect of the normal trading operations of an organisation. (Handelskrediteure)

Trading account: That part of an *income statement* which deals with the determination of the *gross profit* of a trading concern. (Handelsrekening)

Trading trust or business trust: an *inter vivos trust* created as a vehicle for a trading concern. (Saketrust)

Trust: A body formed by a founder who divests himself of certain assets, either by selling them or giving them to the trust where they are to be held for the benefit of named or determinable beneficiaries. The trust can be either an *inter vivos trust* or a *testamentary trust. (trust)*

Trustee: A person appointed to administer a trust. (Trustee)

Ultimate holding company: In the case of a large group of companies it may be found that there are holding companies which are themselves subsidiaries of other holding companies. In a case like this it may be that a company has a holding company, but is ultimately controlled by the company which controls its holding company. This latter company is then its ultimate holding company.

Unappropriated profits: see *Retained earnings*

Underwriters: When shares are being issued the promoters may obtain the services of someone, usually a financial institution, to guarantee that all shares not taken up by the public to whom the shares are offered will be bought by that person or institution. For this service, known as underwriting the issue, a fee is charged, whether or not the shares are actually taken up by the underwriter or not.

Undistributed profits: see *Retained earnings*

Undrawn profits: The term used in the financial statements of a *close corporation* which is equivalent to *retained earnings* in a *company*.

Value added statement or wealth created statement: A statement purporting to show the wealth created by an undertaking over a period and the distribution of that wealth to the various parties who contributed to the making of that wealth. (Toegevoegde waardestaat)

Value added tax: A tax on transactions whereby the tax payable is determined by reference to the value added by the organisation concerned. This is normally the difference between tax paid on inputs to the firm and the tax payable on the outputs of the firm. (Toegevoegde waarde belasting)

Wear and tear allowance: The amount allowed by the tax authorities as a deduction from taxable income in respect of *depreciation*. It is a purely arbitrary percentage of the original cost and does not necessarily bear any meaningful relationship to the economic life of the asset. (Slytasietoelaag)

Working capital: the net current assets of an undertaking, which is the difference between current assets and current liabilities. (Bedryfskapitaal)

Appendix 4

Recommended further reading

Chapter 1

1. Anthony, Robert N *Tell it like it was* 1983 Richard D Irwin Inc
2. Burden, Tom, Reg Chapman and Richard Stead *Business in society* 1981 Butterworths & Co (Publishers) Ltd

Chapter 2

1. Taylor, Ian R, Leon Kritzinger and Leon Puttick *The principles and practice of auditing* 1983 Juta & Company Ltd Chapters 1–6
2. Nobes, Christopher and John Kellas *Accountancy explained* 1990 Penguin Books (British oriented but generally applicable to South Africa)

Chapter 3

1. Everingham G K and B D Hopkins *Generally accepted accounting practice—A South African viewpoint* 2nd edition 1982 (updated regularly) Juta & Company Ltd

Chapter 4

1. Cilliers H S et al *Enterprise Law* 1993 Butterworths Ltd
2. van Niekerk J A S *Co-operative theory and practice* 1988 South African Agricultural Union

Chapter 5

1. Both Juta and Butterworth publish books and periodicals on South African and foreign taxes. Because of the frequent changes in tax law it is advisable to contact the publishers to determine what is available at any time.
2. The Old Mutual guide to South African tax is published annually and contains all the information a non-specialist could want.
3. Similar guides have been published by other undertakings, including Standard Trust, Sanlam and Deloittes.

Chapter 6

1. Any introductory text on accounting. Most of these are aimed at the potential accountant and may be rather technical for those who simply want a general background.
2. Weil, Sidney *Accounting skills* 1989 Juta and Company Ltd (Highly recommended)

Chapter 7

1. Louvau, Gordon and Marjorie Jackson *Computers in Accountants' Offices* 1982 Lifetime Learning Publications (The classic book in this field, but now rather dated)
2. Mawdudur, Rahman and Maurice Halliday *Accounting Information Systems* 1988 Prentice Hall
3. Page, John and Paul Hooper *Accounting and information systems* 4th edition 1990 Prentice hall

Chapter 8 and chapter 9

1. Everingham, G K *Corporate Reporting* 3rd edition 1990 Juta & Company Ltd

Chapter 10

1. Any introductory text on accounting.

Chapter 11

1. Hawkins, David F *Corporate financial reporting and analysis* 3rd edition 1986 Prentice Hall

Chapter 12

1. Parker Lee D *Financial reporting to employees* 1988 Garland Publishing Inc
2. Nobes, Christopher *The Baring Securities guide to international financial reporting* 1991 Basil Blackwell Ltd
3. Radebaugh, Lee H *International aspects of segment disclosures* 1987 Glasgow Business School, Glasgow University
4. Belkaoui, Ahmed *The new environment in international accounting* 1988 Quorum Books
5. McGee, Robert W *Accounting for inflation* 1981 Prentice Hall

Chapter 13

1. Warren, B O *Financial analysis* 1991 Renall Publishers

Chapter 14

1. Foster, George *Financial statement analysis* 2nd edition 1990 Prentice Hall

Chapter 15

1. Hawkins, David F *Corporate financial reporting and analysis* 3rd edition 1986 Prentice Hall
2. Schilit, W Keith and Howard M Schilit *Blue chips and hot tips* 1992 New York Institute of Finance
3. Helfert, Erich A *Techniques of financial analysis* 1987 6th edition Richard D Irwin
4. Harrington, Diana R and Brent D Wilson *Corporate financial analysis* 3rd edition 1989 Richard D Irwin

Chapter 16

1. Jaedicke, Robert K and Robert T Sprouse *Accounting flows: income, funds and cash* 1965 Prentice Hall (Still the classic work on this topic)
2. Any intermediate course accounting textbook. It is also a good idea to read GAAP statement AC118.

Chapter 17

1. Welsch, Glenn A *Budgeting: Profit planning and control* 4th edition 1976 Prentice Hall
2. Sizer, John *An insight into management accounting* Revised edition 1985 Penguin Books Ltd

Chapter 18

1. Uliana, Enrico et al *Financial management* 2nd edition 1992 Juta & Co Ltd
2. Nunes, Morris A *Operational cash flow management and control* 1982 Prentice Hall
3. Van Horne, James C *Financial management and policy* 7th edition 1986 Prentice Hall

Chapter 19

1. Van Horne, James C *Financial management and policy* 7th edition 1986 Prentice Hall
2. Brigham, Eugene C and Louis C Grapenski *Financial management* 6th edition 1991 The Dryden Press

Section 4 generally

1. Guerard, John and H T Vaught *The handbook of financial modelling* 1989 Probus Publishing Company
2. Findlay, M Chapman and Edward E Williams *An integrated analysis for managerial finance* 1970 Prentice Hall (Only for the mathematically inclined)
3. Pappas, James L and Mark Hirschey *Managerial economics* 6th edition 1990 The Dryden Press (Chapters 6–9 and 13)

General

1. The financial press—Business Day, Financial Mail, Finance Week, Finansies en Tegniek, Sunday Times Business Times, Sake Rapport and the financial pages of the daily press.
2. Griffiths, Ian *Creative Accounting* 1986 Firethorn Press (A review of certain fraudulent/near fraudulent practices in presentation of financial statements).

Appendix 5

Answers to test-yourself questions

Part One

Chapters 1–3

1. Scorekeeping, attention-directing and problem solving
2. *(c)* This one is a bit tricky. The holder of a CA (SA) is not automatically entitled to carry out such an audit but has first to register with the Public Accountants and Auditors Board. Only CA's may do this, but many never do.
3. *(d)* The statements are issued by the SAICA, but the Accounting Practices Board, which is a sub-committee of the SAICA but also has representatives from other interested bodies, actually prepares them.
4. *(b)* Only the CA(SA) has a formal period of training. The other institutes require practical experience, but do not lay down formal rules for obtaining this.
5. *(d)* Members of professional bodies which have a disciplinary code and which are recognised by the Minister of Finance may act as accounting officers. At the date of writing (June 1994) the ACCA had not applied for such recognition.
6. *(c)* See the definition in AC103
7. *(b)* Because it violates consistency the effects of such changes have to be specifically disclosed.
8. *(c)* While depreciation was once regarded as making provision for replacement of an asset, economic conditions, particularly the effects of inflation, have made this provision meaningless and this is the definition which is now accepted.
9. *(d)* More properly, perhaps, the answer should have been either of the above.
10. *(a)* This is a requirement introduced by the Companies Act of 1973.

Chapter 4: Forms of organisation

1. *(b)* No written agreement is necessary, but there must be a profit objective.
2. *(a)* The only documents on public register are the founding statement and any amended founding statements. The liability of members of CC's is limited in the same way as that of shareholders in a company, and distributions by a CC are treated in exactly the same way as dividends paid by a company.
3. *(b)* The shareholder has no right other than to vote at meetings. He only becomes entitled to a dividend when the dividend is declared, which the company does not have to do, and has no right of access to the company's records other than the annual financial reports (and interim reports where applicable).
4. *(c)* These are two of the major differences between the two forms.
5. *(b)* A partnership has no legal existence except in the persons of its partners.
6. *(a)* The voting procedures are the opposite of those described, while a co-operative may sell its shares to anyone unless it chooses specifically to limit its membership.
7. *(a)* A partnership must register for purposes of value added tax, but cannot own fixed property (such property belongs to the partners, not the

partnership) and does not pay income tax, which is paid by the each of the partners on his own share of the net income.

8. *(c)* A sole trader is not a legal entity. The owner of the business is a legal entity and has responsibility for the affairs of the sole trader business. The owner is also the taxable entity.

9. *(d)* Free conversion between the various forms of company and close corporation is permitted as long as the requirements of the new form are met eg a public company with ten or less shareholders, all of whom are natural persons, may convert to a close corporation.

10. *(b)* Partners are jointly and severally liable for all the debts of the partnership, but a partner paying the partnership debts is entitled to recover their proportionate share from each of the other partners. They are liable for all debts, even those specifically incurred by other partners in contravention of a partnership agreement.

Chapter 5: Taxation

1. *(b)* Incorporated bodies pay income tax in their own right, while sole traders and partners pay tax on their own income, which may include more than just the income from the businesses.

2. *(a)* This is specifically laid down as not taxable in South Africa. Royalties are subject to income tax in the country where the book was written (Olive Schreiner's case) and the interest on the fixed deposit will be deemed to be South African income unless the contrary can be proven.

3. *(d)* Any of the options may lead to the benefit of the assessed loss being cancelled.

4. *(a)* If the Receiver decided that it was John's intention to renovate the house in order to sell it at a profit he would become liable for income tax on the difference between the selling price of the house and the total cost of the house and renovations.

5. *(b)* Regardless of whether or not they are married in community of property, the wife's income other than investment income is taxed in her own hands.

6. *(c)* Interest of less than R2 000 per year is exempted from tax, as are dividends. Running a business, regardless of the level of income generated, incurs liability for registration as a provisional taxpayer.

7. *(d)* All of the above apply. Note that if only part of the income of the trust is paid out to the beneficiaries the trust will be taxed on the amount not paid out.

8. *(b)* 1995. While the money has been earned during the 1994 tax year there is as yet no certainty that Betty will be getting any of it, and the amount that she will be getting is subject to the quantity of returned goods and cannot be determined with certainty at the end of February 1994. It will therefore only be taxed in the year in which the amount becomes certain.

9. *(d)* would be the normal answer. Note that if a person is regarded as a professional gambler by the Receiver he may have trouble with his

winnings from the casino, and that if a person is regarded as a speculator in shares he may also have trouble with the sale of the inherited shares.

10. *(b)* The amounts laid down do often seem to be arbitrary, but the basis is that the taxable value of any fringe benefit should be equal to the cost to the employer granting that benefit.

Part Two

1. True. The asset "equipment" would increase, but the asset "cash" would decrease by the same amount.
2. True. A one man business may not be a legal entity but it is an accounting entity.
3. False. The capital of a business equals assets minus liabilities.
4. False. Take another look at the accounting equation.
5. True. Cost of goods sold may be shown in the trading account, but it remains an expense of the undertaking.
6. True. That's what the ledger is for.
7. False. An increase in expenses can be balanced by a decrease in assets or an increase in liabilities or capital.
8. False. Source documents are used to make entries into the journal.
9. False. Money drawn out of a business by the owner is an appropriation of profit or a withdrawal of capital.
10. False. The expense is incurred when the goods are purchased. Payment of the account is simply reduction of a liability.

Part Three

1. True. The cash flow statement simply summarises the financial effects of the operating activities rather than reporting on them.
2. False. The ratios help in the interpretation of the figures on the statements, but the statements contain a great deal of information which would not be available from the ratios alone.
3. True, generally. However, decreases could also be due to seasonal or cyclical factors such as increased economic well-being. One cannot say what a ratio implies without examining all the relevant circumstances.
4. False, false, false! Businesses differ, economic times differ, customs in different countries differ so how can there be universal norms???
5. False. The one year period is an arbitrary one imposed on all businesses by tax and company law, but it does not determine the natural cycles for a business.
6. False. The current ratio is calculated by dividing the current *assets* by the current *liabilities*.
7. False.If the accounts receivable collection period remains constant it will be directly proportional to sales.
8. True, generally. It could also be caused by other factors—see 3 above.
9. True. If stock increases, purchases are greater than cost of sales and vice versa.
10. False. Gearing describes the relationship between a firm's debt and its owners' equity.

Part Four

1. True. The disposal value of an asset forms a cash inflow for purposes of evaluation of a project.
2. False. The higher the hurdle rate the higher the return the company wants, and therefore the lower the price it wishes to pay for a particular cash inflow stream.
3. True. As the hurdle rate increases (or as the term becomes longer) the residual values at the end of the project become smaller and are less likely to influence the investment decision.
4. False. A net present value becomes negative as soon as the discounted cash inflows are less than the discounted cash outflows. A negative value would call for rejection of the project on financial grounds.
5. False. Variable costs fluctuate directly in proportion to volume of production.
6. True. The result of relaxing credit terms usually has two consequences, both of which tend to lead to an increase in debtors. They are slower payments from debtors and increased sales.
7. *(d)* All of the costs mentioned are a direct result of carrying the stock.
8. F. A decrease in a share's beta value simply means that the share's price will show smaller fluctuations in the future in relation to movements in the market as a whole. This lower volatility may lead to increased institutional buying of the share which will eventually force up the price.
9. A repayment schedule such as the following can be constructed:

Year	Amount (R000)	Sum of the inflows
1	8 000	8 000
2	16 000	24 000
3	25 000	49 000
4	45 000	94 000
5	35 000	129 000

It can be readily seen that R49 000 has been recovered after 3 years and that the balance will be recovered early in the fourth year, actually 6/45 or 2/9 of the way into that year. Payback period is therefore 3,22 years.

10. A present value table like the following can be constructed:

Year	Net cash flow (R000)	Present value
0	2 500 neg	− 2 500
1	800	690
2	850	632
3	830	537
4	1 200	663
		12

Since the value is positive (only just), the project is acceptable.

Appendix 6

Present value tables

Tables for determining the present value of R1 payable at some time in the future and for determining the value of an annuity of R1 per year payable for a number of years at different rates of discount are included here. These tables are not very comprehensive and are here more for purposes of demonstration than anything else since it is presumed that most users of this book would prefer to work out present values using the functions built into their calculators.

Present value of R1 per year for n years

Years \ Percentage	4	6	8	10	12	14	16	18	20	22	24	26
0	1	1	1	1	1	1	1	1	1	1	1	1
1	0,96153	0,94339	0,92592	0,90909	0,89285	0,87719	0,86206	0,84745	0,83333	0,81967	0,80645	0,79365
2	1,88609	1,83339	1,78326	1,73553	1,69005	1,64666	1,60523	1,56564	1,52777	1,49153	1,45681	1,42353
3	2,77509	2,67301	2,57709	2,48685	2,40183	2,32163	2,24588	2,17427	2,10648	2,04224	1,98130	1,92343
4	3,62989	3,46510	3,31212	3,16986	3,03734	2,91371	2,79818	2,69006	2,58873	2,49364	2,40427	2,32018
5	4,45182	4,21236	3,99271	3,79078	3,60477	3,43308	3,27429	3,12717	2,99061	2,86363	2,74538	2,63507
6	5,24213	4,91732	4,62287	4,35526	4,11140	3,88866	3,68473	3,49760	3,32551	3,16691	3,02047	2,88497
7	6,00205	5,58238	5,20637	4,86841	4,56375	4,28830	4,03856	3,81152	3,60459	3,41550	3,24231	3,08331
8	6,73274	6,20979	5,74663	5,33492	4,96763	4,63886	4,34359	4,07756	3,83715	3,61926	3,42122	3,24072
9	7,43533	6,80169	6,24688	5,75902	5,32824	4,94637	4,60654	4,30302	4,03096	3,78628	3,56550	3,36565
10	8,11089	7,36008	6,71008	6,14456	5,65022	5,21611	4,83322	4,49408	4,19247	3,92318	3,68185	3,46480
11	8,76047	7,88687	7,13896	6,49506	5,93769	5,45273	5,02864	4,65600	4,32706	4,03539	3,77569	3,54349
12	9,38507	8,38384	7,53607	6,81369	6,19437	5,66029	5,19710	4,79322	4,43921	4,12737	3,85136	3,60594
13	9,98564	8,85268	7,90377	7,10335	6,42354	5,84236	5,34233	4,90951	4,53268	4,20276	3,91238	3,65551
14	10,5631	9,29498	8,24423	7,36668	6,62816	6,00207	5,46752	5,00806	4,61056	4,26456	3,96160	3,69485
15	11,1183	9,71224	8,55947	7,60607	6,81086	6,14216	5,57545	5,09157	4,67547	4,31521	4,00129	3,72607
16	11,6522	10,1058	8,85136	7,82370	6,97398	6,26505	5,66849	5,16235	4,72956	4,35673	4,03330	3,75085
17	12,1656	10,4772	9,12163	8,02155	7,11963	6,37285	5,74870	5,22233	4,77463	4,39076	4,05911	3,77051
18	12,6592	10,8276	9,37188	8,20141	7,24967	6,46742	5,81784	5,27316	4,81219	4,41866	4,07993	3,78612
19	13,1339	11,1581	9,60359	8,36492	7,36577	6,55036	5,87745	5,32624	4,84349	4,44152	4,09671	3,79851
20	13,5903	11,4699	9,81814	8,51356	7,46944	6,62313	5,92884	5,35274	4,86957	4,46026	4,11025	3,80834
21	14,0291	11,7640	10,0168	8,64869	7,56200	6,68695	5,97313	5,38368	4,89131	4,47562	4,12117	3,81614
22	14,4511	12,0415	10,2007	8,77154	7,64464	6,74294	6,01132	5,40990	4,90943	4,48821	4,12997	3,82233
23	14,8568	12,3033	10,3710	8,88321	7,71843	6,79205	6,04424	5,43211	4,92452	4,49854	4,13708	3,82725
24	15,2469	12,5503	10,5287	8,98474	7,78431	6,83513	6,07262	5,45094	4,93710	4,50700	4,14280	3,83115
25	15,6220	12,7833	10,6747	9,07704	7,84313	6,87292	6,09709	5,46690	4,94758	4,51393	4,14742	3,83424

Present value of R1 due after n years

Percentage / Years	0	4	6	8	10	12	14	16	18	20	22	24	26
0	1,00000	1,00000	1,00000	1,00000	1,00000	1,00000	1,00000	1,00000	1,00000	1,00000	1,00000	1,00000	1,00000
1		0,96153	0,94339	0,92592	0,90909	0,89285	0,87719	0,86206	0,84745	0,83333	0,81967	0,80645	0,79365
2		0,92455	0,88999	0,85733	0,82644	0,79719	0,76946	0,74316	0,71818	0,69444	0,67186	0,65036	0,62988
3		0,88899	0,83961	0,79383	0,75131	0,71178	0,67497	0,64065	0,60863	0,57870	0,55070	0,52448	0,49990
4		0,85480	0,79209	0,73502	0,68301	0,63551	0,59208	0,55229	0,51578	0,48225	0,45139	0,42297	0,39675
5		0,82192	0,74725	0,68058	0,62092	0,56742	0,51936	0,47611	0,43710	0,40187	0,36999	0,34110	0,31488
6		0,79031	0,70496	0,63016	0,56447	0,50663	0,45558	0,41044	0,37043	0,33489	0,30327	0,27508	0,24990
7		0,75991	0,66505	0,58349	0,51315	0,45234	0,39963	0,35382	0,31392	0,27908	0,24858	0,22184	0,19833
8		0,73069	0,62741	0,54026	0,46650	0,40388	0,35055	0,30502	0,26603	0,23256	0,20376	0,17890	0,15741
9		0,70258	0,59189	0,50024	0,42409	0,36061	0,30750	0,26295	0,22545	0,19380	0,16701	0,14427	0,12492
10		0,67556	0,55839	0,46319	0,38554	0,32197	0,26974	0,22668	0,19106	0,16150	0,13689	0,11635	0,09915
11		0,64958	0,52678	0,42888	0,35049	0,28747	0,23661	0,19541	0,16191	0,13458	0,11221	0,09383	0,07869
12		0,62459	0,49696	0,39711	0,31863	0,25667	0,20755	0,16846	0,13721	0,11215	0,09197	0,07567	0,06245
13		0,60057	0,46883	0,36769	0,28966	0,22917	0,18206	0,14522	0,11628	0,09346	0,07539	0,06102	0,04956
14		0,57747	0,44230	0,34046	0,26333	0,20461	0,15970	0,12519	0,09854	0,07788	0,06179	0,04921	0,03933
15		0,55526	0,41726	0,31524	0,23939	0,18269	0,14009	0,10792	0,08351	0,06490	0,05065	0,03968	0,03122
16		0,53390	0,39364	0,29189	0,21762	0,16312	0,12289	0,09304	0,07077	0,05408	0,04151	0,03200	0,02477
17		0,51337	0,37136	0,27026	0,19784	0,14564	0,10779	0,08020	0,05997	0,04507	0,03403	0,02581	0,01966
18		0,49362	0,35034	0,25024	0,17985	0,13003	0,09456	0,06914	0,05083	0,03756	0,02789	0,02081	0,01560
19		0,47464	0,33051	0,23171	0,16350	0,11610	0,08294	0,05960	0,04307	0,03130	0,02286	0,01678	0,01238
20		0,45638	0,31180	0,21454	0,14864	0,10366	0,07276	0,05138	0,03650	0,02608	0,01874	0,01353	0,00983
21		0,43883	0,29415	0,19865	0,13513	0,09255	0,06382	0,04429	0,03093	0,02173	0,01536	0,01091	0,00780
22		0,42195	0,27750	0,18394	0,12284	0,08264	0,05598	0,03818	0,02621	0,01811	0,01259	0,00880	0,00619
23		0,40572	0,26179	0,17031	0,11167	0,07378	0,04911	0,03292	0,02221	0,01509	0,01032	0,00710	0,00491
24		0,39012	0,24697	0,15769	0,10152	0,06588	0,04308	0,02837	0,01882	0,01257	0,00845	0,00572	0,00390
25		0,37511	0,23299	0,14601	0,09229	0,05882	0,03779	0,02446	0,01595	0,01048	0,00693	0,00461	0,00309

Index